THE LIFE AND LEGACY OF

ALEXANDER CARMICHAEL

The Life & Legacy
of
ALEXANDER CARMICHAEL

Edited by
Domhnall Uilleam Stiùbhart

Proceedings of a conference arranged by
The Islands Book Trust

Published in 2008 by The Islands Book Trust.
www.theislandsbooktrust.com

Acknowledgements

The Islands Book Trust is grateful to Bòrd na Gàidhlig, Catherine McCaig's Trust,
The Russell Trust and The Edinburgh University Library for their assistance in the
publication of this volume.

Disclaimer

The opinions expressed in this volume are those of the authors, and do not necessarily
represent the views of The Islands Book Trust.

ISBN-13: 978-0-9555420-0-8

The Islands Book Trust
10 Callicvol
Port of Ness
Isle of Lewis
Western Isles
HS2 0XA
Tel: 01851 820946

Printed and bound in Great Britain by Nevisprint Ltd.

Cover photographs of Alexander Carmichael and Mr and Mrs Carmichael at Taynuilt
courtesy of the National Museums of Scotland

Price £15

Contents

Illustrations

Contributors

DONALD BLACK is a scholar of the history and traditions of his native Lismore, and author of *Sgeul no Dhà às an Lios/A Tale or Two from Lismore* (2006).

RONALD BLACK is a scholar and a journalist. Among the books he has recently edited are *Eilein na h-Òige: the Poems of Father Allan McDonald* (2002), *The Gaelic Otherworld* (2005), the anthology of eighteenth-century Gaelic verse *An Lasair* (2006), and *To the Hebrides: Samuel Johnson's Journey to the Western Islands and James Boswell's Journal of a Tour to the Hebrides* (2007).

HUGH CHEAPE is Principal Curator and Head of the Scottish Material Culture Research Centre, National Museums of Scotland, and Lecturer in Material Culture at Sabhal Mòr Ostaig. He is the author of *Tartan: the Highland Habit* (1995) and *The Book of the Bagpipe* (1999).

MEGHAN COTE is the former Archival Assistant for the Carmichael Watson Project at Edinburgh University Library Special Collections.

WILLIAM GILLIES is Professor of Celtic Languages, Literature, History and Antiquities at the University of Edinburgh. He has written numerous articles on Gaelic literature and history, and is presently preparing an edition of the Books of Clan Ranald.

JEAN-DIDIER HACHE is Executive Secretary of the Islands Commission of the Conference of Peripheral and Maritime Regions, and the author of *The French MacDonald: Journal of a Marshal of Napoléon in the Highlands and Islands of Scotland* (2007).

NORMAN JOHNSON is a member of Comann Eachdraidh Uibhist a Tuath and a scholar of the history and traditions of his native North Uist.

CALUM LAING is a retired head teacher and a scholar of the history and genealogy of the Uists and Benbecula.

CATHLIN MACAULAY is the Sound Archivist at the School of Scottish Studies, University of Edinburgh, and editor of the journal *Tocher*.

MURDO MACDONALD is Professor of History of Scottish Art, University of Dundee, and a director of the interdisciplinary project *Window to the West/Uinneag dhan Àird an Iar*. He is the author of *Scottish Art* (2000).

ISA MACKILLOP is a retired head teacher and a member of Comann Eachdraidh Uibhist a Tuath. An expert on the songs of her native North Uist, she is a part-time music tutor at Colaisde Bheinn na Faoghla.

CALUM MACNEIL is a scholar of the history, traditions, and genealogy of his native Barra, and a member of Comann Eachdraidh Bharraidh agus Bhatarsaidh.

THE VERY REV. ANGUS JOHN, CANON MACQUEEN is a Gaelic scholar and parish priest of St Barr's on the Isle of Barra.

DONALD MEEK is Professor of Scottish and Gaelic Studies at the University of Edinburgh. He is the author of *The Quest for Celtic Christianity* (2000) and *The Kingdom of MacBrayne* (2006), and editor of the poetry of *Màiri Mhór nan Òran* (1998) and the nineteenth-century Gaelic verse anthology *Caran an t-Saoghail* (2003).

PETER MORRISON is a retired Procurator Fiscal with an interest in Morrison genealogy.

JOHN RANDALL was formerly Registrar General for Scotland and is now Chairman of The Islands Book Trust, living in Lewis.

DOMHNALL UILLEAM STIÙBHART is Principal Researcher for the Carmichael Watson Project at the University of Edinburgh, and Lecturer in Material Culture at Sabhal Mòr Ostaig.

Abbreviations

AC	Alexander Carmichael
CG	*Carmina Gadelica*
CW	Edinburgh University Library, Carmichael Watson collection (GB 237 Coll-97)
GUL	Glasgow University Library
NAS	National Archives of Scotland
NLS	National Library of Scotland
PSAS	*Proceedings of the Society of Antiquaries of Scotland*
SSS SA	School of Scottish Studies, Sound Archive
SGS	*Scottish Gaelic Studies*
TGSI	*Transactions of the Gaelic Society of Inverness*

Introduction and Conclusions

JOHN RANDALL

BACKGROUND

This volume is based on contributions to a highly enjoyable and informative conference about the great collector of Gaelic folklore Alexander Carmichael, organised by The Islands Book Trust and held in Benbecula in July 2006. That the conference was judged successful by all who attended was partly a reflection of the wide range of perspectives represented—including eminent academic scholars, local residents from Benbecula and Uist, and descendants of families who gave Alexander Carmichael material in the nineteenth century. The Book Trust seeks to bring together people from different backgrounds with an interest in the history of Scottish islands in the belief that the sharing of knowledge from different perspectives can provide new historical insights. On this occasion we were certainly not disappointed and I should like to thank everyone involved, not least the people of Benbecula who made us so welcome.

Over the course of the four days of the conference, we not only listened to formal presentations by some wonderful speakers, but also heard first-hand from the descendants of families who knew Carmichael, attended an inspirational ecumenical service in Griminish, visited places in Benbecula, South Uist, and Eriskay associated with Carmichael and other collectors, and enjoyed a cèilidh at Nunton Steadings featuring songs and music from many local people. We have tried to capture some of the spirit of these wider events, which helped so much to make the conference a success, by including contributions from them in this book. I hope the outcome will be a way of recording more permanently and making available to a larger audience the proceedings of a very enjoyable few days.

FINDINGS

It is very difficult, even foolhardy, to attempt to sum up such a wide-ranging event. Each of the contributions in this volume will repay close study. All I can do here is set out a few points which struck me while listening to the various contributions. Some are no doubt blindingly obvious, others may be more controversial.

1. First, it is evident that Carmichael found a particularly rich treasure-house of traditional hymns, incantations, stories, and folklore in Benbecula and Uist. During his career as an exciseman, he visited and collected material from many other areas, but he was clearly impressed, as others such as Margaret Fay Shaw have been since, by the extent to which old customs, songs, and lore were preserved and still alive amongst the Gaelic-speaking people here. The fact that he chose to live in Benbecula or Uist for some seventeen years before moving to Edinburgh is itself testimony of this.

2. Why this should be so is an interesting but ultimately unresolved question. No doubt the area's relative remoteness from other 'modernising' influences emanating from the mainland was a factor. In addition, historical reasons such as the encouragement given to Gaelic culture by the Clanranald landlords for many years, as shown for example by the pre-eminence of the MacMhuirich bards (see William Gillies' contribution in this volume), may have been influential. More complex, but possibly also relevant, is the impact of religion. It is clear that Carmichael found the mainly Catholic areas of South Uist and Benbecula particularly fruitful, even if many of his informants were from North Uist and other Protestant areas. Certainly, as Donald Meek's chapter brings out, he was struck by the detrimental effect of Presbyterian religious revivals in Skye and elsewhere on the willingness of local people to recount old stories and customs.

3. The material collected by Carmichael in Benbecula and Uist was varied and had a number of sources. It seems possible that many of the longer stories were based on the work of the MacMhuirich bards or at least influenced by the cultural environment which their professional activities encouraged. In contrast, the traditional hymns, charms, and incantations which form such an important part of *Carmina Gadelica* appear mainly to be the product of a genuine folk-culture. Many of these reflect a long-standing belief in the supernatural amongst ordinary people, the simple rhythms of daily and seasonal routines, and the need to take any action possible to ward off illnesses and disasters, in an environment which, even today with all our modern comforts, can be challenging and hostile. Carmichael's achievement in taking down and preserving so much of this rich heritage, only part of which was published in the six volumes of *Carmina Gadelica*, was by any standards a remarkable one.

4. Whatever the circumstances in which Carmichael carried out his collecting in Benbecula and Uist, and what this tells us about the society and life of the people there, the production of his great work *Carmina Gadelica*, the first two volumes of which were published in 1900, must however be seen against the background of more general political, social, and linguistic factors affecting the Gaelic world in the late nineteenth century. As Donald Meek brings out so clearly in his chapter, these wider developments, the subject of strenuous intellectual debate and effort in the circle of the Gaelic literati with whom Carmichael associated himself in Edinburgh after 1882, explain the way in which it was eventually decided to present Carmichael's work to the world.

5. Essentially, Carmichael and those who influenced him were engaged in a grand project to demonstrate to a wider and often sceptical outside audience that Gaelic culture was worthy of the deepest respect. There was a conscious attempt by the literati to present the Gael in an appropriately dignified and Christian light, despite remarks made by George Henderson, a key figure in the title given to Carmichael's work, which betray a patronising or insulting attitude to the Highland people. This may account for many of the amendments and additions made to the original recordings, for example the 'smoothing' of texts with the aim of presenting an image of Celtic Christianity, more uniform and ecumenical in character than the variety of the originals might support (again, see Donald Meek). It also accounts for the high quality artistic style adopted in *Carmina Gadelica* which, as Murdo Macdonald brings out, can be regarded as the pinnacle of Celtic revival book design, with letters based on a variety of earlier sources such as the Book of Deer.

6. Carmichael became very much part of the 'Gaelic establishment' scene in the Edinburgh of the 1880s, 1890s, and 1900s, a well-known figure in antiquarian as well as literary circles. His interest in and contribution to the preservation of the material culture of the islands is illustrated in Hugh Cheape's chapter.

7. It may be that Carmichael was particularly susceptible to the influence and arguments of the literati who used him as a conduit between Edinburgh and the Gaelic world. As Donald Black shows in his account of Carmichael's Lismore background, there was an ambivalent attitude in his native island towards Carmichael, both his family and his activities. This, together with Carmichael's lack of academic qualifications, may have bred an insecurity which made him open to arguments which resulted in significant changes being introduced for presentational reasons. In any case, as Ronald Black demonstrates, the issue of 'improving' or editing original recordings for a wider audience is an issue which has faced almost all folklore collectors.

8. This sets the scene for the controversy which erupted in the academic world in the 1970s when differences between Carmichael's original notebooks and his published work were exposed. A tendency to over-react to these revelations is reflected in the title of Ronald Black's contribution: 'I thought he made it all up!' Further work is now under way by Domhnall Uilleam Stiùbhart at the University of Edinburgh on the Carmichael Watson papers (see Meghan Cote's chapter) which is shedding more light on the extent of these differences. Ronald Black's provisional conclusion is that the prose content of *Carmina Gadelica* is the most suspect, while the Gaelic verse (particularly shorter material) is the most authentic. This might be interpreted to mean, for example, that *Carmina Gadelica* i and ii are relatively 'clean', while *CG* iii is perhaps less so. Hopefully, more work on the Carmichael Watson papers will provide more answers to these questions.

9. Interestingly, while there are still memories of Alexander Carmichael alive in Benbecula and Uist (with some descendants of the families he collected from now living elsewhere—see the contributions by Peter Morrison and Calum Laing, as well as those by Calum Macneil, Isa MacKillop and Norman Johnson), *Carmina Gadelica* itself seems to have been rather rarely read in the islands, and so the academic controversy of the 1970s made little impact here. This reinforces the fundamental division between Carmichael's original collecting and the publication of *Carmina Gadelica*.

10. In conclusion, there can be no doubt that Carmichael's collecting of folklore material and the publishing of *Carmina Gadelica* were both massive achievements. But the two achievements were very different projects, and the links between them not straightforward. Carmichael, with others, did his best to advance the cause of the Gael politically and culturally in the late nineteenth century, but in doing so he allowed himself to a significant (but as yet unknown) extent to move away from the authenticity of his original recordings.

Acknowledgements

The Islands Book Trust would like to thank the University of Edinburgh, Western Isles Enterprise, Comhairle nan Eilean Siar, and Comunn na Gàidhlig for financial support towards the conference; and the Dark Island Hotel, Lìonacleit School and Education Centre, and Nunton Steadings for providing accommodation, venues, and logistical support. We are also very grateful to the Church of Scotland and Roman Catholic Church and the ministers/priests involved in the ecumenical service; to everyone who took part in the cèilidh; and to those who helped with transport arrangements throughout the time of the conference. A special thank you goes to Alasdair and Jean MacEachen, who supervised the administrative arrangements and organised the céilidh; to the University of Edinburgh and Donnie Morrison for help with the exhibition on Carmichael and display boards at the conference; and to Calum Macdonald, our Gaelic placement student who helped to make the conference run smoothly. Finally, we are indebted to all the speakers and contributors to this book, to everyone who attended the conference and participated in the discussions, and to the people of Benbecula and Uist whose help and enthusiasm contributed so much to the success of the conference.

1

Alexander Carmichael and *Carmina Gadelica*

DOMHNALL UILLEAM STIÙBHART

Dòmhnall Eàirdsidh Dòmhnallach: *Nach robh sibh ag innse dhomh gu robh ur n-athair a' toirt naidheachdan is rannan do Charmicheal?*

Màiri Anna NicAonghais: Bha.

DED: *'S tha cuimhn' agaibh fhéin air a' seo?*

MANA: O, tha cuimhn' agam fhìn air, tha.

DED: *Có bhliadhna a bhiodh a' sen, saoilidh sibh?*

MANA: O, chan eil sian a chuimhn' agamsa, m' eudail, cha robh mi ach òg. Òg, òg. Cha robh, ach gur cuimhn' agam air Carmichael, le feusag mhór bhàn air. Duine mór mór àrd, garbh. Agus breacan air a' ghualainn agus éileadh beag air. Sin agad na bheil de chuimhn' agams' air Carmicheal.

Donald Archie MacDonald: *Weren't you telling me that your father gave stories and verses to Carmichael?*

Mary Ann MacInnes: *Yes.*

DAMD: *And you remember this yourself?*

MAMI: *Oh yes I remember, yes.*

DAMD: *What year would this be, do you suppose?*

MAMI: *Oh, I really don't remember, I was only young. Very young. I don't remember that, but I remember Carmichael, with a long white beard. A very big tall man, thick-set. And wearing a plaid on his shoulder and a kilt. That's what I remember of Carmichael.*[1]

* * * * *

Charms—I have taken down many charms and incantations up and down these islands. Some of these I communicated to 'Nether Lochaber' who in his own captivating manner has published them in the *Inverness Courier.*

I have always thought that a faithful account of these charms and incantations would be interesting, and, properly considered, mayhap instructive. I have not hitherto however, felt myself equal to the ~~con-genial~~ task congenial to me of giving them to the public, although many scores, if not hundreds of them, lie scattered up and down my manuscripts among masses of other rubbish.

I am not myself superstitious, beyond perhaps the latent superstition inherent I believe ~~in~~ to every Highlander. Nevertheless, down to a friendly feeling for the believers and users of these charms and incantations. Literally,

'We have been friends together
In sunshine and in shade.'

For when a cold world would frown upon our 'dark doings' under the shade of the house ~~within~~ and the darker shade of the smoke within we would betake ourselves to the friendly shelter of a hillock outside and there, 'air chul gaoith agus air aodan greine'—behind the wind and in front of the sun, we would write down our 'mystical lore' unmolested. These mystical beliefs and observances with their hoary origin far back the stream of time, probably contain interest possibly wisdom, had we only the industry of the bee to seek and extract their treasures.[2]

Alexander Archibald Carmichael, folklorist, antiquarian, and author, was born on 1 December 1832 in Taylochan on the Island of Lismore, the ninth and youngest child of Hugh Carmichael, farmer and publican, and Elizabeth (Betty) MacColl. The Carmichaels prided themselves on being the oldest family in the area, his particular branch being descended from the barons of Taigh Sgurrain in Lismore, the last of whom was said to have been swindled out of his estate in the early seventeenth century by the notoriously acquisitive Dòmhnall Dubh nan Àird, Donald Campbell of Airds.[3]

After attending the local island school, the young Carmichael apparently completed his formal education in Greenock. His early years on Lismore remained a touchstone for him, and during the coming decades, we find him time and time again returning to and recreating the nostalgic world of his childhood, the songs, the stories, the people who told them. Here, for instance, Carmichael—quite conscious of the story's symbolism—reminiscences about the Lismore version of that most protean of Gaelic tales, the 'Cave of Gold': *Uamh an Òir.*

I will remember that tale you speak of about, the piper and the dog. So rigidly, indeed, did it take hold of my memory in childhood, that nothing can ever erase it therefrom while I live. The cave into which the piper and the dog entered—as the story goes in our place—is on what was once the property of Sir Duncan Campbell of Barracaldine. It is about two miles from the Roman Catholic College, or rather what was the Roman Catholic College, in Liosmor. My own ancestors and people had Baile-ghrunnail, on which the cave is, and the lands round about there, which perhaps assisted my childish interest in the story. It is told in our place, that when the piper and the dog, went into the cave a considerable distance, it closed its portals for a time; and that the piper was heard playing, when going along under ground, at a place called Creaganich, the well known tune:—

'Cha till, cha till, cha till mi tuille,
Cha till gu brach, gu la na cruinne.'

It is a large cave, directly opposite and looking across, to Dunstaffanage. I can never forget, when some of my bold youthful companions, 'so trusted and true', and myself, would visit the cave, our dreadful suspence when one of us, with infidelic temerity, would, against all remonstrances, go a few yards farther in than the rest, to get a peep at the dark recess.

So much impressed was my boyish fancy with the story, that if I were to go into the cave, even at this distance of time, I would much rather be not too particularly questioned, about the state of my palpitating heart, when exploring the dark recesses of the cave…[4]

On another occasion he relates how:

A Highland fisherman on leaving shore turns his boat '*deiseil*'—sunwise. I remember well when a ~~boy and~~ restless 'laddie' ~~when my beard was not so long nor mo fhalt cho tana~~ as today how fond I was of being allowed the pleasureable privilege of going out to fish, in concert with others, with two old men, *Iain Mac Rob agus Dughall Mor (an aoil)* John MacGrigor and Dugald MacCorquadale. These old men always made a point of turning our little craft sunwise, on leaving land. I remember another old man Dugall *Donn—Dugall* MacIntyre—when building his stacks, that he always built sunwise.[5]

Despite such idyllic memories, Carmichael's childhood in Lismore would have been disturbed by two momentous events. Firstly, there was the almost total clearance of people, many family and school friends doubtless among them, from the southern half of the island in the early 1840s following its purchase by William Cheyney, a process apparently occasioning at least one major fracas by the islanders.[6] Again, the second half of the decade was overshadowed by the effects of the Great Famine, not so much upon the now underpopulated island itself, but rather the surrounding districts about the Firth of Lorn. Much of Carmichael's later sympathy with more radical elements in the crofters' cause can be traced back to his childhood experiences growing up in Lismore.

It was in Greenock, in 1856, that Alexander Carmichael took up his first station with the civil service as an exciseman, the customs in that town being then a virtual Highland fiefdom. The post was apparently 'obtained through the influence of his uncle', the Rev. Alexander MacColl, minister of Durness.[7] Some idea of his character may be grasped from the following anecdote:

> A clergyman from the Highlands had occasion to be in Edinburgh during a '*Sanct Aindrea*' anniversary. He got an invitation to attend the dinner in St Andrew's Hall and which was presided over by the Duke of Argyle. It was customary on such an occasion for each member of the Society to repeat a few lines of poetry when admitted, suited to the occasion. This clergyman was not aware of this and was only told of it as he was passing into the Hall. He however composed a few lines extempore which not only admitted him but led the Duke to place him on his right hand next to himself at the table. I hope I am doing no unkindness to the clergyman's memory by saying that he was my mother's brother.
>
> I had this some years ago from a Mrs Stewart in Greenock—a *real* Highland lady, alas! a class now getting rare.   A.A.C.[8]

Alexander Carmichael was subsequently transferred over to Dublin, where he worked alongside his fellow Argyllshire Gael John Murdoch (1818–1903).[9] The older man, already launched upon his alternative career as a prolific radical campaigning journalist, evidently took Carmichael under his wing, introducing Carmichael to the lively and disputatious intellectual culture of the Irish capital, in particular to the cluster of scholars then laying the foundation of the discipline of Celtic studies, as well as to his Irish political and journalistic contacts. The discussions in which he took part kindled within him an awareness of the wider context of Gaelic language and culture—not to mention a desire to defend the claims of Scottish Gaeldom to the Ossianic lays against the forceful claims of Irish cousins.[10] For Carmichael, ever the youngest child, Murdoch was one of the first of several mentors: energetic, assertive, entrepreneurial, worldly wise, well-read and well-connected older men who encouraged him in his interests, and provided a public outlet for the fruits of his labour. Carmichael may have felt Murdoch's influence in other ways too: in his zealous temperance, his wariness of institutionalised religion, and his enthusiasm for the kilt, a garment he was to wear for the rest of his life.

Given Carmichael's friendship with John Murdoch, it is unlikely to be a coincidence that his next posting was to Murdoch's childhood home, the whisky-producing Isle of Islay. It would be a crucial juncture in his life. In the summer of 1860 the 'very enthusiastic Highlander'[11] volunteered to join the team of pioneering folklorists collecting stories for the four-volume *Popular Tales of the West Highlands* (1860–2). The project was directed, compiled, and indeed inspected under the auspices of the tireless polymath and civil service mandarin John Francis Campbell (1821–85), himself inspired by the recently published *Popular Tales of the Norse* (1859) translated by George Dasent (1817–96).

The principles of 'storyology' inculcated by 'Iain Òg Ìle'—the necessity of recording the performance accurately, accompanied by details concerning place and time of performance, the reciter, and where he or she (usually he) first heard the item—exerted a fundamental influence upon Carmichael's collecting practices for the rest of his life.[12] Nevertheless, such principles, focussed firmly upon the contingent circumstances of the individual performance, were to clash with Carmichael's self-confessed 'romantic disposition'[13], his artistic, spiritual, idealistic, and perfectionist cast of mind. Throughout his life Carmichael was strongly motivated by the desire to redeem Gaels and their traditions both from the odium of outsiders 'who hate—cordially hate—everything that has the misfortune in their *impartial* eyes, to be Highland or having a Highland tendency'[14], and from the perceived hostility of a harsh Highland evangelical church, as well as being spurred by the conviction that it was his duty not only to record the present, but also to retrieve and reconstruct a glorious Gaelic past already vanishing before his eyes. Such proclivities would eventually lead Carmichael to create works very different in character from Campbell's rigorously audited surveys. Nevertheless, the example of Iain Òg Ìle remained a stimulus and an inspiration, not just with regard to collecting and recording procedures, but also in the compilation and presentation of the material collected. The *Popular Tales*, 'a museum of curious rubbish, given as it was gathered in the rough'[15], in which the most outlandish and extraordinary data are arrayed as if within the report of an official commission, would cast a long shadow on *Carmina Gadelica*.

Alexander Carmichael spent some eighteen months gathering and writing up tales for John Francis Campbell, firstly in Islay, then at a new posting in Carbost on the Isle of Skye. There he was 'getting on famously with collecting tales' until an evangelical revival swept the island, as a result of which

> Ever since then I cannot get a tale. Since then my most persevering efforts have been unavailing. The people here have got frightened and their memories with their stores of ancient lore have forsaken them in a most unaccountable manner.[16]

Although by their very nature such awakenings were temporary, Carmichael was clearly somewhat unnerved by the experience and further confirmed in his aversion to Highland evangelicalism.

Three traits come through plainly in Carmichael's letters of the period. Firstly, there is his chronic lack of confidence, his reticence and reluctance to commit any opinion or for that matter any material he had gathered to print. Related to this is his acute perfectionism, impelling him to 'have written and rewritten all the tales' he sent Campbell 'at least five or six times'[17] after he had gathered additional expressions or even additional words from other informants. Finally, there is his omnivorous collecting, considerably more comprehensive than any of his contemporaries and indeed going well beyond folklore alone. Having 'always made a point of refusing nothing I heard'[18], Carmichael amassed a large collection of proverbs, riddles and individual words as well as the tales he had gathered[19]—not to mention a collection of geological specimens.

While engaged to collect for John Francis Campbell, Alexander Carmichael was also recording folksongs for another of his early mentors. The *Treatise on the Language, Poetry and*

Music of the Highland Clans (1862) was a panoptic cultural survey compiled by the Greenock-based journalistic litterateur and Ossian enthusiast Lieutenant Donald Campbell.[20] However, only one of the 52 songs which the young 'enthusiastic Highlander'[21] recorded for him—and it is surely significant that they were taken down entirely from 'lady friends in various places'[22]—was deemed worthy by the old soldier of inclusion in a volume firmly focussed on the prestigious Gaelic literary canon as established by John Mackenzie's *Sàr Obair nam Bàrd Gaelach* (1841).

Reflecting upon his first collecting expeditions, Carmichael refers to:

> the many dark and disagreeable nights I have travelled for many miles going into bogs, going headlong into ditches and yet never able to get such tales as others more fortunate. Yet I can honestly say this that *I have done my best.*[23]

In retrospect, Alexander Carmichael's strenuous efforts during nearly two years of collecting may have been something of a disappointment. Little of what he had collected and transcribed had made it into print: just one folksong, two brief tales, and a jejune essay on Ossian.[24] It is possibly not altogether surprising that his next posting took him far from the Highlands, to the port of Wadebridge in Cornwall. Although Carmichael may well have intended to turn to researching Cornish Celtic folklore, he was to be disappointed. The two-year interlude he spent in the south did however give him an invaluable opportunity to contemplate what he had learnt about his own culture, and to devise plans for the future. His eventual decision was to have momentous consequences, for himself and for Gaelic culture.

At the very end of 1864 Alexander Carmichael returned north. This time, doubtless at his own request, he was assigned to the Uists. His new post, initially based in Lochmaddy and covering the entire Outer Hebrides south of Tarbert, Harris, allowed him to undertake arduous journeys through some of the richest areas for folklore in western Europe, 'a mine of antiquities mental and material'[25], above all the Catholic heartlands of South Uist and Barra. Carmichael 'landed at Lochmaddy by packet from Dunbheagain on the 27 December 1864.'[26] A fortnight later he began collecting, recording his first item, a version of the ballad *Am Bròn Binn* sung by John MacLeod, Ìochdar, South Uist on 10 January 1865.[27] Over the following decades he was to scribble down in a series of field notebooks an extraordinary diversity of material ranging from long Fenian tales and ballads, through historical narratives, songs, hymns, and charms, to anecdotes, observations, proverbs, riddles, and unusual words. Carmichael grasped the opportunity with gusto, a driven man recording in the field when his work would permit, and, back at his lodgings in Lochmaddy, copying out the long prose tales he had recorded during his time in Skye.

> In the Outer Isles, Dr Carmichael's adventures by ford and by ferry were proverbial, and were regarded with awe by a people who had oftentimes to risk, and who sometimes lost, their lives doing such things. … A painfully real one, this sacrifice of toil, physically as well as mentally; it meant oftener than one cares to think, hunger and cold, footsore days and sleepless nights.[28]

Alexander Carmichael soon became well-known throughout the islands for his interest in gathering in old lore. During his sixteen years in the Outer Hebrides his collecting methods, and the material he gathered, were to change a great deal. We might note three key figures under whose tutelage Carmichael reached maturity.

Firstly, under the somewhat demanding and astringent supervision of the naval surveyor and antiquarian Captain Frederick W. L. Thomas, Carmichael began to spend an increasing amount of his time surveying local archaeological sites—especially *dùintean* and *taighean-làir*, brochs and souterrains—and recording their associated traditions. He also dispatched various relics and artefacts, including a font, querns and sculptured stones, to the Museum of Antiquities in Edinburgh under the auspices of the historian William Forbes Skene (1809–92).[29]

Secondly, there was John Francis Campbell, then finishing off the first, and indeed the only volume of *Leabhar na Féinne*, his comprehensive study of Fenian ballads. In September and October 1871 he undertook an adventurous collecting expedition in Uist and Barra, including three days storm-stranded on the remote island of Mingulay. Carmichael accompanied him— quite possibly the only time these two giants of Gaelic folklore collecting actually met—acting as a guide introducing Campbell to eminent local *seanchaidhean* such as Hector MacIsaac in Càrnan, Ìochdar, whom he evidently had already recorded at least twice. Campbell's fieldnotes hint at the fascinating relationship between the 'kilted warrior'[30] and one of his temperamental informants, concerning whom Carmichael had noted on an earlier visit on 24 April 1866:

> Hector MacIosag despises mythological tales and says they are great rubbish in which I fear many men of greater pretention [*sic*] will concur. But of the Fingalians tales he declares them to be worthy [of] the attention of princes—that they are the most elegant excellent and delightful tales that man could listen to. He says that he heard tales read as repeated by persons whom he knows and that the tales were so garbled and mangled that he hung down his head and closed his ears for very shame. He declares that When [he] is done planting his potatoes he will ~~come~~ travel over the F[ord]—a dis[tance] of about 21 m.—to give me a proper opp[ortunity] of taking down any word he has before he dies. He says he [has] neither son nor dau[ghter] except one little girl to whom he can leave his legacy of prose and poetry. And as he likes me better than any other person in the world he is desirous I should become poss[essor] of this invaluable legacy. Ind[eed] he considers it an imper[tinence] that his young daug[hter] does not exhibit a wish to become poss[essor] of these tales of the Feine in prose and poetry. He dec[lares] that there is no man from the Butt of Lewis to Barra Head—200 m.—who has the history of the Fing[alians] so well as he. Re[citers] are the most egotistical set I have ever met. Each thinks himself much better than his neigh[bours] in reciting. Each declares that other re[citers] are only garbling the tales.[31]

'I am Eachan MacCiosaig no man can tell you as I can'[32]:

> His wife made a song. I have this but Alasdair wrote it. Your tune is right. … I have the lay— Alasdair has written it. Sings it. … The lay of the Maiden. Alasdair has this long ago from me. … *Mac Rìgh na Iorasmaile*. There is a lay on that. I had it but I forget it. I don't think that Alasdair got that from me. … Muireartach. Alasdair has this from others. I had it she is very long.[33]

Carmichael's expedition with Campbell appears to have galvanised the younger man to begin publishing once more, as we see from a letter he wrote in December:

> I am alone at present—my wife having gone to Edin[burgh] at long last. As I have got our cottage so much to myself I am trying to bring up my arrears. But I believe it would occupy my undivided time for six or eight months to transcribe all my rubbish…[34]

In quick succession Carmichael dispatched for the *Transactions* of the new Gaelic Society of Inverness three prose narratives he had collected, as well as composing an archaeological paper—based upon a first draft by Campbell himself—describing a recently discovered North Uist souterrain.[35]

Finally, there was Alexander Carmichael's wife. Carmichael reined back his recording further following his marriage to Mary Frances MacBean (1841–1928), in Edinburgh in January 1868. A civil engineer's daughter from the Black Isle, brought up an episcopalian and working as housekeeper to Bishop Alexander Penrose Forbes at Burntisland when she met Alexander, Mary Carmichael was, in the words of a friend of the family:

> an accomplished person—educated and refined in every way a most desirable acquisition to the small society of this island … who I am much inclined to say is even superior to himself in every way…[36]

Alexander Carmichael had married up in the world. It is no exaggeration to say that his future life and achievements were to be quite dependent upon the work, advice, artistic taste, and social skills of his new wife:

> it was his wife who, first, by her good management made it possible for him to bear the financial strain of his adventure, and to wander about through Isles and mainland as the spirit moved him, and who, again, when the collected material was being arranged for publication, by her cultured ear and artistic hand added greatly to the beauty of the work.[37]

Alexander and Mary Carmichael were to have four children: Alexander (Alec) (1868–1941), Elizabeth (Ella) (1870–1928), Eoghan (1876–1966), and Iain (1878–1928). In 1870 they moved to Trumaisgearraidh Manse in North Uist, the minister, the Rev. Neil Macquarrie, being a bachelor. At the end of 1872, after a brief stay in Ìochdar in South Uist, the family at last set up home in Creag Goraidh in the Isle of Benbecula. The Carmichaels were soon supervising the rebuilding of their new house: 'We enlarged and restored it, and created its surroundings till the place was said by all who saw it to be the prettiest in the Long Island.'[38] It should be noted that it was situated close by the Creagorry Inn where islanders would wait until the South Ford between Benbecula and South Uist could be crossed. Carmichael could still gather much from passers-by.

Alexander Carmichael soon became well-known throughout the islands as one interested in old lore, as we can see, for example, in a note concerning the seanchaidh John Stewart of Baile Sear, North Uist, who had died in 1868 aged 78:

> This John Stewart had a great store of old things. He heard of my search for old things and often reg[re]t[ted] that I was not coming the way so that he might unburd[en] his mind to me ere he died. I never saw him altho I often wished.[39]

Carmichael's achievement as a folklore collector is all the more unexpected given his occupation as an exciseman. Nevertheless, Carmichael's work clearly did curtail his vocation. When posted in Skye he describes of how John MacKenzie from Coll, a skipper on a notoriously fast cargo smack clearly undertaking smuggling operations on the side, refused to allow him on board for evening céilidhs:

> It was well known—for it could not be concealed—that 'Maighstir Carmicheil', or 'Gaidsear an fheile' ['the kilted gauger'] was always writing down whatever he could hear for some mysterious purpose, possibly for printing them and exposing their names for telling the 'foolish tales' and of course it would not do to let him hear anything.[40]

Indeed, Carmichael's own opinions about his work both official and personal, albeit expressed relatively soon after his arrival in Uist, were not at all sanguine:

Those old people with the marvellous memories are the only parties from whom I have been in the habit of receiving any sympathy or co-operation. And this sympathy is perhaps all the more genuine because we are both proscribed—they openly and I silently.[41]

We cannot deny the existence of counter-traditions in some families in Uist at least—and possibly especially among the younger generation—which were rather less sympathetic to Alexander Carmichael than later hagiography might have it. In order better to understand the position the young exciseman found himself in, it might be worth examining in greater depth a single revealing tale. In 1968 Andrew Nicolson of Griomasaigh was recorded telling a lengthy anecdote, clearly patterned after the events, concerning how Carmichael had been outwitted by a local smuggler:

Anndra MacNeacail: Sin, ma-thà, 's bu mhath leam stòiridh innse dhuibh air fear ris an canadh iad Alasdair Bàn an Eilean Ghriomasaigh a' Chinn a Tuath. Tha e coltach gu robh e math air dèanamh uisge-beatha aig an àm. Tha cuimhn' a'm m' athair a bhith 'bruidhinn air an duine. Bha m' athair mu h-ochd bliadhna a dh' aois 'nuair a thachair a' stòiridh a tha mi 'dol a dh' innse dhuibh. Rugadh m' athair ann an 1860.

A' latha bha seo bha Maighstir Carmichael air tighinn dhan dùthaich dhan a' *Chustoms and Excise* agus bha e air dèanamh a-mach gum beireadh e air Alasdair Bàn. 'S ghabh e droch shìde airson sin a dhèanamh—thàinig e nuas air Fadhail Chàirinis air iom' bàthadh, agus nochd e 'n taigh Alasdair Bhàin gun for aca gu robh a leithid a dhuine 'dol a thighinn idir. Ach bha Alasdair Bàn a-siod fhathast, agus thuirt e ri Carmichael gu robh e toilicht' fhaicinn aig a dhachaidh bochd, agus gu robh e duilich cho fliuch 's cho fuar 's a bha e.

'Agus, a dhuine chòir', ars' esan, 'man téid sibh a lùib an taighe a rannsachadh bu toigh leam dram de dh' uisge-beatha math a thoirt dhuibh a bhlàthaicheadh sibh agus a chuireadh caran toileachas a's an inntinn agaibh.'

Agus rinn e sin. Thug e glainne dha, agus man do thàrr i bhith sìos dhùin na sùilean aig Carmichael agus dh' iarr e àit' a's a sìneadh e e fhéin. Agus fhuair e sin air a' bheingidh ann an taigh Alasdair Bhàin agus cuibhrige briagha Gàidhealach a shnìomh iad fhéin, 's a chàrd iad agus a dh' fhigh iad cuideachd, a chàradh air. Agus chaidil e airson ceithir uairean an uaireadair.

'Nuair a dhùisg e bha na bha 's an taigh air a chuir an dara taobh far nach fhaiceadh esan na duin' eil' e. Agus bha cuideachd a' phoit-dhubh, mar a chanadh iad, a bha pìos an tao' muigh dhen taigh aig Abhainn an t-Searraich, bha i air pìosan a dhèanamh dhith aig a' bhodach, Alasdair Bàn Dòmhnallach, agus air a caitheamh dh' a' loch air beulaibh an dorais. Agus bha h-uile sìon dhe sin seachad 'nuair a dhùisg Carmichael, agus dh' iarr Alasdair Bàn air an taigh a rannsachadh 's rinn e sin. Chaidh e fo na leapannan fhéin, ma dheireadh, air a ghlùinean ach chan fhac' e sìon a' sin. Cha robh dad ann—dh' fhalbh a h-uile sìon. Agus thuirt e gu robh e duilich gun do chuir e dragh air…

'Ach air an ath thuras', ars' esan, 'glacaidh mi sibh.'

'O', ars' Alasdair Bàn, 'cha bhi 'n ath thuras ann, a charaide. An ath thuras 's ann dhan ùir a bhios sinn a' dol, agus 's cinnteach gur e mis' théid an toiseach ann—tha mi sean co-dhiùbh.'

Ach beagan as a dhéidh sin bha Carmichael air an fhadhail a' dol a-null a Bheinn na Faghla. Agus bha taigh ann an Gramasdal an uair sen, taigh-òsda ris an canadh iad Taigh Ghramasdal—tha 'n tobht' aige fhathast ri faicinn—agus … bha e 'dol air adhart a-null chon an taighe agus e air faighinn a-mach gu robh deoch a' dol dhan taigh sin a feadhainn dhen fheadhainn a bha 'dèanamh an uisge-beatha ann a' falach aig na dachaidhean. Agus gun do thachair bràthair ris … an duine bha e 'rannsachadh an taigh aige beagan lathaichean roimhe sin—seann duine gasda aig an àm, Gilleasbaig mac Lachlainn Dòmhnallach, bràthair Alasdair Bhàin.

Thug e 'm pige far a mhuin agus bha e 'dol 'ga thoir leis go Càirinis, ach rug Gilleasbaig mac Lachlainn air a' sgòrnan air agus thug e ruith mhath air agus chuir e 'na chadal e. 'S thug e air a mhuin e do dh'Eilean na Mnà Mairbhe, dhan Chaiginn, agus chaidil e ann a shin gu robh 'n ath thràigh ann, agus dh' fhalbh e air a shocair dh'a chois go Loch nam Madadh. 'S ghabh e air a' phacaid a' làrna-mhàireach, 's chan fhacas tuilleadh an Uibhist Carmichael.

Sin sibh, ma-thà.

Andrew Nicolson: *Now then, I would like to tell you a story about a man who was called Alasdair Bàn, in the island of Griomasaigh, North Uist. Apparently he was good at making whisky at the time. I remember my father speaking about the man. My father was about eight years old at the time of the story I'm going to tell you. My father was born in 1860.*

This day Mr Carmichael had come to the district for the Customs and Excise, and he had decided to catch Alasdair Bàn. And he had picked a bad day for doing this—he came over the Càirinis ford, nearly getting drowned in the process, and arrived at Alasdair Bàn's house where they hadn't expected that sort of person to come. But Alasdair Bàn was still there, and he told Carmichael he was happy to welcome him to his humble home and he was sorry he [Carmichael] was so wet and cold.

'And, good man,' he said, 'before you go to the trouble of searching the house, I would like to give you a dram of good whisky to warm you, and perhaps give you a little pleasure.'

And he did this. He gave him a glass, and before it had gone down [his throat], Carmichael's eyes were closing and he asked for a place where he could lie down. And he got this on the bench in Alasdair Bàn's house, with a lovely Highland bed cover they had spun themselves, and carded and woven too, put over him. And he slept for four hours.

When he woke up anything that was in the house had been put out of the way where neither he nor anyone else would find it. And the black pot, as they called it, [the still] which was a bit away from the house at Abhainn an t-Searraich, had been taken apart by the old man, Alasdair Bàn MacDonald, and thrown in the loch in front of the door. And this had all been down by the time Carmichael woke up, and Alasdair Bàn asked him to search the house and he did that. He even went under the beds, in the end, on his knees but he saw nothing there—there wasn't anything there, it was all away. And he said he was sorry he had troubled him…

'But next time,' he said, 'I'll catch you.'

'Oh,' said Alasdair Bàn, 'there won't be a next time, my friend. Next time it's to the grave we'll be going, and I'm sure I'll be the first to go—I'm old anyway.

But a short time after that Carmichael was crossing the ford to Benbecula. And there was a house in Gramasdal then, an inn called Gramasdal House—the walls are still to be seen—and … he was going towards the house and he had found out that drink was being supplied to the house by some of the people who were secretly making whisky at their homes. And he met a brother … of the man whose house he had searched some days before—a fine old man at that time, Archie son of Lachlan MacDonald, the brother of Alasdair Bàn.

He [Carmichael] took the jar off his [Archie's] back and he was going to take it to Càirinis, but Archie, son of Lachlann, caught him by the throat and gave him a good going over and knocked him unconscious. And he carried him on his back to Dead Woman's Island, to the Caigeann [half-way across the North Ford], and [Carmichael] lay there until the next tide went out, and then he went quietly on foot to Lochmaddy. And he took the packet boat [out] the next day, and Carmichael was never seen in Uist again.

There you are then.[42]

Evidence from Carmichael's field notebooks show that Alexander Carmichael recorded material in Gramasdal several times: certainly sometime during 1866; on 28 October 1870; and on 3 January 1872.[43] He was recording, or more likely transcribing existing material written down by a local collector some three years previously, from Lachlan MacDonald, Griomasaigh, in February 1866.[44] Seeing that the 1866 recording in Gramasdal was made from none other than 'Mrs Marion Macdonald, Innkeeper', it is tempting to suggest that Andrew Nicolson was around two years out in his dating of the story. If so, then Carmichael probably visited Griomasaigh early in 1866, in mid-February, and subsequently paid a visit to the inn, possibly in April or even in November of the same year. What may be telling is that Carmichael did not appear to have recorded any more material in Griomasaigh until 1877[45]—the year of Archibald MacDonald's death.

What did the anecdote mean to contemporaries? Firstly, we should remember Mary Ann MacInnes' memory, at the beginning of this paper, concerning Alexander Carmichael's imposing appearance. The basic thrust of the story is that Archie MacDonald, at nearly sixty years of age, fought, beat, and knocked unconscious the tough, brawny exciseman, twenty-five years younger than himself and giving every appearance of being a bonny fechter, who had recently arrived in the island.

If the anecdote is unpacked still further, however, some rather more disquieting conclusions might suggest themselves. What was Alexander Carmichael doing with Alasdair Bàn in the first place? In another letter to Captain Thomas, written on 8 March 1870, Carmichael writes:

> And yet my strictly official duties would be comparatively easy were it not for the self-imposed   task of endeavouring to keep so many hundreds of poor people all over my station from coming within reach of the law.[46]

Surely this is just what the exciseman was doing with Alasdair Bàn, paying him a visit not so much to catch him in the act, but rather in order to give him a subtle warning, through an elaborate charade, that his smuggling activities would no longer go unpunished. No matter how remote the island, no matter how inclement the weather, the excise would find a way. Alasdair Bàn evidently understood the bargain, and apparently acquiesced. With his poit dhubh, his whisky still, in pieces at the bottom of the nearest loch, 'cha bhi 'n ath thuras ann, a charaide', 'there won't be a next time, my friend.'

If Carmichael's strategy seemingly paid off with Alasdair Bàn, his encounter with Alasdair's brother Archie went catastrophically wrong, resulting in an episode of intense violence which ended with his being knocked unconscious and stranded in the middle of the ford on the significantly named Eilean na Mnà Mairbhe, a humiliation which, doubtless grown in the telling, would have afforded much amusement in the local céilidh houses. Carmichael might not have left on the packet steamer the following day, but as far as the Griomasaigh people were concerned he might as well have done.

The anecdote is woven around the different behaviour of Alexander Carmichael towards the two brothers. His indulgence to Alasdair Bàn pays off. In Alasdair's gracious words of greeting to the exciseman, we perhaps hear an echo of the kind of welcome and hospitality with which Carmichael would have been received many times in his travels throughout the islands: 'thuirt e ri Carmichael gu robh e toilicht' fhaicinn aig a dhachaidh bochd, agus gu robh e duilich cho fliuch 's cho fuar 's a bha e'; 'he told Carmichael he was happy to welcome him to his humble home and he was sorry he [Carmichael] was so wet and cold.' But what is especially interesting is the apparently rather arbitrary emphasis the seanchaidh places on the coverlet under which Carmichael sleeps:

> Agus fhuair e sin air a' bheingidh ann an taigh Alasdair Bhàin agus cuibhrige briagha Gàidhealach a shnìomh iad fhéin, 's a chàrd iad agus a dh' fhigh iad cuideachd, a chàradh air. Agus chaidil e airson ceithir uairean an uaireadair.

> *And he got this on the bench in Alasdair Bàn's house, with a lovely Highland bed cover they had spun themselves, and carded and woven too, put over him. And he slept for four hours.*

This reference can only be a deliberate allusion, perhaps added slightly later but nevertheless preserved in Andrew Nicolson's narrative, to the Highland Home Industries charity work organised by Carmichael's future wife Mary, and by wives of the local Uist gentry. If Mr Carmichael was celebrated throughout the islands as a collector of folklore and antiquarian traditions, Mrs Carmichael was no less well-known for her work among the poorest section of the population, encouraging knitting and weaving—a major and hitherto overlooked source of income for crofters and cottars in the late nineteenth century. Alasdair

Bàn's blanket, an object freighted with meaning, indeed imbued with a certain perspective on paternalistic (or rather, maternalistic) class relations in the island, expressly recalls this for the narrative's audience. At this distance in time we are unable fully to grasp how contemporary listeners would understand the object's significance in the narrative. Was the seanchaidh intending to point up the irony of Carmichael's supposed errand being partly thwarted by the type of bed cover whose production his wife would zealously promote, or else suggesting that under the new dispensation Alasdair Bàn and his like would effectively 'go legitimate' and make a living weaving textiles rather than distilling whisky?

What we do have in Andrew Nicolson's anecdote is a local evaluation of two possible approaches taken by the authorities, and indeed by Alexander Carmichael himself, towards the islanders—and indeed two strategies carried out by the islanders themselves: lenience and reciprocal accommodation, or else violent confrontation. One strategy—one might even describe it as 'exercising the prerogative of mercy'—would pay dividends, with exciseman and tenant following a mutually understood ritual of courtesy and deferential obeisance; the other, provoking robust resistance, would surely, and disastrously, miscarry. Both, as has been seen, contain elements of what we might describe as ritual activity. It is clear which approach Carmichael preferred to adopt. It was only when it was impossible for him to turn a blind eye, as with Archie MacDonald, that he was forced to act otherwise.

For another example of how, when carrying out his duties, Alexander Carmichael would go to some lengths not to antagonise islanders, we might turn to an anecdote recorded by the Australian singer and song-collector Clement Hosking during his visit to Uist in 1937:

> The hulk of an old cargo ship—mute witness to the danger of the Hebridean seas—lay partially submerged a few hundred yards from the shore. Probably it rested on what was once *Balesiar.* An amusing story of this old barque was related to me by a native of Baleshare, therefore none from this island should find it offensive. Years ago, laden with a cargo of whisky, it was wrecked here. What happened to the crew I never heard, but the Balesharians rescued most of the precious cargo. Highlanders as they were, they proceeded to enjoy this very real gift of nectar from the gods until some jealous busybody from North Uist made it his business to inform the excise authorities of what had happened. At once an officer was sent to Baleshare with instructions to pour away all the whisky. This excise officer, I understand, was none other than Alexander Carmichael, who had gathered his *Carmina Gadelica* among these people. He obeyed his instructions to the letter, if not in the spirit (this is not intended as a pun), pouring the precious fluid away, but as he poured he allowed it to flow into the troughs, tubs, buckets and vessels of every description which the folk of the island could procure.[47]

Alexander Carmichael was zealous not only in discharging his occupation, but also in attempting to protect islanders both from fiscal burdens, for instance in persuading the Board of Inland Revenue to abolish the onerous taxes on carts and on dogs kept for herding[48], and from the rigours of legal punishment. Despite Carmichael's fastidiousness about applying the law, his position nevertheless demanded that he occasionally did so. A praise poem by Flora MacLeod, Fionnghal nighean Chaluim, Baile Sear, North Uist, crows over the arrest and imprisonment for smuggling of a hated neighbour—in the very village where tradition has it that Carmichael consented to the islanders' plundering a cargo of whisky:

> Tha mo cheist air an lasgair
> Shiubhlas aotram fraoch is machair,
> 'S e Carmichael tha mi cantainn,
> Gu math fad' e fallainn beò.

Gu math fada fallainn buan e
Bho'n a ghlac e 'phacaid chuagach.
'S ann a chuir e dha'n taigh fhuar i,
Com na truaillidheachd leis an òl.

My praise is of the young spark
Who travels lightly over heather and machair,
It's Carmichael I mean,
May he have a long, healthy life.

May he last long and be healthy
Since he caught the limping wee package.
He put her to the cold house,
A body wrecked by strong drink.[49]

The very ambiguities generated by his work and his vocation, of course, may have made Carmichael a less welcome and altogether less trusted visitor in certain localities. Enforcing the excise was clearly a lonely task, and an arduous one: Carmichael's field notebooks demonstrate how his collecting was by no means a regular practice, but rather an opportunity snatched during spare hours or evenings when his duties permitted—or indeed those of his informants. Writing down the lay of the Muileartach from Donald MacLellan of Hàcleit a Deas, Benbecula, on 20 October 1871, Carmichael concludes:

> Note—much of this is difficult to understand. The reciter is an old man (84) and his enunciation is low and impaired. I had much difficulty in writing this.
> The reciter is a little man—not 5 ft. I should think. He is very active and all his faculties unimpaired he is so active and industrious that I could hardly keep him in from the cattle while writing this.[50]

Of course, he was not only responsible for combatting illegal distilling, but for much routine drudgery such as supervising dog licences and organising agricultural returns.[51] We see, for instance, Carmichael recording a story from Alexander MacNeil of Ceann Tangabhal, Barra, on 22 March 1871, then remarking:

> Wrote this tale while granting tax Licences at Castlebay during spare minutes & intervals[52]

Tedious and repetitive though such work was, it offered Carmichael an unrivalled opportunity to get to know the islands and their inhabitants—and to investigate possible new informants.

Even after Carmichael had been collecting throughout the Uists and Barra for several years, he remained uncertain about what to do with what he had gathered. In his correspondence with Captain Thomas he appears diffident, unsure of his ability to compose anything worthy of being printed, dependent upon the approval and emendations of others:

> I have been end[e]avouring to procure as many measurements of old duns as possible before the winter came in and this must partly plead my excuse. I have a good deal of antiquarian lore and many antiquarian sketches procured for you. I only require time to arrange and copy them. This is to me the most distasteful part of this whole work. Perhaps I can bring materials to the building as well as others but I cannot build myself. I must however set to work soon and send you a package of 'old stuff'.

> I had the pleasure of seeing Mrs Thomas here yesterday. She told me that you are putting some work through the press. If you should desire any remarks of mine worth printing may I ask you to see that they are correctly worded? I write you without any regard to form or correctness. Consequently I know my papers must necessarily be very lame indeed. In truth I can hardly even look at my own productions. If I do I am sure to be so dissatisfied with them that I must rewrite. And as this entails time and delay I just keep from looking at them and send them as they are.[53]

The younger Carmichael had followed the fashion of his contemporaries in according especial value to long prose narratives, the longer the better, generally recorded from men: an echo of the prestige of the hefty triple-decker novels so beloved of the mid-Victorian generation.[54] For various reasons, these judgements were to change.

The fundamental reason may well be that, having been recording and copying long prose tales for well over a decade, Alexander Carmichael was rather losing interest in the genre. Maybe he felt that he had done all the collecting he could; again, with the best reciters in the islands when he had first arrived already dying off, it was a painful matter to record from their apprentices the inevitable waning of that particular tradition. Also, it is likely that his earlier Ossianic enthusiasms had swiftly and painfully dissipated with the publication in 1872 of Campbell's *Leabhar na Féinne*, which effectively debunked Macpherson's claims.

> Your book is invaluable to all persons interested in Gaelic ballad poetry and who wish to arrive at the honest truth regarding Ossian.
>
> For my own part I must candidly own that my faith in MacPherson's 'Ossian' is more shaken than is at all pleasant.[55]

In fact, Carmichael may have increasingly felt that the soul of the culture was not to be found in the epic prose tales tailored for public recitation so celebrated among contemporary folklore collectors. Indeed, the rest of his collecting career may be read as a reaction to and a recoil from the Ossianic question, a turn away from the public, epic, masculine rhetoric of a 'martial race', almost from the rough materials of an embryonic national literature, to the private, the personal, the spiritual. Having dwelt among the people of Uist for a number of years, and having won a measure of trust, he was now in the unusual position of being able to gather private and personal lore, the reciters of which 'were more rare and reticent'.[56] Much of this material, of course, was possessed by women, and the evident attractiveness of this enthusiastic, candid, ingenuous and above all sympathetic folklore collector to the opposite sex should not be overlooked.[57]

Again, from 1873 Carmichael contributed various short articles as a correspondent for the *Highlander*, the new radical crofting newspaper edited by his one-time mentor John Murdoch. Its columns offered an outlet for shorter, quirkier, more anecdotal lore, items which were easier for the hard pressed family man to write up than long prose narratives, material designed to entertain and to provoke a response from the readership.

Another crucial factor in helping to explain Carmichael's change of tack is surely the social status of his wife, and the work she undertook, following the example of Captain Thomas' wife, as a promoter of 'home industries'. This not only encompassed charity work in itself, but was imbued with a strong moral and reforming stance. Indeed, Alexander Carmichael's later labours systematically collecting, polishing and promoting Gaelic spiritual material can be read as a somewhat oblique contribution to the same 'reformation of popular culture' as was envisaged in the 'home industries' programme.

Carmichael was of course hardly unaware of the poverty suffered by the people of the islands at the time, as can be seen from his horrified remarks in a field notebook concerning Donald Mackinnon, an old man of 98 in Dalabrog who suddenly fainted in front of him while reciting a tale:

> here poor old Donald MacInnon fell on the floor off his stool in a swoon & I thought he was dead. There were only two little children in a boy & a girl & I request them to run for the neighbours I raised the old mans head & placd a bag with some *diasun* bere heads under his head. He vomited ~~spe~~ A neigh[bouring] woman came but she seemed as scared as myself I placed 2/- in his hand & left. Poor man! Death would be a relief from such wretched poverty & rags & disorder & dirt. Wretched! wretched! wretched![58]

Mary Carmichael's work as 'a ministering angel'[59] in island society surely allowed her husband to make contact with the very poorest stratum of island society, especially the old women from whom he was to gather so many of the charms and prayers which were to form the core of the first two volumes of *Carmina Gadelica*.

During the 1870s Carmichael was also increasingly preoccupied with the idea of compiling a guidebook, or indeed a series of volumes, concerning the natural history, the history, and the culture of the Outer Hebrides, working up for the general public the 'mass of stuff about birds beasts fishes and antiquities', the 'plenty of raw materials scattered over a backload of scrapbooks'[60] he had gleaned throughout the islands over the years. Such an ambitious project would require considerably more leisure than he could afford in his exacting position. His attempt to secure Bhàlaigh farm in North Uist for this purpose met with a rebuff from the estate. This blow, coupled with his increasing disillusion regarding the philistine and repressive 'Uist gentry', and a concern to ensure a better education for his children, led him to quit the Hebrides in 1878 and to take up a new posting on the mainland, in the port of Oban. On the eve of their departure, however, disaster struck when the City of Glasgow Bank suddenly collapsed:

> We sold nearly all we had at Creagorry to Mr Norman Macdonald Bank Agent and Mr Nicol his brother-in-law, Accountant in the Bank. They paid Mr Carmichael with a deposit receipt of their own Bank three days before the failure was announced. I suppose we will get nothing, though I believe they paid nothing into the Bank.
>
> As Mr C. dealt with the City Bank, so far as remitting Revenue money only and had no private account there he immediately handed the deposit receipt to the Caledonian Bank at Lochmaddy and since we came here it has been returned dishonoured.[61]

The refusal of Mrs Gordon, proprietor of South Uist, to compensate them for the money spent in improving their home in Creag Goraidh, meant that, after a somewhat wearisome stay in Oban, the Carmichaels found themselves in April 1880 'under the painful and humiliating necessity of selling our furniture to pay our debts'[62] and having to leave the town. Spurning the Inland Revenue's offer of a prestigious and better-paid post in London, and taking a pay cut of some £70 in the process, Carmichael took his family back to Uist. Instead of returning to Mrs Gordon's estate, however, he chose to settle in Scolpaig on Sir John Campbell-Orde's estate of North Uist. The (furnished) house and its grazings were given to him rent free by the factor, John MacDonald of Newton and Scolpaig, in Carmichael's opinion 'one of the best and shrewdest men in the Western Isles. To me he is dear as a brother.'[63]

Carmichael had returned to the Hebrides because 'I feel that I should place on record what I know of the natural history and antiquities of these islands and in the belief that I could do this better on the spot.'[64] It was in Scolpaig, drawing upon local knowledge concerning the remaining townships in the islands where the runrig system was still practised, that Carmichael at last, after much postponement and vacillation, finished a project which was to change his career: his appendix concerning Hebridean land customs written for the third volume of *Celtic Scotland* (1876–80), the *magnum opus* of William Forbes Skene.[65] In summer 1882, having spent some two extra years in the Hebrides, Carmichael moved to Edinburgh for the sake of his children's schooling.

> [On] the very day he left the island to take up his residence on the mainland, he was suddenly called on to pay an account amounting to within a few shillings of one hundred pounds for stores ordered on behalf of people whose own orders would have been dishonoured by the merchants.[66]

In Edinburgh he was to pass the remaining three decades of his life.

A central theme of W. F. Skene's work is its focus on traditional customary law. Carmichael's heartfelt, somewhat idyllic, but nevertheless detailed and authoritative picture of the few Hebridean townships which retained remnants of the older system represents a core text in the development and rehabilitation of communitarian ideologies which were to loom so large in Highland politics during the following decade. The liveliness of his agrarian descriptions caught the eye of Francis, Lord Napier (1819–98): indeed, he later credited the chapter with first inspiring in him an interest in Highland affairs. As a result, in 1883 Napier requested Carmichael to contribute a similar piece for the *Report* of the Crofting Commission. His two appendices appeared in the *Report* the following year.[67]

The 1870s saw increasing stress on the Highland land question, itself part of a broader 'Gaelic question', a topic subsuming economic, political, cultural, educational and religious issues: what was to be the position of Gaels within Scotland, and within the wider British state? How could, and should Gaels engage with the English-speaking world outwith the Gàidhealtachd?

A significant factor in this was the emergence of a more self-confident, self-conscious, and indeed more argumentative generation of Gaels, a generation familiar with formal institutions and their conventions, not only living in the Highlands, but in Lowland cities, in London, and overseas. This cadre had spent their formative years in a region racked by famine, disruption, and despair. Since then the Gàidhealtachd had changed dramatically. Improved communications networks of steamer, rail and telegraph, of the post and of newspapers, facilitated contact and allowed fora for discussion and debate. Increased literacy in Gaelic and in English had fostered a publishing industry which had created and promoted Gaelic literary canons and developed Gaelic identities. Crucially, there was the spread of the institutions of state and church. Endowed with the charisma of power, backed by the prestige of print, and employing techniques of individual socialisation through discipline and rote-learning, these functioned as innovative, dynamic, even liberating 'communities of memory', promoting new histories, calendars and celebrations, rituals, signs and symbols, the acquisition and cultivation of new habits of social behaviour, conduct, and bodily practices, new registers of language, even a new language itself to replace the old. Promoting coherent narratives of secular and religious progress, these institutions brought individuals into a much more equivocal relationship not just with a 'traditional' past, but an unsatisfactory present, offering them a new community with new goals. Cultural, educational, religious, political and economic changes promoted the integration of the local into wider national and imperial perspectives, not only in a geographical sense, but in a temporal one too: the Highlands were oriented towards the future, towards progress.

Above all, surely, the new generation possessed expectations. Having learnt the relevant entrepreneurial, organisational and oratorical skills, with experience, discipline, social standing and bureaucratic contacts, they could attempt to negotiate with and negotiate around the British state, to demand a voice and a place within it. Crucially for their status as a special interest group, they had not only to be able to articulate their grievances, but to translate their case and to present it and narrate it in terms explicable and acceptable to the English-speaking world outside. The concept of translation, translation between traditional oral Gaelic and the burgeoning written registers of the language, and translation between the Gaelic and English tongues, a two-way traffic not only a matter of words but of concepts, of literature of all genres and degrees, of beliefs, claims and counter-claims, of knowledge and of narratives, is of crucial importance for understanding the period and, indeed, for understanding the later career of Alexander Carmichael.

A key marker of identity for this new generation was a self-conscious distance from the past, even at the same time as it refashioned and redeployed memories of previous injustices in the service of the crofters' cause. During the couple of decades after the mid-century, throughout much of the western Gàidhealtachd, an older generation raised in communally-worked townships during the twilight of the chiefs gradually ceded social, cultural, and moral authority to a younger cohort, much more mobile, much more conversant with the outside world, brought up under a new dispensation in a more individualistic crofting system, under the sway of incoming landlords possessing none of the residual traditional prestige of their predecessors. For Alexander Carmichael, the resulting generation gap between the older people from whom he collected traditional material, and the—in his eyes at least—uninterested young, was quite palpable.

In the Highlands, gradual but fragile economic improvements, in wages, housing, and diet, perhaps especially deriving from the growth in the fishing industry during the 1870s, had by no means benefited the entire population. Modest gains had thrown into sharper relief the plight of those left behind, especially those in the older generation who were the recipients of the 'home industries' charity of the likes of Mary Carmichael. Although contemporary Gaelic communitarian ideologies may have been heavily influenced both by tradition and by religious principle, rising inequalities among the people themselves may have given questions of social welfare and mutual aid a new inflection, a new urgency. Indeed, perhaps the increasing animus felt across the Highlands against the landlords during the period is not so much due to rank incomprehension of their motives and actions, but rather reflects an increasing ability to understand them all too well.

Alexander Carmichael's personal experience in Uist had left him with a heartfelt rancour against the local gentry and a sympathy with people 'who to my thinking have been for many years past discouraged repressed and tyrannized over the negative kindness of the proprietor notwithstanding.'[68] This was especially the case with the poorest section of the Uist population, upon whom 'probably Mrs C. spent more time, trouble, and means, in alleviating distress and sickness among the people than all other persons together, the paid doctors alone excepted.'[69]

Carmichael took up Napier's offer with enthusiasm, but embarked upon a rather unusual course of action, rounding off his second paper, 'Grazing and agrestic customs of the Outer

Hebrides', with a rhyme, a hymn, two prayers, three blessings, and four songs, two of them milking lullabies, in order to illustrate his subjects' grace, refinement, and piety: 'a touching dedicatory old hymn'; a 'beautiful little prayer'; 'singularly chaste, beautiful, and elevated' verses which:

> indicate, I think, the wonderful natural refinement of the people who could appreciate, preserve, and repeat these, and whole libraries of similar oral literature throughout the past ages. … I have never heard, either in this or among the people, an unbecoming word or an impure story.[70]

As we have seen, Carmichael's attitudes towards spirituality, hardly dormant beforehand, had nevertheless undergone a sea change over the previous decade.[71] In Uist, having gained the trust of the people among whom he lived, and possibly owing in part to his wife's charity work, he was now aware of and able to gain access to more private, devotional lore. There may have been another inspiration too. In autumn 1878, newly arrived in Oban, Carmichael, his wife, and some friends 'went to Iona, a party of six and were fortunate in getting a little cottage all to ourselves, near the landing place.'[72] Iona Cathedral and Nunnery had recently been cleared and restored as a result of a major programme of works at the expense of the Duke of Argyll, under the direction of W. F. Skene and the Society of Antiquaries. His visit to the 'cradle of Christianity' in the Gàidhealtachd clearly stimulated Carmichael to further research on the island, culminating in a study of Iona place-names drawing also upon the comprehensive and intensive work he had done for the previous two years on the toponymy of Harris, the Uists, and Barra for the Ordnance Survey.[73]

Alexander Carmichael refused to present evidence directly to the Napier Commission, though the tenor of the peroration to his second appendix suggests, despite his earlier praise of the communal system, that he also envisaged the creation of a layer of respectable middle-ranking small farmers—possibly such as he himself aspired to be in Bhàlaigh:

> Therefore go back to the old order of things under improved conditions. Unloosen their cords, and allow the people to expand by filling up the central rungs in the land ladder, all of which are at present absent, rendering it impossible for a crofter, however industrious, to rise higher than he is. To my thinking it is impolitic, as well as unjust, to hem the people into a corner, thereby impoverishing the many to enrich the few. The people of the Outer Hebrides are admirable workers by sea and land, and if they are less persevering than they might be, it is the fault of circumstances.[74]

The pieces he forwarded to Napier make a strong cultural statement, one perhaps somewhat disconcerting to us today, offering a spiritual perspective on the land question which stressed how deeply imbricated Gaels' lives were with the landscape in which they lived. The other crucial element in the 'Grazing and agrestic customs' is the emphasis on respectability.

> To me these meetings of the crofters were highly interesting, as showing the ability of the people, their logical and legal acumen, their readiness of resource, and, I am happy to add, their invariable courtesy towards one another.
>
> In seeing these respectable industrious crofters quietly, friendly, and judiciously thus arranging their farming affairs, often wet, weary, and hungry, without food, without rest, without having been home since early morning when they left for their work, I have felt that they were cruelly maligned.[75]

Carmichael's piece was specifically intended to engage his readers' interests and sympathies. Leaving overt political attacks to others, he aimed to win over as many as possible. His indirect approach certainly paid off. The appendix proved remarkably popular, an uncontroversial oasis in exceptionally contentious volumes:

> At the last meeting of the Crofter Royal Commission, the members discussed the various papers that had come before them. 'Some praised one paper and some another', said Professor Mackinnon, 'but there was only one opinion among us all that your paper, Mr. Carmichael, is *the* paper of the Commission—a paper which will live as long as the English language lasts. I was asked to tell you this, and to thank you for it.'[76]

Carmichael pursued the topic in his paper 'Uist old hymns', presented to the Gaelic Society of Glasgow on 24 December 1888.[77] The enthusiastic reception accorded the piece, and a promise of financial support, encouraged him to embark upon a much more comprehensive work on the subject. As ever, though, Alexander Carmichael did not feel that the material he had was ready for the press:

> I have finished or nearly finished the translations of the old hymns collected in the Outer Hebrides. But before sending them to press I am anxious to collate them with the memories of the old people and to try and get if but an additional verse, line, or even word or variation.
> For this purpose I must go among the few the very few remaining dear old people of the kind hearts the wonderful memories and the courteous manners.[78]

In the autumn of 1890 Carmichael spent 'ten weeks in Skye, Bearnary (Harris), North Uist, South Uist, Barra, Bunawe and Lochaber, in search of new hymns and new versions.' In July of the following year, as he recounts to in an appreciative and encouraging letter to the young Lady Evelyn Murray (1868–1940), then in the middle of her meteoric folklore collecting career, he was able to send to the Clarendon Press 'a compilation of ancient hymns charms and incantations collected in the Outer Hebrides where I lived for nearly thirteen years. These ancient hymns are of a high order—higher than anything known to me either in Gaelic or in English.' Nevertheless, the editing work would clearly take considerably more time and effort than he had originally envisaged:

> I have translated and retranslated ~~the old~~ revised and rerevised the old hymns and inca[n]tations but I am far from satisfied with my own work and yet I cannot make it better. It is di[s]heartening! Words and phrases occur, especially in the incantations that are not only obsolete but archaic, and these have caused me much trouble.[79]

It is a telling passage. In fact, the first two volumes of the work would take Carmichael nearly a decade to complete, and he would continue to labour on the project for the last twelve years of his life.

As has been seen, in the initial stages of Alexander Carmichael's collecting career charms, hymns, prayers, blessings, and other spiritual material did not loom particularly large. His first intention had been to publish a guidebook to the Hebrides, incorporating not only cultural but archaeological and natural historical material. This idea subsequently expanded, possibly under the influence of Skene's *Celtic Scotland*, into a projected three-volume account: 'The 1st say, the Geology and fauna; the 2 social and domestic; and the 3[d] antiquities.'[80] Carmichael certainly did collect some charms during his early years in Uist, but it was not until later in the 1870s that he began recording them systematically—possibly after he had heard about the herbalist descendants of the Beaton medical family still living in South Uist, and had sent the Rev. Alexander Stewart, 'Nether-Lochaber', *Eòlas an Torranain*, the torranan charm, as a curiosity to use in his newspaper column in summer 1874.[81]

To say the very least, charms were a rather neglected genre in Gaelic literary collections up until Carmichael. This was not only because the preponderance of educated clergymen among the collectors led to such semi-literate low magic or occult superstitions being spurned on principle.[82] Another of John Francis Campbell's team, the entrepreneurial collector par excellence John Dewar (1802–72), was possessed of a rather caustic opinion of them, ascribing their invention to 'Druids' who duped the people with tales:

> that the fairies had the power of being either visible or invisible, as they thought proper, and that they had the power of enchanting people, and of taking them away and make fairies of them; and that the Druids had charms which would prevent that… The Druidical priests pretended that they had charms that would prevent the witches from doing aney harm, and they would give a charm for payment. … Beil or Beul was the name which the Druids gave their god, and the Druids of Beil pretended to be the friends of the people; they pretended to have charms to cure different kinds of diseases, and also charms to prevent fairies, ghosts, and witches, from annoying or harming people. It is a well-known fact, that the superstitions of the Druids has been handed down from generation to generation for a great maney ages, and is not wholy extinct yet…[83]

At best, charms were simple curiosities remembered from childhood, a province of the old and credulous. At worst, summoning up images of the evil eye and the irrational superstition of a more primitive age, charms were far from welcome in the modern Gaelic canon. Nevertheless, despite religious disapproval and neighbourly derision, in times of trauma and anxiety charms and charmers were resorted to by all sections of the community—just as was the case, in fact, in many other areas of Victorian Britain. Carmichael's early error, perhaps, was to believe that he had stumbled across the last hidden remnants of a genre which in some respects remained just as strong among the strict presbyterian communities of Easter Ross as it was among the islanders of South Uist and Barra.

Even after he had moved to Edinburgh, Carmichael continued to collect spiritual material on his travels through the Gàidhealtachd, especially back in Uist. Nevertheless, it should not be forgotten that a good number of items in the first two volumes of the *Carmina* were in fact gathered by other hands, such as Father Allan McDonald of Eriskay (1859–1905), the Rev. John Gregorson Campbell of Tiree (1834–91), and most notably John Ewen MacRury (1853–1909) from Torlum in Benbecula, 'a highly intelligent man for whose knowledge of old lore I am deeply indebted in this work.'[84] Possibly inspired by Carmichael, MacRury had himself been collecting since the mid-1870s. In 1889 he posted to Edinburgh a parcel of Uist charms; during the winter of 1894–5, he compiled through reminiscence, recording, and indeed composing, a substantial collection of lore for Carmichael. Though none of the specific items which MacRury gathered appeared in the first two volumes of *Carmina*, Carmichael made much of the information he recorded, and, it appears, of the writer himself. Strewn in great profusion throughout the Carmichael Watson collection are draft notes for *Carmina Gadelica*, many apparently in the hand of John Ewen MacRury.[85]

During the final decade of the nineteenth century, Alexander Carmichael, now approaching retirement, further consolidated his position not only as doyen of Edinburgh's Gaelic intellectual community, but also as a crucial player in Scotland's Celtic Renaissance. In order better to understand the milieu in which *Carmina Gadelica* was compiled and created, the

Rev. Donald Lamont's reminiscences of the Carmichael household during these years is worth quoting:

> I was privileged to see a little of the home of the Carmichaels during my student days in Edinburgh, and the chief recollections of it that remain with me now are these: the hospitality of their table; the unwordly ideals of life that prevailed there; the golden atmosphere through which the Highland people and all Gaelic things were seen; and the number of interesting people who might be seen there.[86]

Carmichael's own character had matured into a striking personality:

> what one saw first and last in Dr Carmichael's personal appearance was a fine stateliness touched with emotion. When he entered a room, every eye seemed to say: This is a great Celtic gentleman, one who has lived in statelier and courtlier days. But such as knew him could always see the tenderness glowing through the stateliness, though the one never really blotted out the other. In his most tender moments, he was the stately gentleman; in his stateliest moods he attracted through his tenderness. It is difficult to get an English word to describe him exactly, though in Gaelic one would naturally use the word *uasal*—high thoughts and high deeds transfiguring person and manner.[87]

Alexander Carmichael's collection of spiritual lore had inspired the folklorist and secretary of the Crofters' Commission William Mackenzie (1851–1919), the historian Alexander MacDonald (1860–1928), and the scholar Alexander Macbain (1855–1907), to investigate further and to categorise such material.[88] For Macbain especially, imbued with the ideology of cultural evolutionism and convinced that Gaelic society was only recently, and imperfectly, Christianised, Gaelic charms offered a royal road back 'to the times of primitive Aryan unity.'[89]

> Superstition is nearly all a survival of Paganism into Christian times; and in the incantations the names of Christ, his apostles, and the Virgin Mary took those of the old heathen gods.[90]

For Macbain, one man's work was central:

> In this connection, the beautiful hymns collected by Mr Carmichael in Uist at once occur to one. Some of them are just on the indefinable borderland that separates Christianity and Paganism, and others again incline to a doubtful position between a literary croon and an incantation.[91]

Such articles caught the jackdaw eye of the Symbolist poetaster William Sharp (1855–1905), or rather that of his alter ego Fiona MacLeod, the doyenne of the Celtic Twilight movement. Sharp plundered Carmichael's work for examples of charms, concentrated, bejewelled fragments of prose poetry saved from the wreck of a dying civilisation, proof of the supernatural affinity between the visionary, passionate, soulful, intuitive Celt and an emblematic nature, a spirited rejection of modern rationalism and progress, a symbolist genre *avant la lettre*.[92] Sharp's position as literary adviser to the publishing firm owned by the polymathic visionary Patrick Geddes (1854–1932) may have led to Carmichael contributing to Geddes' seminal journal *Evergreen* (1895–6) an entertaining, somewhat meandering, 'locally enthusiastic'[93] article about his homeland culminating in eye-catching assertions concerning Robert Burns' supposed Highland ancestry.[94]

Carmichael's own dignity and piety inspired both Gaelic students and scholars, and members of the intellectual and artistic circles of *fin de siècle* Edinburgh. In turn, they exerted a major influence on Alexander Carmichael's greatest and most enduring work. They propagated the romantic notion of the mystic, visionary, sequestered, primitive 'Spiritual Celt', constructed by the scholars Ernest Renan (1823–92) and Matthew Arnold (1822–88) but owing much to James Macpherson's Ossian.[95] They shared the fascination and attraction felt by the late Victorian generation towards spiritualism and psychical research, offering comforts and insights denied to scientific materialism. Of course, *Carmina Gadelica* also represents an intervention in contemporary domestic religious debate, endeavouring to portray, or even to construct, an ecumenical, tolerant, and mystical indigenous tradition of Gaelic—or indeed Celtic—Christianity in opposition to evangelical Highland Presbyterianism on the one hand, and, on the other, the widespread belief in the Lowlands that a dogmatic, biblicist, sabbatarian Calvinism was representative of the religion of the region as a whole. But most important of all for Carmichael was his political goal, nothing less than to redeem his people:

> I had another secret hope in my soul—that by making the book up in as good a form as I could in matter and material, it might perhaps be the means of conciliating some future politician in favour of our dear Highland people. For example, had the book been in the hands of Mr. Gladstone some twenty years ago, who knows but it might have interested him still more in our dear lovable people. These aspirations come in upon me and waylay me to my sore detriment.[96]

In *Carmina Gadelica* Alexander Carmichael compiled and edited a substantial collection of sacred pieces, hymns, blessings, prayers, and charms, expressedly intended to illustrate the refined spirituality, the crepuscular rhapsodic mysticism, the visionary qualities of the spiritual Celts amongst whom he had lived for nearly two decades. The process of finding a publisher was a long one. As *Idylls of the Isles*, the book was first offered to the Clarendon Press in 1891, and subsequently retracted. It was placed under the auspices of Archibald Sinclair's Gaelic press in Glasgow, and withdrawn again, but not before Sinclair had printed a consignment of flyers in 1897 in order to gather subscriptions for *Òr agus Òb*, as the project was now called. In December of that year Carmichael finally retired from the Inland Revenue, after over 41 years of service.

The editing of the literary side of the project—indeed its very title—was indebted to the encouragement and advice of Carmichael's protégé the scholar George Henderson (1866–1912). The creation of the volumes themselves was in hands of the publisher Walter Biggar Blaikie (1847–1928), Carmichael's wife Mary who illustrated the letters, and his daughter Ella. Together, they were able to fashion a landmark in Scottish publishing, a stately, sumptuously produced *magnum opus*, whose illustrations and hand-made paper were surely intended to recall early Christian manuscripts, to represent to the reader the original numinous experience of hearing the original chants and lays. This was intended not just as a treasury of lore, but as an object of beauty in itself: 'the book, when seen, will command its own market & be a possession.'[97]

The first two volumes of *Carmina Gadelica* were published in October 1900, in a limited edition of 300, at 3 guineas a copy. Special handmade volumes were presented to his wife Mary, to whom the work was dedicated, to his four children, to John Henry Dixon who had first offered to pay for the printing of 'Uist old hymns' some twelve years earlier, and to Queen Victoria.[98] In his gift to his wife, Carmichael wrote the following inscription:

To thee,

    Mary,
    The gifted woman,
    The devoted mother,
    The perfect wife,
I, thy grateful husband, owe
more than words can tell.
Mo ghaol, mo ghaol mo ghaol fhein thu
Mo ghaol an diugh mar an de thu
Mo ghaol gach oidhche 's la dh eireas
    Mo ghaol air thalamh agus neimh thu.
My love, my love mine own love art thou
My love to-day as yesterday art thou
My love every night and day that arise art thou
    My love of earth and of heaven art thou.
    Alexander.
30th Oct 1900[99]

Carmina Gadelica shows the influence of such art books as those published by Patrick Geddes, of the beautiful *Records of Argyll* edited by Lord Archibald Campbell (1846–1913) in 1885 to which Carmichael had himself contributed, and, perhaps, of the tourist souvenirs published by the little Iona Press. As an artistic achievement, it stands in the very first rank.

The myth of *Carmina Gadelica* was planted; and continued more or less unchallenged throughout the publication of volumes three to six. Carmichael's editing methods were eventually roundly challenged in 1976 with the publication in *Scottish Gaelic Studies* of Hamish Robertson's somewhat notorious article 'Studies in Carmichael's *Carmina Gadelica*'[100], in which Carmichael was accused of meddling with and altering original texts, of archaising, of polishing, even of invention and of deception. Searching for surviving manuscript copies of charms in the third and fourth volumes of *Carmina*, Robertson found that 'hardly one had not been touched up in some way, sometimes quite drastically.'[101] Robertson's forceful indictment called forth an equally vigorous response from John Lorne Campbell in the next issue, wherein several of the former's more extreme accusations were rebuffed. Nevertheless, although Carmichael's editing practices, and the motivations behind them, can certainly only be understood with reference to his own times and circumstances, both when collecting and when writing up, the fact remains, in Campbell's words, that:

> Much of the first three volumes of the *Carmina* must be taken as a literary and not as a literal presentation of Gaelic folklore.[102]

In connection with the continuing controversy, a brief examination of Carmichael's papers may be apposite here.

Alexander Carmichael's papers form the core of the Carmichael Watson collection in Edinburgh University Library. The sheer size of the collection is somewhat daunting: nine linear metres of shelf space in the library strong room, comprising volumes, notebooks, scrapbooks, ledgers, and a few printed books, sixty boxes filled to the brim with an astonishing variety of materials, generally bundles of paper of various ages and conditions in envelopes or tied with cord. The other striking feature of Carmichael's own manuscripts is the sheer heterogeneity of the types of paper used, taking in tiny scraps, pages ripped out of diaries, hundreds of little slips, jotters, notebooks, the large blue foolscap sheets he uses so often in his early fieldwork, the large excise forms on which he would scribble rough drafts of letters and petitions, the double-paged lined jotter paper on which he would edit and re-edit items for *Carmina Gadelica*, and indeed *Carmina* page proofs as well.

Paper was scarce in the Hebrides. Alexander Carmichael had to use and often reuse what he could. He would then hoard and transcribe fieldwork material for future use, a habit he was to follow scrupulously for the rest of his days. In Carmichael's manuscripts we can trace a life through paper, and also trace how, through bureaucratic paperwork, the reach of the Victorian state was extending even into the remotest corners of the kingdom. The profusion of material recorded is paralleled by the profusion of the types of paper on which it is recorded. Challenging to conserve, to catalogue, and to research, the physical nature of Alexander Carmichael's manuscript collection makes it quite unlike any other contemporary archive.

Scholars researching Carmichael's editing practices have focused upon locating two types of material: the original field notes; and the original drafts for the two volumes of *Carmina Gadelica* published in 1900.

In their attempts to unearth original 'field notes', scholars have spent much time trying to track down loose sheets. In fact, most of the surviving material gathered in the field is written down in notebooks, or, to use Carmichael's own description, 'scrap books'. John Mackechnie, the collection's original cataloguer, certainly noted down several of them, while Professor William Matheson was well aware of at least one of the items, drawing upon it for his edition of the songs of Ruairidh MacGilleMhoire, the seventeenth-century Blind Harper.[103] A search through the archive reveals some 26 notebooks, mainly taken up with original material, as well as a couple of others containing some original items. These books can be categorised into three phases: those which Carmichael used in the early 1860s while stationed with the excise at Carbost in Skye[104]; the numerous books he used while working in the Outer Hebrides between 1865 and 1882[105]; and those he used to record material either from Gaels in Edinburgh, where he spent the last thirty years of his life, or else when summer touring around the Highlands.[106] Carmichael's appalling handwriting has so far prevented these items from being accorded the recognition they deserve. Many researchers will sympathise with John Francis Campbell's exasperated remark when first confronted with material written by him, that 'I cannot make anything of this mans writing till I copy it.'[107]

Carmichael's return to the Highlands in 1864, to Uist, certainly led to a change of approach in his collecting methods. As he well knew from experience, it was far from easy to travel through the Outer Hebrides, whether for excise work or for fieldwork. It was for this reason that he bought a set of robust, softback notebooks specifically for the task. Compared to loose foolscap sheets or jotters, they were convenient to carry around; they were much less likely to get lost, torn, or damaged; they were relatively waterproof; and they were much easier to write on resting on his (kilted) knees, whether in the black house or without.

These field notebooks allow us to open the 'black box' of Carmichael's years in the Outer Hebrides, to trace where he went and when, with whom he worked, how his fieldwork changed over his lifetime. They allow us to go right to the heart of Alexander Carmichael's collecting endeavours, to look over his shoulder as he records for the first time from his informants the multifarious materials he would spend the rest of his life transcribing, contemplating, and editing. They are among the most valuable folklore manuscripts in the country, of international importance.

However, it would be somewhat premature simply to label these notebooks as the original core of the collection. The very earliest field notebooks from Uist, for example, do not contain roughly scribbled items we might expect from later examples, but material rather neatly written out in pen. The fortuitous survival of a torn scrap of paper now catalogued as CW MS 423 hints at a possible solution. The page contains part of a tale 'Righ Eirean' narrated by Donald MacPhee in Ìochdar, South Uist, on 21 February 1866. This is clearly the original of the unfinished story 'Righ Eirinn' in the notebook CW MS 104 fos.32–5: it is by the same reciter, and, when it is remembered that Carmichael understood 'Faoilleach' to be the month of February rather than January, it bears the same date.

Donald MacPhee's tale recorded in the notebook breaks off after three folios, followed by a short account by one John Mackenzie, clearly originally from Gairloch, regarding a relation of his who fought at the Battle of Sheriffmuir. Carmichael then resumes with another tale by MacPhee. It is possible that Carmichael was transcribing the story in pen into his notebook from the original loose leaf copy when he was interrupted by Mackenzie, who had an anecdote which he then recorded in pencil. Given the somewhat racy nature of MacPhee's first tale, it is tempting to imagine that the seanchaidh was testing his prudish young visitor by retailing one of the more uncouth tales from his repertoire. Then again, the beginning of the story resembles a tale which Carmichael had taken down from Alasdair MacNeil in Barra the week before.[108] The two men may have been discussing what Carmichael had just recorded in Barra, and MacPhee may have determined to give his audience a similar tale. Whatever the case might be, Alexander Carmichael decided not to finish transcribing the tale, but, after having taken down a historical anecdote, he then copied out in full a second tale by MacPhee. This time, however, he recorded MacPhee's narration in pencil first, before writing over it, in pen, one line above the original all the way through. Although Carmichael clearly polished the first tale, improving its flow, when transcribing it into the notebook, this is not the case with the second tale. We should also note that Mackenzie's Sheriffmuir anecdote is itself rewritten and edited in pen at the end of the field notebook.[109] The diverse techniques Carmichael was using to record and transcribe his material at this time suggest that he was in something of a quandary regarding his collecting and transcribing methods. Soon afterwards, he begins to record his material straight from the reciter into the notebooks in pencil.

This particular episode suggests that we should resist the temptation to be dogmatically certain concerning the unchanging nature of Alexander Carmichael's fieldwork methodologies. There are simply too many gaps in the collection, as well as the prospect of unexpected items being rediscovered. Certainly, there are plenty of dated items in later transcriptions or even in *Carmina Gadelica* which have no corresponding matter recorded in the field notebooks. Again, we have some material which Carmichael recorded straight onto paper during the years when he was using his notebooks. These are either catalogued as separate items, or else tipped into the notebooks. We can see that one item at least was written by Carmichael on an unattached sheet after he had come to the end of a notebook the day before and thus had no more space.[110] Suspicious clusters of dates of later transcriptions, without their original recordings, might suggest missing field notebooks, but we will never be able to state this with absolute certainty.

Even when original items in the field notebooks have been located and recorded, the researcher then has to contend with Alexander Carmichael's transcription notebooks.[111] Since Carmichael would write down not only the date of the original recording in his field notebook, but would also enter a transcription date if the item was transcribed, the researcher is in a position to trace how his interests changed over the years. At first, most copies were made for other people: for the edition of *Ossian* by the Rev. Archibald Clerk (1813–87) in 1870; for John Francis Campbell's *Leabhar na Féinne* in 1872; and for the fortnightly column written by the Rev. Alexander Stewart (1829–1901), 'Nether-Lochaber', for the *Inverness Courier*. Later on in the

1870s we find Carmichael transcribing for his own ends, firstly for newspaper articles, for research into Hebridean landholding, then increasingly for charms and hymns. These transcriptions also reveal how even the earliest material Carmichael recorded and circulated—especially Ossianic lays—could be tainted by his desire to shore up the claims of James Macpherson's productions.

In a sense, the problem, if that is what it is, dates back to Carmichael's formative years as a collector. For the young Carmichael, poets were:

> like lapidaries. They get hold of a gem no matter how or where and make it their own, and they polish and shape it to suit their own tastes. It was once fixed in a brooch it is now in a necklace. It once confined the modest folds of a village maiden it is polished reset and now adorns the snowy bosom of a courtly countess.[112]

Obsessive artistic polishing, the search for the perfect, and necessarily collated, *Urtext*, is the key characteristic of Carmichael's attitude towards material he sends to his editors. To return to one of his letters to John Francis Campbell explaining why he is hesitating to send him the tales he has promised:

> But there is another reason why I have not sent you before now some proofs of my attachment to the work you are engaged upon. I am exceedingly desirous of getting every tale as full and complete as I possibly can. In consequence of this and in consequence of always getting some additional words or expressions I have written and rewritten all the tales I now send you at least five or six times. When travelling amongst the people for my tales I have frequently heard from them some additional particulars some additional words to tales I already had. Instead of cutting them short—so to speak—by telling them that I had those tales already I always listened to them and if they had anything which I had not before, I took it down.[113]

Campbell, it should be noted, appears to have been rather suspicious of material sent him by Carmichael, requesting copies of original field notes, and in fact using very little of what Carmichael sent him for his anthologies.[114]

Again, in 1872 when sending in a tale, or rather several versions of a tale, for the first time to the Gaelic Society of Inverness—the exceptionally important 'Toirioc na Taine'—Carmichael warns:

> This tale is written from the dictation of the 'Seanachaidh' with all the seanachaidh's tautology. I would therefore strongly recommend to the Council of the Gaelic Society of Inverness to rewrite the tale blending all the versions into one and omitting all the unnecessary repetitions.
> For this purpose let them hand over the M.S.S. to the able hands of 'Sgiathanach' [i.e. Rev. Alexander MacGregor].[115]

In the end, the exigencies of pressing time and the presence of a waiting editor meant that the younger Carmichael would have to send off his texts whether he felt they were ready or not—although it should be noted that he could blame lack of time too. In a letter to Rev. Archibald Clerk, Carmichael artlessly remarks of his version of the *Laoidh Chlann Uisne* he recorded from the smith Donald MacPhee of Breubhaig, Barra:

> In transcribing this poem I did so as much as I could from memory without looking at my *Sgialac* book more than I could avoid being in a hurry at the time. It is therefore possible I may in some instances have inserted the words of the printed book.[116]

After he came to live in Edinburgh, however, Carmichael had much more time, and no editor but himself. In addition, his old folklore mentors, more exacting scholars such as John Francis Campbell and his erstwhile tutor and colleague Hector Maclean (1818–93), were now dead.

Carmichael was certainly somewhat apprehensive about the work he had recorded being read by Gaelic speakers; he was much the more discomposed by the prospect of his texts appearing in English. The prose narratives he sent as contributions to the *Transactions of the Gaelic Society of Inverness* in the early 1870s were printed in Gaelic alone. When, however, he renewed his connection with the society in the late 1880s after he had moved to Edinburgh, he supplied not only a Gaelic 'original' of the story he sent them—the romance of *Deirdire* recorded in 1867 from Iain MacNeil in Buaile nam Bodach, Barra—but forwarded an English translation just over a year later.[117] This may have been inspired in part by rivalry with the Rev. John Gregorson Campbell of Tiree, who had been making a name for himself with a series of narratives he had collected, edited, and translated in various Gaelic periodicals, including the *Transactions*.[118]

If Carmichael intended to surpass the minister, he certainly succeeded: *Deirdire* is a complex narrative related in an ornate, even archaic style, remarkably rich in idiom, in one sense a fusion of the long prose narratives which had fascinated him in his earlier collecting career with the delicate sensibilities of the more private material he had gathered more recently. The publisher and folklore scholar Alfred Nutt (1856–1910) went so far as to tell him 'that this was the finest story ever got in Scotland or in Britain equal to anything of the kind in the ancient classics of Greece or Rome.'[119] When, however, we compare the printed text to the original recorded text, we find that Carmichael has not only polished up MacNeil's oral account, but effectively rewritten it, even to the extent of interpolating a major episode quite absent in the original. In his study of Carmichael's narrative, Alan Bruford emphasises:

> the thoroughness with which, having taken down a complete text, he revised every sentence, almost as if he were trying to evade copyright restrictions.[120]

One key difficulty is that Alexander Carmichael had not in fact taken down a complete text. As a narrative, the original *Deirdire* is extremely problematic. Half of it was taken down from MacNeil by Carmichael himself on 16 March 1867. Then he broke off, 'on account of having made an appointment with Dr MacGillivray to go out shooting with Dr W. E. MacLellan and to dine at Eoligearry house in the evening.' The remainder of the story was written down later by 'Mr Donald MacRae of Buaile nam Bodach', posted to Carmichael afterwards, transcribed, and then retranscribed by an amanuensis in 1872.[121] *Deirdire* was an awkward text from the start, and this perhaps is why Carmichael felt able to rewrite it substantially for his presentation to the Gaelic Society of Inverness.

Carmichael's English translation of *Deirdire*, and the poetic version he made for the *Transactions* in 1889 of the associated ballad *Laoidh Chlann Uisneach*[122] are similarly elaborate, high-flown, and archaic. He was determined to make an impression on an English-speaking readership, and we might suspect the influence of a series of lectures in rhetoric and literary style he attended between October and December 1886, probably at the University of Edinburgh.[123]

It is also clear that Carmichael was confronted with a similar quandary in presenting and translating the spiritual material he had collected. He writes frankly about this predicament in the drafts he prepared for the projected later volumes of the *Carmina*:

> These poems seemed finer / better when sung or recited or intoned. The music / recitatives intonation improved the words and the listener / hearer was charmed / ear and mind were charmed and affected. In reducing the powers to paper they lost the music the rhyme and the rhythm and much of the charm with which the reciter endowed them. The reciters too lost the thread and the control of their words and their memories when the music was lost to the words. The words / the poem did not appear the same thing at all when sung and when reduced to paper.[124]

Alexander Carmichael felt that the charms and other pieces he had recorded could not do justice to the reciters, to the circumstances of collection, to their greater meaning, or to the mysterious story, the 'referent image', so often lying behind them. When reduced to words on a bare page, they simply weren't numinous enough for *Carmina Gadelica*. Where, as was generally the case, several versions of the same charm type existed, one possibility was to try to collate them and attempt, as it were, to reconstitute a putative ideal original—not at all an unusual approach at the time or indeed for several generations afterwards when editing oral poetry. Using his remarkable knowledge of Gaelic tradition, and with the help of his family and friends, Carmichael set to work on the material he had at hand. It is clear from Carmichael's manuscripts that he was prepared to hone, polish, even rewrite substantial portions of his original material before publishing, smoothing metre, cadence, and rhyme, heightening and refining language, adding esoteric referents, even introducing obscure vocabulary and archaic names in order to enhance the impact which the hymns and charms—and indeed the quotations from the informants themselves—would exert upon the reader of *Carmina Gadelica*. As before, Carmichael took especial care with the English versions of his material: indeed, even for the very first charm he had had published, back in 1874, we find him, quite uniquely, experimenting with translations in a field notebook.[125] Although his earlier editing processes are fairly minor in nature, it is likely that some later material was substantially rewritten or even virtually composed by the author—though some of these apparently concocted items were winnowed out by later editors. We might note the rather guileless confession by Rev. Kenneth MacLeod (1871–1955) to Carmichael's son-in-law Prof. William J. Watson (1865–1948) concerning one of the more artificial creations:

> The Achan Mathar is really a hybrid. I worked it up from a few stray lines, and from such conversational suggestions as 'Bha i guidhe cuideachd nach biodh e 'na dhallaran-ceo anns a' bhlàr'. Several old people in Skye, Uist and Eigg knew about it, but none of them could give me even one complete verse. Dr Carmichael liked it greatly and added touches to it.[126]

Alexander Carmichael's original field notes—or a large proportion of them—survive in his archive. This may well be true of many of the long sought after original drafts of the first two volumes of *Carmina Gadelica*. Printer's proofs for the second volume certainly exist in the collection, but, as we might expect, they tell us little.[127] The actual editing, polishing, or rewriting, was carried out at an earlier stage of the process.

On examining the Carmichael collection, the researcher begins to notice something rather unexpected. Throughout the collection there is a great quantity of material, scribbled out and reworked, on the reverse or verso side of the folios. This material, still uncatalogued, is where many of the apparently lost drafts of *Carmina Gadelica* i and ii are in fact to be found. As we have seen, during his years in the Highlands Alexander Carmichael would often preserve and reuse sheets of paper.[128] Indeed, all his life he had the habit of turning used sheets of paper over—tearing them in half if too large—and effectively recycling them. After the publication of the first two volumes of *Carmina*, Carmichael made another fieldwork expedition to the Outer Hebrides, before commencing work on a further two volumes.[129] In preparing this work, he reused the drafts of the earlier volumes. Scholars searching for the earlier drafts simply needed to turn the pages over once more. Because these drafts went unmentioned in the catalogue, however, they were effectively invisible.

These verso first drafts are scattered throughout the collection; related items, indeed parts of the very same item, can be found hundreds or even thousands of folios apart from each other. In addition, not all the relevant pieces are necessarily on the verso side. Some sheets were not reused; others were catalogued with the later piece on the verso side, and the earlier draft left on the recto; again, it is plain that by no means all or perhaps even most of the earlier drafts have survived: indeed, it is most unlikely. The collection is something of a giant jigsaw puzzle—with crucial pieces missing forever—and it will be some time at least before we will be able to attain a reliable picture.

Fortunately, it is very easy to distinguish earlier drafts from later ones. Carmichael's handwriting altered dramatically following the publication of the first two volumes of *Carmina*, becoming much more of a scrawl, to some extent because of the different, thinner nib he was using. Again, with practice it becomes relatively straightforward to distinguish new types of writing paper from old.[130]

While editing the third and fourth volumes of *Carmina Gadelica* in early 1940, James Carmichael Watson (1910–42) describes in a letter to his cousin Michael Carmichael how the *Carmina Gadelica* drafts contained 'four handwritings', as well as two different typewriter fonts.[131] Alexander Carmichael's own hand is immediately identifiable, as is his wife's. One of the remaining scripts, somewhat angular in character—if indeed it is a single hand—would appear to be that of John Ewen MacRury from Torlum in Benbecula, an old acquaintance of Carmichael at that time working in the Lowlands as a clerk. The other—again, if it is from the same pen—may be that of the young Kenneth MacLeod, although it may be confused with Ella's hand. I have found no evidence of a typewriter being used in compiling the original drafts of *Carmina Gadelica*.

There are four categories of early draft material in the collection: the items themselves; the introduction; the notes at the end of the second volume; and the table of informants.

In drafting items, Carmichael and his collaborators appear to have employed the same editing techniques from the 1890s onwards, both for the publication of the first two volumes of *Carmina Gadelica*, and also in preparing the later projected volumes. On a double spread of loose lined paper, as if made for a jotter, the item—a charm, hymn, prayer, or song—would be written out and edited in Gaelic on the left, with the English translation on the right. Both would, apparently, take shape at the same time. If the layout became too chaotic and cluttered, the process would be continued on a fresh sheet. When the item was judged to be ready, it would be written out in a fair hand, possibly by Ella, and—as is suggested by the absence of such neat versions for the earlier two volumes in the collection—dispatched to the publisher to be typeset. Plenty of such neat drafts destined for the later, abandoned volumes still exist in the collection. Unfortunately, however, it appears that few actual working drafts of items printed in *Carmina Gadelica* i–ii have been preserved.[132] It seems as if many of these rough working copies simply did not make it into the collection as it exists today. Whether extant drafts survived because they had already been reused for later editing work and thus, effectively 'in hiding', escaped being disposed of along with the rest, is a moot question. It should be stressed, however, that very few of these early drafts, especially the editing drafts of the charms, prayers, and hymns which make up the core of *Carmina Gadelica* i–ii, survive in their original state without having been turned over and 'recycled' later. As matters stand, we cannot tell whether the remainder of these draft items, of which there must once have been more than two hundred, were used for household purposes, or else calculatingly disposed of. We may never know.

The various drafts of the introduction to *Carmina Gadelica* volume i are scattered throughout the collection. This is in contrast to the drafts for the introduction for the projected third and fourth volumes, composed around 1904: most, but not all, of these appear to be found in CW MS 126. Early drafts are relatively easy to identify: numbered jotter sheets of continuous prose written out in thick black ink, some paginated with letters of the alphabet, others in a numerical order. There are in fact several stages in the composition of the first introduction, probably dating back as far as the early 1890s, judging by the scratchy pen with which Carmichael wrote out the earliest version.[133] Indeed, in the *Carmina* introduction we can discern the faded outline of the introduction to another book, or books, Carmichael never managed to write: the history and natural history of the Outer Hebrides on which he was working fitfully during his last years in Uist in the late 1870s and early 1880s.[134] The *Carmina* introduction takes up and develops ideas, themes, and verbal riffs which Carmichael had been working on since he commenced his folklore collecting career in the early 1860s, *idées fixes* which had clearly taken on deeper, personal connotations. Just as with the draft items, we can observe Carmichael working closely with his collaborators, especially, it seems, with his young protégé Kenneth MacLeod. MacLeod may well have rewritten or even added to parts of the final *Carmina* introduction, lending certain passages, especially the notional dialogues, an unmistakable, and occasionally rather sentimental, flavour.[135]

Various drafts for the notes at the back of *Carmina* ii are strewn in great profusion across the collection.[136] Most of these are composed by two hands: that of Alexander Carmichael himself; and an angular, somewhat capricious hand which may be John Ewen MacRury's. It is unclear to what extent MacRury was acting as Carmichael's amanuensis or copier, or as an author himself. As before, there must have been a final written draft sent off to the publishers, an intermediate stage between the still extant earlier versions, and the printer's proofs now preserved in MS 239.

Fourthly, and easiest of all to recognise, are the various drafts of the catalogue of reciters printed at the very end of the second volume of *Carmina Gadelica*. These sheets, dispersed in clumps, allow us to trace the development of the structure of *Carmina Gadelica*. Most interestingly—in contrast to Carmichael's early treatment of the hymns as effectively anonymous in his Napier Commission and 'Uist old hymns' articles—Carmichael began work on *Carmina Gadelica* not so much with the items, but rather with the reciters.[137]

Indeed, *Carmina Gadelica* is as much a book of people as it is of folklore in itself. Presiding over everyone else is the personality of Alexander Carmichael, for whom *Carmina Gadelica* was a personal testament. This is a constant theme in the reviews of *Carmina* preserved by Ella in her scrapbook CW MS 245. *Carmina Gadelica* is Carmichael's book, the 'splendid consummation of the love-labour of a whole diligent life-time' in the words of one reviewer:

> a great religious work, piously perfected by a man, every fibre of whose body and being vibrates to the beauty of holiness, and, as one might say, to the holiness of the beauty which he found in the life of even the most humble of his own people.[138]

Other reviews struck the same note:

> Two things strike one forcibly in connection with the work—the charming personality which pervades it and which will always form one of its chief attractions—and the devout piety the passionate self abandonment to the Almighty—a clumsy phrase I cannot find a better—displayed in the songs.[139]

> No one can read the work, or the notes, or gaze upon the portrait of Mr Carmichael in his everyday Highland dress, without feeling: 'Here is a charming personality, I would like to know that man. Here is a new world.'[140]

> Since Macpherson's *Ossian*, nothing has appeared in connection with the literature of the Highlands which can be in any sense compared with it. But even in this the comparison fails. This is beyond question the genuine thing; the other is not beyond doubt in certain respects. This is the very marrow of the life of our people in its far-reaching merit and simplicity and honesty—for which we thanks Mr. Carmichael with all our heart. He has done a noble work nobly.[141]

All his life Carmichael had been to say the least diffident about putting material into print, whether texts he had written himself or, as we have seen earlier, texts he had recorded from others. His letters to John Francis Campbell show how apprehensive he was having his Ossianic essay printed in *Popular Tales*.[142] As has been seen, in 1871 John Francis Campbell, on tour in the Uists, drafted an entire article in Carmichael's name in return for hospitality, information, and advice. By the time Carmichael was ensconced in Edinburgh as one of the doyens of the Celtic Revivalist scene, he was effectively a literary celebrity, and literary property, himself. It comes as something of a shock to see that the article appearing under Carmichael's name in Patrick Geddes' *Evergreen* actually underwent its final draft at the hands of Ella Carmichael and Kenneth MacLeod.[143] By the 1890s one could say that Alexander Carmichael had himself become a brand, sustained not only by his own pen, but also by those of his family and friends. From the manuscript evidence in the Carmichael Watson archive, *Carmina Gadelica* should be regarded as a collaborative enterprise, nurtured, developed, and brought to fruition not only by Carmichael himself, but by his wife Mary, his daughter Ella, and Kenneth MacLeod. Indeed, the figure of Alexander Carmichael himself might be considered as something of a collaborative enterprise, perhaps even as a persona occasionally adopted by his assistants in the editing process.

Little public criticism of *Carmina Gadelica* was voiced during Alexander Carmichael's lifetime, or indeed while his wife and daughter were still living. Nevertheless, some of their contemporaries were uneasy about his editing techniques. Both Father Allan McDonald and the Rev. John Gregorson Campbell were clearly uncomfortable with his earlier treatment of material with which they themselves were already well acquainted[144]; we might also note the Celtic scholar Alexander Macbain's significant remark that some of Carmichael's spiritual items inclined to 'a doubtful position between a literary croon and an incantation.'[145] It was Macbain who read out to the Gaelic Society of Inverness a paper which caused Carmichael the most hurt, and may have contributed to his inability to prepare further volumes of the *Carmina* in his lifetime.

John L. Robertson (1854–1927) had translated, under the title 'Ossianic heroic poetry', the comprehensive survey 'Die ossianischen Heldenlieder' written by the German scholar Ludwig Christian Stern (1846–1911) for the *Zeitschrift für vergleichende Litteraturgeschichte* 8 (1895). Stern only briefly mentions Carmichael's *Deirdire* as having been published 'not without factitious admixture of book learning.'[146] When this remark eventually came to Carmichael's notice, he was clearly stung by it and in April 1901 drafted a letter in reply:

> New terror will be added to the lives of men who try and sacrifice much in trying to rescue old lore among them by critics who sit at home in judgement upon them.
>
> I published some poems possibly Probably some [of] these poems are in manuscript possibly in print but I took my part of them from neither manuscripts nor from print whatever present or future critics may so allege but from the dictation of unlettered men and women who said that they heard them when young / in youth from the lips of unlettered old men and women.[147]

Nevertheless, comments such as Stern's had clearly hit home. Among Carmichael's papers concerning the further volumes of the *Carmina* on which he was working between 1904 and 1906 are a number of drafts of the introduction, demonstrating how preoccupied he was with justifying his editing techniques:

> Any poetry not written down is soon apt to get mangled in oral transmission. And even poems in print suffer in oral tradition—words and phrases and whole lines being more or less different from the those of the poet. This is inevitable among unlettered people words and lines are taken up wrongly and others are substituted (in their place).
>
> Many words and phrases and lines in these poems are old worn and unintelligible to the listener. It is only long intercourse among the people that enables me to place many of these words and phrases on paper and to render them with more or less accuracy.
>
> I was often at a loss how to render sounds into words and what these words might mean/meant. Sometimes the reciters were able to help the writer and sometimes they were not. If I have not always succeeded I have made an effort. ~~What~~ Whether I should have written/printed the words in the forms in which I found them I do not know. I have followed the advice and example of ~~Mr Carmichael~~ Mr Campbell of Islay and I have the approval of home/British and Continental scholars
>
> Besides the original difficulty of understanding much of what the old people said and comprehending it sufficiently to take it down ~~many~~ most of the books in which the lore was written down from the people got more or less wet on my person from rain water on land salt from sea spray at sea and from salt water in crossing fords rendering the pencil writing often difficult and sometimes impossible to decipher. Much time has been lost/spent ~~of~~ over these small but vexatious difficulties.
>
> No one can be more conscious or can more regret than I ~~do~~ myself the imperfections of the taking down the blurred condition of the writing and the inadequate translations of these poems.
>
> I have found it difficult to act. Had [I] space and means at my disposal I would have given all the different versions with all their different and innumerable divergences and incongruities. This plan would have suited my mind but not my means as it would have filled many instead of few volumes.
>
> I collected all the versions I possibly could and then collated all these versions as well as I possibly could words lines phrases and verses.
>
> Collecting entailed much time much trouble much expense and much travelling in all sorts of places and in all sorts of weathers and in all sorts of damps.
>
> But all these combined were nothing to the work and the worry of connecting and collating and combining all the different and divergent versions into one.
>
> I am more than conscious that I have not succeeded although I have again and again gone over the ground and over the work.[148]

Whether because of old age, the sheer amount of material, or inability to defend his treatment of what he had gathered, Alexander Carmichael was unable to create further volumes out of the great mass of paper he had accumulated during his lifetime. Perhaps pointedly, the next item he published after *Carmina Gadelica* was the tale of 'Caol Reathainn', in the new *Celtic Review* edited by his daughter Ella. It was the first piece he had ever had printed, at the beginning of his career some forty years previously.

In 1905, the year he published a book-length edition of *Deirdire*, Alexander Carmichael and his wife were granted a Civil List pension.[149] The following year, he was awarded an honorary LL.D. by the University of Edinburgh. Carmichael continued to contribute to the *Celtic Review* for the rest of his life, and carried out collecting expeditions almost until the year of his death.[150] Many of his new informants were mainland Ross-shire contacts of his son-in-law William J. Watson, who had consulted them while gathering information for his ground-breaking *Place-Names of Ross and Cromarty* (1904). What was clear from his journeys to the eastern Gàidhealtachd is that far from being confined to the remoter Catholic islands of the Outer Hebrides, charms were in fact widespread throughout the Gàidhealtachd, even in the most traditionally presbyterian districts.

Carmichael did not see the further volumes of *Carmina Gadelica* he originally envisaged through the press. It was left to his daughter Ella to bring out a new edition of the first two books of the *Carmina* in 1928, the year of her death. A third and fourth volume, edited by his grandson James Carmichael Watson, appeared in 1940–1, while a fifth was edited by Angus Matheson (1912–62) in 1954. The series was rounded off with the magnificent sixth index volume, a landmark in Gaelic scholarship, edited by Angus Matheson and seen through the press by his brother William (1910–95) in 1971.

Although both contemporary and later scholars cast some doubt on the treatment of the material he had gathered, Carmichael's great work, and his manuscript collection as a whole, remain an indispensable treasure-trove, the fruits of a lifetime spent tirelessly in the service of his own people, gathering, preserving, communicating, and interpreting Gaelic culture, history, tradition, and lore for the wider world and for future generations. Carmichael's collecting work was not only exceptionally arduous and demanding; it must never be forgotten that it was also carried out at a time when habitual contempt of Gaels, their language and culture, was widespread and publicly expressed, when many Gaels themselves had little interest in and no time for the traditions of their people.

We can only begin to understand Alexander Carmichael by attempting to read his life and work in the context of his own times, above all by acknowledging his endeavours to defend and vindicate his people through the extraordinary strategy of rehabilitating a despised genre hitherto of little more than curiosity value. Carmichael understood the intrinsic worth and dignity of this 'lost lexicon of piety'[151]; not only this, but he was able to persuade people to let him write it down, a remarkable achievement as he was well aware himself:

> It is my pride that they entrusted me, a Protestant, not only with these poems but with many other things which they often declared they would trust to the priest alone.[152]

Controversial as *Carmina Gadelica* remains, the way he, his wife, his daughter, and his circle of friends presented Gaelic spiritual lore ensured that it would last.[153] Again, although he certainly altered his material, he preserved all his archive, from field recordings to transcriptions to editing drafts. Alexander Carmichael did not destroy his papers. These allow us to put his achievement in its proper perspective, to value it all the more, to understand that

'*Carmina Gadelica* is not a monumental exercise in literary fabrication nor, on the other hand, is it a transcript of ancient poems and spells reproduced exactly in the form in which they survived in oral tradition.'[154] No-one with an interest in any aspect of Gaelic Scotland can ignore *Carmina Gadelica*. 'No true book lover but will prize *Carmina Gadelica* among his chief treasures.'[155]

Alexander Carmichael died in at his home in Edinburgh on 6 June 1912, and is buried at St Moluag's on his native island of Lismore.

> The coffin, covered in Carmichael tartan, was carried by relays of mourners along George Street in Oban to the North Pier for the boat to Lismore. Michael Carmichael [Alexander's grandson] says that the tartan used on the coffin was the fabric from Alexander's two kilts, which his wife, Mary, and daughter-in-law, Laura, unpicked for use as a pall.[156]

The memorial was designed by his son Eoghan:

M'ANAM · A'BHI · AN · SITH
AIG · SORCHAIR · NA FRITHE ·
MICHEIL · CRODHAL ·
AN · COMHDAIL · M'ANAMA:

CHUM · CLIU · DHE
AGUS · AIR · CUIMH
NE · AN · OLLAMH ·
ALASDAIR · MACGILLEMHI
CHEIL: LISMORE · 1833
DUNEIDEANN · 1912
ALEXANDER · CAR
MICHAEL · LLD:

> Be my soul in peace with thee, Brightness of the mountains.
> Valiant Michael, meet thou my soul.[157]

Many people have given me invaluable help and advice while compiling this article. I would especially like to thank the following: Donald Black; Ronald Black; Ray Burnett; Grant Buttars; Hugh Cheape; Meghan Cote; Catrìona Garbutt; William Gillies; Jean-Didier Hache; Anette Hagan; Bill Innes; Calum Laing; Cathlin Macaulay; Allan MacColl; Murdo Macdonald; Alasdair MacEachen; John MacInnes; Margaret Mackay; Isa MacKillop; Donald John MacLennan; Mary Macleod; Angus Macmillan; Calum Macneil; Fiona Marwick; Donald Meek; Catrìona Muir; John Randall; Sylvia Robertson; Priscilla Scott; John Shaw; Arnott Wilson; Andrew Wiseman; and Stefan Zimmer. Mo bheannachd aca uile. Bu mhath leam taing shònraichte a thoirt dha mo mhnaoi Abi airson cho fad-fulangach 's a bha i fhad 's a bha mi an-sàs ann an saoghal Alasdair MhicGilleMhìcheil.

Thanks also to the staff of the following archives for their knowledge and patience: National Archives of Scotland; National Library of Scotland; Sabhal Mòr Ostaig; the School of Scottish Studies; Strathclyde University Archives; Glasgow University Special Collections; Atholl Archives, Blair Castle; and especially to Edinburgh University Library Special Collections with whom I am working at present studying the Carmichael Watson collection. This research is being funded by the generosity of the Carnegie Trust for the Universities of Scotland, and the Scotland Inheritance Fund.

[1] School of Scottish Studies, SA1963/67 A2: Mary Ann MacInnes of Stadhlaigearraidh, recorded by Donald Archie Macdonald.

[2] CW MS 230 fos.176–8 (3 Dec 1881).

[3] CW MSS 113 fos.4ᵛ–6; 383 fo.175; Donald Mackinnon, 'Alexander Carmichael, LL.D.', *CG* iv, xxi; but see CW MS 106 fo.7ᵛ; also John MacInnes, *Dùthchas nan Gàidheal: Selected essays* (Edinburgh, 2006), 477–8.

[4] NLS Adv. MS 50.2.1 fos.303–4, AC, Carbost, to John Francis Campbell, 17 Jan 1861.

[5] CW MS 118 fos.21ᵛ–22.

[6] Dòmhnall MacIlleDhuibh, *Sgeul no dhà às an Lios: A tale or two from Lismore* (n.p., [2006]), 41–8. See also NAS GD1/126/8/2 fo.73, AC, Oban, to W. F. Skene, 9 Jul 1879: 'Nearly the half of Lismore belongs to the Duke [of Argyll]. This is almost wholly a wilderness so rendered by the Duke's predecessor where in my young days there was a fine middle class tenantry.'

[7] Mackinnon, 'Alexander Carmichael', *CG* iv, xxii; *Fasti* vii, 103. MacColl may have made use of Campbell connections on his mother's side. Carmichael writes of how he 'had the felicity of spending some of my boyish happy days among the hills and dales of Sutherland-shire': CW MS 451 fo.3.

[8] CW MS 118 fo.49.

[9] John Murdoch, ed. James Hunter, *For the people's cause* (Edinburgh, 1986), 22–5, 86–91, 149–50.

[10] NLS Adv. MS 50.1.12 fos.163ᵛ, 182–3; CW MSS 103 fo.17ᵛ; 502, 'Oisein'; see John Francis Campbell (ed), *Popular tales of the West Highlands* (new ed. 1890–3: Alexander Gardner, 4 vols, Paisley), iv, 226: 'I believe in them myself—fully believe. I am literally convinced that Fingal lived and that Ossian sang.'

[11] NLS Adv. MS 50.1.14 fo.490a, Hector MacLean, Ballygrant, to John Francis Campbell, 9 Aug 1860. Carmichael had first come across John Francis Campbell's project when he was asked to take down a couple of stories—'Caol Reidhinn' and 'Mac an Luinn'—from Peter Anderson, 'Pàdraig Buidhe', Port Charlotte, on behalf of the retired excise officer John MacLean, Cultorsay: NLS Adv. MS 50.1.4 fos.58a–59; fo.60, John MacLean, Cultorsay, to John Francis Campbell, 19 Jul 1860.

[12] *CG* i, xxxi.

[13] NLS Adv. MS 50.2.1 fo.303a, AC, Carbost, to John Francis Campbell, 17 Jan 1861.

[14] NLS Adv. MS 50.1.12 fo.123, same to same, 19 Dec 1860.

[15] Campbell (ed), *Popular tales of the West Highlands*, i, iii–iv.

[16] NLS Adv. MS 50.2.1 fo.333a, AC, Carbost, to John Francis Campbell, 9 Mar 1861.

[17] NLS Adv. MS 50.2.1 fo.332ᵛ, same to same; cf. Campbell (ed.), *Popular tales of the West Highlands*, iv, 211–12.

[18] NLS Adv. MS 50.2.1 fo.334ᵛ, same to same.

[19] See CW MS 454 fos.1–3. The proverbs Carmichael had collected were sent to his friend Sheriff Alexander Nicolson (1827–93), then working on his *Collection of Gaelic proverbs and familiar phrases* (Edinburgh 1881): see CW MS 105 fos.67–92; 113 fo.62ᵛ; also AC, 'Alexander Nicolson, LL.D. Advocate. (From a fellow-worker and a friend of twenty-eight years' standing).', *Celtic Monthly*, i, no.7 (April, 1893), 111; Rev. Kenneth MacLeod, 'Our interpreter', *CG* iv, xxxii.

[20] Examples of these songs: CW MSS 244 fos.384–5, 454–5, 470; 369 fos.166, 261ᵛ; 499 fos.28, 58, 208. For other Campbell contacts of Carmichael in his youth, see Mackinnon, 'Alexander Carmichael', *CG* iv, xxi–xxii.

[21] Lieut. Donald Campbell, *A treatise on the language, poetry and music of the Highland clans* (Edinburgh, 1862), 190.

[22] CW MS 244 fo.690.

[23] NLS Adv. MS 50.2.1 fo.367a, AC, Carbost, to John Francis Campbell, 3 Dec 1861.

[24] Campbell (ed.), *Popular tales of the West Highlands*, iii, 119–26; iv, 209–26 [original, NLS Adv. MS 50.1.6 fos.607–45].

[25] CW MS 107 fo.16.

[26] CW MS 494 fo.344ᵛ.

[27] CW MS 113 fo.9.

[28] MacLeod, 'Our interpreter', *CG* iv, xxxiv, xxxv.

[29] AC, 'Donation of baptismal font from Chapel of St Maelrube, Lochaoineart, Skye', *Proceedings of the Society of Antiquaries of Scotland [PSAS]*, viii (1868–70), 237–9; 'Notices of Teampull Michael, Keallun, North Uist, and of sculptured stones in Bearnarey, Harris, and in Benbecula; an 'Abrach' quern, and quarry for querns, Heisgeir, North Uist, &c. By Alexander A. Carmichael, Esq., Lochmaddy, in a letter to W. F. Skene, Esq., LL.D., F.S.A.

Scot.', ibid., 276–86, also 415. Carmichael's private collection of artefacts is now in the West Highland Museum, Fort William.

[30] NLS Adv. MS 50.4.6 fo.143.

[31] CW MS 104 fo.83.

[32] NLS Adv. MS 50.2.4 fo.182.

[33] NLS Adv. MS 50.2.4 fos.200ᵛ–1, 30 Sep 1871; see CW MSS 90 fo.17ᵛ; 104 fos.83ᵛ–6; 341 fo.64ᵛ–65; 468; GUL MS Gen. 1090/18(8); *CG* i, xxiv. For Campbell's 1871 expedition, see NLS Adv. MSS 50.2.4, 50.2.21, 50.4.6. While in Mingulay both collectors took down the poem 'Gum beannaicheadh Dia taigh mór Thunga' from Roderick MacNeil, 'Ruairidh an Ruma', apparently the only occasion in the nineteenth century we have two different recordings of the same recitation: CW MS 119 fo.55; NLS Adv. MS 50.2.21 fo.64ᵛ.

[34] NLS Adv. MS 50.2.8 fo.29, AC, Ìochdar, to John Francis Campbell, 19 Dec 1871. Mary Carmichael had probably gone to Edinburgh with her new daughter Ella.

[35] AC, 'Toirioc na Taine', *Transactions of the Gaelic Society of Inverness* [*TGSI*], ii (1872–3), 25–39; 'Laoidh nan Ceann', ibid., 46–9; 'Fionnladh Choinneachain, Mac na Bantraich', ibid. v (1875–6), 19–37; 'On a hypogeum at Valaquie, Island of Uist', *Journal of the Anthropological Institute of Great Britain and Ireland*, iii (1874), 272–5; see CW MSS 362 fos.259–61ᵛ; 465; also AC, 'Sgrios nam Piocach, bho Aonas Macaonais, Craoitear, Smearceit, Uist-a'-Chinn-a'-Deas. [Sgriobhta le Alasdair G. MacGilleMhicheil, air an 13mh là de cheud mhios na bliadhna, 1865.]', *An Gaidheal*, i, no.10 (Dec, 1872), 266–7.

[36] NAS GD403/90/1, transcription of a letter by John MacDonald to Sir John Campbell-Orde, 20 Oct 1876.

[37] MacLeod, 'Our interpreter', *CG* iv, xliv; also James Carmichael Watson, 'Mary Frances MacBean', ibid., xli–xlv.

[38] NAS GD1/126/8/2/95, AC, Oban, to Skene, 13 Apr 1880.

[39] CW MS 107 fo.31.

[40] CW MS 470 fo.4.

[41] CW MS 472 fo.1, AC, Lochmaddy, to Capt. Thomas, 28 Mar 1867.

[42] SA1968/223, A9–10; 'Alasdair Bàn agus an géidseir', *Tocher*, 48/9 (1995), 416; see Bill Lawson, *Croft history: Isle of North Uist* iii (Northton, Isle of Harris, 2001).

[43] CW MSS 160 fos.103–14; 116 fos.47ᵛ–49ᵛ; 90 fos.9ᵛ–?12ᵛ.

[44] CW MS 104 fo.12.

[45] CW MS 108 fos.5–?7.

[46] CW MS 362 fo.204, AC, Lochmaddy, to Capt. Thomas, 8 Mar 1870; see MacLeod, 'Our interpreter', *CG* iv, xxviii: 'In Uist, which forty of fifty years ago was even poorer than it is to-day, he paid the excise dues and filled the meal-chest of many a poor crofter and of many a poorer cottar'.

[47] Clement Hosking, *Fine song for singing: a Celtic odyssey* (Sydney, 1950), 56.

[48] Mackinnon, 'Alexander Carmichael', *CG* iv, xxiii.

[49] GUL MS Gen.1090/14(49). From the references on the other page in the manuscript to Taynuilt (where Carmichael had a summer house) and Glen Lonan, it may well have been written down from the recipient's own recitation. For Fionnghal nighean Chaluim, see CW MSS 107 fos.29ᵛ–31; 111 fo.20; *CG* i, 316–17; ii, 16–17, 86–9, 378; v, 87; Linda Gowans, *Am Bròn Binn: an Arthurian ballad in Scottish Gaelic* (Eastbourne, 1992), 21–2.

[50] CW MS 119 fo.61.

[51] See for example CW MS 90 fos.1ᵛ–7, 28ᵛ.

[52] CW MS 119 fo.19.

[53] CW MS 362 fos.193–4, AC, Lochmaddy, to Capt. Thomas, 7 Nov 1867.

[54] See, for example, CW MS 472 fos.1–3, AC, Lochmaddy, to Capt. Thomas, 28 Mar 1867; *CG* i, xxii.

[55] NLS Adv. MS 50.2.17 fos.25ᵛ–25a , AC, Ìochdar, to John Francis Campbell, 4 Nov 1872.

[56] *CG* i, xxxii; cf. ibid. iii, 48–9.

[57] See MacLeod, 'Our interpreter', *CG* iv, xxx–xxxi, xxxiii.

[58] CW MS 119 fo.43ᵛ, Mar 1871.

[59] NAS GD1/126/8/2/96, AC, Oban, to Skene, 22 Apr 1880.

[60] CW MS 362 fo.172ᵛ, AC, Creag Goraidh, to Capt. Thomas, 12 Mar 1877; ibid., fo.179, same, Oban, to same, 22 Jan 1879.

[61] NAS GD1/126/8/2/132, Mary Carmichael, Oban, to Skene, [4 Nov 1878].

[62] NAS GD1/126/8/2/96, AC, Oban, to Skene, 22 Apr 1880.

[63] NAS GD1/126/8/2/62, same to same, 19 Dec 1879; also NAS GD403/90/6x, H.H. Mackenzie to James Carmichael Watson, 15 Jul 1941.

[64] NAS GD1/126/8/2/97, AC, Scolpaig, to Skene, 27 Jul 1880.

[65] William Forbes Skene, *Celtic Scotland* (Edinburgh, 3 vols, 1876–80), iii, 378–93.

[66] MacLeod, 'Our interpreter', *CG* iv, xxviii.

[67] AC, 'Farming customs in the Outer Hebrides', and 'Grazing and agrestic customs of the Outer Hebrides', *Report of Her Majesty's Commissioners of Inquiry into the condition of the crofters and cottars in the Highlands and Islands of Scotland* (Edinburgh, 1884), 213–16; 451–82.

[68] NAS GD1/126/8/2/78, AC, Oban, to Skene, 26 Jul 1879.

[69] NAS GD1/126/8/2/95, same to same, 13 Apr 1880.

[70] AC, 'Grazing and agrestic customs', 470, 474, 481; see CW MS 487 fos.45, 62ᵛ.

[71] See, for instance, 'Beath-eachdraidh Choluim Chille. Ceud abstol na Gaidhealtachd', *An Gaidheal*, i, no.1 (Jun 1871), 3–5; no.2 (Sep 1871), 23–4, two articles about St Columba by 'A.C., Loch na Madadh, Uist, 1871'. The series, however, appears to have been rounded off by another hand: 'Beath-eachdraidh Chaluim-Chille', *An Gaidheal*, i, no.5 (Jul 1872), 115–17; also the intriguing collection of early sermons in CW MS 354. Note also the interesting fact that Carmichael's parents appear to have been friendly with Father James Macgrigor, the last professor in the old Lismore Catholic seminary: Mackinnon, 'Alexander Carmichael', *CG* iv, xxi; AC, 'Grazing and agrestic customs', 462.

[72] NAS GD1/126/8/2/60, Mary Carmichael, Oban, to Skene, 4 Nov 1878.

[73] AC, 'The place-names of Iona', *Scottish Geographical Magazine*, ii (1886), 461–74; iii (1887), 80–7, 242–7; see CW MSS 125 fos.103, 107, 114; 225 fos.1–91; 230 fos.122–7; 362 fos.1–8; 369 fos.1–4, 199–201; 487 fos.77, 134–48; 502 fos.205–13; 519; MacLeod, 'Our interpreter', xxxiii–xxxiv; NAS (West Register House), RH4/23/106–9.

[74] AC, 'Grazing and agrestic customs', 473; see *CG* i, xvii.

[75] AC, 'Farming customs', 214.

[76] CW MS 510 fo.9.

[77] AC, 'Uist old hymns', *Transactions of the Gaelic Society of Glasgow*, i (1887–91), 34–47; see CW MS 487 fo.65, John Murdoch, Glasgow, to AC, 24 Jul 1885: 'Go on with your paper, it is of the utmost value at this moment.' See Murdoch, ed. Hunter, *For the people's cause*, 194–6.

[78] CW MS 510 n.f., AC, Edinburgh, to Alexander Macbain, 25 Sep 1889.

[79] Blair Castle, Atholl Archives, 1474, AC, Edinburgh, to Lady Evelyn Murray, 84 Eaton Place, Westminster, 11 Jul 1891. My thanks to Sylvia Robertson for kindly drawing my attention to this letter. For Carmichael's 1890 expedition, see CW MS 1, fos.1–12.

[80] CW MS 362 fo.173ᵛ–4, AC, Scolpaig, to Capt. Thomas, 29 Jul 1880.

[81] CW MS 111 fos.13ᵛ–14; 'Nether-Lochaber', *Inverness Courier*, 6 Aug 1874; also 8 Oct 1874.

[82] See Deborah Davis, 'Contexts of ambivalence: The folkloristic activities of nineteenth-century Scottish Highland ministers', *Folklore*, 103 (1992), 207–21.

[83] Campbell (ed.), *Popular tales of the West Highlands*, i, lii.

[84] *CG* ii, 350; my thanks to Calum Laing for kindly forwarding information concerning his great-uncle.

[85] CW MSS 1 fos.12ᵛ–111; 124 fos.27–30; 126 fos.237ᵛ–238

[86] Rev. Donald Lamont, 'Elizabeth Catherine Carmichael', *CG* iii, xxii.

[87] MacLeod, 'Our interpreter', *CG* iv, xxvii–xxviii.

[88] Alexander Macbain, 'An old Gaelic charm', *Celtic Magazine*, xii (1886–7), 236; idem, 'Highland superstition', *TGSI*, xiv (1887–8), 232–72; idem, 'Gaelic incantations', ibid., xvii (1890–1), 222–6; idem, 'Incantations and magic rhymes', *Highland Monthly*, iii (1891–2), 117–25, 174–81, 222–31, 290–7, 341–8; Alexander Macdonald, 'Medical spells and charms of the Highlands', *Celtic Magazine*, xiii (1887–8), 34–40; William Mackenzie, 'Gaelic incantations, charms, and blessings of the Hebrides', *TGSI*, xviii (1891–2), 97–182; also idem, 'Leaves from my Celtic portfolio iv', *TGSI*, viii (1878–9), 100–28; see also Rev. Archibald MacDonald, 'Notes on the religion and mythology of the Celts', *TGSI*, xix (1893–4), 37–49; Rev. Malcolm MacPhail, 'Folklore from the Hebrides IV', *Folk-Lore*, 11 (1900), 439–50.

[89] Macbain, 'Incantations and magic rhymes', 223.

[90] Ibid., 229; see *CG* i, xxxiii–xxxiv.

[91] Ibid., 232.

[92] See especially NLS MSS 8779 fos.59–71; 8782 fo.32ᵛ; 10563 fo.21.

[93] Strathclyde University Archives, T-GED 8/1/8, 26, *Dundee Advertiser* review of *Evergreen*, i, July 1895.

[94] AC, 'The Land of Lorne and the satirists of Taynuilt', *Evergreen*, i (Spring, 1895), 110–15; see Strathclyde

University Archives, T-GED 8/1/8, 1, 2, 4.

[95] See especially Donald Meek, *The quest for Celtic Christianity* (Edinburgh, 2000), 38–78.

[96] AC to Father Allan McDonald, 15 Mar 1898, in John Lorne Campbell, 'The text of *Carmina Gadelica*', *Éigse*, viii (1956), 261; idem, 'Notes on Hamish Robertson's "Studies in Carmichael's *Carmina Gadelica*"', *Scottish Gaelic Studies* [*SGS*], xiii(1) (1978), 1.

[97] CW MS 487 fo.308ᵛ, William Jolly to AC, 28 Nov 1897; for the publishing history of the *Carmina*, see CW MSS 527, 528A; John Lorne Campbell, '*Carmina Gadelica*: George Henderson's corrections and suggestions', *SGS*, xiii(2) (1981), 183–218; Laura S. Sugg, 'The experience of God in everyday life in Alexander Carmichael's *Carmina Gadelica*' (University of Edinburgh, Ph.D., 1997), 53–8, 275–87; note also an article, almost a trial for the *CG* indices: Æ.J.G. Mackay and AC, 'Notes on a pair of pampooties, or shoes of raw hide, from Aran More, Galway Bay, by Æ.J.G. Mackay, LL.D., F.S.A. Scot., Sheriff of Fife and Kinross. And on cuaran and other varieties of shoes used in the Highlands and Islands of Scotland, by Alexander Carmichael, Corr. Mem. S.A. Scot.', *PSAS*, xxviii (1893–4), 136–50.

[98] Sugg, 'Experience of God', 61–4, 288–92. The two volumes Carmichael dedicated to the Queen were not sent before her death in January 1901. They are now preserved in the library of Sabhal Mór Ostaig, Isle of Skye.

[99] Sugg, 'Experience of God', 65, 292; see CW MS 87 fo.22.

[100] Hamish Robertson, 'Studies in Carmichael's *Carmina Gadelica*', *SGS*, xii(2) (1976), 220–65.

[101] Ibid., 231.

[102] John Lorne Campbell, 'Notes on Hamish Robertson's "Studies in Carmichael's *Carmina Gadelica*"', 13; this echoes the folklorist Calum Maclean's judgement in his review of *CG* v in *Arv*, 11 (1955), 153: 'He was in a sense more of a litterateur than a student of folk-tradition.'

[103] William Matheson (ed.), *The Blind Harper* (Edinburgh: Scottish Gaelic Texts Society, 1970), 229.

[104] CW MSS 109 (four paperback notebooks); 224 (a sheet of this manuscript was sent by Carmichael to John Francis Campbell, and is now catalogued as NLS Adv. MS 50.1.12 fos.208–9). The notebooks in MS 109 may, however, be neat copies.

[105] Five of these he bought in late 1864, before he left his previous excise post in Wadebridge, Cornwall: CW MSS 104, 105, 107, 113, and 114. When these were filled, over the following years he would use the notebooks now catalogued as CW MSS 90, 106, 108, 111, 115, 116, 119, and 150.

[106] CW MSS 89, 110, 117, 120, 122, 126(f) and (g), and 178.

[107] NLS Adv. MS 50.1.12 fo.138.

[108] CW MSS 104 fos.1ᵛ–12; 476.

[109] CW MS 104 fos.35, 91.

[110] Loose sheets include CW MSS 244 fo.149ᵛ; 461; 512, 'notes from Lewis'; 519, 'Mac a' Phì a' Choin Duibh' and 'Airi na h-aon oich'. MS 115 is a school jotter apparently acquired in Ness when Carmichael found himself without paper on a visit there in October 1873: see CW MS 114 fos.89–90.

[111] This category includes CW MSS 7, 87, 112, and 154.

[112] CW MS 107 fo.14ᵛ, 16 Oct 1865.

[113] NLS Adv. MS 50.2.1 fo.332, AC, Carbost, to John Francis Campbell, 9 Apr 1861.

[114] See NLS Adv. MSS 50.1.11 fo.326; 50.1.12 fos.162ᵛ, 163ᵛ, 174, 203ᵛ, 209, 214–15, 233, 250; 50.7.6 fos.26ᵛ–27.

[115] CW MS 341 fo.67.

[116] CW MS 103 fo.17ᵛ.

[117] AC, 'Deirdire', *TGSI*, xiii (1886–7), 241–257; 'Deirdire, English Translation of Deirdire', ibid., xiv (1887–8), 370–87. One should also note another translation of the same text, perhaps by Alexander Mackenzie, in 'The story of Deirdre [English translation] part I' in Alexander Macbain 'The hero tales of the Gael', *Celtic Magazine*, xiii, no.146 (December, 1887), 69–77; ibid., no.147 (January, 1888), 129–38.

[118] See John Gregorson Campbell (ed. Ronald Black), *The Gaelic otherworld* (Edinburgh, 2005), 654, 664–9.

[119] CW MS 527 n.f., 25 Apr 1901.

[120] Alan Bruford, '"Deirdire" and Alexander Carmichael's treatment of oral sources', *SGS*, xiv(1) (1983), 4.

[121] CW MSS 114 fos.29ᵛ–42ᵛ; 154, 4–29; cf. 103 fo.17ᵛ.

[122] AC, 'Laoidh Chlann Uisneach', *TGSI*, xv (1888–9), 206–15.

[123] CW MS 151.

[124] CW MS 126 fo.100; cf. *CG* iii, 41.

[125] CW MS 111 fos.13ᵛ–14.

[126] CW MS 502 fo.159, Kenneth MacLeod, Gigha, to William J. Watson, 22 Nov 1930.

[127] CW MSS 239 fos.1–128; 485.

[128] There is a possibility that Carmichael did at least some of the editing of *Carmina Gadelica* in the Highlands, at his summer home in Taynuilt.

[129] See CW MS 110 for details of this tour.

[130] For Carmichael ordering foolscap quarto essay paper in August 1898, see CW MS 500 fo.675^v.

[131] Sugg, 'Experience of God', 67.

[132] For examples, see a draft of *Rann romh Urnuigh*, *CG* i, 2–3: CW MSS 391 fo.1^v and 503 fo.835^v; an English draft version of *Ruin*, *CG* i, 51: CW MS 126 fo.60; a draft of *Coisrig Cadail*, *CG* i, 81: CW MS 126 fos.53–4, 57; two successive drafts of *A' Choich-Anama*, *CG* i, 92–3: CW MS 230 fo.142^v, then CW MSS 170 fo.20^v and 244 fo.489^v; a draft of *Ho m' aghan!*, *CG* i, 266: CW MS 126 fo.55; and, possibly, an early English version of *Cronan Bleoghain*, *CG* i, 273: CW MS 126 fo.56. CW MS 494 fo.152^v is a draft, probably for a later projected volume, of a version of *An t-Aingheal Diona*, *CG* i, 48–9, an item related to *A' Choich-Anama*. Among the many later drafts are copies of the songs *A phiuthraig mo rùin*: CW MS 503 fos.38–46; and *Cumha Mhic an Tòisich*, ibid. fos.628–46; also the charm *Òra Ri Shul*: CW MS 494 fos.334–6; also CW MSS 368; 494 *passim*; 499 fos.147–64, 492–500.

[133] Many of these can be found in CW MSS 160, 244 and 502.

[134] CW MS 362 fo.172^v, AC, Creag Goraidh, to Capt. Thomas, 12 Mar 1877; ibid., fo.179, same, Oban, to same, 22 Jan 1879.

[135] Compare, for example, Carmichael's draft CW MS 339 fo.128^v with MacLeod's at CW MS 503 fo.583^v; also the draft acknowledgements, possibly in the hand of Ella Carmichael, CW MS 502 fo.316^v, with MacLeod's later version, CW MS 499 fo.341^v. Note also MacLeod's telling additions at CW MS 125 fo.25^v.

[136] Drafts of the notes occur in abundance throughout the collection: for just a few examples, see CW MSS 124 fos..30^v, 31^v; 244 fos.39^v, 40^v; 339 fos.63^v, 64^v, 67^v, 68^v, 71^v, 91^v; 359 fos.72^v, 73^v, 74^v, 78^v, 80^v; 491 fo.28^v; 493, fo.173^v; 369 fos.55^v, 73^v, 176^v, 182^v; 500, fos.63–5; 503 fo.683^v.

[137] See, for example, CW MS 499 fos.576^v, 577^v. Two different calculations of the structure of *CG* are compared on CW MS 124 fo.74^v. Various versions exist: two of the earliest are preserved in CW MS 124 (something of a workshop for *CG* i–ii) fos.1–9. Two others are in Mary Carmichael's hand: compare an earlier initial page (CW MS 218 fo.50^v) with a later one (CW MS 125 fo.23^v). What may be the final initial page, torn in two and reused as were most of Carmichael's double-page spreads, can be reconstructed from CW MSS 124 fo.80 and 244 fo.243^v.

[138] CW MS 245 fo.250: Dr H.C. Gillies, *Highland News*, 8 Dec 1901.

[139] CW MS 245 fo.264^v, Andrew Ross to Ella Carmichael, 9 Aug 1900.

[140] CW MS 245 fo.289: George Henderson, *Oban Times*, 9 Feb 1901.

[141] CW MS 245 fo.272^v: Dr H.C. Gillies, *Caledonian Medical Journal*, Jan 1901.

[142] NLS Adv. MSS 50.1.12 fo.204, AC, Carbost, to John Francis Campbell, 17 Dec 1861; 50.2.1 fos.364–7, same to same, 3 Dec 1861.

[143] AC, 'The Land of Lorne', 110–15; see CW MS 217 fos.76–83. Kenneth MacLeod was drawing upon material concerning the poet band the Cliar Sheanchain which John Ewen MacRury had recorded the previous year in Uist, possibly acting as amanuensis for Carmichael: CW MS 1. See also CW MSS 2, 3, 126(n).

[144] See CW MS 245 fos.244–5; Campbell (ed. Black), *Gaelic otherworld*, 668, 674–9.

[145] Macbain, 'Incantations and magic rhymes', 232.

[146] J.L. Robertson, 'Ossianic heroic poetry', *TGSI*, xxii (1897–8), 300; Ludwig Christian Stern, *Zeitschrift für vergleichende Litteraturgeschichte*, 8 (1895), 150: 'übrigens nicht ohne Zutun von Buchgelehrsamkeit.' See Alexander Carmichael, 'Deirdire', *TGSI*, xiii (1886–7), 241–257; 'Deirdire, English Translation of Deirdire', ibid., xiv (1887–8), 370–87.

[147] CW MS 527 n.f., 25 Apr 1901; see also *CG* i, xxxiv.

[148] CW MSS 126 fos.30^v, 44, 82–3; 365 fos.3–4; see *CG* i, xxxiv.

[149] Sugg, 'Experience of God', 250. A letter by Carmichael to Patrick Geddes on 6 May 1904 offering to sell his collection of 'a number of stone implements belonging to the stone period of our Scottish history' he had collected 'in the Western Isles during my long residence there' to the Carnegie Trustees might suggest that the couple were then in financial difficulties: Strathclyde University Archives, T-GED 9-538.

[150] AC, *Deirdire and the Children of Uisne* (Edinburgh, 1905); 'The Ruskins', *Celtic Review*, iii (1907), 343–51; 'Naoimh Chinntaile', ibid., iv (1908), 371–2; 'The Barons of Bachuill', ibid., v (1909), 356–75; 'Some unrecorded incidents

of the jacobite risings', ibid., vi (1910), 278–83, 334–48; 'Thugar maighdean a chuil-bhuidhe', ibid., vii (1911), 138–43; 'Traditions of the Land of Lorne and the Highland ancestry of Robert Burns', ibid., viii (1912), 314–33.

[151] MacInnes, *Dùthchas nan Gàidheal*, 477.

[152] CW MS 502 fo.325ᵛ.

[153] Compare the fate of a similar collection of Gaelic lore, compiled by another protestant but recorded in a rather more favourable environment, where a straightforward, considerably less artistic presentation of the material has led to its continuing neglect: Dúbhglas de hÍde (ed.), *The religious songs of Connacht/Abhráin diadha chúige Connacht* (Dublin, 1906).

[154] MacInnes, *Dùthchas nan Gàidheal*, 491.

[155] Nutt, review of *CG*, 421.

[156] Sugg, 'Experience of God', 14.

[157] *CG* i, 66–7; Sugg, 'Experience of God', 14. 'To the honour of God and in memory of Dr Alexander Carmichael, Lismore 1833 [*recte* 1832], Edinburgh 1912'.

2

Alexander Carmichael: The Influence of Lismore

DONALD BLACK (DOMHNALL MACGHILLEDHUIBH)

Alexander Carmichael of *Carmina Gadelica* fame was recognised as one of the great collectors of folklore—not just in Gaelic Scotland but in the wider European context. He was born on the island of Lismore in 1832 at Croit an Lochain ('the croft by the lochan'). That Alexander collected so little on his native isle is to be regretted—his profession, as an excise officer, appears to have been a barrier which precluded contact with his fellow islanders. They were not actually 'Carmichaels' but MacMichaels, who had no real connection with the Lowland family of that name. Alexander's father Hugh was known locally as Eoghann Greusaich ('Hugh the Cobbler'). By coincidence, an emigrant from Lismore, also a Carmichael, was a cobbler in Antigonish, Nova Scotia. Many families followed particular trades for generations, and their émigré representatives would continue plying their trade in their new environment.

The indigenous Carmichaels, who claimed to be the original branch of this family on Lismore, are said to be descended from the family line of 'an t-Easbaig Bàn MacGhilleMhìcheil' ('the Fair-haired Bishop Carmichael') as he is remembered with respect. Local tradition credits him with inspiring the building of the Cathedral of Argyll on this island. The site on which the cathedral was sited was said to have been gifted by King Haakon (1204–63), whose wishes were honoured by Ewen MacDougall of Lorn around 1241; the cathedral itself was built sometime between then and 1320. Unfortunately, these 'originals' always considered themselves superior to the 'common herd', 'standoffish'—a characteristic which could have also contributed to any suspicion on his native isle regarding his motives.

Alexander's family were said to be land-owning on Lismore in a place called Creag an Sgurrain, the location of which is now uncertain. The view from Croit an Lochain where Alexander spent his childhood looks across Balnagown Loch towards a rectangle of trees known as Coille nam Bàrd ('the wood, or grove, of the bards') and in the same area are Cnoc na Clàrsaich and Tobar na Clàrsaich—surely perpetuating the memory of an ancient cultural college or centre? Little wonder that our friend was almost destined to become a folklorist! His ancestors had inherited the title Barran Tigh' an Sgurrain (Baron of Sgurran) possibly an ecclesiastical 'title' similar to the MacDhùnShléibhe/MacLeay/Livingstone Barons of Bachuil who were almoners to the early Church.

Near the family home are the ruins of Sgoil Shomhairle ('Samuel's School') where Alexander would have been first introduced to formal education. Fortunately, he would have been educated in Gaelic and English. My old grand-uncle Calum, though he remained a crofter, was literate in both languages through his time at Samuel MacColl's School—this was an ability not granted to the next generations, which was really tragic.

Another family of Carmichaels appeared on Lismore several centuries later and were disparagingly always referred to as 'na Cìobairean' ('the Shepherds'). They were said to have arrived on Lismore due to a rather odd set of circumstances, deported to this island which had few sheep. Legend again tells us why this happened. Government troops were searching the mountains of Appin and Lochaber for a highwayman who was terrorising and robbing lawful travellers. Eventually they surprised and captured the ancestral 'cìobair', who was only a common sheep stealer, also operating in this huge area. An astute politician, he promptly turned King's evidence and incriminated the highwayman: whether deservedly or not is uncertain.

This 'Cìobair' or Carmichael received a partial pardon—and exile to the almost sheepless island of Lismore—not too severe a sentence! Many readers may well have roots in the islands, and will understand how family honour and reputation can be influenced by ancient tales, or just unproven rumours, which in time have legendary implications. For this reason, I would suspect, something of a slur followed them for several generations, probably unfairly. Time heals, and subsequent intermarriage with the indigenous Carmichaels, though somewhat frowned on, blurred most bloodlines. Nevertheless, some prejudice did linger into the twentieth century—unfortunately, even to my own time. I might suspect Alexander, son of Eoghann Greusaich, inherited and was saddled with the residue of this ancient prejudice towards his perceived 'mixed lineage'. This traditional memory might well have been one reason for his lack of success in recording folklore on Lismore, combined with the suspicion aroused by his profession as an excise officer. His fellow Liosaich, some of whom I remember—many of them very sensible and otherwise moderate people—remained deeply suspicious of Alexander's motives.

The Carmichaels of Lismore certainly excelled in a variety of fields over the centuries: for example, Dugald Carmichael (1772–1827), a botanist of note who qualified in medicine but who joined the army as a foot-soldier in order to travel the world. On his journeys he recorded a huge number of plants and trees. Natural history had become his real forte. In the twentieth century the brothers Dr Hugh and Dr Donald Carmichael became nuclear physicists, Hugh having the doubtful honour of working on the project which produced the atom bomb. Whatever one's sentiments are on this controversial subject, Dr Hugh was considered of sufficient importance to be one of the élite assembled at Los Alamos.

A good old friend of my own, the late John David MacColl with whom I spent many happy evenings, in response to my question on this very subject—the suspicion with which Alexander was regarded—said: 'it was not just that he appeared to be prying into old forgotten things—he always overstayed his welcome. He'd have his dinner and might well be still there at bedtime!'

His grandson Michael Carmichael MRCVS and I became friends after a doubtful start! Some years ago I contributed some short Gaelic articles (with an English translation) to the *Oban Times*, one on this very question: the lack of material from Lismore. Within days I had received a reply from Michael, a retired vet living in Fort William. He had no definite answer either. On the suspicion aroused by Alexander's profession, Michael's reply was: 'the "old man" would possibly turn a blind eye, if someone had some valuable lore, or a good story to tell.' Whether this tactic worked with his fellow Liosaich is problematic. However, he mentions meeting an old Uibhisteach shepherd who said the 'Gadger' was well-received there and considered reasonably tolerant—and was ready to turn a blind eye to any illegal activities if the suspects had songs, incantations, or some interesting legend or other to relate. When stationed in Uist Alexander was never affected by religious prejudice, and became friendly with Father James MacGregor who was one of the final group of students to study for the priesthood in the Seminary of Cille Chiarain on Lismore.

Michael and his cousin James Carmichael Watson (1910–42), who was posted missing in action in the Second World War, paid a visit to Lismore in 1937 and was surprised—or shocked—by the stony silence their questions concerning their grandfather and *Carmina Gadelica* met with. James's mother Ella Carmichael (1870–1928) was born at the family home at Kilandrist, Lismore. She later married William J. Watson (1865–1948), Professor of Celtic at the University of Edinburgh. I have come across a rather odd comment regarding this marriage, which came from the pen of a certain MacGregor: 'I have always thought it is a great tragedy for Gaeldom, as well as for my late mother, that my father, on his return from India did not marry Ella Carmichael.' Strange logic indeed! Maybe Ella Carmichael would not have been eager to react favourably to any proposal of marriage from this gentleman, and was happy to marry Professor William Watson. Ella was born in the old family home at Croit an Lochain—unlike the rest of Alexander's family.

Michael gifted Comann Eachraidh Lios Mór with the six volumes of *Carmina Gadelica* in memory of his grandfather: a most generous gesture. Maybe we, in our own small way, can keep the candle burning; in doing so, many interesting remnants of Lismore's oral traditional are coming to light. We have also build up a worldwide membership, mostly expatriates whose ancestors emigrated as far back as the South Carolina migration in 1775, as well as descendants in the rest of the USA, and in Canada, Australia, and New Zealand.

This was also the time when so many Gaels began to turn their backs, as it were, on their language and heritage, not passing it to their children and grandchildren. Some families inherited nothing whatsoever, but fortunately there were exceptions, and I was rather fortunate in my own family: my grandmother, parents and a well-loved bachelor grand-uncle, Calum Beag Òg. Little wonder that many islanders and Highlanders became embarrassed by their undervalued culture and language.

Alexander Carmichael was said to have kept an open door for students of Highland or Island origin, and was not at the close of his life's journey a wealthy man. He produced a paper which contributed to the passing of the Crofters Act, and was also a contributor to the Gaelic Society of Inverness, the *Gàidheal*, and the *Highlander*. Certainly Scots, whether Highland or Lowland, seemed to respond more favourably to collectors from outwith their homeland, who it must be said were honourable and well-intentioned people, though fated to look from the outside! Well, we've all heard comments like 'A kent his faither', or from the north-east, 'Fa' does he think he is?' Or as they would say in Lismore 'An gàidsear le 'cheistean!'—meaning our friend Alexander.

Indeed a great deal was lost due to this strange attitude. To quote from a recent publication: 'Lismore is an island, where each ruin and knoll carries some tale, or some secret tradition unique to that spot: even evidence of cultivation is a memorial to some long-departed ploughman, and another agricultural system.'

Alexander Carmichael's last resting place is to be found in the western end of the old cemetery at Clachan Lios Mór, where he is surrounded by his clan. This Celtic cross was designed by his son Eoghan (1876–1966), an architect by profession. On it is the following epitaph, now barely legible:

A MHICHEIL MHIN NAN
STEUDA GEALA: A CHOISINN
CIOS AIR DRAGAN FALA:
GAOL DHE IS PIAN MHIC
MUIRE: SGAOIL DO SGIATH
OIRNN, DIAN SINN UILE

This is my own inadequate translation of these words:

PEACEFUL MICHAEL OF THE WHITE STEEDS,
WHO CONQUERED THE DRAGON OF BLOOD,
LOVE OF GOD AND THE PAIN OF MARY'S SON,
SPREAD THY WINGS OVER US AND SHELTER US ALL.

Bha fàidh riamh gun urram 'na dhùthaich fhéin: The prophet was always without honour in his own land.

* * * * *

Despite being urged by Rev. Archibald Clerk (1813–87) to compile a history of his native Lismore [CW MS 103 fos.151–2], Alexander Carmichael was never able to do so. He certainly recorded a great deal from the island and its environs, right from the very beginning of his career as a collector, when in late summer 1860 he took down items from Dougall MacCombie and Kate and Duncan Lawrie in Port Appin on his way to take up his new posting in Skye [CW MS 474 fos.8–13; NLS Adv. MS 50.1.12 fos.126, 129, 202]. Again, on his return from Cornwall to the Gàidhealtachd, on his way over to the Uists, on 14 December 1864 he records in one of his new field notebooks Ewen Carmichael, Druim na Mòine, Appin—evidently a kinsman—relating details of their shared genealogy [CW MS 113 fos.5–9; see also Charles H.E. Carmichael, 'Epitaphs abroad: John (Carmichael), Bishop of Orleans', *Notes and Queries*, 3rd series, ix (234) (23 June 1866), 514]. Family ties clearly remained strong— the Carmichaels' daughter Ella was born in Lismore on 9 August 1870, with Alexander apparently seeing her for the first time on 2 September. During this visit he jotted down seventeen extremely valuable pages of island lore and antiquarian descriptions [CW MS 106 fos.5–21]. He had returned from his work to Lismore once again by 12 November, probably to take his wife and new daughter back to the Uists [CW MS 7 fo.0ᵛ].

It was not, however, until Alexander Carmichael began to rent a summer home in nearby Taynuilt, after he had left the Hebrides for Edinburgh, that he took up recording the traditions of Lismore again. He took down various pieces of lore from the local minister on 14–15 August 1883 [CW MS 120 fos.1ᵛ–5ᵛ], and we find him again on the island, at Achanduin, on 23 August 1886 [CW MS 122 fo.12]. On 5 October 1892, at Bachuill, Carmichael records the well-known story of how Stewart of Appin was murdered by Maclean of Duart and the corpse rescued by the Livingstone Baron of Bachuill and his two 'red-haired fine daughters' [CW MS 126 fo.199]. Nevertheless, in spite of all the material Alexander Carmichael recorded concerning his native island and indeed his own family, both in the notebooks and in the many sheets now gathered together as CW MSS 231, 242, and 382–3, he clearly felt unable to work them up into extended prose. Newspaper and journal articles there may have been, as yet unlocated; a book there was not. Carmichael evidently felt a great deal of affection for and emotional ties to the island of his birth, his childhood, and his own people, even ending *Carmina Gadelica* ii with a *Fuigheal* from John Stewart of Lismore, 'still an island of much interest, and anciently of much importance' [*CG* ii, 216–17, 381]. Whether because his work in the Outer Hebrides had first claim on his heart, or because he was simply too close to his native *dùthchas* and its people to write about them in print, Alexander Carmichael's Lismore remains, for the time being at least, in manuscript.

Domhnall Uilleam Stiùbhart

3

Carmichael in Barra

CALUM MACNEIL

Those who take it upon themselves to write about a serious subject will inevitably attract criticism. Some critics will be mild and objective, others will criticise without giving due cognisance to either the times, or the conditions under which the materials for such writings were gathered. Some who criticised others for 'improving' material were themselves guilty of errors; however as the saying goes, those who have never made mistakes have probably never done much of anything in their lives.

I personally have no difficulty accepting Alexander Carmichael's works, warts and all, despite the fact that there are errors in some of the genealogy of the Barra parish informants. Indeed, on the contrary, I owe a debt of gratitude to Alexander Carmichael, for in his introduction to the story of Deirdre he gives a physical description of JOHN MACNEIL (Iain Donn), Buaile nam Bodach, and also of his brother ALEXANDER MACNEIL of Ceann Tangabhal—my great-great-grandfather on the paternal side. A glance at the personal histories of these two brothers shows the nomadic existence which was led by the indigenous population of Barra.

Iain Donn was born at Earsairidh, lived subsequently at Theiliseigh following his marriage, and then at Cille Bharra, Allathasdal, over to South Uist, back to Theiliseigh, Fuidheigh, Bréibhig, over to Mull, then back to Buaile nam Bodach, where he died in 1875 aged about 95. Alexander was born at Earsairidh, also lived at Theiliseigh for a time, and then at Cliad, over to South Uist, Morghan, Bogach, Fuidheigh, Bréibhig, Gleann, and finally Ceann Tangabhal where he died aged 94. They were two of at least seven sons of Ruairidh Bàn Eachainn Òig Sheumais Ruairidh Dhuibh Laird of Barra.

This was a period of kelp boom and bust, which together with the vagaries of both the shark and the cod and ling fishing, and also the demoralising effect of insecurity of tenure, forced emigration; the result being that families were divided, lack of money dictating that they could not all go.

Many of their uncles and aunts had emigrated to Cape Breton and Prince Edward Island, and three of their brothers went to Cape Breton too, where they were joined by Iain Donn and Alexander's oldest children. Small wonder that people who had been through such hardships found solace in reciting tales to while away long winter nights; after all, it was one of the few things that a rapacious landlord or his minions could not charge monies for. Their nomadic existence would of course have given them not only opportunities to acquire new lore, but would also have provided them with fresh audiences at regular intervals.

We are indebted to Alexander Carmichael for recording customs as well as tales, some of which have resonance with present practice: fishing customs, for example. Carmichael noted the practice of dividing the fishing grounds at the beginning of the season Féill Brìghde.

Historically, the Barra fishermen began their long line fishing in February, weather permitting. They would start working north-west of the sound of Barra, or the Caolas Uibhisteach, as they termed it. They would fish along the 60 fathom mark 'a-muigh air an trì fichead', and southwards, following the migratory route along this contour until they reached the Sgrìob Bhàn, south of Barra Head. Then they worked their way north into the Minch, coming much closer inshore as the season progressed.

During Carmichael's early visits to Barra, the fishermen used locally-built boats of the skiff type. They were lightly built for easy rowing and buoyant when empty, but were also small, with a poor carrying capacity and an inability to tack effectively due to their rig and lack of forefoot. By the 1870s the earlier east coast models, the Scaffie and Fifie were utilised. These were much larger and stronger, with a much improved carrying capacity. As more lines were worked it became imperative to have a system of shooting their lines, to avoid shooting over each other, as this might result in conflict. Stone cairns were therefore erected on strategic hillsides to assist in these demarcations.

The present intensive use of hundreds of creels shot in long strings and the use of miles of tangle nets has led to fishermen shooting in an agreed direction west of Barra when working in close proximity to each other.

During a visit to Barra in 1870, Carmichael states that he prevailed upon a woman to do the 'tuiream'. A close look at the death records for 1869–71 would lead one to believe that it may have been the funeral of Roderick MacPhee of 20 Gleann (the lighthouse packet master), who was drowned off the entrance to the sound of Vatersay, along with his two shipmates, Donald MacNeil aged 38, and John MacNeil aged 16, on 28 May 1870 while on their way to service the Monach light.

Roderick was born in 1834 and was married to Joan MacGill in 1859. They had a young family. Roderick's body came ashore in Crogearraidh, according to P.F. report. Perhaps his remains were returned to Bàgh a' Chaisteil/Castlebay by the relief packet, thus causing the dramatic scenes described by Carmichael. More tragedy befell the family, when the widow Joan passed away in 1874, leaving the children orphaned. It appears that they went to Glasgow to live with some of Joan's family. Some of their descendants have been back in touch over recent years.

The following is an attempt to identify the Barra Parish informants more fully:

ALEXANDER MACNEIL

[*CG* ii, 381n.13: 'Mr. Iain Campbell of Islay and, for him, the distinguished scholar Mr. Hector Maclean, Islay, took down many tales from this reciter. I wrote down many more, but all three of us made little impression upon the old man's abundant lore. I noted from him the names and characters of several score of long heroic tales, any or all of which he was ready to dictate to me. Amongst them was a very long, complete and wondrously fine version of Deirdire. Alexander MacNeill said that the version of this tale which I had already taken down from his brother Iain Donn was only a fragment. Yet this fragment of the story of Deirdire has been pronounced by critics equal to any ancient or modern critic.'

(*CG* ii, 212–13, *Am Breid*, although attributed to Alexander in the index, was evidently recorded from Peggy MacAulay, Tobha Mór, South Uist).

CW MS 113 fos.14ᵛ–?44ᵛ [18, 21 Jan 1865]: *Bhalantaigh is Hoiseantaidh*; ?*Laoidh Chaoilte*.

CW MS 104 fos.1–12 [13 Feb 1866]: *An t-Òg Chraobh*.

CW MS 479 [1 Dec 1870]: *Ciadais mac Rìgh Àlainn*.

CW MS 119 fos.5–19 [21–2 Mar 1871]: *Laoidh na Ceàrdaich*; *An Gruagach Bàn, mac Rìgh Éireann*. 'Heard this from his father when a boy. Alxr MacNeill is 72. Wrote this tale while granting tax Licences at Castlebay during spare minutes & intervals'.

Alexander's wife MARY gave Carmichael an òran-sìth *Is moch an-diugh a rinn mi éirigh* on 6 July 1869, when she was 72 years of age.]

JOHN MACNEIL

[*CG* iii, 310–11: *A' Ghrian.*

CW MS 114 fos.29ᵛ–42ᵛ [16 Mar 1867]: *Eachdraidh Chlann Uisne.*

possibly CW MS 7 fo.13ᵛ [6 Nov 1870]: *Is toil leam, 's toil leam.*]

CATHERINE MACINTYRE of Bearnaraigh, Barra, was the wife of Donald Macintyre (Mac Eòghainn Craigston). She was the daughter of Iain Mór MacInnes and Margaret Macintyre Bhàslain.

[*CG* i, 34–5: *Achanaidh Grais*]

MATALY CAMPBELL of Pabaigh was the daughter of Domhnall Alasdair Morrison from Cille Pheadair. She was married to John Campbell, Mac Dhomhnaill Ruaidh Néill Eachainn Mhiughalaigh, and they removed to Vatersay after the Land Raids.

[*CG* i, 36–7: *Achanaidh Comhnadh*]

JOHN CAMERON was the son of Donald Cameron and his first wife Margaret Mackinnon. He was born at Allathasdal, was married, probably first to Catherine Salmin, and then to Mary MacNeil. He died at Borgh.

[*CG* i, 42–3: *Carraig nan Al*; *CG* v, 208–9 [8 Oct 1868]: *Tàladh Mhic Leòid*; *CG* ii, 375n.5: 'The Camerons came to Barra as 'leine-chneis' with Jane, daughter of Cameron of Fassifearn, and sister to Colonel John Cameron, of whom Scott, Byron, and others have sung in undying verse.'

CW MS 87 fo.2 [7 Oct 1868]: *Gòrag nach deach thu dh' Iain Dubh*]

RODERICK MACNEIL, Ruairidh an Rùma, of Mingulay was the son of Donald MacNeil and Ann MacNeil of Grinn. He was a grass keeper at Sanndraigh when he married Fionnaghal MacNash, the daughter of Eòin 'ic Dhiarmaid from Grinn.

[*CG* i, 138–9: *Heire Bannag*; *CG* iii, 110–13: *Duan Nollaig*; also *CG* i, xxiv; ii, 352: 'a famous story-teller and a man wondrously endowed mentally and physically.'

CW MS 114 fos.63–85 [Aug 1867]: 'my friend old Ruairi'; history of the island; 'Ruary has Laoi mhic Ceallair remarkably correct. He appreciates it highly.'; *Slàn iomradh a ghaisgich*; 'Nighean Rìgh na Spàinne agus MacGillEathain Dhubh-Àird'.

CW MS 150 fos.11ᵛ–20ᵛ [22 May 1869] *A phiuthrag, Àpran duibh o bu horo huile ohò*: 'Heard from Ruairi mac Dhonil who says that his fath[er] who lived in Bearnara heard this under the floor of his house one night while he was lying awake.'

CW MS 119 fo.55ᵛ [Sep 1871]: *Gum beannaich Dia Taigh Mór Thunga*: 'Ruari's father heard this in America'.]

NEIL MACNEIL, a herd at Eòlaigearraidh, Niall mac Iain Bhàin Dhomhnaill Mhóir, originally from Cille Bharra. He was married to PEGGY MACDONALD, daughter of Iain Duallach and his wife Chirsty MacNeil Bhàslan. This good couple led a typically nomadic life around the northern half of Barra and the offshore isles.

[*CG* i, 122–3: *A Ghealach Ur*; ibid., 268–9: *Thoir am Bainne.*

CW MS 87 fos.24ᵛ, 26–7, 29 [?Sep 1885]: *Ho! m' aghan, ho! m' agh donn*; *I hòileagan, hì hò m' aighean*; 'Neill Macneill now an old man was 'topsman' as was his father before him for Macneill of Barra.'

CW 504 fos.71–6 is an anecdote about how a cow hid its calf from him for some days.

Also, possibly, *The Highlander* (Aug 1881), *Cumha an t-Sealgair*, recorded by AC on 1 Dec 1870.

Neil's wife Peggy, mistranscribed as 'Mary' (clearly a mistake for Margaret), gave AC a cattle charm, *Buachaille Naomh Chaluim Chille*.]

ALEXANDER MACDONALD, Borgh, was possibly the son of Mac Iain and Marion Galbraith of Baile na Creige. He was married to Margaret Mackinnon, daughter of Gilleasbuig of Borgh and he died in 1866.

[*CG* i, 192–3: *Laoidh an Triall*; *CG* iii, 76–7: *Ìos an Cuartaiche*; also *CG* ii, 377n.9: 'Mr Campbell of Islay said that this noble-minded man resembled, when speaking, the celebrated French preacher, Mirabeau.'

CW MS 104 fos.12ᵛ–27 [15–16 Jan 1866]: *Còmhrag Fhinn agus Mhànais*; *Laoidh na Muirgheartaich*; *Laoidh Dhiarmaid*; *Duan an Deirg*]

GILLEASBUIG MACKINNON of Earsairidh, shoemaker, was possibly the son of Mac Dhomhnaill and Catherine Nicholson from Bhàslan. He was married to Mary MacNeil, daughter of Uilleam Iain, and died in 1869.

[*CG* i, 150–1: *Cairioll Callaig*; also *CG* ii, 377n.4: 'This intelligent man dictated to me the names of thirty-seven consecutive generations of the Macneills of Barra.']

JOHN PEARSON was the son of John MacPherson and Mary MacPhee of Ceann Tangabhal. According to the baptismal record, John was born in 1814, was married to Catherine Nicholson, gave evidence to the Napier Commission, and died in 1885. Oral tradition has it that he led a very colourful life indeed.

[*CG* i, 222–3: *Duan an Domhnaich*; *CG* ii, 40–1: *Eolas Gradhaidh*; *CG* iv, 316–17: *Giullan Geal Thír*; ibid., 356–9: *Guidhe nan Leòdach*.

CW MS 7 fos.16ᵛ–17 [2 Dec 1870]: *Giullan Gealù* [also CW MSS 244 fo.149ᵛ; 499 fos.161–4]; fo.17ᵛ [Dec 1870]: *Eòlas Beum Sùla*.

CW MS 119 fos.19–22 [23 Mar 1871]: 'Niall Glùn-dubh'; *M' fheadan is m' eòin is m' uighean*; 'Coinneach nan Tarbh'; 'Mac Mhic a' Phì Cholasa'; 'An Luideag'; 'Domhnall Gorm Mór agus Domhnall Gorm Óg Shléite'; 'Nighean MhicGilleChaluim Ratharsair'.

CW MS 90 fos.37ᵛ–46 [24–5 Sep 1872]: *Eòlas Gràdhaich*; *Tuiream Tòrraidh*; *Eòlas Sgéith Féithe*; *Duan an Dòmhnaich*; Barra and family history.]

His sister CATHERINE also gave stories to Carmichael. She was married to Ali MacFarlane, a soldier, and she had a reputation for witchcraft. She was reputed to have placed a curse on a neighbouring family over a dispute about access to a well. Allegedly she cursed the five sons of the family, stating that water would be the cause of all their deaths, and it so came to pass that they all perished by drowning, two of them being lost together, the others in separate incidents. Not a lady to be trifled with, she was born in 1807 and died in 1880.

[*CG* iv, 356–9 [14 Mar 1873]: *Guidhe nan Leòdach*; *CG* v, 86: *Am Bròn Binn*; ibid., 344–5: 'bean-tuirim'.

CW MS 491 fos.48–9 [21 Jun 1870]: 'MacNéill Bharraigh agus "For"'.

CW MS 119 fo.22 [23 Mar 1871]: *'S ann a ghabh mi mo chead dhiot*.

CW MS 90 fo.37ᵛ–9, 47–8 [24 Sep 1872]: *Mo ghaoil òig a' chùil duinn/Gur e mo ghaol-sa Shawfield*; *Gòrag nach téid thu dh' Iain 'n-diugh*; *Ach a phiuthair sin 's a phiuthra*; Barra and family history; *Am Bròn Binn*; *Cha till, cha till MacCruimein*; *Cuim' nach togainn guth àrd?*; *'S mis' tha gu tùirseach/'S tric snigh' air mo shùil*]

ISABELLA GALBRAITH of Sgallairidh was the daughter of Murdo Mackinnon of Nasg, Mac Fhionnlaigh Mhóir. Finlay had come to Barra to work for MacNeill of Barra; he was a native of Elgol in Skye. Isabella was born in 1824 and was married to John Galbraith, Mac Chalum Iain. She died in 1907.

[*CG* i, 108–9: *Earna Mhoire*; ibid., 110–11: *Failte a Mhoire*]

NEIL CAMPBELL of Mingulay was probably Mac Eachainn Néill Eachainn. He married Marion MacNeil, daughter of Coinneach Mhìcheil Ruairidh, ex-Sanndraigh. He was born in 1825 and died in 1889.

[*CG* i, 250–1: *Beannachadh Fuiridh*]

RODERICK MACLACHLAN should have read Roderick [mac] Lachlainn, Ruairidh Bàn. A gardener for MacNeil, he was reputed to be from Mull. He married Flora MacPhee, daughter of Gilleasbaig, the ferryman at Cille Bharra. He died in 1897 aged 85 years.

[*CG* i, 264–5: *Ho Hóiligean, Ho m' Aighean*.

A story concerning a cow hiding her calf from Ruairidh is recorded in CW MS 504 fos.68–70]

CAIRISTINE/CAIRISTÌONA MACDONALD of Earsairidh was the daughter of Alasdair MacNeil and Margaret MacPhee from Allathasdal. She was born in 1814, married to Roderick Mór MacDonald, Mac Iain, and died in 1895.

[*CG* i, 270–1: *Cronan Bleoghan*.

CW MS 87 fo.28 [28 Sep 1885]: *Thig a Mhoire ?mhios na bò-sa* [as above]; *Na bi t' aonar, na bi t' aonar, Iomall buaile, bò gun laogh!*]

MARY MACKINNON of Sanndraidh was Mary MacNeil, daughter of Domhnall Mór Ruairidh Bhàin Eachainn Òig. She was born at Theiliseigh in 1814, married Hector Mackinnon, Mac Ghilleasbaig, shepherd at Sanndraigh, and died in 1891.

[*CG* ii, 76–7: *An Eidheann-mu-Chrann*]

MARY MACDONALD from Mingulay, who made an impression on Carmichael, was the daughter of Ruairidh Chaluim, a crofter. She became the third wife of Donald Boyd, natural son of Neil Boyd and Isabella Campbell, daughter of Iain Chailein.

[*CG* ii, 166–7: *An Oigh agus an Leanabh*; *CG* v, 60–1: *Seathan mac Rìgh Éireann*.

CW MS 150 fos.13–14ᵛ, 15ᵛ–18 [22 May 1869]: *Seathan mac Rìgh Éireann*; *Chì mi a' ghrian a' falbh gu siùbhlach*; *A Mhòr a ghaoil*; *'S ann an-raoir nach d' fhuair mi 'n cadal*; *Chuala mi do ghèadh 's a' bhinneach*; *A bhean ud thall gu dé th' air t-aire?*; *Ùisdein mhic 'Illeaspa Chaluim*]

ISABELLA MACNEIL of Ceann Tangabhal was the daughter of Alex MacNeil, Mac Ruairidh Bhàin, already noted, and his wife Mary MacDougall, daughter of Neil MacDougall and Isabella MacAulay of Uist. Isabella was born in 1834, remained single, and died in 1913.

[*CG* iii, 286–7: *Gealach Ùr*]

MÒR, her sister, who was also an informant, was born in 1843 and died in 1927. She was the second wife of Murdo MacLean, Mac Eòin Eachainn Eileanach, of Borgh.

[*CG* v, 2–5 [8 Mar 1869]: *Craobh nan Ubhal*; ibid., 22–7 [2 Dec 1870]: *Iain Òg mac MhicNéill*; ibid., 60–1: *Seathan mac Rìgh Éireann*.

CW MSS 244 fos.608–9, 668–9; 339 fos.135–6 [8 Oct 1868]: *Òran Mhic 'ic Ailein*; *Ge Grianach an Latha*; *Seathan mac Rìgh Éireann*.

CW MS 107 fos.22ᵛ–23ᵛ [8 Mar 1869]: *Craobh nan Ubhal*.

CW MS 160 fos.92–3, 118–20 [6 Jul 1869]: *Creagag Mhic Iain mhic Sheumais*; *Dh' fhalbh mo rùn ás a' chala*.

CW MS 218 fos.26–8 [6 Jul 1869]: *Gura diombach mis' 'm buachaill'*.

CW MSS 7 fos.14–15; 244 fo.422 [2 Dec 1870]: *Iain Òg mac MhicNéill*.

CW MS 90 fos.49–51 [25 Sep 1872]: *Cumha Mhic an Tòisich*.]

MARY CAMPBELL, daughter of Gilleasbaig Dhomhnaill (1822–74), was married to Donald MacLean, Mac Alasdair Ruairidh Phàdraig (1813–93), both of Ceann Tangabhal.

[CW MS 90 fo.46 [24 Sep 1872]: 'Got the roilein [i.e. runs] from Mairi Chaimbeul wife of Don. Maclean Ceantangval Barra']

JAMES CAMPBELL was Mac Iain Chailein, but referred to as Seumas Chailein. He was born in 1800, married Chirsty MacNeil, and died in 1876. They were cleared from Gleann in 1850 and lived in Nairn for a while, but eventually returned. Seumas and Chirsty were my great-great-grandparents.

[*CG* v, 216–25 [26 Sep 1872]: *Tàladh Mhic Leòid*.

CW MS 90 fos.51ᵛ–52ᵛ [26 Sep 1872]: *Tàladh Mhic Leòid*]

WILLIAM SINCLAIR was the inn keeper at Bàgh a Tuath/Northbay, although he was recorded by Carmichael in Vatersay. He died there aged 75, one year younger than he was recorded as in the 1871 census. The natural son of Mary MacIsaac, he was married to Mary MacEachen, both of them from Arisaig.

[CW MS 113 fos.54–5 [15 April 1865]: *Chuir Fionn a mheur fo dheud fios*]

Without the dedication of Alexander Carmichael and his assistants, our knowledge of our ancestors and their customs, beliefs and way of life would be quite sparse. He treated his informants with courtesy, sympathy, and respect (something that is lacking in some modern scholars and historians working from cosy offices). I take my hat off to him.

* * * * *

Hector Maclean, John Francis Campbell, Alexander Carmichael, and Barra

Since the time of the first major Scottish Gaelic folklore project, the collecting and publishing enterprise carried out under the auspices of the great polymath John Francis Campbell of Islay (1821–85), the people of Barra have played host to several generations of scholars drawn by the extraordinarily rich culture of the island.

The Islay schoolmaster Hector Maclean (1818–93) was the first of these: he made two trips to Barra for Iain Òg Ìle, during which he noted down lengthy stories, as well as Fenian material, from the major male *seanchaidhean* on the island at the time. Those whose lore he mainly recorded were Hector Boyd, fisherman, Bàgh a' Chaisteil; Alexander MacDonald, Borgh; Roderick MacLean, tailor, Ceann Tangabhal; Alexander MacNeil, fisherman, Ceann Tangabhal; John MacNeil, 'Iain Donn', Buaile nam Bodach; Roderick MacNeil, 'Ruairidh an Rùma', Mingulay; Roderick MacNeil, labourer, Gleann; and Donald MacPhee, smith, Breubhaig.

On his first expedition to the Outer Hebrides, in July and August 1859, Hector Maclean spent a fortnight in Barra, followed by a week in South Uist and another week in North Uist. He arrived in Barra from Tobermory on 13 July 1859, and set to work searching for potential informants and the tales they could tell. The local minister, the Rev. Henry Beatson (1811–89), a Gaelic learner from Greenock, was somewhat discouraging:

> [He] does not seem to know very much about them though he is very fond of Gaelic literature. … He doubted if I could succeed well in the island as he said he liked to hear what the people had to say on traditionary matters but thought it was all incoherent and fragmentary.

On the other hand, the local schoolmaster, Allan MacDonald, Ailean Aonghais Duinn, from North Uist:

> seems to be well acquainted with the manners and amusements of the people and he tells me that there are plenty of them. I have spoke to several and they seem to have them in scores only yesterday a man disappointed me who promised to come but went to the fishing. The rest of the boats crew he said were unwilling to let them away. There is no working on them here without whisky. I see It is the only thing that will put them in tune and humour whatever they get besides. They are pretty anxious to know what they are to get…
>
> I am informed of an endless number of persons who can recite an endless number of tales all the way up from this to Harris. MacDonald the Schoolmaster is very obliging and lend me his assistance. He is not the least bigotted. He is well acquainted in the Long Island being a Native of North Uist and he thinks that Barra is as good if not better than any of them as it is the more purely Roman Catholic district.[1]

MacDonald's optimism was borne out; when MacLean returned from his journey he informed Campbell that '[i]n Barra I was more successful than in the other places.'[2] Indeed, by mid-October he had copied out from his notes 376 pages of tales from Barra alone to send to Campbell.[3]

Among these pages, now preserved in the John Francis Campbell manuscripts in the Advocates manuscripts in the National Library of Scotland, are some exceptional examples of the storyteller's art. From Alexander MacNeil, whom Maclean clearly visited several times during his visit, were recorded *Maghach Colgar*[4]; *An Gruagach Bàn*[5]; *An Dà Sgiobhair*[6]; *An Gadaiche Dubh*[7]; *An t-Iasgair*[8]; *Nighean Iarla a' Ghliocais*[7]; *Mac na Banntraich Bharraich*[10]; and *Conall*[11]. Most, if not all, of these stories had been learnt by MacNeil from his father Ruairidh Bàn, who had died some twenty years earlier at the age of eighty; from Donald Macintyre, tenant at Allathasdal, who died about forty years previously 'at a very advanced age'; and from Diarmuid Gillies. 'Three of Alexander MacNeill's brothers can recite these tales but one of these brothers is in America and the other in Australia.' Hector Boyd told Maclean two stories: *Na Trì Saighdearan*, learnt 'from John MacNeill, who has left Barra, and from Neil Mackinnon, Ruagh Lias'[12]; and *Na Trì Bantraichean*[13]. Alexander MacDonald, Borgh, apparently gave Maclean *An Dà Chìobair*[14]; while four short anecdotes and a longer narrative—*Baile Bhuirgh*, *An Tulman*, *Eilean Phabaidh*, *Seanntraigh*; and *Na Féinne*[15]—were told 'by four individuals, Alexander MacDonald, tenant, Barra, Bailebhuirgh, who heard them from his grandmother, Mary Gillies, about forty years ago, when she was more than eighty; Neill MacLean, tenant, ditto, who learnt them from Donald MacNeill, who died about five years ago, about eighty years of age; John Cameron, ditto, who heard them from many, but cannot name any in particular. They state that these tales were very common in their younger days.'[16]

At the end of August the following year Hector Maclean embarked upon a second expedition.[17] His purpose this time was not only to collect fresh material, but also to ensure that the page proofs for the forthcoming first two volumes of *Popular Tales of the West Highlands* were approved as accurate by the ultimate authorities: the *seanchaidhean* themselves. He appears to have arrived in Barra on 18 September 1860[18]; the fascinating letter he wrote to Campbell four days later is worth quoting at length:

> Coming across the sound of Barra to Barra I read Conall to men and women in the boat who were delighted with it and declared there was not a word wanting. They gave it as their opinion that it was fully better in the book than it was generally recited. I read it to Alexander McNeill himself the next day after my arrival at Castle Bay and excepting a few words not very mportant he admitted it was all there only there might be a little wanting in the sound in some parts. McNeill's memory is so good that he missed a single incident if omitted. The night before last I read all his tales at his own house and he is satisfied that no incidents are missing. We had a crowded house but he was for keeping the juvenile portion of the community out as he thought they would not keep quiet. I desired him to let them all in, that I would rather have them. This he did not seem willing to do but to keep them out he found impossible and then he gave it up for a bad job. They behaved very decently however and listened with great attention not a syllable was to be heard not the least noise made. I had not any interruption but on the contrary the pleasure of having all eyes intent upon me. The number of youngsters present would have formed a goodly school. I wish I had such attentive and obedient pupils at home likely I should were I to read tales for them. I read his own tale to Boyd and he is satisfied that it is all there fully as well as he recited it. He laughed as much at it as though it had been a new tale to him. I read *his* to Alexander McDonald also and he said there was nothing to correct or add, that I had them as he gave them. I have taken down several fables from Boyd I hope they may be to your purpose. I have got another version of the Chest from McNeill richer in some parts than the other.[19]

On 30 September Maclean wrote another letter to his patron, telling of an intrepid expedition he had just made to Mingulay to interview the famous Roderick MacNeil, Ruairidh mac Dhomhnaill, better known as Ruairidh an Rùma 'from his having found at some time 3 hogsheads of rum on the shore':

> I was over at Minglay last week and saw Roderick McNeil who is so celebrated among the people here as a story teller. I have written several of his tales which appear to me to be remarkable for vivid and pointed dialogue. He is an animated and spirited old man and though crippled to a certain extent by rheumatism his vivacity is not the least damped and the vigorous activity of his mind is not the least impaired 74 and not a trace of dotage. He hobbles about bareheaded and barefooted and is said not to have worn shoes for the last fifty years. He tells his tales with extraordinary effect being a capital natural elocutionist using pause emphasis gesture and inflection of the voice to express passion sentiment and character fully as well as though he had been trained by some of the best actors of the day. His Gaelic is excellent but his style is of the plain simple kind. He has obviously an aversion to anything obscure or mystical and gives a clearness and reality to the greatest extravagance. He is I think the opposite of McPhie more dramatic than narrative in his manner a moderniser of the antique and a realiser of the ideal. He has many tales borrowed from other sources than Highland but he gives them all a Highland form.[20]

As we have seen, during Maclean's first visit to Barra he collected most of the extended narratives from one man: Alexander MacNeil, Alasdair mac Ruairidh Bhàin. Now, with much deeper experience of collecting and analysing folklore, not to mention the status afforded him by the imminent publication of the first two volumes of *Popular Tales*, and indeed his better grasp of Barra Gaelic, Maclean was able to record from a number of different Barra *seanchaidhean*.

As seen from his letter, Maclean took down from Alexander MacNeil a second, expanded version of *Nighean Iarla a' Ghliocais* on 21 September 1860[21]—thus giving folklorists the unaccustomed luxury of possessing two different tellings of a tale from the same nineteenth-century informant; while on 4 October he recorded from the same reciter a much simpler, much more widespread story, *An Sìthichean 's an Tàillear*[22]. The day before he had recorded a long narrative *Gille nan Spleadh 's Gille nan Spuachd* from Alexander's brother John at Buaile nam Bodach.[23] It is clear that it wasn't easy for Iain Donn to tell his story at dictation speed:

> John McNeill one of the story tellers who lost occasionally the thread of his narrative when reciting slowly for me said 'Nam faighinn-sa dol air m' aghaidh ['s] na ropaichean leis bhiodh a chùis gu math.' If I could get going on with the ropes to leeward the matter would be well.[24]

John had learnt this story from his maternal grandfather Kenneth Gillies about 60 years previously. Gillies, apparently about a century old, died *c.*1811. This John may well be identical to two additional John MacNeils recorded during Maclean's visit: 'John MacNeill, labourer, Barra', whose version of *Conall*—a narrative also recorded from Alexander MacNeil—was written down on 2 October[25]; and, probably, the John MacNeil who gave him *A' Bhruighinn Chaorainn*, learnt 'from Hector MacVicar, Cuibhn, Barra, about 60 years ago'.[26] MacVicar had died more than fifty years previously aged around eighty.

It is possible, but not certain, that it was on Maclean's second trip that he recorded a series of tales from Roderick Maclean, tailor, Ceann Tangabhal, Barra: a man whose trade had evidently led him a rather peripatetic life. From the tailor were written down *Nighean Rìgh fo Thuinn*, a story he had heard frequently recited by old men in South Uist about fifteen years previously[27]; *Alasdair mac an Ìmpire*[28]; *Grùthan an Eòin 's an Sporan Òir*[29]; *Gille a' Bhuidseir*[30]; *An Dà Chraoibh Ghaoil*, learn from a mason at Petty, Inverness[31]; as well as *An Nighean a Reiceadh* and *An Leanabh gun Bhaisteadh*, two stories learnt from Alexander MacPherson, eighty years old, living 'at no great distance from the reciter, but … now bedridden and unable to recite himself.'[32] It is likely that the fisherman Hector Boyd gave Maclean some further stories: *An Duine Bochd Beairteach*[33]; *Na Trì Léintean Canaich*[34]; as well as a number of short children's stories: *Am Madadh Ruadh 's am Bonnach Beag*, 'learnt from one John Campbell who died three years ago'; *Am Buideal Ìme*, 'learnt from Neil McNeill, Vatersay, and from many other old men. Neil McNeill died ten years ago, past eighty years of age'; *An Gobhar Glas*; *Am Madadh Ruadh 's an Coileach*; *A' Chearc*, 'learnt from Donald McKinnon, Laidhinnis, Barra, who died twelve years ago at the age of sixty'[35]; as well as *Am Fàinne Òir*, also told by his father Neil Boyd[36].

John Francis Campbell evidently compiled the printed index to *Popular Tales of the West Highlands* in something of a hurry, and the (probably at least) three Roderick MacNeils from whom Maclean recorded in Barra have become confused. From a fisherman of the name at Bàgh a' Chaisteil he recorded *A' Bhràth*.[37] From Roderick MacNeil, labourer, Gleann, he recorded *Bràthair Bochd*[38]; *Cod Cawdy*, a version of *An Gille Carach* learnt from Domhnall mac Mhìcheil mhic Néill about 21 years previously, the original reciter being past sixty at the time— he emigrated to North America some sixteen years ago[39]; *Bilidh*[40]; *Iosbadaidh (Na Trì Gillean Nach Dealaicheadh)*[41]; *An Nighean Bhrèagha Leisg*[42]; *Iain Mac Rìgh na Frainge*[43]; *Siarlas Òg Mac an Ridir' Aimbheartaich*[44]. From a Roderick MacNeil, labourer, Ceann Tangabhal, Maclean wrote down *Ridire nan Ceist*.[45] MacNeil gives as his own sources Donald MacNeil (probably the Domhnall mac Mhìcheil noted above); John MacNeil, Ceann Tangabhal, 'who died aged 53 11 years ago'; and Roderick MacNeil, Mingulay—the celebrated Ruairidh an Rùma.

During the three days, 25–27 September 1860, that Maclean spent on Mingulay, he apparently recorded five stories from Ruairidh: a version of *An Gille Carach* learnt from one Neil Campbell about thirty years previously[46]; *Brian Breugach*[47]; *Mac Rìgh Éirinn agus Nighean Rìgh na Grèige*[48]; *An Gobha*, learnt from John MacNeil, Sanndraigh, who had died seven years previously aged 76[49]; and *An t-Each Dubh*, learnt from Roderick Gillies, Borgh, about twenty years previously, Gillies then being 25 years old—an unusual example of an older *seanchaidh* learning from the recitation of a younger.[50]

Hector Maclean also recorded a great deal of Ossianic material in Barra, reflecting his patron John Francis Campbell's growing, albeit somewhat reluctant, interest in the genre. On his previous visit to Barra he had taken down a version of *Oisean an déidh na Féinne*, but seems to have neglected to record the name of the reciter.[51] Matters were rather different in 1860. His main informant was Donald MacPhee, the smith in Breubhaig, the best reciter of Ossianic poetry Maclean had ever heard, from whom he recorded a large number of items.[52] From Alexander MacDonald, Borgh, he wrote down *Laoidh Dhiarmaid*, a lay the informant had heard from his mother Marion Galbraith. MacDonald then traced it back six generations to one of his ancestors who had come from Kintyre to Barra.[53] Maclean also apparently received a version of *Conn Mac an Deirg* from MacDonald's recitation the following year.[54] Indeed, the fact that on the Old New Year of 1862 Hector Maclean sent Campbell a *Duan Chollainn* originally recorded on 21 September 1860 from Alexander MacNeil, Ceann Tangabhal, suggests that he had taken down considerably more material in note form which he had not later written up for his patron—manuscripts now doubtless lost forever. The *Duan* 'was composed by the reciter's great-grandfather to the young Hugh MacNeill in Barra, great-grandfather of Alexander MacRory the white [i.e. Alasdair mac Ruairidh Bhàin], and son of the brother of MacNeill of Barra.'[55]

When Alexander Carmichael first arrived in his new posting in Loch nam Madadh at the end of 1864, it is hardly surprising that he wasted no time whatsoever in travelling south to Barra and recording from the informants who had already given so much to Hector Maclean. Within three weeks he was on the island; there, in Breubhaig, for only the second time in his life he saw a hand-quern being operated.[56] The first informant Carmichael called on seems to have been Alexander MacNeil, from whom he recorded the extended narrative *Bhalantaigh agus Hoiseantaigh* on 18 January 1865, and possibly also the Fenian lay *Laoidh Chaoilte* three days later.[57] Carmichael appears to have already begun collecting Ossianic material for the Rev. Archibald Clerk (1813–87) at this time; hence on his next visit, later on that year on 6 October, he took down *Laoidh Caragain* [i.e. *Earragain*] *Mhóir Mhic Rìgh Lochlainn* from Lachlann MacIsaac of Ceann Tangabhal.[58] The following year, 1866, Carmichael, now clearly more familiar with the demands of his work, was able to spare more time to renew his acquaintance with MacNeil, from whom he recorded the narrative *An t-Òg Chraobh* on 13 February. Two days later he was also able to meet Alexander MacDonald, Borgh; the *seanchaidh* gave him the Fenian lays *Còmhrag Fhinn agus Mhànais*, *Laoidh na Muirgheartaich*, *Laoidh Dhiarmaid*, and *Duan an Deirg*.[59] More Ossianic items were recorded from Donald MacPhee, the smith at Breubhaig, during a visit on 10 December.[60] Carmichael records how MacPhee had heard most of his lays from Hector MacNeil, the famous 'Dall Mór Eòlaigearraidh':

> 'Eachunn Mac Neil' a blind man who lived with MacNeil of Barra in the triple capacity of musician, historian, and genealogist. MacNeil was a big powerful good looking man. He lost his sight in boyhood from the smallpox. He lived in the family of MacNeil for a long time till the last chief's affairs went wrong. At this time Hector MacNeil would be about eighty years of age. He saved a few hundred pounds of money upon which he retired. He married when he was considerably past eighty, a young woman of thirty. He was considered the best violin player in the Western Isles. Donald MacPhie says that MacNeil could repeat a very great deal of the poems attributed to Ossian, and that too in a style he never heard equalled by any other person. He says that MacNeil could repeat much of Ossian's poetry that was neither so easily remembered as the 'lays' attributed to Ossian but that the language and sentiments were exceedingly fine. MacNeil delighted in these and in explaining them to his hearers. Surely these poems could have been nothing else but the proscribed 'epics'? MacPhie says that he could remember a good deal of this poetry some years ago but being an old man now—he can only remember snatches here and there except the lays which are simple and more easily remembered. MacPhie mentions several others from whom also he hears Ossian's poems but Hector MacNeil was the principal person from whom he heard them. From all I have heard of MacNeil he must have had much Ossianic lore in prose and poetry and that too of the genuine stuff.[61]

The mention of Hector MacNeil here reminds us of how the older generation in the islands at the time had been brought up under, and still felt the influence of, the social and cultural framework of the now vanished pre-crofting, chiefly world.

Alexander Carmichael was clearly taken with Donald MacPhee, and spent three days recording from him the next time he visited Barra, on 13–15 March 1867.[62] The following day, however, he travelled to Buaile nam Bodach where he wrote down—or rather, began to write down—the most famous piece recorded in Barra: the long narrative *Eachdraidh Chlann Uisne*, or *Deirdire*, from the recitation of the 83-year old John MacNeil, Iain Donn, brother of Alexander.[63] Carmichael only recorded a part of Iain Donn's story before having to break off:

> Left off here, on account of having made an appointment with Dr MacGillivray to go out shooting with Dr W. E. MacLellan and to dine at Eoligearry house in the evening.[64]

The remainder was recorded and sent to Carmichael the following month by 'Mr Donald MacRae Buaile nam Bodach' (a tacksman in that township)—the first perplexity in this most problematic of texts.

Up until now Carmichael had been following the programme initiated by John Francis Campbell and his colleagues, recording long narratives and Fenian lays, generally from male *seanchaidhean*. This would change with his next visit to Barra, or rather to the islands south of Barra. The novelty of his visit to Mingulay and Berneray in mid-August 1867, and his growing interest in island antiquities as a result of a correspondence begun at the end of the previous year with Capt. F.W.L. Thomas, led him to record a considerably broader range of material—including songs, traditions, and archaeological remains—than he had done previously. One suspects also the influence of two forceful personalities: Roderick MacNeil, Ruairidh an Rùma—'my friend old Ruary'—who acted as guide on his visit to Mingulay; and also, possibly, Mary Frances Macbean, his future wife whom he first met on a trip to Bernera Lighthouse, probably on 12 August 1867. They would be married only five months later, in Edinburgh on 13 January 1868.[65]

It is probably no coincidence then, that following his marriage Alexander Carmichael turned away from recording longer stories and Ossianic verse, and increasingly began to record women's songs. On his next visit to Barra, on 29 April 1868, he recorded a series of waulking songs from Marion MacPherson, the daughter of Iain mac Dhomhnaill Bhàin, in Gleann[66], while later on in the year, on 7–8 October, he recorded from John Cameron, crofter, Borgh—'full of old lore and … a good intelligent story-teller'—the fairy song *Gòrag nach deach thu dh' Iain Dubh*, and a version of *Tàladh MhicLeòid*.[67] Later on, probably in the evening of the 8 October, Carmichael seems to have attended a remarkable céilidh at Ceann Tangabhal, where Marion MacNeil, nighean Alasdair 'ic Néill, sang *Òran Mhic 'ic Ailein, Ge Grianach an Latha*, and *Seathan Mac Rìgh Éireann*.[68]

In March 1869 Carmichael was back once more in Barra, taking notes on the archaeological remains of the island, and, on 8 March, recording a version of *Craobh nan Ubhal* from Mary MacNeil, Ceann Tangabhal.[69] Just over two months later, on 21 May 1869, he was once more recording Donald MacPhee in Breubhaig; this time, however, his intention was to write down historical anecdotes and songs—*Seathan* and *An Fhìdeag Airgid*—rather than the Ossianic material for which the smith was famous.[70] One same day he took down three songs from Marion MacNeil, Gleann—apparently Mòr nighean Domhnaill Bhàin: *Fhir mhóir á sliabh a' Chuilinn*; a fairy song *Rinn mi'n cadal*; and a love song to Murchadh mac Fhearchair Thiristich.[71] On 22 and 23 May he was recording once more on Mingulay: historical information and songs from Ruairidh an Rùma once more—*A phiuthraig nan rùn*; the song of Seumas mac Eòin 'ic an Ollaimh Ìlich, one of his favourites; and *Àpran duibh*, a fairy song heard by his father in Bernera coming from under the kitchen floor. Carmichael also took down a version of *Seathan* from Mary MacDonald, Màiri nighean Ruairidh Chaluim, and Mary wife of Angus Campbell; as well as more songs from the former: *Chuala mi do ghèadh 's a' bhinneach; A bhean ud thall; Ùistein mhic Gilleasbaig Chaluim*.[72]

Henceforth Alexander Carmichael's interests would be firmly focused upon songs and shorter items, rather than the long narratives and Ossianic verse which had so preoccupied John Francis Campbell's team. These interests can be traced in the notes which follow each of the informants tracked down in Calum Macneil's important article above. One brief episode, however, should be mentioned in the way of a conclusion: Campbell's expedition to the Uists and Barra in 1871, collecting material for his forthcoming book of Ossianic lays, *Laoidhean na Féinne*. Although his thanks to the local minister in the first volume of *Popular Tales*[73] might suggest that he had visited Barra before, this was to be John Francis Campbell's one extended stay on the island.

The expedition began dramatically, when Campbell and his guide Alexander Carmichael found themselves storm-stranded on Mingulay for three nights between 20–23 September, a time Campbell passed in writing down stories from Ruairidh an Rùma:

> There is not a bird in the islands that Rory does not know all about and this man told us a horse-riding story. It was curious to find out whence the story came. I made Rory tell it and then found that he got it from a soldier who had been 7 years in the West Indies. In his regiment they used to tell stories in barracks every night. From that soldier he also learned a story about certain Blue Mountains. A son of his a sailor was many years in the East Indies and learned the language. One day a comrade to him came out here and harkened to a man who is telling the Blue Mountains as your father used to tell it in Minglay. Now here is something about the diffusion of popular tales. East Indies Minglay and West Indies bridged and an old man who can neither read nor write in the middle with a head full of Eastern and Western Lore.[74]

The men were eventually picked up from Mingulay on 23 September. Carmichael returned to his no doubt anxious wife in Uist, while that evening Campbell, in his lodgings in Bàgh a' Chaisteil, recorded from Alexander MacNeil, Alasdair mac Ruairidh Bhàin, in English translation, *How the Feinn was set up; Pàdraig Rìgh Éirinn who marries Oisein's daughter*; as well as several shorter stories.[75] 'There is none in Barra who has this but me' according to Alasdair, a declaration evoking Campbell's sardonic comment: 'But he spoke the thing that is not for his brother has them better."[76] Times were changing in Barra with the recent development of the main village as a bustling fishing port: while the recording was going on, Campbell notes:

> chorus going on. A cat mewing incessantly a door slamming another creaking every time it is opened a tame seagull skirling continually, a child crying a dozen of drunken fishermen singing a gaelic song with a stamping chorus, then in hobnails trampling up & downstairs and stamping on the floor over head. A man abusing the mistress for more whisky, two men fighting, and men at intervals rushing in at the door to look at me with fishy eyes and go out again suddenly shy and frightened at my silent gaze—such are the ways of literature in Barra when the herring fleet has fared well and come home in funds.[77]
>
> Tell a robber story in return gave my man a couple of shillings. Hear that he is the owner of a stone in Cill Bharrai which I was looking at the other day and that his people are buried under it. That they took it from Iona because their people MacNeills of Barra were buried under it there. That gentlemen have tried to buy it Priests and all but that he will never part with it while he can keep that stone, which none can read, with its leaves and deer & wonderful work. Shake hands and send him home. Then despairing of sleep with the row of the fishermen set to work and wrote these three capital stories—Half past 11 pm.[78]

Two days later Campbell was recording Fenian material, and a long narrative *Cath Sliabh Magh na Muchdrain* from John Cameron, Borgh.[79] Meanwhile, according to his notes:

> John MacNeil brother of Alexander sent up by ~~the~~ Carmichael from the North end. 89. walked ~~two or three or four~~ [*supra*: 5] miles—~~distance unknown~~ from Baile tuath.—disturbs the Cameron who goes off—in a fit of jealousy.[80]

With John Cameron having stormed off in a huff, Iain Donn recited for John Francis Campbell *An Duine Bochd Beairteach*, the same story Maclean had recorded from Hector Boyd more than ten years previously, and *A' Bhruighinn Chaorainn*, before launching into a long *tour d'horizon* of recent Barra history:

> My Father and the Colonel were grandsons of two brothers. MacNeills of Barra. Tannaistear Bharra was my great grandfather. Long were the Clan MacNeill in Barra. I am nearest to them & they were chiefs of the MacNeills. MacNeill of Canna is illegitimate. MacNeill of Colonsay is not the chief. Then breaks off with a whole history of the loss of Barra purchase of commission, portions to daughters who they married & all about them.
> I was there when all was taken.[81]

Regrettably, Campbell had to leave for South Uist the following day.

We are most fortunate that John Francis Campbell, Hector Maclean, and Alexander Carmichael collected and preserved such an extraordinary wealth of evidence concerning the people of Barra, their exceptional culture, and their fascinating history. I hope that this short piece might hint at something of the treasures waiting to be unearthed. Much research remains to be carried out, by scholars in Barra and scholars in the university working together, in partnership.

My thanks to Calum Macneil for his kind assistance. Any errors remaining are of course my own.

Domhnall Uilleam Stiùbhart

---

[1] NLS Adv. MS 50.1.14 fos.237–237a, Hector Maclean, Bàgh a' Chaisteil, to John Francis Campbell, 16 Jul 1859. Calum Macneil informs me that Allan MacDonald was the brother of Margaret, Mairead Aonghais Duinn,

Malacleit, the subject of Isa MacKillop and Norman Johnson's contribution to this volume. His work not only as schoolmaster, but also as sub-postmaster and Inspector of the Poor would have made MacDonald particularly acquainted with the people of Barra.

[2] Ibid. fo.279ᵛ, same, Ballygrant, Islay, to same, 31 Aug 1859.

[3] Ibid. fo.298ᵛ, John Francis Campbell, Niddry Lodge, London, to Donald Munro, 14 Oct 1859.

[4] John Francis Campbell (ed.), *Popular tales of the West Highlands* (4 vols, Paisley, 1890–3) [henceforth *PTWH*] i, 181–202.

[5] Ibid. ii, 424–50; see NLS Adv. MS 50.1.14 fo.490.

[6] NLS Adv. MS 50.1.10 fos.249–60; J.G. Mackay (ed.), *More West Highland Tales* (2 vols, Edinburgh, 1940–60) [henceforth *MWHT*] i, 372–92.

[7] NLS Adv. MS 50.1.8 fos.231–51; *PTWH* i, 157–9.

[8] NLS MS 50.1.8 fos.157–75; see *PTWH* i, 102; George Henderson, *The Celtic dragon myth* (Edinburgh, 1911), 155–72.

[9] NLS Adv. MS 50.1.9 fos.17–20.

[10] *PTWH* ii, 120–40.

[11] Ibid. ii, 148–80.

[12] NLS Adv. MS 50.1.8 fos.279–90; *PTWH* i, 195–6.

[13] Ibid. ii, 232–52.

[14] Ibid. ii, 94–7.

[15] Ibid. ii, 47–55, 85–93.

[16] Ibid. ii, 92.

[17] NLS Adv. MS 50.1.14 fo.490, Hector Maclean, Ballygrant, Islay, to John Francis Campbell, 23 Aug 1860.

[18] NLS Adv. MS 50.2.1 fo.224aᵛ, same, Poll a' Chàrra, South Uist, to same, 18 Sep 1860; see NLS Adv. MSS 50.1.14 fos.479–82; 50.2.1 fo.99.

[19] Ibid. fos.225–225a, same, Bàgh a' Chaisteil, Barra, to same, 22 Sep 1860.

[20] Ibid., fo.226, same, Bàgh a' Chaisteil, Barra, to same, 30 Sep 1860.

[21] NLS Adv. MS 50.1.9 fos.1–15.

[22] Ibid. fos.41–4.

[23] NLS Adv. MS 50.1.12 fos.157–87.

[24] NLS Adv. MS 50.2.1 fo.256aᵛ, Hector Maclean, Ballygrant, to John Francis Campbell, 26 Nov 1860.

[25] NLS Adv. MS 50.1.9 fos.55–66. This version of *Conall* was apparently learnt from an old man at Dréimeasdal, South Uist, almost 30 years previously.

[26] Ibid. fos.69–81.

[27] NLS Adv. MS 50.1.10 fos.125–37.

[28] Ibid. fos.138–48; *MWHT* i, 168–86.

[29] NLS Adv. MS 50.1.10 fos.149–58; *MWHT* i, 188–209.

[30] NLS Adv. MS 50.1.10 fos.159–67; *MWHT* i, 210–27.

[31] NLS Adv. MS 50.1.10 fos.194–202; *MWHT* i, 278–90.

[32] NLS Adv. MS 50.1.10 fos.203–11; *MWHT* i, 292–307; NLS Adv. MS 50.1.10 fos.221–4; *MWHT* i, 308–29.

[33] NLS Adv. MS 50.1.10 fos.225–36; *MWHT* i, 330–45.

[34] NLS Adv. MS 50.1.10 fos.237–48; *MWHT* i, 346–70.

[35] *PTWH* iii, 103–19.

[36] NLS Adv. MS 50.1.9 fos.177–80. These last two were recorded on 4 October 1860, while the others were taken down on 20 September.

[37] Ibid. fos.45–6.

[38] NLS Adv. MS 50.1.8 fos.311–15.

[39] Ibid. fos.345–50; recorded on 24 September 1860.

[40] NLS Adv. MS 50.1.10 fos.97–103; *MWHT* i, 118–29.

[41] NLS Adv. MS 50.1.10 fos.104–14; *MWHT* i, 130–47.

[42] NLS Adv. MS 50.1.10 fos.115–24; *MWHT* i, 148–67.

[43] NLS Adv. MS 50.1.10 fos.168–93; *MWHT* i, 228–77.

[44] NLS Adv. MS 50.1.11 fos.471–8; also recorded on 24 September 1860.

[45] NLS Adv. MSS 50.1.9 fos.21–31; 50.14 fo.490.

[46] NLS Adv. MS 50.1.8 fos.335–44.

[47] NLS Adv. MS 50.1.9 fos.93–104.

[48] See *PTWH* iv, 420–1, no.327.

[49] NLS Adv. MS 50.1.11 fos.339–50, 479–83.

[50] Ibid. fos.450–9.

[51] *PTWH* ii, 113–17.

[52] NLS Adv. MS 50.2.1 fo.382, Hector Maclean, Ballygrant, Islay, to John Francis Campbell, 31 Dec 1860. See *PTWH* iii, 46–9, 309–11, 320–47, 397–406; iv, 414–19, nos.219, 241, 249, 277–82, 303. Maclean appears to have visited Donald MacPhee towards the end of his second stay on Barra, on 1 October 1860.

[53] NLS Adv. MS 50.1.12 fos.88–93.

[54] Ibid. fos.51–6, 3 Jul 1861.

[55] NLS Adv. MS 50.1.12 fos.267–8; *PTWH* iv, 426–7, no.381.

[56] *CG* i, 254.

[57] CW MS 113 fos.14ᵛ–44ᵛ.

[58] CW MS 105 fos.20ᵛ–23.

[59] CW MS 104 fos.1–31.

[60] CW MSS 103 fos.7–9, 11–12ᵛ; 339 fos.123, 132.

[61] CW MS 103 fo.9. See AC's note to *Duan an Deirg*, CW MS 114 fo.11: 'Heard this from Eachun MacNeil a blind man who lived in MacNeil of Barra's house as musician and historian. Hector MacNeil was a big powerful man and considered the best fiddler in Scotland. He married when he was considerably past 80 years. He had £200 saved from his salary. Had no family.' Among MacPhee's other sources were, for *Laoidh Mhànais*, 'Iain mac Fhearachair Iain Johnson a little old man who lived at Cille Bhara' [Ibid. fo.18]; and, for *Teanntachd Mhór na Féinne*, the celebrated catechist from North Uist Roderick MacQueen, Ruairidh Ruadh [Ibid. fo.25].

[62] CW MSS 103 fos.10, 14–17; 114 fos.6–29; 375 fos.35–40.

[63] CW MS 114 fos.29ᵛ–42ᵛ.

[64] Ibid. fo.42ᵛ.

[65] Ibid. fos.58–88; 362 fos.238, 241–2, 246, 253, 266; *CG* ii, 229, 278; iv, xlii.

[66] CW MS 519, not foliated.

[67] CW MS 87 fo.2; *CG* v, 208–9.

[68] CW MSS 244 fos.608–9, 668–9; 339 fos.135–6.

[69] CW MS 107 fos.17–23ᵛ.

[70] CW MS 150 fos.3–5.

[71] Ibid. fos.7–11.

[72] Ibid. fos.11ᵛ–22.

[73] *PTWH* i, cxxx.

[74] NLS Adv. MS 50.4.6 fo.148; see also NLS Adv. MSS 50.2.11, 98–100; 50.4.6 fos.143–50; 50.1.21; CW MS 119 fos.55–6; *CG* ii, 352–3.

[75] NLS Adv. MS 50.2.4 fos.77–96.

[76] Ibid. fo.86.

[77] Ibid. fo.91.

[78] Ibid. fos.96–7.

[79] Ibid. fos.97–110, 115–37.

[80] Ibid. fo.144.

[81] Ibid. fo.156; see fos.65, 144–55.

4

I Thought He Made It All Up:
Context and Controversy

RONALD BLACK

Everyone agrees that Alexander Carmichael really existed. Unfortunately the same cannot be said for the contents of *Carmina Gadelica*. The problem is best summed up in the words of a person who should have known better, namely my wife, who cheerfully remarked to me just a few weeks ago: 'Oh, I thought he made it all up!'

This, as every politician comes to realise, is the difference between complex reality and public perception. When it leaks out to the public that a great collector has been found guilty of fiddling with some of his hard-won materials, the whole lot becomes tainted. As James Boswell said about Macpherson's Ossian: 'Antiquaries, and admirers of the work, may complain, that they are in a situation similar to that of the unhappy gentleman whose wife informed him, on her death-bed, that one of their reputed children was not his; and, when he eagerly begged her to declare which of them it was, she answered, "*That* you shall never know;" and expired, leaving him in irremediable doubt as to them all.'[1]

Ossian is a good place to start, because it reminds us of some basic facts. One is that the word 'translation' has a wide spectrum of meaning. Another is that there were exactly 100 years between Macpherson's *Fragments* of 1760, a monument to unscientific fieldwork and loose translation, and John Francis Campbell's *Popular Tales of the West Highlands* of 1860–2, a monument to scientific fieldwork and literal translation, which marked Carmichael's début as a collector. Another is the accusation that Carmichael was 'a firm believer in MacPherson's *Ossian*', the rebuttal of which by John Lorne Campbell formed part of the controversy about *Carmina* in the 1970s.[2]

Halfway between the *Fragments* and the *Popular Tales* both in time and in spirit are the *Kinder- und Hausmärchen* of the brothers Grimm, better known to us as Grimms' fairy tales, the first volume of the first edition of which was published in 1812. This event marks the beginning of folklore scholarship as we know it today. Jacob Grimm, the philologist, lived from 1785 to 1863, and Wilhelm, the literary scholar, from 1786 to 1859. Their original purpose, as enunciated by Jacob, was to salvage what was left of a priceless resource stored in the heads of the ordinary people of a politically divided German nation. But they began making changes even between the manuscript and the first edition. When *Sneewittchen*, Snow White, meets the dwarves for the first time in the manuscript, they ask merely that she cook their meals in return for shelter, but when printed in 1812, their terms have escalated in a way that seems to reflect the brothers' idea of contractual relations between men and women: 'If you will keep house for us, do the cooking, make the beds, wash, sew, knit, and keep everything neat and clean, you can stay with us and you won't want for anything.'[3]

One reviewer described the collection as mostly rubbish, and even a friend of the Grimms commented privately: 'If you want to display children's clothing, you can do that quite well without showing an outfit with buttons torn off, smeared with dirt, and the shirt hanging out of the trousers.' Jacob took little more to do with it, but through six more editions Wilhelm polished the prose, altered the content, and fleshed out the texts till some of them were double their original length. Writing in his brother's name as well as his own, he ceased to insist on fidelity to oral tradition, preferring to point out that the collection was a 'manual of manners' (*Erziehungsbuch*) and had been made suitable for children.[4]

So each edition was a little further from the original than the one before. The failings of motherhood were a particular problem, so in the second edition Snow White's mother became her stepmother, and in the fourth edition the same fate befell Hänsel and Gretel's mother, whose crime was child abandonment.[5] The seventh and last edition, which has of course become definitive, appeared in 1857, two years before Wilhelm's death, six years before Jacob's, and at precisely the time when Carmichael was beginning to collect. It is interesting to note that Wilhelm's friend Professor Benecke of Göttingen liked the bogus, very twee style of the Irish stories collected and retold by Thomas Crofton Croker, but approved rather less of the arch but honest approach adopted by William Grant Stewart in his *Popular Superstitions and Festive Amusements* of 1823, the seminal work on Gaelic and Highland folklore. Stewart was so close to the earthy-sounding traditions he was describing that he needed to use archness and irony as a distancing device. Benecke told Wilhelm in 1826 that Edgar Taylor, whose English translation of the Grimms' tales also appeared in 1823, had much to teach Croker and even more to teach Stewart.[6]

Thanks to the Grimms, two separate strands had emerged in the publication of folktales by the time the term 'folklore' was invented by the Englishman William Thoms in 1846.[7] On the one side were the literary creations and recreations practised by writers and poets like Ernst Hoffmann (1776–1822) and Hans Christian Andersen (1805–75). Andersen, like Stewart, grew up amongst poverty and folklore, and used the latter to create a more perfect world of his own—some of his 156 fairy tales and stories are recreations, but the vast majority, like 'The Ugly Duckling', are his own invention.[8]

On the other side is the strand of authenticity represented by Jacob Grimm. This can be found in, for example, the Danish tales collected by Just Matthias Thiele and the Norwegian ones collected by Peter Asbjørnsen and Jørgen Moe. This leads us to Gaelic. The English scholar George Dasent met Jacob Grimm when on diplomatic business in Stockholm in 1840 and found him inspirational. Subsequently he met Asbjørnsen, Moe, and John Francis Campbell (1822–85). Dasent's *Popular Tales from the Norse* appeared in 1859, and by then Campbell, too (whom I will call JFC from now on), was hooked on what he liked to call 'storyology'.[9]

JFC's attitude to authenticity was crystal clear from the beginning. In the introduction to the first volume of *Popular Tales of the West Highlands* he wrote: 'The following collection is intended to be a contribution to this new science of "Storyology". It is a museum of curious rubbish about to perish, given as it was gathered in the rough, for it seemed to me as barbarous to "polish" a genuine popular tale, as it would be to adorn the bones of a Megatherium with tinsel, or gild a rare old copper coin. On this, however, opinions vary, but I hold my own that, stories orally collected can only be valuable if given unaltered.'[10]

Civil Service mandarin as he was, JFC ran the operation with masterly efficiency. First he recruited a team of fieldworkers. 'I begged,' he wrote, 'for the very words used by the people who told the stories, with nothing added, or omitted, or altered.' Then he played the inspector, getting a selection of informants to retell their stories while he compared them to the transcript on his knee. One of the fieldworkers subjected to his scrutiny was Alexander Carmichael.[11]

JFC's rigorous approach influenced his successors and informed the collecting of other types of material. In particular, in a correspondence with the Rev. John Gregorson Campbell, published in 1895, JFC wrote: 'I am much obliged by your promise to put some one to write for me. If he writes from dictation will you kindly *beg him to follow the words spoken* without regard to his own opinion, or to what they ought to be . . . If you are sceptical I hold to my creed of the people. But creed or no creed I want to get the tradition as it exists and I would not give a snuff for "cooked" tradition.'[12]

The culinary metaphor made a big impression on John Gregorson Campbell (whom I will now call JGC). When he published *Duan na Muilgheartaich* in 1881 he wrote: 'For archæological or other scientific purpose, it is essential that ballads of this kind, and indeed everything got from oral sources, should be presented to the reader "uncooked", that is, without suppression or addition, or alteration, which is not pointed out.'[13] Elsewhere, dropping the metaphor, he wrote: 'The object of the writer has always been, in all matters affecting Celtic antiquities, to make whatever he deems worthy of preservation, as available and reliable to the reader as to himself, without addition, suppression, or embellishment.'[14]

JGC was busy applying JFC's mantra to a variety of folklore contexts, particularly charms and miscellaneous superstitions. On one occasion he even criticised his mentor. He wrote: 'The attributes of the *fuath* are different in different tales, and Mr Campbell (*Tales of the West Highlands*, ii. 191) has fallen into the error of conjoining attributes ascribed in several stories and representing the *fuath* as a water spirit having web-feet, tail, mane, etc. The name of a desolate moor near Ullapool in Ross-shire, *Leathad Leacanta nam Fuath* ("the Flat-Stoned Declivity of Fuaths"), is alone convincing it was not deemed particularly a water spirit.'[15]

JGC's accuracy as a scholar is important to us here, for two reasons. One is that he tangled with Carmichael over the issue. The other is that in 1983 Alan Bruford attacked JGC's standards of accuracy in the same article in which he attacked Carmichael's.[16] As JGC's editor and biographer I had to deal with this. My conclusion was that Bruford was wrong, and that JGC in fact developed a procedure consisting of immediate transcription from his notes followed by the checking of points of detail on subsequent visits to his informant. As minister of Tiree this was not difficult, since most of his informants were his own parishioners. However, I was not satisfied with this, and made a detailed comparison between JGC's manuscript of a tale, his published version and his English translation. I concluded that JGC was in the habit of writing 'etc.' in his transcripts where a 'run' occurred which could be filled in at leisure, for example by copying from an earlier point in the text, and that he used a variety of techniques to avoid offending Victorian sensibilities—altering a Gaelic word to one less well known (such as *magairle* becoming *leth-chollainn*), bowdlerising the English translation, or omitting the phrase altogether. In this respect he was no different from JFC. The folklorist's mantra of 'writing without suppression, addition or alteration' fell silent at the portals of public performance and publication.[17]

Now for JGC's brush with Carmichael. This was in 1889. Quite worryingly, it looks as if the latter had sent him drafts of one, two or perhaps all three of the charms which subsequently appeared in *CG* ii as *Eolas an Torranain, An Torranan* and, again, *Eolas an Torranain*. At that stage, however, Carmichael did not have it as *torranan* at all but *foraman*. JGC replies: 'I have heard about the plant "*Foraman*" in Skye as being fennel where fresh water falls into the sea but I do not know its scientific name. But without entering into these subjects at any great length, I cannot but think that in point of value it is necessary, that the words of these rhymes are given by you exactly as they came to hand without addition, or suppression, or emendation. This will give them greater weight, & value as actually found in popular lore. I think therefore it would not be wise for me to interfere even if I could.'[18]

This was a rebuke. It was ignored by Carmichael, and the three charms duly appeared in *Carmina* with *torranan* and 'figwort' in big letters. There is no mention of *foraman*, of fennel, or of JGC. Instead there is a rambling six-page introduction connecting the plant with St Torranan of Uist, St Ternan of Banchory, the isle of Taransay, and Taranis, the thunder god of the Gauls. I see no reason to doubt the overall authenticity of the three charms, but in this introduction Carmichael stirs such a speculative blend of history and topography into his basic ingredients, including the streams in Benbecula called the Gamhnach and the Deathachan, that the flavour of genuine oral tradition is overwhelmed.[19]

In other cases we have the actual texts and translations that went back and forth between JGC (1834–91) and Carmichael, and the most striking thing is that Carmichael's texts were shifting sands. *O'n Ti tha shuas* 'from Him on high' in 1891 becomes *o'n Tri tha shuas* 'from the Three on high' in 1900. Similarly *a chur fais* 'to give growth' becomes *a chur failt* 'to welcome', the angels Gabriel and Raphael become Ariel and Gabriel, *bhuam* 'from me' becomes *bhuainn* 'from us', and *geamhradh* 'winter' becomes *gaillionn* 'storm'.[20] This sort of thing is wearily familiar to all of us who have followed the controversy about *Carmina* in these thirty years since it began in 1976.

Before we come to the controversy, however, I have to round off my picture of the context. Carmichael's half-century of activity was a golden age of Gaelic folklore collecting. Sheriff Alexander Nicolson (1827–93) and the Rev. Duncan Campbell (1854–1938) collected proverbs. The outstanding collectors of tales were JFC and his assistants Hector MacLean (1818–93) and John Dewar (1802–72), also the Revs James MacDougall (1833–1906) and Duncan MacInnes (*c*.1820–1903). JFC also collected Ossianic ballads. Finally, the leading collectors of superstitions and general folklore, in order of age, were JGC, Dr Robert Craig Maclagan (1839–1919), the Rev. Neil Campbell (1850–1904), Father Allan McDonald (1859–1905), and the extraordinary Lady Evelyn Stewart Murray (1868–1940), who went on a collecting explosion for just one year of her sad aristocratic life, 1891.[21] Also worth a mention is Lord Archibald Campbell (1846–1913), who on JFC's death in 1885 shouldered his legacy as motivator, organiser and editor.[22] Finally there is Carmichael himself, renowned by the end of his life as one of the greatest specialists of the group, the king of charms and incantations. By the time *Carmina* came out in 1900 he was the second-oldest survivor. Only MacInnes was older.

Thanks to the two Campbell aristocrats, the group's published output was prodigious, and nearly all of it came out before *Carmina*. There were four volumes of *Popular Tales* in 1860–2, then JFC's *Leabhar na Féinne* in 1872, Nicolson's *Gaelic Proverbs* in 1881, and Lord Archibald's *Records of Argyll* in 1885, consisting mainly of the 'historical tales' genre which JFC had deliberately excluded from *Popular Tales*, although John Dewar had collected dozens if not hundreds for him. *Records of Argyll* included some of the charms and incantations sent by Carmichael to the Napier Commission and published in 1884 in the appendix to their report. Between 1889 and 1895 there appeared five volumes of collected folklore published as the *Waifs and Strays* series, consisting of the work of MacInnes, MacDougall and JGC, with Lord Archibald as general editor. A posthumous collection by MacDougall, *Folk Tales and Fairy Lore*, appeared in 1910.

But it is what happened in 1900 and 1902 that is of the greatest interest to us. *Carmina* did not appear till October 1900 but was well flagged up in advance.[23] JGC had been dead since 1891, but his devoted sister Mrs Jessy Wallace knew Carmichael well. JGC's long work on superstitions had been ready for the press since about 1874, but Carmichael had used it, and this would have worried Jessy. So the appearance of JGC's book in 1900 and 1902 bears all the hallmarks of haste. It is badly edited, cheaply produced, and the publisher, James Maclehose, even insisted that it be divided artificially into two so that he could test the market with one volume before publishing the other. Worst of all, he cut out the original texts of all the charms, which were of enormous value. Ironically, he then showed them to Carmichael, who copied them out, and it is thanks to this manuscript in the Carmichael Watson Collection (CW MS 241) that I have been able to restore them to JGC's text, now republished as *The Gaelic Otherworld*.[24]

The reason I draw attention to these fifteen classic works of Gaelic folklore published between 1860 and 1910 is that close study of them furnishes the immediate context for Carmichael's practices. In the main, thanks to JFC's inspiration, they seem to be an accurate rendering of the people's words. But each collector has his own personality, and in the case of one in particular, James MacDougall, every so often an outrageous romanticism seems to get the better of him, and tales are told in a way which certainly does not represent the authentic voice of the people. I am thinking for example of *Nighean Righ a' Churraichd Ruaidh*, 'The Daughter of the King of the Red Cap', which has impossible place-names in it like *Eilean Mòr Spiorad a' Cheò*, even though, like everything else in the volume, we are told that it was got from Alexander Cameron, a native of Ardnamurchan who was the roadman between Duror and Ballachulish.[25]

Two other kinds of context deserve mention. One is the publication of traditional verse. Two of the greatest of nineteenth-century anthologists, John Mackenzie and the Rev. Alexander Maclean Sinclair, are known to have meddled with their texts in the interest of perceived virtues like decency, good grammar and the elimination of loanwords.[26] The other context is charms and incantations themselves. There was an explosion of activity in the last two decades of the nineteenth century, nearly all of it in journals. William Mackenzie, first secretary of both the Gaelic Society of Inverness and the Crofters' Commission, published nine items in 1879 and another ninety or so in 1892.[27] The scholar Alexander Macbain published seven in 1888 and another forty-eight in 1891.[28] Alexander Macdonald, 'Gleannach', published seven in 1888 and another nine in 1914.[29] The Rev. Archibald MacDonald, Kiltarlity, published four in 1893.[30] The Rev. Malcolm MacPhail published three in 1900.[31] And there are forty-one charms in English only in JGC's *Witchcraft and Second Sight* of 1902, to which I restored the Gaelic originals in *The Gaelic Otherworld*.[32] If we total these up the number of items comes to 218, which is the equivalent of more than a volume of *Carmina*—*CG* i has 157 items, *CG* ii has 107 with many extra bits and pieces in the dictionary of Gaelic folklore, *CG* iii has 182, and *CG* iv has 190. *CG* v has 132, but less than a dozen of these could be described as charms or incantations.[33]

Another important source for hymns, prayers, rhymes, charms and incantations is Father Allan McDonald's collection of general folklore. This consists of five notebooks, CW MSS 58A and 58B in Edinburgh University Library ('Folklore MSS I and II'), Gen. 1090/28 and 1090/29 in Glasgow University Library ('Folklore MSS V and VI'), and CH2/1/1/13/128/1 in Canna House ('The Strange Things MS').[34] For some years now Mrs Flora Komori and I have been transcribing these notebooks and publishing our work in monthly instalments in the Uist community newspaper *Am Pàipear*.[35] If we are spared, the result should be a substantial volume, perhaps published in twelve or fifteen years' time. But there is no reason why the relevant material should not be available meanwhile to cross-fertilise with studies in *Carmina*.[36]

Now for the controversy. It began in 1976 with a paper by Hamish Robertson in *Scottish Gaelic Studies*. His interest was in the study of religion rather than of text, and he was deeply disappointed to discover that his idol had feet of clay. Having compared some of the texts in *CG* iii and iv with drafts in the Carmichael Watson Collection, he denounced Carmichael as a 'romantic dilettante'. Very importantly, he remarked: 'There is no trace of material existing for Vols. I and II among the manuscripts of the Carmichael-Watson collection, except for a few rare passages which belong to the notes in the second volume.'[37] One of the most important tasks of the new Carmichael project should be to establish whether this is true, and more generally to prepare a catalogue of *Carmina* texts with links to their surviving manuscript sources. And future *Carmina* scholarship should begin by assessing Robertson's textual criticisms in detail.

Robertson's tirade drew a response in 1978 from Dr John Lorne Campbell (whom I will call JLC). He pointed out, as I have just done, that Robertson's own work required critical enquiry, and refuted the younger man's evidence on various matters of detail. But he also reminded us of the intellectual atmosphere of the time in which Carmichael lived: a time when the cultural inheritance of the Gael was slighted, abused and set at naught every minute of the day and in every place from Highland schoolrooms up through churches and courts to Parliament itself. Carmichael's aim was to raise the prestige of the Highlanders to a level at which those in authority such as Gladstone would pay attention to what they had to say—an aim which, in JLC's opinion, was entirely honourable.[38] Incidentally, this is why Carmichael's presentation of the four great quarter-days of the Gaelic calendar is strangely skewed—*Latha Fhéill Brìghde* (1 February), *Bealltainn* (1 May) and *Lùnastal* (1 August) are lovingly presented, but the greatest of them all, *Samhain* (1 November), which is essentially a celebration of pagan primalism and anarchy, is conspicuous by its absence.

The trouble with this argument is that *Carmina* emerges as a work of propaganda rather than of folklore. JLC did not deny that Carmichael tinkered with what he had collected, but defended the practice by alleging that this was the normal custom of his time. This I find even scarier than Robertson's allegations. He said: 'Much of the first three volumes of *Carmina* must be taken as a literary and not as a literal presentation of Gaelic folklore.'[39] To which I would say, why three and not four or five, and also, with friends like that, who needs enemies?

JLC makes other points which deserve commentary if not criticism. He says that Carmichael's ignorance of Roman Catholic devotional literature 'is revealed by his printing a Gaelic version of the "Hail Mary" as if it were a traditional Gaelic poem (i:110)'.[40] That is unfair. Carmichael prints the item without comment, and could not possibly have been ignorant of the Hail Mary. JLC also says: 'From a modern point of view, the only volumes of *Carmina* that are adequately edited are the last two.'[41] I think this is a fair criticism of James Carmichael Watson's work as editor of *CG* iii and iv, less so of *CG* i and ii which never really had an editor. In 1900 they consist of a gifted collector doing his best with difficult materials, and in 1928 his daughter Ella makes a few minimal changes. Some books cannot be edited—they should be allowed to stand as monuments or follies, depending on one's point of view, and different books should be written to grapple with the issues they raise.

Even more importantly, JLC says: 'Carmichael . . . admitted that he was collating and combining different versions and using some to mend the imperfections of others, as we have seen. The modern enquirer can take it for granted that this process was going on, especially in the material that makes up the first three volumes of *Carmina*.' The sole basis for this allegation appears to be a letter written by Carmichael to Father Allan McDonald in 1904, when material for the projected *CG* iii was being got together. Carmichael says: 'I have many versions of things and they give me much bother. For example, *Tàladh Muime Dhomhnaill Ghuirm* is the grandest thing that I know in the Gaelic language. I have some ten or twelve versions of that, all differing more or less. How to deal with them all is hard to say. I cannot give all the versions separately. To give all the versions of all poems separately would be ruinous. I must therefore collate them all and give the result alone—not at all an easy matter.'[42]

In my opinion, JLC is stretching the evidence too far. *Tàladh Dhòmhnaill Ghuirm* is quite a well-known song. The process Carmichael is talking about has been applied since then in all the Scottish Gaelic Text Society editions of verse, where a primary text is selected or even created, and sources and variant readings are given in an apparatus. Since his books were aimed at a popular as well as an academic readership, Carmichael was probably planning to dispense with the apparatus. But we cannot assume that this was the process he applied to the charms and incantations in *CG* i and ii, all of which are ascribed to named informants. The proof of this is the fact that over and over again he gives separate treatment to variants of the same charm. Charms were hard to get, and were not to be treated in the same way as songs, which were still ten a penny. We have to ask ourselves whether the man who wrote the following words about Mary Cameron of Sgiathairigh in Glenelg in *CG* iv, 231, had the instincts of a forger: 'I went to her from Ardchattan in Lorne, travelling up Glen Orchy, down the Black Mount, by the Moor of Rannoch, Lochaber, Fort William, through the Garbhchrioch (Rough Bound) and Arasaig on to Mallaig. Thence I took boat by night along the Linne Shléiteach (Sound of Sleat), past Cnòideart (Knoydart), and into Loch Shubhairn (Loch Hourn), arriving at Arnisdale late at night. Next morning I took boat for Sgiathairigh near Ceann Loch Shubhairn (Loch Hourn-head). I found Mary Cameron a pleasant and hospitable woman, but on no account would she repeat to me "Eòlas a' Chaimein", though I tried every possible means to persuade her. She said that the "eòlas" was entrusted to her for no foolish purpose, and she was not going to impart it for any foolish purpose to any person. On the following morning I took boat to Eilean Diarmaid (Isle Ornsay) to meet the steamer for Mallaig, whence by train to Edinburgh. It was a long, costly and, alas, disappointing journey, like many similar ones.'

This still leaves the editor of *CG* iii and iv, Carmichael's grandson Professor James Carmichael Watson, looking exposed. JLC excused him on the grounds of fidelity to his grandfather, ignorance of Uist and Barra tradition, and wartime conditions. In 1941, when *CG* iii and iv were safely through the press, he joined the Navy, and on 26 March 1942 he was posted 'Missing Presumed Killed' when his ship, HMS *Jaguar*, went down in the Mediterranean.[43]

In a further article in 1981 JLC got down to detail, documenting the help received by Carmichael from the scholar George Henderson between 1892 and 1900. Henderson's advice was only partially and often reluctantly accepted. This article is an invaluable contribution to the lexicography of *Carmina*. The mysterious word *bràc*, for example, 'haunts the first four volumes of *Carmina* with various interpretations', and 'with the meaning "reindeer" is now in both MacBain's and Dwelly's dictionaries, on the sole authority of *Carmina*'.[44] In future when we have forgotten the polemics we can get down to the serious business of analysing Carmichael's work, charm by charm and incantation by incantation, beginning with the insights provided by articles like these.

But in 1984 Alan Bruford returned to the heart of the dispute. If Carmichael 'repaired' the texts he had collected, what was the nature of these 'repairs'?

To find this out, Bruford carried out a comparison between the tale 'Eachdraidh Chlann Uisne' ('The Story of the Children of Uisne') as told to Carmichael on 16 March 1867 by John MacNeil at Buaile nam Bodach in Barra, and as published by Carmichael in 1887. We have a transcript of Carmichael's field-notes made by his 'Preventive Man' Robert Urquhart in Ìochdar in 1872. The results are amazing. Carmichael made changes big and small in nearly every line. These are changes for the sake of improving the language, cleaning it up, heightening the style, developing the story, archaising, and for the sake of change itself. Where MacNeil used the anglicised idiom *anns an spot* ('immediately') Carmichael substituted *air larach nam bonn*. Where MacNeil said *gus am faigh mise greim oirrese* ('until I can get hold of her') he substituted *agus feuch am faic mise Deirdire* 'so that I may behold Deirdire'. Where MacNeil said *chuir e air a ghualainn i agus cos air gach taobh ga mhuineal* ('he set her on his shoulders with a leg on either side of his neck') he substituted *chuir Naois Deirdire air fras-mhullach a ghuaille* ('Naoise placed Deirdire on the very summit of his shoulders').[45]

It is particularly distressing to find the familiar diction of *Carmina* constantly surfacing on top of the Barra man's words. Where he said *thug e suas an deò* ('he gave up the ghost') Carmichael substituted *leig e osna ghoirt a' bhais agus sgain a chridhe* ('he heaved the sore sigh of death and his heart rent'). Where MacNeil used no adornment at all we find exclamations like *O bhith 's aodaich!* ('Oh, food and clothing!') or *a Righ na gile 's na greine* ('O King of the moon and of the sun').[46]

Worst of all, one small part of the story—ten lines of print—is enlarged to take up a dozen pages of Carmichael's book. This can only be described as Alexander Carmichael trying his own hand at writing a folktale, while ascribing it to John MacNeil. Dr Bruford's conclusion is that 'there is reason enough here to apply stringent critical standards to everything that Carmichael published or prepared for publication . . . we are entitled to accept, if not expect, the possibility of "improvement" or even forgery'.[47]

This is uncannily in line with what scholars like Maria Tatar have found the Grimms, Wilhelm at least, doing through the seven editions of their stories. She says: 'The Grimms actively and deliberately altered the folkloric material they claimed to have tried so hard to preserve in its pristine state. At times, those changes seem oddly arbitrary.' But in a passage where for 'Grimms' we may read 'Carmichael' and for 'German' we may read 'Gaelic' she says: 'The Grimms wanted to give the public a document of German folk culture in its most admirable form. To make it appear all the more German, every fairy (*Fee*), prince (*Prinz*), and princess (*Prinzessin*) was transformed into a more Teutonic-sounding enchantress (*Zauberin*) or wise woman (*weise Frau*), king's son (*Königssohn*), and king's daughter (*Königstochter*). Proverbs were added to give the collection a more folksy texture, and the proper moral sentiments were woven into the text, for this collection was to be in many ways a showcase for German folk culture. Thus a king condemns his wife to be burned at the stake in the first edition, but he does so only with the greatest regrets in the second edition: he stands at a window and watches her with tears in his eyes, "because he still loved her so much".'[48]

The difference between the two Grimm brothers, the scientist and the nation-builder, is also the difference between JFC and Carmichael.

I have to point out here that Bruford was careful to make no claims about *Carmina*. He says: 'The only way in which Carmichael seems exceptional—in this publication: I cannot speak for others—is the thoroughness with which, having taken down a complete text, he revised every sentence, almost as if he were trying to evade copyright restrictions.' Equally thought-provoking is Bruford's remark that in his twelve-page interpolation Carmichael was 'trying his hand at writing a Gaelic story in the traditional style with some success in prose, less in the poems'.[49] It sounds as if writing charms and incantations may not have been his *forte*. So now I want to turn to the case studies from *Carmina* that I have carried out myself over the years, beginning with the Curse of Neist.[50]

The Curse of Neist was said to have been used by a MacLeod witch in the 1530s to drown a boatful of marauding Clan Ranald MacDonalds off the most westerly point of Skye. Over and above the version in *CG* iv, 356–9, I have identified five versions written down by five different people between the 1850s and the 1950s, all in Skye. They vary in length from ten lines to four. So what are we to make of the *thirty-four*-line version in *Carmina*?

In this case there are documents in the Carmichael Watson Collection to help us. They consist, firstly, of four scraps, varying in length from eighteen lines to six, written out in Carmichael's own hand in what is now CW MS 495, and secondly of a draft of the full thirty-four-line version, written in ink in copperplate with pencil annotations, also now in CW MS 495, and clearly used by Professor James Carmichael Watson in assembling the published volume. I do not know whose hand it is in.

I have been unable to track down Carmichael's original field-note of any of the scraps. But we do know from whom he got them, because there are names attached to most of the scraps, and these names are then gathered together under the heading in the draft and in the published book, as follows: 'Reciters: Archibald Maclellan, master-mariner, Loch Boisdale, South Uist; John Pearson and Catherine Pearson, cottars, Ceann Tangabhall, Barra, 14th March 1873; and others in Kintail in 1903.'[51] This is unique for *Carmina*, because throughout the whole of the five volumes there is no other instance of a multiple named source in which the contributions of individuals are completely unmarked.[52] However, taking this together with additional ascriptions given with the scraps, we can work out that the first scrap was got from Capt. Maclellan, the second from the MacPhersons (Pearsons), the third from Mrs Flora Maclennan (*née* Matheson) in Dornie, and the fourth from an unknown person or persons in Dornie.

Now let us examine the text. The first four lines in *Carmina* are:

> *Gaoth an iar*
> *Air fiacail Feiste,*
> *Gaoth is corr,*
> *Ceò is uisge.*

Wind from the west / On the tooth of Neist, / Wind and more, / Mist and rain.

These are a distillation of different fragments given to Carmichael by the MacPhersons and Mrs Maclennan. Some images are missing from *Carmina*. Both informants offered the image of the west wind on the point of Neist, and also added a line about *gaoth gun chiall* 'a senseless wind, a raging wind', which *Carmina* lacks. Mrs Maclennan lacked the tooth image, but made up for it by throwing in a line about *bochunn baisteach/baistidh* ('a swelling surge of rain'). Carmichael's *Gaoth is corr*, 'Wind and more', is a very lame summing-up of these sources. The actual word *còrr* does not appear in them at all.

Two lines, *Muir a falach / Talamh is athar*, are added in pencil to the draft, and these words duly appear in *Carmina* with the translation: 'Sea concealing / Earth and heaven.' Where did they come from?

Next *Carmina* has:

Clann Domhnaill
Air bhordach briste,
Gun sgòd dh'an tuigse—
An glaodh leam cha mhisde!

Clan Donald / On broken planking, / No shred of sense left them— / I pity not their bawling!

Both the MacPhersons and Mrs Maclennan have the image of broken planks. In fact Mrs Maclennan has it twice. But where does *sgòd* come from? Mrs Maclennan provides the answer. She has: *Leom(sa) cha leon 's cha mhisde / Am beoil bhi leonta briste / 'S am por (bhi) gun sgot nan eigin. / Am por gun sgot dh'an ceille / S am poor bhi sgite sgeitse.* It means something like: 'I'm not pained or bothered / By their mouths being wounded and broken, / Their seed being destitute, / Their seed being senseless, / Their seed being exhausted, worn out.' Mrs Maclennan's *sgot dh'an ceille* becomes Watson's *sgòd dh'an tuigse.* So again we find that one word in *Carmina* is a distillation of several lines of text.

There is also a question about the *Carmina* line *An glaodh leam cha mhisde*. All the sources, including the draft text in front of Watson, have the word for 'bawling', in the form *glaodh, gaoire, gaoireachd* or *gaoirich*, coming last in the line. For example, the MacPhersons have: *Am por bhi sgite/sgiota / Am beoil bhi briste / An ceo bhith silteach / Us deoir / 'S na deoir air am mnathan ceile. / Leom cha leon an gaoire.* ('Their seed being exhausted / Their mouths broken / Their mist oozing / And tears / And tears being shed by their wives. / I'm not pained by their distress.') The evidence suggests that it was Watson himself who chose which of the four words to use, and changed its position in the line while he was at it. It was a bad decision, because the verse should have finished *glaodha, gaoire, gaoireachd* or *gaoirich* to provide end-rhyme with the rest of the text. When I looked at the curse in *Carmina* and compared it with the fragments, it dawned on me that Carmichael had distilled it into four verses, linked by end-rhyme on *glaodha, gaoire, gaoireachd* or *gaoirich* to rhyme with *saor dhaibh, sgaoilte* and *dhaoine.* His grandson, despite being the editor of *The Gaelic Songs of Mary MacLeod*, had failed to notice that.

The second verse as it appears in *Carmina* consists of eight lines:

Coit chaol chorrach,
Crainn ard reamhar,
Seòil phait phlaideach,
Luchd bharaillean falamh,
Cathadh mara
Dol dh'an adhar,
Sàl dh'an dalladh,
Is Cuan nan Gallan saor dhaibh.

Skiff crank and narrow, / Masts tall and stout, / Sails coarse and bulging, / Cargo of empty barrels, / Spindrift flying / Up to heaven, / Brine blinding them, / And Cuan nan Gallan free to them.

The first three lines correspond to the sources except that *reamhar* 'stout' should read *reamhach* 'thin'! *Luchd bharaillean falamh* is in none of Carmichael's own sources, but I know that he saw it around 1906 in JGC's papers.[53] Did he steal it? As for the last four lines, I cannot find them anywhere, but I do not believe that he made them up, because *Cuan nan Gallan saor dhaibh* sounds so unlike a curse.

The third verse in *Carmina* again has eight lines. I have only been able to identify one source for it, the five lines which Carmichael took down at Dornie from person or persons unknown. There are three issues here. First of all, the first three lines in *Carmina* are basically the first three lines collected in Dornie:

> *Taoim gu tobhtach,*
> *Taoman bristeach,*
> *Seòil a' stracadh.*

> Bilge to thwarts, / Bailer brittle, / Sails ripping.

Secondly, the fourth line noted in Dornie, *Ceo ghan tacadh* 'Mist choking them', becomes four lines in *Carmina*,

> *Sgeò a' sacadh,*
> *Sneachd a' tachdadh,*
> *Muir ag atach,*
> *Fir a' rachdadh.*

> Fog suffocating, / Snow choking, / Sea swelling, / Men straining.

Watson was a bit doubtful about one word, writing on the draft 'rachdadh? technical term'. And thirdly, the line *Stiuir/Steoir gun ocar feuma* noted at Dornie, meaning something like 'Helm insecurely anchored', was thrown out by whoever prepared the draft, presumably Carmichael himself, and replaced with *Agus gach aitim sgaoilte*. I can see one good reason why this was done: Carmichael had clearly perceived a metrical dynamic at work in some of his sources and was trying to do justice to it by ending each verse, as I have pointed out, with a disyllabic rhyme on the sound *ao*. He achieved this by drafting in the line *Agus gach aitim sgaoilte* from somewhere else, despite the fact that it would appear on the face of it to mean 'And every tribe dispersed'. Then he translated it 'And every orifice open'.

For verse four, our main source is Captain Maclellan, who says: *Sgioba bhras bhrothach/bhorb / Gun urram coin dha cheile. / Gun mhodh a choin dha cheile. / Gun mhodh nan/na troich dha cheile. / Guidh buan nan Leodach / Do shluagh Chlann Dòmhnuill eitidh.* In other words, skipper-like, he offers a line 'A rash scabby crew', variations on the theme 'Without a dog's (or dwarf's) respect for each other', and a dignified conclusion: 'The MacLeods' eternal wish / For the folk of frightful Clan Donald.' The MacPhersons throw in *urram muic* 'a pig's respect'. Carmichael liked the 'crew' idea but did not seem to care for how it was done, and *Carmina* reads:

> *Sgioba lag-lamhach,*
> *Ardanach aineolach,*
> *Mór-bhriathrach,*
> *Beag-chiallach,*
> *Gann-rianach,*
> *Dall-ghnìomhach,*
> *Mì-sgiamhach,*
> *Gun urram Dhia na dhaoine!*

> Crew weak-handed, / Haughty, ignorant, / Big of speech, / Small of sense, / Scant of reason, / Blind of action, / Ugly of form, / Without respect to God or men!

Almost the only concessions to our sources are in Watson's notes on the draft—in particular, he altered the last line to *Gun urram fir dha chéile*, 'Without respect of man for his neighbour', which happens to be JGC's last line—but then he changed it back again!

I think therefore that in this last verse of the Curse of Neist, as published in *CG* iv, we have pinpointed some lines concerning which a charge of fabrication *can* be levelled. The arguments are these. We seem to have copies of Carmichael's field-notes, but these words do not appear in any of them. We also have several versions of the curse collected by others between 1850 and 1950, and these words do not appear in any of them either. These words reflect an *idea* in our other sources for the curse and are therefore unlikely to have been drafted in from some other text.

Having made our case for the *fact* of the crime, we may now turn to *motive*. This is supplied by the demands of poetic form. Carmichael wanted an eight-line stanza with seven short lines linked loosely by rhyme, this rhyme feeding into the middle of the long eighth line, which must finish on disyllabic end-rhyme on *ao*.

Although I have used the word 'crime', I have to point out that neither Carmichael nor his grandson knowingly committed one. I have made it clear that the Curse of Neist is in *CG* iv. What we see here is Carmichael enjoying himself in his old age by constructing a cohesive text out of some fragments. It would be useful to know for sure whose is the handwriting of the draft: it is not Alexander's, it is not James's, so I assume it is that of Ella Carmichael Watson (1870–1928), Alexander's daughter and James's mother. We can see from Ella's contributions to the *Celtic Review*, which she herself edited, that she was a confirmed Celtic Twilightist and may very well have encouraged her father to experiment in this way. This point needs further research, but it has to be emphasised that Alexander Carmichael *did not publish this text*.

As for Watson, he was two years old when his grandfather died. He had no way of knowing what was authentic and what was not. He published this text in good faith. He wrote: 'In the fifth volume I hope to explain fully how I have dealt with the material and to what extent I am responsible for the final form of the work. Every circumstance makes this desirable—the unprepared state of most of the original manuscripts, the nature of the material, and the Collector's unequalled knowledge and power of interpretation. But lest the opportunity should be withheld, I say now without reserve that I have made as little change as possible. To the Gaelic text no word has been added, and, save that a few broken lines or stanzas have been omitted, no word has been taken away. . . In translating I have tried to follow, as best I could, my grandfather's usage in the first two volumes; but certain departures have been necessary and have been deliberately made, and I have not strained after mere verbal consistency.'[54]

We must therefore put under the microscope something that Carmichael himself published, that is, something from *CG* i and ii. Some years ago I subjected the short carol *Dia na Gile, Dia na Greine* 'God of the Moon, God of the Sun' (*CG* ii, 168) to detailed analysis. I established that Carmichael's translation was highly suspect, and that the item contained several Gaelic words (some of which found their way into Dwelly) which never really existed.[55] What happened throughout *Carmina* is that Carmichael provided facing-page translations, thus creating a direct linkage between Gaelic ghost-words which had no meaning and real English words which did have meaning. This had elevated the ghost-words to the status of real words, and whenever we see the letters 'AC' ('Alexander Carmichael') in Dwelly we should be suspicious. The best comment about all this is in a letter to Carmichael from Father Allan, dated 20 September 1900, after receiving his presentation copy: 'The translation is marvellous. It is a puzzle to me how you were able to interpret what I know the reciters themselves would tell you they could not understand, and yet when I read any such piece and look at the translation I say "Yes, it must be that". Your Gaelic intuition must be extraordinary.'[56]

Was Father Allan capable of irony? As an editor of his poems, I can tell you that the answer is yes.

When the Carmichael Watson Collection yields no field-notes, transcripts or drafts for a particular item in *Carmina*, we cannot question the authenticity of a published text. We simply have to accept that it is what Carmichael heard, or thought he heard. Structure and semantics are no help as a mark of authenticity in folklore terms. A charm or incantation as Carmichael heard it may not have had perfect rhyme or made perfect sense. It might well be corrupt in various ways. We can of course start improving the structure, substituting words to make better rhyme or better sense, and finessing our basic translation. That may well be a legitimate exercise in restoring a lost original. It is what Carmichael, encouraged perhaps by Ella, did in private with the Curse of Neist. If we find that an item does not have perfect rhyme or make perfect sense, we are entitled to take this as evidence that Carmichael did not tamper with it. We are equally entitled to take it as evidence that he may have misheard it in the first place. Either way, if there is no help to be had in the Carmichael Watson Collection, we must accept that the text is an honest record of a folklore event, and try to place it beside records of related folklore events for comparison and contrast. That is a process whereby the *value*, as opposed to the *authenticity*, of a text begins to emerge.

So let me now present another little case study, a text which exists in different versions both within and outwith *Carmina*.[57] This is the sequence of three related Christmas hymns at *CG* i, 126–37 (all of which begin basically with the words *Beannaicht' e, beannaicht' e*, 'Blessed is He, blessed is He'), along with two earlier versions of the first of the three, one published by Carmichael himself in 1874 and one by William Mackenzie in 1880.[58] Mackenzie does not say where he got his version, but Carmichael informed *Highlander* editor John Murdoch that 'the following Christmas Carrol was taken down this year from the dictation of Mr. Angus Gunn, a pauper aged 85, residing at Dail-fo-thuath, Ness, Lews'.[59] In *Carmina* he was still more informative: 'The three poems which follow were taken down from Angus Gunn, Ness, Lewis, then over eighty-four years of age. Angus Gunn had been a strong man physically and was still a strong man mentally. He had lived for many years in the island of North Roney, and gave a graphic description of it, and of his life there. He had much oral lore which he told with great dramatic power.'

While admitting that it is 'really a sort of benediction, referring specially to the birth of the Saviour', Mackenzie was careful to point out that it was used as a *duan Callainn*, that is, a rhyme chanted by young lads as they went carousing around the houses at Hogmanay, driving off evil spirits by banging on a sheepskin, seeking hospitality, and cursing anyone who refused it.[60] Already in 1874 we find Carmichael on the opposite tack, expressing to Murdoch 'his regret that the fasts and festivals connected with Christmas have been to such an extent suppressed, that now there are many who do not know the origin of the very name', and his belief that 'it would have been well to preserve those practices, as they led people to reflect upon the great Christian events, and to benefit by meditation on the lessons inculcated'.[61]

To analyse this material it is necessary first to examine the main differences between the versions of 'Gunn no. 1' (if I may call it that) published in 1874, 1880 and 1900. I will refer to these as A, B and C. The translations given for A and C are Carmichael's. Mackenzie did not offer a translation, so I supply translations for B in square brackets.

A *Ho-Rí! Ho-Rí! Beannaicht E, beannaicht E.* 'Hail to the King! hail to the King! / Blessed is He, blessed is He!'

B *Ho Righ! Ho Righ! Beannaicht' e, Beannaicht' e!* ['Ho Righ! Ho Righ! Blessed is he, blessed is he! (*or* Let it be blessed, let it be blessed.)']

C *Ho Ri, ho Ri, / Beannaicht e, beannaicht e.* 'Hail to the King, hail to the King, / Blessed is He, blessed is He.'

This is a constant refrain throughout A, B and C. The most that can be said of *Rí, Righ* or *Ri* is that it is a pun. *Ho-rì* and *hi-rì* are regularly found in Gaelic song as meaningless vocables. Carmichael restricts himself to *Rí* or *Ri* but translates as if it were *Righ*: 'Hail to the King!' This is a case of translation being misused to prove a point. Mackenzie spells the vocable *Righ* but does not offer a translation.

A *Iomairst do Dhia e eadar bhrat' us aodach, / Slainte dhaoine gu' ro' ann.* 'With its covering and clothing, / And the health and welfare of all herein.'

B *Thugadh do Dhia e eader bhrat is aodach, / Slainte dhaoine gu robh ann.* ['It was given (*or* May it be given) to God between cover and clothing, / Be the health of people in it.']

C *Iomair do Dhia, eadar bhrat is aodach, / Slainte dhaoine gun robh ann.* 'Consign it to God from corslet to cover, / Be the health of men therein.'

Carmichael's *iomairst* looks like a misunderstanding of *iobairt* 'sacrifice'. In 1874 he did not attempt to translate it at all. Mackenzie's word *thugadh* is totally different, either because he was using Carmichael's published text and felt entitled to adhere to it in spirit if not in fact, or because his text is from an independent source. In 1900 Carmichael emended *iomairt* to *iomair* as glossed by Dwelly under *imir*: 'Need, behove, must, require. 2 (AC) Deliver.' The theological subtlety of this couplet appears to have escaped Carmichael: the words *brat* and *aodach* refer primarily to the Christ child, their relevance to domestic architecture being by no means obvious. 'Be He God's sacrifice between mantle and bedclothes, / May men's salvation in Him be.'

A *Gu mu sin ceann sguilb 'is taigh, / Daoine slan sa bhuntair.* 'Many be the stakes in the roof-tree, / And joyous be all within.'

B *Gu mo lionmhor cabar 'san fhardaich, / Is daoine slana a' tamh ann.* ['May there be rafters galore in the dwelling, / And healthy people living in it.']

C *Gum bu liuth crann's an tigh, / Daoine tamh 's a' bhunntair.* 'Many be the stakes in the house, / And men dwelling on the foundation.'

Carmichael's original text makes little sense except perhaps for *ceann sguilb* 'a thatching pin'. The other texts bear little relationship to it beyond maintaining the general architectural theme. Again it is impossible to know for sure whether Mackenzie has an independent source. His version has *aicill* rhyme *fhàrdaich : slàna*. In 1900 Carmichael struggles to extract some sense from his original. He rejects *ceann sguilb*, but by opting for *bhunntair* rather than *mhuinntir* (*Daoine slàn sa mhuinntir* 'Healthy people in the household') he stays faithful to his field-note in one respect at least. Once again, note Dwelly: 'bunntair,(AC) *s.m.* Foundation of a house.' Both *ceann sguilb* and *bunntair* reappear however in Gunn no. 3: *Gu mu liuth dul 's ceann sguilb 's an aros, / Daoine tamh 's a bhunntair.* 'Many be the ties and stakes in the homestead, / People dwelling on this foundation.'

A *Noc oiche Nollaig Moire, / Rugadh mac na Moir Oighe.* 'This is the eve of the great nativity. / Born is the Son of Mary the Virgin.'

B *Nochd Oidhche na Nollaige Mòire, / Rugadh Mac na h-Oighe Muire.* ['This is the Eve of Christmas Day, / The Son of the Virgin Mary is born.']

C *Nochd Oichdhe* [sic] *Nollaige moire, / Rugadh Mac na Moir Oighe.* 'This night is the eve of the great Nativity, / Born is the Son of Mary the Virgin.'

Nollaig Mhòr is Christmas Day, *Nollaig Bheag* is New Year's Day.[62] Mackenzie's version has *aicill* rhyme *Mòire : Òighe*. Yet again, it is impossible to say whether this is because he possessed a better source than Carmichael or because he was a more astute editor.

A *Rainig a bhonnan an lar.* 'The soles of His feet have touched the earth.'
B *Rainig a bhonnan an lar.* ['His soles have reached the ground.']
C *Rainig a bhonnaibh an lar.* 'The soles of His feet have reached the earth.'

This suggests that Mackenzie *was* basing his text on Carmichael's. It also highlights Carmichael's liking for spurious archaisms (dative plural *-ibh* wrongly used as nominative).

A *Shoillich fearann, shoillsich fonn, / Chualas an fhonn (am fonn?) eir an traigh.* 'Shines on the sea and shines on the land, / And loudly sounds the chorus of the strand.'
B *Shoillsich fearann, shoillsich fonn, / Chualas am fonn air an tràigh.* ['Earth has lit up, land has lit up, / The tune has been heard upon the strand.']
C *Shoillsich fearann, shoillsich fonn, / Chualas an tonn air an traigh.* 'Shone the earth, shone the land, / Heard was the wave upon the strand.'

This seems to confirm that Mackenzie was following Carmichael, but also reveals Carmichael as the more astute editor. It occurred to him on further reflection that *an fhonn*, which he first thought he heard, was Gunn's Lewis pronunciation of *an tonn*.

A *Beannaicht mo Righ, / Gun toiseach gun chrioch, / Gu sumhuin gu sior, / Gach linn gu brach!* 'This this eve is the glorious nativity. / Hail! hail! all hail, O! King to Thee, / Through the limitless bounds of eternity.'
B *Beannaicht' mo Righ, gun toiseach, gun chrich! / Gu sumhainn, gu sior, gach linn gu brath!* ['Blessed be my King, without beginning, without end! / Eternally, everlasting, all ages for ever!']
C *Beannaicht an Righ, / Gun tus, gun chrich, / Gu suthainn, gu sior, / Gach linn gu brath.* 'Blessed the King, / Without beginning, without end, / To everlasting, to eternity, / To all ages, to all time.'

This appears to confirm that Mackenzie's source was Carmichael's text in *The Highlander*. It also shows Carmichael going completely beyond the score in 1874 to emphasise the Christmas element in the text. His translation in that year bore almost no relation to the original.

Having established beyond reasonable doubt that the versions of 'Gunn no. 1' published in 1874, 1880 and 1900 are one and the same, I can now go on to compare Gunn nos. 1, 2, and 3.

The first verse in no. 1 is a blend of motifs relating to the Nativity, to the blessing of the house, potentially also to the blessing of the first-foot or other visitor. The second is devoted to the blessing of the house, the third and fourth to the Nativity. One wonders what *Chualas an tonn air an traigh* 'Heard was the wave upon the strand' has to do with Christmas, but Gunn no. 2 holds the key.

> *Shoillsich frith dha, shoillsich fonn dha,*
> *Nuall nan tonn le fonn nan tragh,*
> *Ag innse dhuinne gun d' rugadh Criosda*
> *Mac Righ nan righ a tir na slaint;*
> *Shoillsich grian nam beannaibh ard dha,*
> > *Ho! ro! biodh aoibh!*

Carmichael translates: 'The mountains glowed to Him, the plains glowed to Him, / The voice of the waves with the song of the strand, / Announcing to us that Christ is born, / Son of the King of kings from the land of salvation; / Shone the sun on the mountains high to Him, / All hail! let there be joy!' This brings *fonn* and *tonn* together as joyful sounds that partake in celebrating the birth of the Saviour.

By contrast, Gunn no. 3 reads far more like a *duan Callainn* than a Christmas carol. There is nothing in it about the birth of Christ. *Beannaicht' e* could refer either to God or to the house. The word which Carmichael translates as 'Hail King' is now spelt *Hoire*—is this not simply 'Hurray'? Above all, it reads as a house-blessing from start to finish, and would sit comfortably with the first-footing tradition. The words *brat* and *aodach* each appear twice, the first time in exactly the same theological phrase as in Gunn no. 1, the second time more fully incorporated into the domestic environment, so that they come to refer in some way to the plenishings or contents of the Highland home, perhaps the loom.

> *Iobair dh 'an Ti eadar bhonn agus bhrat,*
> *Eadar chuaill agus chlach agus chrann;*
> *Iobair a ris eadar shlat agus aodach,*
> *Slanadh shaoghal a dhaoine th' ann.*

Carmichael translates: 'Offer to the Being from found to cover, / Include stave and stone and beam; / Offer again both rods and cloth, / Be health to the people therein.'

Thanks to these three versions, we appear to see a Christmas hymn slowly turning into a secular *duan Callainn*: Gunn no. 2 first, then Gunn no. 1 (with its variants from 1874 and 1880), then Gunn no. 3.

What have we learned from this? Firstly, that the comparison of texts can throw up unexpected results. Secondly, that Carmichael's translations are suspect once again. Faced with choices between sacred and secular, archaic and modern, Christian and pagan, he will choose the sacred, the archaic and the Christian. And thirdly, that Carmichael was actually very good at citing his sources. Not only does he give us Angus Gunn's name and place of origin but he tells us a bit about the man generally. He tells us the source for all the main texts in *CG* i and ii, that is, basically everything except the scraps which he quotes to illustrate the points he makes in his dictionary of Gaelic folklore in *CG* ii. This is in contrast to Mackenzie, Macbain, JGC and other collectors of similar material, who generally failed to cite sources. As well as Carmichael I exempt Father Allan McDonald from this criticism.

I would now like to try and set up an overall critical framework with which to begin to measure the authenticity of *Carmina*. Straight away I have to emphasise that there are three types of material in the collection, and that these have to be assessed separately. There is what I would like to call *seanchas*, that is, prose narration in English and Gaelic. Then there is Carmichael as 'Our Interpreter' (to use the title given to him by Kenneth MacLeod in the biographical introduction to *CG* iv). This includes Carmichael's introductions, explanations and notes as well as his translations of the charms and incantations. Thirdly and most importantly, there are the charms, incantations, hymns, prayers etc. themselves—the 'verse' texts.

Let us consider the *seanchas* first. Note that the Gaelic and the English of the prose passages are very much in the same category, because really they were created together and so there is no reason why the English should not be a perfectly good translation of the Gaelic. The prose passages are the least authentic thing in *Carmina*. I would argue that this is what Alan Bruford proved in his analysis of *Deirdire*. He did *not* show that Carmichael was a fabricator of charms and incantations, because before the invention of tape-recorders the ways of recording Gaelic prose were many and varied, depending on the skills and inclinations of the informant and the collector, whereas there was only one way to record Gaelic verse, and that was word for word in Gaelic. Carmichael's field-notes show that his basic method was to note the bones of a story in English with key words in Gaelic, then put it back into Gaelic afterwards at his leisure. Sometimes we catch him going through several drafts, each a little more flowery than the one before. The end result is a form of prose which is highly creative, and as Bruford sarcastically remarked, two-dimensional.[63] Here is an example from *CG* iii, 275:

> In leaving the Isles, the writer went to say good-bye to the people who had all been so good and kind, so courteous and hospitable, to him, and of whom the poorest of the poor were not the least near to his heart. When saying good-bye to me, Mór MacNeill ceased speaking, and taking my hand in her two hands, kissed it and watered it with her tears, and curtseying low, said:—Agus tha sibh a nis a' falbh agus a' fàgail bhur daoine agus bhur dùthaich, a luaidh mo chridhe! O ma ta, guma slàn a bhitheas sibh agus guma h-innich a dh'éireas dhuibh gach aon taobh dh'an téid sibh, gach aon cheum dh'an siubhail sibh. Agus mo bheannachd féin leibh, agus beannachd Dhé leibh, agus beannachd Mhoire Mhàthar leibh, gach tràth dh'éireas sibh a suas agus gach uair a laigheas sibh a sìos, gus an laigh sibh a sìos an suain ann an glacaibh Ìosda Crìosda nam buadh agus nam beannachd—nam buadh agus nam beannachd!—And you are now going away and leaving your people and your country, dear one of my heart! Well, then, whole may you be, and well may it go with you, every way you go and every step you travel. And my own blessing go with you, and the blessing of God go with you, and the blessing of the Mary Mother go with you, every time you rise up and every time you lie down, until you lie down in sleep upon the arm of Jesus Christ of the virtues and of the blessings—of the virtues and of the blessings!

This passage would be a good starting-point for the most interesting and important paper that does *not* appear in this collection, 'Alexander Carmichael and Women'.[64]

Next, Carmichael as 'Our Interpreter'. I used to enjoy many a long conversation with his grandson Michael Carmichael, who was a veterinary surgeon in Fort William and came to see me whenever he was in Edinburgh.[65] Michael had a very straight but spluttery way of speaking. Once when I politely referred to his grandfather as a scholar he said: 'Shcholar? He wash no shcholar!'

That is actually true. Carmichael did his very best to interpret things correctly but as far as scholarship was concerned he was an amateur, prone to fall into what we might call undergraduate-type errors. By 1928, thanks to her husband who was Professor of Celtic in Edinburgh University, even his own daughter had realised this. In the first edition (1900) of *CG* ii, under *sgeo* in the dictionary of Gaelic folklore, is a long passage of speculation about the origin of the place-name 'Glasgow', ending with the words: 'I am indebted for this suggestion to my eldest son.'[66] In the second edition this was all swept away and instead we find in square brackets the words: '[These explanations are improbable.]'[67] If we then look under *smeoirn*, we find that Carmichael defines it as 'arrow-head, arrow-point, the destructive end of the arrow', but this is followed in the second edition by a plaintive comment in square brackets: '[The dictionaries make 'smeoirn' the butt end.]'[68]

A sure sign of amateur scholarship is the tendency to cover up one's tracks rather than expose them to scrutiny. Carmichael did this. Nowhere in *CG* i and ii did he make the slightest reference to the collections of Mackenzie or Macbain. Nor does his attitude to lengthmarks do him any credit. On 12 March 1896, following correspondence with the Oxford University Press regarding the possibility of their publishing Carmichael's collection, Henderson wrote to him: 'From the nature of the Gaelic language the Oxford men would not say the work was correct unless the long vowels were carefully distinguished from the short ones. It is so in spoken speech and they take it to be *slovenly* to discard them. There is no way of getting over it.'[69] Carmichael continued to resist, and in 1900 the first two volumes, 300 copies only, were simply 'Printed for the author by T. and A. Constable'.[70]

The third category is the Gaelic originals of the hymns, prayers, charms, incantations etc. themselves. This is the most important thing in *Carmina*, because it is from these originals that all else flows. And I would suggest that on the whole it is also the most authentic thing.

I base my case on two simple litmus tests, augmented by detailed comparative study of the texts themselves. The first test is source and the second is length. With respect to source my argument is that if the source is named, the text is likely to be genuine. With respect to length my argument is this. Most Gaelic charms and incantations, when laid out on the page according to their natural rhythm, are short. The average length of the forty-seven items laid out as verse in Macbain's 'Gaelic incantations' is nine lines. The average length of the ninety-five items laid out as verse in Mackenzie's 'Gaelic incantations, charms, and blessings of the Hebrides' is nine lines. As a rule of thumb, I think we should look with suspicion on any charm or incantation in *Carmina* which is more than forty lines long if unattributed, that is if no source is named, or more than eighty lines long if attributed. Now let us apply this test to each volume in turn.

In *CG* i, which consists of incantations, including sections on seasons and labour, basically all of the 157 items are attributed.[71] The longest items are *Ora nam Buadh* 'The Invocation of the Graces' (6–11) at seventy lines, and *Duan an Domhnuich* 'The Poem of the Lord's Day' (216–21) at seventy-two lines, so in actual fact everything passes my litmus test.[72]

CG ii consists of 107 items, mainly charms. There are also 221 items (verse quotations) in Carmichael's dictionary of Gaelic folklore. The 107 main items are all attributed. This time there are two items over eighty lines long. Firstly, *Eolas a Chrannachain* 'The Charm of the Churn' (144–51) has 104 lines. This has to be questioned. Admittedly there are twenty-eight repetitions of *Thig, a chuinneag, thig*, so if we discount these we are down below eighty lines. But it is still a long charm, and another thing that raises my suspicions is that Carmichael treats us to a rambling introduction of two-and-a-half pages without either talking about his source, Mary Maclellan, Crofter's wife, South Haccleit, Benbecula, or making any remark whatever about the extraordinary length of the charm. Secondly, an item called simply *Taladh* 'Lullaby' (194–201) beginning *Eala bhan thu, / Hu hi! ho ho!* has eighty-seven lines, but as most of these consist of *Hu hi! ho ho!* I think we can take it off our list of suspects.

CG iii consists of 182 items, mainly incantations, of which only fifty-one are attributed. That means that 131 of the items have to pass my forty-line test. Let us see what comes up in the net.

Altachadh Eirigh 'Petition at Rising' (34–9) has forty-two lines. No informant's name is given, but it is clear from the introduction that she is from Beinn Mhór in South Uist. So it may be regarded as a marginal.

Urnaigh Mhadainn 'Morning Prayer' (40–7) has exactly eighty lines. The reciter's name is given (Mary Gillies, crofter, Morar), but Carmichael's introduction has an apologetic tone:

> Mary Gillies sang this poem in a recitative voice. The effect was charming, but the poem was difficult to follow. The music and rhythm were good, but these disappear in the process of writing. Folklore reciters, not being accustomed to being stopped, become confused with the interruptions of writing. When they are allowed to proceed in their own way, music and poetry and pleasure flow back, and all rejoice.

Urnaigh 'Prayer' (58–61) has forty-one lines and is unattributed. It contains no folklore elements except perhaps for one or two items of vocabulary like *caimich mo mhiann* 'enfold my desire' and *comaraich m'aigne* 'keep safe my mind'—it is a hymn, not an incantation, and as such there is no reason why it should not have forty-one lines.

Achan Ìosa 'Prayer to Jesus' (78–83) has seventy-one lines and is unattributed, so it deserves a long hard look.

Leanabh an Àigh 'The Child of Glory' (116–17) is unattributed but has only twenty-four lines, so it passes our test anyway. It is worth mentioning here, however, because it is the famous nineteenth-century hymn by Mary MacDonald from Ardtun in the Ross of Mull. The origins of some other less well-known items in *Carmina* can be identified from Catholic tradition in ways indicated by JLC.[73]

Achan Mhoire Mhàthar 'Prayer to Mary Mother' (118–25) is attributed to Mary MacDonald, crofter, Greater Bohuntin, Lochaber, but it has 104 lines, so I would put it on the list for further investigation. The same goes for *Moladh Moire* 'Praise of Mary' (126–33), 102 lines, attributed to Mary Maclellan, *née* MacDonald, crofter, Beoraidh, Morar, though I note that there are asterisks in place of two lines, which hardly suggests fabrication. In his study of the *Deirdire* forgery Bruford remarks: 'Carmichael did not like to leave any gaps in the narrative.'[74]

Soisgeul Chrìosd 'The Gospel of Christ' (182–9) is attributed and has seventy-seven lines, so it just passes the test anyway, but it is a good example of an item where further work has already been done, because JGC also published a version of it.[75]

Finally from *CG* iii, two items which fail the test, and it is very interesting that they do, because they both belong to the *Òrtha nam Buadh* group of charms which is already under some suspicion.[76] The *CG* iii items are *Òra Buadh* 'Invocation of the Graces' (212–15), no attribution, forty-one lines, and *Sian Bhuadha* 'Charm of Grace' (216–25), which is also unattributed and has a massive 122 lines, making it our most suspicious item of all. Its mesmeric phrases

> *Cha dèan gobha,*
> *Cha dèan ceard,*
> *Cha dèan clachair,*
> *Cha dèan saor*
> *Beart na ball . . .*

> No smith shall make, / No craftsman shall make, / No mason shall make, / No wright shall make / Gear nor tool . . .

were once exquisitely mimicked in a political poem by Derick Thomson which goes in part

> *Cha dean farmad,*
> *cha dean eud,*
> *cha dean càineadh an talamh rèidh.*
> *Cha dean 'mi fhìn,'*
> *cha dean 'mo threubh,'*
> *cha dean 'mo chlas' ach plàsd is cèir.*

> Envy will not, / grudging won't, / slanging can't prepare the ground. / 'I myself', / 'my own clan', / 'my class' are bandages, I've found.[77]

CG iv consists of 190 items, mainly animal incantations and charms, of which only seventy-two are attributed.

An Eala Bhàn 'The White Swan' (28–31) is unattributed and has sixty-two lines, but this comes down to a respectable thirty-three if we do not count repetitions of *Guile guile*.

Cronachdainn Sùla 'Countering the Evil Eye' (158–61) is unattributed and has fifty-two lines, so it is clearly in the red zone.

Am Bansgal 'The Vixen' (322–7) is unattributed and has eighty-eight lines, so it certainly deserves investigation. It is a curse on a named woman followed by a prayer for protection from her—an unusual item which reads more like a consciously creative work than a traditional incantation, although full of traditional features. I imagine that whoever gave it to Carmichael would have asked to remain anonymous.

Binneach nam Beann 'Melodious One of the Mountains' (328–37) is ninety-two lines long and unattributed, but Carmichael says: 'I have taken down several versions, in South Uist and elsewhere.' It is basically a hymn with a story behind it, and is in Father Allan's collection also.

Thàinig na Cait Oirnn 'The Cats are Come on Us' (360–3) is fifty-four lines long and unattributed, but it is a pìobaireachd song and if we disregard all the repetitions of *Thàinig na Cait* we are well within our guidelines.

With *CG* v the intellectual atmosphere changes. Here at last we are given references to other published versions of the texts in question, allowing a relatively pain-free check on authenticity. This volume consists of 132 items, mainly waulking songs, fairy songs, verses connected with specific stories, charms for divination, versions of an Arthurian ballad, and miscellaneous songs, poems and fragments, of which only forty-four are attributed. Perhaps the most obvious thing about its contents is that it contains no hymns, no prayers, and very little of the type of material—charms and incantations—for which my 'litmus tests' are intended.[78] Nevertheless my tests may be worth applying to see what they throw up.

Craobh nan Ubhal 'The Apple Tree' (6–9) is forty-four lines long and unattributed, but this is not exceptional for a waulking song.

The massive 192-line version of *Seathan Mac Rìgh Éireann* 'Seathan Son of the King of Ireland' (66–79), sometimes called 'the Queen of Waulking Songs', was obtained from the Rev. Kenneth MacLeod's aunt, Janet MacLeod, at the schoolhouse, Eigg, in January 1905. It is, I think, the longest waulking song on record. Janet allegedly defended it thus (63):

> 'Seathan son of the King of Ireland' was the choice of waulking songs. The women to-day have only fragments of it; when I first remember, 'Seathan' by itself would be sufficient to complete the waulking, however tough the cloth. I myself remember but little of it to-day, compared with what I knew when no waulking was complete without me.

JLC comments:

> It certainly must have been exhausting to sing, if it really ran to 192 lines, each repeated twice with a different phrase of the refrain each time; but Carmichael may have done some conflation here, as was the case in some other instances.[79]

Version 'A' of *Am Bròn Binn* 'The Sweet Sorrow' (92–9) is 110 lines long (and attributed, more or less), but this is not an unusual length for a ballad.

The fairy song *A Mhór, a Ghaoil* 'Mór, My Beloved' (136–43) is eighty lines long and unattributed, but some other versions in print are longer still.[80]

The section *Tàladh Mhic Leòid* 'MacLeod's Lullaby' (183–233) contains sixteen items, five of which fail the 'litmus test'. This demonstrates that the Fairy Song of the MacLeods, more than any other item or group of items in *CG* v, is ripe for reassessment. Other versions, published and unpublished, must be taken into account, as should the texts which follow it in the volume, *Comhradh eadar Bean-Shìdh agus Bean Shaoghalta* 'Dialogue between a Fairy Woman and a Mortal Woman' and *A' Bhean-Shìdh agus an Leanabh* 'The Fairy Woman and the Child' (236–9), both of which are related to it in different ways.[81]

Cumha Mhic an Tòisich 'Mackintosh's Lament' (346–53) has 100 lines and is unattributed. It is, I believe, the longest printed version of this item. It is clearly to be distinguished from Carmichael's second *Cumha Mhic an Tòisich* (354–9), which has sixty lines and is attributed. I have published a discussion of these Mackintosh laments, but there is much more to be said, preferably by a musicologist.[82]

Finally, *Tàladh* 'Lullaby' (368–73) has seventy-two lines and is unattributed. Discounting repetitions of the line *Nì mo leanabh cadal agus gheibh e 'n t-ian*, it still has forty-nine lines. It has twenty-four verses; the other version to which the reader is referred (published twice by Sinton) has three.[83] Each of the twenty-four verses follows the same simple formula:

> *Tha nead an/a'/na* [bird]
> *San/Fo/Ann*[s] [*an/am/a'/na*] [location],
> *Nì mo leanabh cadal agus gheibh e 'n t-ian.*
>
> The nest of the [*bird*] / Is [in/under/among the] [*location*], / My little one will sleep and he shall have the bird.

Not all the lines are fully rhythmical and not all the rhymes are correct. Alternative readings are given in two places (*Caidil thus, a leinibh, agus gheibh thu 'n t-ian* for the refrain and *thobhtaidh* for *thobhta*). There is a strong likelihood, in my opinion, that this text represents a large modern superstructure imposed on a small traditional foundation, either by Carmichael himself or by a correspondent who gave or sent him the poem in manuscript. The alternative readings are easily explained as the changes of mind to which all poets, good and bad alike, are subject. In the end, the strongest argument for the poem's authenticity is the fact that, except in the refrain, it differs entirely from Sinton's.

My conclusions are as follows. Carmichael did not 'make it all up'. Though taught by JFC, who believed in the honest recording of folklore as a science, he chose to follow the propagandist path first trodden by Wilhelm Grimm. The three participants in the controversy of the 1970s and 1980s were all guilty of hyperbole to some extent. Of the three types of material in *Carmina*, prose narrative is the least authoritative, and Gaelic verse text is the most authoritative, with interpretative material in the middle. It has not been proven as yet that any of the verse texts in *CG* i and ii, the only ones for which Carmichael himself was directly responsible, lack authority.

The time for polemics is over. What is required of the Carmichael Watson Project is a catalogue of the items in *Carmina*, listing references to the notes and drafts that lie behind them. What is required of individual scholars is detailed studies of specific texts such as the *Òrtha nam Buadh* group of charms or the Fairy Song of the MacLeods, based on a threefold structure of sources—*Carmina Gadelica*, Carmichael's notes and drafts, and variants recorded by others. Particular attention should be paid to charms and incantations which fail the litmus test, i.e. those more than forty lines long if unattributed, those more than eighty lines long if attributed.

Finally, I would like an answer to what I would call the Hamish Robertson Question: does the Carmichael Watson Collection contain notes or drafts for anything in *CG* i and ii, and if not, why not?

[1] Robert W. Chapman (ed.), *Johnson's Journey to the Western Islands of Scotland and Boswell's Journal of a tour to the Hebrides with Samuel Johnson, LL.D.* (Oxford, 1970), 423.

[2] John Lorne Campbell, 'Notes on Hamish Robertson's "Studies in Carmichael's *Carmina Gadelica*"', *Scottish Gaelic Studies* xiii (1978–81), 1–17: 8–9.

[3] Maria Tatar, *The hard facts of the Grimms' Fairy Tales* (Princeton, NJ, 1987), 11, 29.

[4] Ibid., 16, 17, 19.

[5] Ibid., 36.

[6] Christa Kamenetsky, *The Brothers Grimm and their critics: folktales and the quest for meaning* (Athens, OH, 1992), 199.

[7] Richard M. Dorson, *The British folklorists: a history* (London, 1968), 1, 80.

[8] Elias Bredsdorff, *Hans Christian Andersen: an introduction to his life and works* (Copenhagen, 1987), 66–7, 119.

[9] Dorson, *British folklorists*, 393.

[10] John Francis Campbell, *Popular tales of the West Highlands* i (Edinburgh, 1860), x–xi.

[11] Ibid., xxi, cxxxiii–cxxxiv.

[12] John Gregorson Campbell, *Waifs and strays of Celtic tradition, Argyllshire Series, no. V: Clan traditions and popular tales of the Western Highlands and Islands* (London, 1895), 139–40, cited in Ronald Black (ed.), *The Gaelic otherworld* (Edinburgh, 2005), xix–xx.

[13] John Gregorson Campbell, 'The Muileartach', *Scottish Celtic Review*, ii (November, 1881), 115–37: 117; idem, *Waifs and strays of Celtic tradition, Argyllshire Series, no. IV: The Fians* (London, 1891), 135; Black (ed.), *Gaelic otherworld*, xx.

[14] John Gregorson Campbell, 'Fionn's Ransom', *Transactions of the Gaelic Society of Inverness* [*TGSI*] xv (1888–9), 46–62: 50; Black (ed.), *Gaelic otherworld*, xx.

[15] Black (ed.), *Gaelic otherworld*, 275.

[16] Alan Bruford, '"Deirdire" and Alexander Carmichael's treatment of oral sources', *Scottish Gaelic Studies*, xiv(1) (1983), 1–24: 3.

[17] Black (ed.), *Gaelic otherworld*, 668–9.

[18] Ibid., 678.

[19] *CG* ii (Edinburgh, 1928), 78–91.

[20] Black (ed.), *Gaelic otherworld*, 680–1.

[21] Sylvia Robertson and Patricia Young, *Daughter of Atholl: Lady Evelyn Stewart Murray 1868–1940* (Dundee, 1997), 13–24. Lady Evelyn's remarkable folklore collection is at present being prepared for the press.

[22] Black (ed.), *Gaelic otherworld*, 635, 668, 685.

[23] John Lorne Campbell, '*Carmina Gadelica*: George Henderson's corrections and suggestions', *Scottish Gaelic Studies*, xiii (1978–81), 183–218: 183, 214–16.

[24] Black (ed.), *Gaelic otherworld*, 643–4, 668, 674–8, 685–6, 687.

[25] Rev. James MacDougall (ed.), *Waifs and strays of Celtic tradition, Argyllshire Series, no. III: Folk and hero tales* (London, 1891), ix, 145–86.

[26] Michael Linkletter, 'The Alexander Maclean Sinclair Papers in NSARM', *Scotia*, 27 (2003), 6–21: 8–10, 19; idem, 'The Gaelic Collection of the Public Archives of Nova Scotia', in Michel Byrne, Thomas Owen Clancy, and Sheila Kidd (eds), *Litreachas & eachdraidh: Literature and history: papers from the Second Conference of Scottish Gaelic Studies, Glasgow 2002* (Glasgow, 2006), 148–60: 154–6.

[27] 'Leaves from my Celtic portfolio IV', *TGSI*, viii (1878–9), 100–28 (eight items); 'Leaves from my Celtic portfolio V', *TGSI*, ix (1879–80), 19–43 (one item); 'Gaelic incantations, charms, and blessings of the Hebrides', *TGSI*, xviii (1891–2), 97–182.

[28] 'Highland superstition', *TGSI*, xiv (1887–8), 232–72; 'Gaelic incantations', *TGSI*, xvii (1890–1), 221–66. A revised version of the latter article appeared in *The Highland Monthly*, iii (1891–2), 117–25, 174–81, 222–31, 290–7, 341–8, under the title 'Incantations and magic rhymes' (117–25) or 'Gaelic incantations' (other pages).

[29] 'Medical spells and charms of the Highlands', *The Celtic Magazine*, xiii (1888), 34–40; *Story and song from Loch Ness-side* (Inverness, 1914), 140–1, 171–82.

[30] 'Notes on the religion and mythology of the Celts', *TGSI*, xix (1893–4), 37–49.

[31] 'Folklore from the Hebrides IV', *Folk-Lore*, xi (1900), 439–50.

[32] This listing does not include items in newspapers, but I would like to think that it covers all the main

contributions to the genre, i.e. articles or books containing three charms or more. A complete listing of all Gaelic charms and incantations in print, beginning with the *seun* published by the Rev. Dr Norman MacLeod in *Cuairtear nan Gleann*, January 1842 (see Black, *Gaelic otherworld*, 212), is a prerequisite for the proper assessment of *Carmina*.
[33] Clearly these figures are arbitrary to some extent, and depend on a precise definition of 'charms and incantations'. The term is scarcely adequate to define this body of material. Carmichael subtitled *Carmina* 'Hymns and Incantations'. This appears on the title-page of all six volumes—including *CG* v, which contains no hymns and very few incantations, and consists mainly of songs! The term 'rhymes' should be introduced to cover, for example, the versified sayings about the calendar in *CG* i and about animals and birds in *CG* iv, the miscellaneous rhymes quoted in *CG* ii, and the verses connected with specific stories in *CG* v. My friend Dr Mary Low, author of *Celtic Christianity and nature* (Edinburgh, 1996) and of many articles on the spirituality of *Carmina*, prefers to distinguish hymns and prayers very clearly from charms and incantations. Against her, it is possible to argue that the hymns and prayers in *Carmina* are simply songs or incantations with a religious purpose. Even so, we would still be left with 'charms, incantations, rhymes and songs'. Given the gradual expansion of *Carmina* from the core of material published in 1900, it is probably best to define its subject matter in terms of concentric circles, with Carmichael's 'hymns and incantations' at the centre, charms and prayers next, rhymes and songs a little further out, *seanchas* and tales towards the outside, and other prose categories (such as onomastics and lexicography) at the extremity.

[34] For a brief account of these manuscripts see Ronald Black (ed.), *Eilein na h-Òige: The poems of Fr Allan McDonald* (Glasgow, 2002), 451. As is pointed out at p. 452 of that work, 'Folklore MSS III and IV', which are believed to have been in the possession of Father Allan's friend the Rev. George Henderson (1866-1912), have disappeared. I believe they are gone forever.

[35] The late John Lorne Campbell's edited transcript of the collection lies in typescript in Canna House. For various reasons, however, I decided that it was better to begin the work afresh.

[36] I am delighted to report that, thanks to an appeal made at the closing session of the Carmichael conference, Mrs Komori and I recruited two highly qualified volunteers to the project: Mrs Catriona Garbutt (Benbecula) and Mr Andrew Wiseman (Fort William and Edinburgh).

[37] Hamish Robertson, 'Studies in Carmichael's *Carmina Gadelica*', *Scottish Gaelic Studies*, xii (1971–6), 220–65: 226, 236.

[38] Campbell, 'Notes', 1–2, 12–13. Campbell had made the same point in his review of *CG* vi: *Scottish Gaelic Studies*, xii (1971–6), 290–9: 297.

[39] Campbell, 'Notes', 2, 13.

[40] Ibid., 15.

[41] Ibid., 12.

[42] Ibid., 2, 14.

[43] Ibid., 4, 5; *CG* iv, xix, xxiii. In 1992, to mark the fiftieth anniversary of his death, I published an account of the last year of his life as related to me by his first cousin Michael Carmichael, who knew him well (Raghnall Macille-Dhuibh, 'Missing Presumed Killed', *West Highland Free Press*, 10 July 1992).

[44] Campbell, 'Corrections and suggestions', 196, 197.

[45] Bruford, 'Deirdire', 2, 8, 16.

[46] Ibid., 9.

[47] Ibid., 17–20.

[48] Tatar, *Hard facts*, 30, 31–2.

[49] Bruford, 'Deirdire', 4, 19.

[50] What follows is a summary of material in Black (ed.), *Gaelic otherworld*, 182, 435–6, and Raghnall MacilleDhuibh, 'The Curse of Neist (1)' and 'The Curse of Neist (2)', *West Highland Free Press*, 28 October and 11 November 2005.

[51] Calum Macneil, Barra, has confirmed to me that Pearson is merely the form of his surname adopted by John MacPherson when in America. He was a corporal in the Confederate army in the Civil War: *CG* ii, 376. This form of the surname was also used by his daughter Catherine (Campbell, 'Notes', 17).

[52] There are only three comparable instances, all in *CG* v. Different parts of *Seathan Mac Rìgh Éireann* 'Seathan Son of the King of Ireland' (60–83) were got from eleven women, ten of whom are named; all three texts printed are ascribed to named informants, only the variant readings being anonymous. *A' Bhean-Shìdh* 'The Fairy Woman' (226–33) was got from two named women, one of whom seems to have furnished the main text, the other the variant readings. *Cumha Mhic an Tòisich* 'Mackintosh's Lament' (354–9) was got from a single named source; two

further named sources 'and others' are represented anonymously in the variant readings.

[53] Black (ed.), *Gaelic otherworld*, 435, 687, 701, 702.

[54] *CG* iii, vii. These words, edited down a little, also appear on the dust-jacket of *CG* iii and iv.

[55] Raghnall MacilleDhuibh, 'God of the Moon, God of the Sun', *West Highland Free Press*, 5 January 1996.

[56] John Lorne Campbell, review of *CG* vi, *Scottish Gaelic Studies*, xii (1971–6), 290–9: 298.

[57] This is a radically altered version of the study first presented as Raghnall MacilleDhuibh, 'A Gaelic carol analysed', *West Highland Free Press*, 22 December 1995.

[58] 'Duain Challuinn', *The Highlander*, 17 January 1874, 3; William Mackenzie, 'Leaves from my Celtic portfolio V', *TGSI*, ix (1879–80), 19–43: 28–9. I am grateful to Mr Calum Laing, Alness, for drawing my attention to the *Highlander* article and sending me a copy of it. The other *duan Callainn* in the article was sent in by 'Iain', who was probably Mr Laing's grandfather's brother John MacRury (1843–1907). He seems to have been working as a *ceann-aiche-siubhail* in Lewis at that time, but later became minister of Snizort. See Black (ed.), *Gaelic otherworld*, 647.

[59] 'This year' presumably means 1873. The date of publication was 17 January 1874, and Murdoch writes: 'Our Uist correspondent sent us the following Carrol for insertion last week, but owing to the wretchedly defective postal provisions and arrangements made for the Outer Hebrides, we are only able to give it this week.'

[60] See, for example, Black (ed.), *Gaelic Otherworld*, 530–1.

[61] 'Duain Challuinn', *The Highlander*, 17 January 1874, 3.

[62] Black (ed.), *Gaelic otherworld*, 529.

[63] Bruford, 'Deirdire', 16.

[64] The writer of such a paper might also wish to take account of the remarks on Carmichael as a 'ladies' man' in Ronald Black (ed.), *An tuil: Anthology of 20th century Scottish Gaelic verse* (Edinburgh, 1999), 710.

[65] His 'beat' covered an enormous area, including Canna. He was a great friend of John Lorne Campbell's, indeed he it was who first introduced me to Dr Campbell (at the opening of the National Library's exhibition on Dr and Mrs Campbell's life and work).

[66] Alexander (Alec) Carmichael (1868–1941).

[67] See also Campbell, 'Corrections and suggestions', 210–11.

[68] I believe I am the first to refer to the 'Notes' in *CG* ii as 'the dictionary of Gaelic folklore', but it seems to me that, by default, they form the germ of precisely such a work. The 'Notes' originated as footnotes or endnotes on specific words in the text, but Carmichael marked the words so glossed by putting them in inverted commas! Henderson advised: 'The printers must be told to put numbers in place of the inverted commas. If you arrange the notes alphabetically, however, there is no need to disfigure the page with anything.' (Campbell, 'Corrections and suggestions', 214.)

[69] Campbell, 'Corrections and suggestions', 214.

[70] Title page. The imprint page of each volume is blank save for the words: 'Three hundred copies printed.' See also J.L. Campbell, review of *CG* vi, *Scottish Gaelic Studies*, xii (1971–6), 290–9: 290.

[71] I use the term 'item' in this paper in a slightly technical sense, defining it as a charm, incantation, hymn, prayer, rhyme or song laid out as two lines or more of verse. In *CG* v, for example, there is no 'item' at all at p. 236, where the key part of the text is laid out as a conversation in prose, whereas p. 238 presents an 'item' of twenty lines contained in a prose text. Separate verse quotations within the same tale are generally counted as separate 'items'.

[72] On *Duan an Domhnuich* see Campbell, 'Notes', 7–8.

[73] See ibid. 3, 7–8, 9–10. There is a version of the prayer *Spiorad Naomh* 'Holy Spirit' (*CG* iii, 88–91) from Mingulay in Ealasaid Chaimbeul, *Air mo chuairt* (Stornoway, 1982), 52.

[74] Bruford, 'Deirdire', 12.

[75] Black (ed.), *Gaelic otherworld*, 215–16, 474–8.

[76] In his preface to the single-volume edition of *Carmina* (Edinburgh, 1992), John MacInnes briefly examined different versions of *Òrtha nam Buadh* and concluded (17) that 'perhaps few texts in *Carmina* are totally free of some editorial repair-work and some, including the "Invocation of the Graces," may have it to a very high degree'. This was my reason for including Carmichael's *Ora nam Buadh* 'The Invocation of the Graces' in *An tuil*. MacInnes's preface has now been reprinted in *Dùthchas nan Gàidheal: selected essays of John MacInnes* (Edinburgh, 2006), 477–91.

[77] Ruaraidh MacThòmais, *Creachadh na clàrsaich* (Edinburgh, 1982), 212–13, reprinted in Black (ed.), *An tuil*, 464–5. The tone, or rather tones (verse and prose), of *Carmina* are so distinctive as to be easily parodied, and Carmichael's contribution to Gaelic literature was not universally admired in the late twentieth century. One critic privately described the inclusion of *Ora nam Buadh* in *An tuil* as 'a carbuncle on the book'.

[78] As I have pointed out, whether 'incantations' can be held to include prayers is a matter of opinion. Mr Calum Macneil pointed out at the conference that prayers at wakes in Barra might go on for hours, the priest arriving at 9 p.m., laymen taking over about midnight and continuing to 3 a.m. or even 6 a.m.: 'Our people were capable of reciting prayers of great length.'

[79] J.L. Campbell (ed.), *Hebridean folksongs* (3 vols, Oxford, 1969–81) ii, 196. For Janet MacLeod see also Black (ed.), *An tuil*, 721.

[80] See also *Oran An Eich-Uisge*, Black (ed.), *Gaelic otherworld*, 704.

[81] See also ibid., index s.v. 'Fairy song of Dunvegan'.

[82] See ibid., 365–8.

[83] Rev. Thomas Sinton, 'Snatches of song collected in Badenoch VI', *Celtic Magazine*, xii (1886–7), 295–304: 299; idem, *The poetry of Badenoch* (Inverness, 1906), 27.

5

Alexander Carmichael and 'Celtic Christianity'

DONALD E. MEEK

In the emergence of what is termed 'Celtic Christianity' nowadays, no influence has been more powerful than the body of material contained in Alexander Carmichael's *Carmina Gadelica*. The material has been recycled endlessly in smaller anthologies and other publications. One has only to read the works of present-day writers such as Esther de Waal and Ian Bradley to realise how powerful *Carmina Gadelica* actually is.[1] It is no more and no less than the Bible of 'Celtic Christianity', and its role in the re-rooting of the so-called 'Celts' in a new spiritual landscape has been immense.

It is quite clear, from even the most cursory examination of the surviving corpus of papers and other material gathered by Alexander Carmichael in the second half of the nineteenth century, and now lodged in Edinburgh University Library, that the published *Carmina* series was constructed along a particular line, a line defined by Carmichael and his helpers before 1900. It is no less evident that his subsequent editors had to toe that line to preserve the thematic cohesion of the published collection. The line was, in short, the making of the 'Spiritual Celt'. In Scotland, at this time, 'Celt' became the in-word for 'Gael', and 'Celtic' the fashionable, upmarket, sanitised word for 'Gaelic'. Similar uses of the words 'Celt' and 'Celtic' can be found in Ireland in the context of the Irish language and its speakers. In the emerging presentation of *Carmina*, 'hymns' were the central concept. As a result of adherence to the paradigm of the 'Spiritual Celt', much material relating to the darker, 'pagan' side of Highland tradition was left out, possibly because it was deemed too 'wild' or unsuitable. The agenda driving the creation of *Carmina Gadelica*, whose first two volumes were published in 1900, was therefore to present a particular view of the Gaels as essentially spiritual beings, who accommodated in their religion both sacred and secular, 'pagan' and Christian, perspectives in an harmonious style. The key point was the ecumenical, tolerant, syncretistic—and also civilised and cultured—nature of the 'Spiritual Celt'.

One has only to look at the amount of material of a 'pagan' nature left out of the *Carmina*, and still lying unedited in Edinburgh University Library, to realise that neither the Gaels nor the editors of *Carmina* were, in fact, as accommodating and as eclectic as the paradigm wanted them to be. Those happy, innocent souls who nowadays construct, unquestioningly, the foundation of what is called 'Celtic Christianity' on the basis of the published *Carmina*, and who bombard the unsuspecting public with recycled texts and all sorts of amazing claims about 'Celtic spirituality' (so-called), need to bear this simple fact in mind.

In defining present-day 'Celtic Christianity', and in emphasising its reconstructed nature, it is vitally important also to understand that it is not necessarily the same thing as the 'popular' form of Christianity which once existed among the Gaelic-speaking people of the Hebrides. It is undoubtedly the case that Hebridean people had a store of prayers, charms and incantations, which they used regularly, as well as traditions about the saints, many of which existed beyond the rituals and ceremonies and liturgies of 'formal' or 'institutional' Christianity. There is no point in denying that; demotic forms of Christianity, in both Catholic and Protestant guises, have always existed. I was well aware of such traditions in my native island of Tiree. From time to time, usually at times of 'stress', the saints would be invoked, and I myself was sometimes 'ticked off' for using (in my innocence) Gaelic imprecations involving their names, especially that of the Virgin Mary. Particular rites, hovering on the boundary between 'paganism' and Christianity, were well remembered. Indeed, I knew a distinguished islander who claimed to be the last *Tirisdeach* to have performed a right of exorcism involving the Evil Eye. He was none other than Captain John C. MacKinnon, M.B.E., the wonderfully genial and kind Master of the MacBrayne motor-vessel, *Claymore* (1955), which regularly linked Tiree to South Uist. On one occasion when I visited the highly educational bridge of the *Claymore*, Captain MacKinnon told me of how, as a boy, he had been dispatched to the local 'healer', *Bigean an Loch* ('The Chick of the Loch') in Earnal, Tiree, to obtain a bottle of holy water for the family cow, which was in a milk-denying predicament. He duly did so, and was instructed to pour the water over the left horn of the cow, while invoking the names of the Father, the Son and the Holy Spirit. This he did, and the cow resumed her production of milk. My father too often spoke of the dreadful challenge which was sometimes assigned to him in identifying the culprit, when a case of the Evil Eye was—allegedly—detected in livestock. As a boy, he had to watch a particular hill, and to pay close attention to the first person who appeared over the brow of that hill. That person was, supposedly, the perpetrator of the animal's ailment. Little rhymes and verses were also used at particular times of the year, principally Hallowe'en and New Year.

Such traditions were found in Protestant, as well as Catholic, communities. What is, however, much more arguable is the manner in which the Gaelic material gathered by Carmichael was manipulated in such a way as to provide a paradigm rather different from what Hebridean people themselves might have understood or recognised. Prayers, charms and incantations were used in the Hebrides in a very harsh and difficult environment, in which people lived close to natural disasters, experienced 'hostile' and supernatural forces as a living, tangible reality, and found consolation in their prayers and rhymes at the ends and beginnings of particular seasons. This is a context very, very different from modern, middle-class suburbia, which is usually afflicted by too much of this world's goods, rather than too little.

In this paper, I wish to consider Alexander Carmichael and the emergence of the 'ideal' paradigm of the 'Spiritual Celt/Gael', which had reached prominence by the late nineteenth century. I will explore some aspects of the theoretical underpinning that Carmichael's published work received from Gaelic ministers and Celtic scholars, and especially from those who had already espoused this paradigm. Finally, I will consider the making of the first two volumes of *Carmina Gadelica*, by taking a closer look at the contribution of Dr George Henderson (1866–1912) to the product.

We can state confidently that the making of the 'Spiritual Celt/Gael', and the religious movement which attached itself ultimately to 'Celts' more generally, involved more minds than that of Alexander Carmichael. Indeed, I would argue that this could be called a 'project' in today's terms. It was an alliance, even a willing conspiracy, of collectors, clergymen and academics, who were seeking a *via media* in the midst of late nineteenth-century ecclesiastical unrest, and who were ready to embrace helpful theories about 'Spiritual Celts'. In this process, material gathered 'locally' in the Hebrides was interpreted 'globally' through 'external' scholars and their theories, and then 're-rooted' in other soil, or even in the native turf.

'Indigenous' lore was thereby subjected to some degree of manipulation, if not retro-engineering, by reconstructionists with wider cultural, and even political, goals in mind. It could, of course, be argued that the 'indigenous' material ceased to be 'indigenous' the moment it was collected by Carmichael, and that it was further divorced from its context when it was conceptually reappropriated by non-Gaels. Scholarly theorising added yet another dimension. Those readers who encounter *Carmina Gadelica* today, and fall in love with the prayers and charms of the people of the Hebrides as a pure and uncontaminated fountain of 'alternative spirituality', need to be aware that this is a consciously reconstructed package. So too do those who may find fault with Carmichael for having, somehow, 'deceived' his readers. Because of the alleged discrepancy between the 'original' versions of the *Carmina* and their printed forms, Carmichael has been perceived as something of a 'second Macpherson', and a miniature 'Carmichael Controversy' has rumbled quietly along in scholarly circles since the early 1970s.[2]

I am reminded here of a story that I once read in a manuscript notebook compiled by the Rev. Duncan MacGregor Campbell, who was for a period a schoolteacher in Griomasaigh, North Uist. According to Campbell's story, Carmichael, who always strutted around in his kilt, was 'on the road' on a frosty morning. Unfortunately, he did not notice the black ice and 'went for a flier' in his grand attire. As he hit the ground in a crumpled heap, a wry youngster who had observed the great man's fall quipped, '*Chan e Car a' Mhìcheil a bhios againn oirbh tuilleadh, ach Car a' Mhuiltein*' ('We will not call you Carmichael any longer, but Somersault'), thus playing wickedly on the element *car* in both *Car a' Mhìcheil* and *car a' mhuiltein*.

In a sense, Carmichael has 'gone for a flier'—second time round—because of the presentation of his charms and prayers in the published *Carmina*. To make him stand straight again, we have to understand the nature of the academic 'black ice', on which he and others were treading over a century ago. The fact is that some sort of theoretical backbone, and also an editorial method, had to be found, if a cohesive set of volumes was ever to emerge from the perplexing mass of material gathered by Carmichael. Carmichael, who was not a scholar but a collector without scholarly training, was faced with an enormous challenge when he set about editing his material. He needed academic support and conceptual reinforcement as he toiled on his forthcoming volumes. At various stages along the road, in the 1880s and the 1890s, we can see him at work, testing the water, soliciting interest, changing his mind, changing publishers, changing titles—and, in his lonely struggle to produce his volumes, leaning heavily on the views of scholars such as Dr George Henderson, to the extent that, in producing his material for publication, he was led along fashionable, and at times rather slippery, academic pathways.

Scholarly concerns

Alexander Carmichael returned to Edinburgh from his posting in the Hebrides in 1882 for the sake of his children's education. For the twenty years from 1861 to 1881 he had been a Customs and Excise officer in the islands, and had spent most of the time in North and South Uist. When he joined the Excise, he was posted to Dublin, Islay, Cornwall, Skye, Uist (twice), and then finally Edinburgh.

The year 1882 was of particular significance in the Gaelic and Highland calendar. Events conspired to enhance the profile of the region and its language. In the spring, the crofters (and especially their womenfolk) in Braes, Skye had taken a stand against the arrival of Sheriff William Ivory and his posse of police, resulting in the famous 'Battle of the Braes'. This brought the crofters' agitation to national prominence, and led to the establishing of the Napier Commission, which issued its great report in 1884. Alexander Carmichael was an important contributor to that report.

In 1882 too, Professor Donald MacKinnon (1839–1914) had been inducted to Scotland's first Chair of Celtic, recently created at the University of Edinburgh. MacKinnon, a native of Colonsay, was an outstanding authority on Gaelic literature, custom and belief. He had gained prestige in the 1870s as the writer of a fine series of Gaelic essays in the journal, *An Gaidheal*, where he sought to expound the hallmarks of 'the Gael'. In doing so, he relied on Gaelic Proverbs and proverbial lore to a considerable extent. Given MacKinnon's interest in proverbs, it is fascinating that in 1881 and 1882 two separate editions of *Gaelic proverbs* by Sheriff Alexander Nicolson (1827–93) were published in Edinburgh. Alexander Carmichael had also contributed to the making of Nicolson's celebrated volume. Soon MacKinnon gathered a like-minded circle around him in his home in Edinburgh. Its number included Alexander Carmichael, Neil MacLeod (1843–1924), the Skye bard, and Donald MacKechnie (1836–1908) from Jura, a fine writer of Gaelic prose.

The year 1882 was therefore a conceptual starting-point for 'focused' Gaelic scholarship in Scotland, centring on Professor MacKinnon and his Chair. Of course, attempts were being made before 1882 to lay the foundations of what was to become our understanding of 'modern Gaelic scholarship'. The first priority of that scholarly venture was to establish who the Gaels themselves actually were, in 'Celtic', ethnic and cultural terms. For MacKinnon, traditional Gaelic lore held the key. In analysing Gaelic proverbs and the wider body of Gaelic literature, especially poetry, he employed a broadly 'bottom-up' approach, constructing his operating framework by means of ready-to-hand Gaelic evidence, rather than 'broken-down Aryan myths'. He was well aware of the critical writing of Matthew Arnold (1822–88), and earlier pioneers, such as Johann Gottfried Herder (1744–1803), appear to have influenced him. Several of the 'new' Scottish scholars were also applying linguistic perspectives supplied by new springs of thought in the universities of Europe, and especially Germany. Major efforts were being made to 'follow the asterisk in the East' (i.e., the asterisk of reconstructed philological forms) and to determine the hallmarks of the Celtic language family in the context of its wider Indo-European kindred. This was signified by the celebrated foundational work by Johann Kaspar Zeuß (1806–56), *Grammatica Celtica*, of 1853.[3] The 'mind of the Celt' could also be reconstructed, along similarly 'comparative' lines, through surviving lore, tales and literature. As an expert in Gaelic tradition, however, Professor MacKinnon did not succumb to the 'lure of the asterisk' and its 'Aryan implications' as easily as some of his contemporaries. He also kept well clear of more controversial theorisers, and he had a healthy scepticism about matters faddishly 'Celtic'. Simultaneously, scholars in other disciplines were trying to determine the nature of 'Celtic' religion and spirituality, and none more conspicuously and successfully than Ernest Renan (1823–92), a Breton who was a brilliant orientalist and a controversial Roman Catholic theologian.[4]

These new perspectives, operating in terms of 'Celts' and matters 'Celtic', had been injected into the academic mainstream by the time Alexander Carmichael reached Edinburgh in 1882, and they were to have a profound bearing on the 'package' which he was to present to the public as *Carmina Gadelica* almost twenty years later. In keeping with the prevailing academic *Zeitgeist*, a more general 'Celtic Revival' was in the air, in political and artistic, as well as scholarly, matters. Time and again, we can see Carmichael interacting with the Gaelic and Celtic scholars who were applying the new learning in Scotland, and especially the paradigm of the 'Spiritual Celt', but we can also perceive the power of the artistic dimension of the 'Celtic Revival' in the fine artwork on the pages of the finished volumes.

'Uist old hymns'

A good place to begin when exploring the emerging morphology of Carmichael's version of the 'Spiritual Celt/Gael', which controlled the shape of the *Carmina* and ultimately of 'Celtic Christianity' itself, is the lecture that he gave on 'Uist old hymns' to the Gaelic Society of Glasgow on 24 December 1888—a day before Christmas, you will note. By 1888, when he gave his talk to the Gaelic Society of Glasgow, Carmichael had been back in the Lowlands, and living in Edinburgh, for six years. The first volume of the Society's *Transactions* carried a report of the paper, a report which had been derived from a newspaper. The introduction to the report in the *Transactions* stated:

> As a Collection of these Hymns will shortly be published, the whole lecture is not available, but we submit the following report of it, which appeared in the newspapers—and which has been revised and extended by Mr. Carmichael.[5]

From these comments alone, it would seem that the definitive published work (if that is what is implied by the 'Collection') was expected very soon. However, it is evident that the process of editing what became *Carmina Gadelica* was still very much ongoing ten years later, and that there were very many uncertainties to be resolved, including a title and a publisher. In fact, it was to be another twelve years before the first two volumes appeared. The point about the 'Collection' at this stage is that it was to be an unpretentious collection of hymns, and it seems that 'Uist old hymns' was probably intended as its title. Carmichael argued that such hymns embraced, and consecrated, the activities of the Gael—and 'Gael' and 'Gaelic' were still his operating words. We cannot fault his understanding of the 'homes and hearths' to which his material belonged. He did not make any special case for their being part of a wider set of 'Celtic' beliefs. That was to come.

The centrality of religion in Carmichael's vision, and especially a certain kind of religion, inclusive and ecumenical in spirit, is, however, very clear in the concluding remarks attributed to him in the report:

> Mr. Carmichael concluded a most interesting and valuable lecture by quoting a beautiful Hymn used before retiring to rest. It would be observed, he said, that all these Hymns belonged to the Roman Catholic times, but they had been admired and considered of great value by such Protestant Divines as the late Rev. Dr. MacLauchlan [*sic*], Edinburgh; the late Rev. Dr. A. Clerk, Kilmallie; and the late Rev. Dr. Cameron, Brodick, and many others.[6]

The 'lateness' of these supportive clergymen may be ominous, as may the fact that both McLauchlan (Free Church) and Clerk (Church of Scotland), like Carmichael himself, were strong supporters of the authenticity of James Macpherson's 'Ossian'—Clerk particularly so.[7] Carmichael had evidently been soliciting the views of some of the earlier ministerial scholars on the 'Uist old hymns'. In other words, he was dependent on the perspectives of leading Presbyterian ministers to find an appropriate religious setting for these compositions. The ministers tended, on the whole, to be in the more broad-minded camp, but to be 'old-fashioned' and, like Carmichael, 'Ossianic' in their scholarly approach.

The report also included the views of the living clergy, who had been present at the Glasgow meeting. In particular, a fulsome tribute to Carmichael came from the Rev. Robert Blair (1837–1907), a distinguished Islayman, Church of Scotland minister, and Gaelic scholar of the pro-Ossian camp, then in retirement in Cambuslang. Blair had edited the commemorative edition of the poems of the Islay bard, William Livingston, which was published in 1882. Blair is reported as saying:

> He had never listened to hymns more touching or beautiful, and they certainly threw much light on the Celtic character. Despite the many references to Angel and Saint worship, of which they as Protestants might not approve, these hymns and prayers proved conclusively that our Celtic forefathers were a deeply religious people. It seemed to him that in consecrating every duty of the day with a suitable prayer or hymn, and so carrying their religion into every detail of life, they proved that they were an educated people. He was of the opinion that the Highlanders had not yet been properly understood by their Lowland brethren. He had held and maintained that the Highlanders were far ahead in the olden times of those who declared them to be nothing but naked savages and barbarians, and the fine tone and culture of these hymns certainly went a long way to prove all that. He would almost defy any people to produce more beautiful prayers or finer hymns. Mr. Carmichael had put all Highlanders under a deep debt of gratitude to him by collecting these exquisite specimens of our ancient lore. These things were fast passing away, and very few of the rising generation felt much interest in them. The spread of English, through our schools and School Boards, was hastening the disappearance of our Celtic folk lore. He felt personally indebted to the lecturer for the intense pleasure he had afforded himself, as well as all present, by the choice selection of Uist old hymns.[8]

Two matters of significance stand out from these remarks in general, and from the comments of Blair in particular. The first is the desire of all to find a broadly-based form of Christian spirituality which embraced Roman Catholicism and Protestantism. It is fascinating to note that two of the supporters of this quest, cited by Carmichael, were leading figures of the Free Church of Scotland, namely Thomas McLauchlan (1815–86) and Alexander Cameron (1827–88). Both had been scholarly men, and had helped to lay the foundations of nineteenth-century Celtic Studies in Scotland. McLauchlan had published an important edition of material from the Book of the Dean of Lismore in 1862. Cameron, who had died only a few months before Carmichael delivered his paper, was a devotee of the new, philologically-based scholarship pioneered by Zeuß.[9] These philological principles were taking root in Scotland through the solid, ongoing work of a group of scholars, including the Rev. John Kennedy (1819–84), another Free Church minister, Alexander Macbain (1855–1907) (teacher of George Henderson), and William J. Watson (1865–1948).[10] Gradually, Gaelic and Celtic scholarship was shedding its older, clerical garb and becoming largely laicised.

The second matter of significance is the desire of some to use the hymns to present Highlanders in a good light. The hymns, according to the Rev. Robert Blair, did precisely that. They challenged the smear of savagery with which Highlanders were tainted by 'Lowland brethren'. The hymns could be used to sing the praises of the Gael, as well as of God. The ministers who were present, however, appear to have been unanimous in converting the 'Gael' into the 'Celt', most obviously when they were emphasising positive qualities. These positive qualities included the 'education' of the 'Celt'. As Blair's comments indicate, 'education' was seen by some as a very important aspect of the 'message' of the 'Uist old hymns', and, as is evident from the later contribution of Dr George Henderson, it helped to shape editorial approaches to the *Carmina*. Blair's reference to 'the spread of English, through schools and School Boards' suggests that he resented, or was at least less than enamoured of, the Education

(Scotland) Act of 1872 and its consequences for Gaelic (which the Act failed to mention). The Act was likewise an issue for Professor Donald MacKinnon, who wrote his well-known essay, 'Seann Sgoil' ('Old School'), on the different concepts of education represented by his 'old school' in Colonsay, on the one hand, and by the 1872 Act on the other. MacKinnon's deep unease with the Act and its implications is evident in the essay.[11] The Act had created fissures, if not faultlines, cultural and political, which had to be crossed, or somehow negotiated, by university-trained clerical and academic Gaels, who now had to respond to accusations that the generality of Gaels were not 'properly educated', presumably in post-1872 terms. Presbyterian ministers, in particular, would have been aware of a long-standing connection between religious knowledge (through the reading of the Gaelic Bible) and 'education', as inculcated by the succession of church-related schools in the Highlands prior to 1872. In Blair's mind, therefore, 'Spiritual Celts' were also 'educated Celts', and 'Uist old hymns' integrated both strands.

Among the audience that night was a representative of the new post-1872 order in Scottish education, namely the inevitable Mr William Jolly, H.M.I.S. (1838–1915), who occupied the chair. Mr Jolly lived up to his name by giving rousing speeches at dinners of the Gaelic Society of Inverness, founded partly to meet concerns about Gaelic created by the 1872 Education Act, and he could always be relied on to be positive and practical, even if he had no Gaelic and no means of accessing directly, or of understanding, the material which caught his fancy. It was the practical side of the hymns that he liked, and particularly 'the practical nature of the religion of the composers of these hymns'.[12] And the helpful dimension was not lacking: 'He was sure it would be interesting to the meeting to hear that a cultured English gentleman, on the shores of Loch Maree, was so impressed with the beauty of these old hymns that he had offered to bear the whole expense of publishing them.'[13] The gentleman, it would seem, was John Henry Dixon (1838–1926), who had recently published *Gairloch in North-West Ross-shire … with a Guide to Gairloch and Loch Maree* (Edinburgh, 1886), and had directed that 'the profits, if any, from the sale of this book will be applied in aid of Poolewe Public Hall'. Here, then, was a solution to the other bugbear with which a collector had to contend—finance to publish the finished volumes.

So, as early as 1888, the wider design of the 'Collection' was being worked out by Carmichael, and a patron, known for his generosity and evidently familiar with the poetry, place-names and history of the Gairloch area, had been found by the ever-helpful Mr Jolly. This makes it all the more perplexing that it took longer than another decade to bring the first two volumes of the 'Collection' to their final form. Perhaps Carmichael was just too busy to proceed quickly—a problem not unknown to scholars today! Were matters really as far advanced as Carmichael claimed when he spoke to the Gaelic Society of Glasgow, or was he flying a kite to see who would be attracted by it, and how the audience would respond to it? Was he testing the water, or perhaps even looking for those who could provide him with sufficient 'water' to float the project?

My own hunch is that, in his first few years in Edinburgh, Carmichael probably did not know what to do with the mass of material that he had gathered in the Hebrides. There were those, however, who were willing and able to fill his theoretical void. Certainly he found strong backing among the scholarly Gaelic clergy, and learned from them. Robert Blair's comments are very close to Carmichael's own views when he wrote to another clergyman, Father Allan McDonald of Eriskay (1859–1905), a decade later about his purpose in publishing *Carmina Gadelica*: 'that by making this book up in as good a form as I could in matter and material, it might perhaps be the means of conciliating some future politician in favour of our own dear

Highland people'.[14] They also chime closely with his introductory remarks on 'the ill-understood and so-called illiterate Highlanders of Scotland' in the first volume of the *Carmina*.[15]

I am not aware of any specific evidence that indicates why Carmichael chose to focus so strongly on the 'hymns' of the Gaels as a theme for the collection by which he would make his name. There were probably a number of factors. He was a collector of very wide interests and it is likely that he would have encountered religious material among the lore available in many districts. It certainly looks as if the years in Uist, and in particular his period in Benbecula and South Uist, influenced him very deeply. Moving between Protestant North Uist and Roman Catholic South Uist is likely to have given him a desire for an ecumenical presentation which, like the causeways now linking these islands, could cross the divisions of the post-Reformation period. As Professor William Gillies has suggested to me, it is quite possible that he may have come to question the adequacy of 'the comfortably, overwhelmingly Protestant faith he grew up with in Lismore'. It is clear that he had a strongly religious bent in his own nature, tempered with a desire to achieve a balanced position. If he was inclined to move towards Roman Catholicism, he was also courting the opinion of broad-minded Presbyterian clergymen such as Thomas McLauchlan, Archibald Clerk, and Alexander Cameron.

In terms of the wider scholarly ethos of the time, too, the spirituality of the so-called 'Celt' was a much-admired phenomenon, which had been emphasised by Ernest Renan and again by Matthew Arnold in the mid-1860s.[16] Carmichael was familiar with Renan's paradigm of the 'Celt', and actually alludes to it in his introduction to *Carmina Gadelica*. 'If this work does nothing else,' he wrote, 'it affords incontestable proof that the Northern Celts were endowed, as Renan justly claims for Celts everywhere, with 'profound feeling and adorable delicacy' in their religious instincts'.[17] The time was ripe to demonstrate the spirituality of the so-called 'Hebridean Celt' as part of a much wider religious parcel, which, it was argued, was tolerant of secular culture—unlike aggressive, evangelical Presbyterianism, with which Carmichael had collided head-on in Skye at the outset of his labours.

Reacting to religious revival: Carmichael's early work

It was important to Carmichael to exalt God and the Gael, but it was no less important to him to strike a new accord *between* God and the Gael, because of the apparently negative attitudes to tales and traditions which he had encountered as a collector in the mid-nineteenth century, when evangelicalism began to take strong root in the Highlands and Islands in the context of religious revivals. Carmichael began his career as a collector within the enterprise of the celebrated John Francis Campbell of Islay (1821–85), and he gathered tales and heroic ballads, two types of lore in which Campbell had a particular interest. He managed to fulfil his desire of 'giving his name a place' in Campbell's book, namely *Popular Tales of the West Highlands*, published between 1860 and 1862. Volume 3 contained two tales contributed by him; volume 4 also contained material, this time Ossianic, from Carmichael, who had moved to Carbost in Skye by 1861.[18]

Carmichael's move to Carbost coincided with a religious revival in the district, and he wrote on 9 April 1861 to J. F. Campbell to describe how it affected his attempts to collect tales:

> I was getting on famously with collecting tales till about two months ago. About that time the revivals began in the next parish to us here where some most extraordinary scenes were and still are taking place. Ever since then I cannot get a tale. Since then my most persevering efforts have

been unavailing. The people here have got frightened and their memories with their stories of
ancient lore have forsaken them in a most unaccountable manner. Still I would get something
amongst a few of them yet if gossiping tongues would but keep silent. For instance two old wives,
two of my friends whom I used to go to see after some of their neighbours got frightened[,] have
been told by the said neighbours for their edification that they were two old wives of the d——
and that he was sure to come for them if they did not give over their ungodly tales.[19]

Similar reports were sent by Donald K. Torrie (1832–78), another of Campbell's collectors,
who commented in the same month, 'I hope I may be successful in driving their Free Kirkism
out of the them [i.e. informants in Torrin and Strathaird, Skye]'.[20] Carmichael himself was
ready to point the finger at Free Church ministers: 'I find that the clergy—especially the Free
Church clergy, are much against *sean sgeulachdan* and denounce them as "ungodly" &c.'[21] In the
introduction to the first volume of the *Carmina*, he specifically mentions what evangelicalism
had done to secular Gaelic tradition in Lewis.[22]

What is noteworthy here is the confrontational nature of Highland evangelicalism in
revivalist mode, and its impact on collectors like Carmichael. What is even more significant is
that Carmichael became the champion of an ecumenical and tolerant form of religion, which
is epitomised in *Carmina*, and that there were Highland clergymen who were prepared to back
him by 1888. In the twenty years or so after 1861, the Free Church, helped into existence in
1843 by a powerful pulse of religious revival, had become the home of different theological
positions, and the morphology of nineteenth-century evangelicalism was assuming more
culturally benign forms. Far from being opposed by Free Church ministers in 1888, Carmichael
was claiming to have gained the sympathy, and the understanding, of two of their leading (but
now deceased) Gaelic scholars, McLauchlan and Cameron. The Free Church of Scotland,
however, was (by the 1870s) in the process of being disturbed by strife between the
'constitutionalists' and the majority who wished to unite with the United Presbyterian Church.
In a contentious era, 'Uist old hymns' may have been seen as a road to peace on various fronts
of ecclesiastical strife. It is ironic and significant that, in the very year (1900) that the first two
volumes of the *Carmina* were published, the majority of ministers in the Free Church left the
institution, and joined the broader, more tolerant United Free Church of Scotland, where they
enjoyed the liberty of singing hymns—*carmina* of another kind. The residual Free Church
adhered strictly to the metrical Psalms.

Carmichael, Henderson and the invention of Čarmina Gadelica

It will be remembered that 'Uist old hymns' was the title of Carmichael's lecture to the
Gaelic Society of Glasgow in 1888. 'Uist old hymns' may have been what he had in mind as a
title for his collection in 1888. However, the first stab at producing a specimen printed text
appears to have been made around 1897, the year of Carmichael's retirement, when the work
was given a very different title (*Òr agus Òb*), and a title page was produced, indicating that it was
to be published by the distinguished Glasgow publisher of Gaelic material, Archibald Sinclair
(1850–99). But it did not materialise. Precisely why this attempt at publication failed, as did an
earlier approach to the Clarendon Press, I do not know—possibly Sinclair's death intervened.
Carmichael was, however, known to be thrawn and difficult in his orthographic understanding.
That, together with lack of finance, may have scuppered the Sinclair venture. Sinclair, an
Islayman to the core, was a most supportive printer, publisher and promoter of Gaelic works,
but it is possible that subscribers did not appear in sufficient numbers.

In 1897, Sinclair prepared a batch of flyers for the book, in sumptuous black and red print, but many were later recycled by Carmichael for the writing of his drafts. They appear, rather oddly, among his papers, with the printed side scored through and the backs, the versos, re-used (and then re-used again!) for his characteristic large scrawl. Carmichael got nothing out of the deal, except an apparently welcome and very usable pile of scrap paper. The final publication, by T. &. A. Constable, of the first two volumes of what we now call *Carmina Gadelica* was very much a touch-and-go affair, with a great deal of hesitation and changing of mind on the part of Carmichael, his potential publishers, and (as we shall see) George Henderson. Carmichael himself had to fund the venture: despite the earlier offer of patronage by John Henry Dixon, the 'cultured English gentleman' of 1888, he did not avail himself of this 'generous appreciation'.[23]

Carmichael, then, had found a name and a potential publisher for his collection by 1897, but he had a very different publisher and a very different title by 1900. Semantic challenges also reared their heads. Carmichael's scholarly advisers saw problems with the term 'hymn', and tried to steer him towards a broader and more inclusive agenda, although the broadly religious emphasis remained intact.

Here, in particular, we can see the influence of Dr George Henderson. Henderson, a native of Kiltarlity, was educated at Raining's School, Inverness, under Alexander Macbain, and at Edinburgh University. He was also the first Celtic scholar from Scotland to study on the Continent, at Leipzig and Bonn, and then at Vienna, where he gained his Ph.D. From 1906 to 1911, Henderson was lecturer in Celtic at Glasgow University. Henderson gave Carmichael a great deal of help as his editorial labours progressed, especially in the final stages of editing. He read the introduction and notes to the forthcoming work, and tightened and corrected the material very thoroughly. Henderson appears to have been wholly familiar with the contents of the first two volumes as they took shape, possibly because he contributed a fair amount.

According to the Rev. Kenneth MacLeod (1871–1955), author of *The Road to the Isles*, and a close associate of Carmichael's, the relationship between Carmichael and Henderson was *dìreach mar gum biodh an t-athair agus am mac ann* ('just as if father and son were there').[24] The first volume of *Dàin Iain Ghobha*, the poems of John Morison of Harris, edited by George Henderson and published in 1893 by Archibald Sinclair, Glasgow, carries a dedication to Alexander Carmichael,

> whose devotion to the rescue of ancient Celtic literature is not inferior to his piety and wisdom; whose love of the idylls of the isles and of the Highland people is equalled only by his affection for whatsoever things are pure and lovely and of good report wherever found; who has always encouraged me in my love for the Gaelic tongue, its prestige and its beauty, and to whose friendship among other benefits I owe my first acquaintance with a noble poet's mind…

As the introduction to the second volume of Morison's songs, published in 1896, makes clear, Henderson was a devotee of the 'Celtic Church', which he described in a discursive explanation of the background to the 'Latin Loan Words used in Iain Gobha'—an excellent example of the tangential scholarship then in vogue, and Henderson's predilection for Latin, soon to affect Carmichael's labours. 'The Celtic Church had width, variety, and freedom,' writes Henderson; 'the story of the Gospels surpassed the native rites . . . Every element not contrary to the essential nature of the doctrine of Jesus was allowed to remain as heretofore.'[25]

Given his commitment to the 'Celtic Church', Henderson was well suited to the task of advising Carmichael in the interpretation of his material. It seems possible that Henderson was the ghost-writer, or at least the key conceptualiser, of much of the introduction to *Carmina Gadelica*. At the very least, he supervised the project closely, and helped to keep it on track when, under Carmichael's unsteady hand, it tended to wander off into 'diffuseness'.

Through Henderson, who had contacts in Oxford, we can also see the input of a Welsh scholar whose contribution to the shaping of *Carmina Gadelica* has not been acknowledged hitherto, and requires to be underlined. This was the palaeographer, John Gwenogvryn Evans (1852–1930), who produced foundationally important editions of early Welsh manuscripts. Evans was evidently in Oxford when Henderson was there in the mid-1890s, and Henderson asked Evans for advice on the title and layout of the title page of Carmichael's proposed work.

Henderson wrote to Carmichael in 1896: 'Evans is of opinion that *Hymn* is misleading in this case and should be avoided.' Evans was evidently consulted about the title that was printed on the flyer of 1897, and suggested as a subtitle 'The Lays and Incantations of the Gael'. The difficulty for Henderson and evidently for Evans was to find a way of expanding the term 'hymn' to embrace what Henderson called 'spells'. He wrote: 'The Spells you give are a unique feature and you could explain in your preface that Òr means prayer, hymn or sacred metrical entreaty, and spell charm'.[26]

Gradually, in the course of the discussion, the title itself changed from *Òr agus Òb*, to *Lyra Gadelica*, and finally to *Carmina Gadelica*, suggested by Henderson. When finally *Carmina Gadelica* was agreed, Henderson was cock-a-hoop, as he wrote to Carmichael:

> I feel more and more how fitting *Carmina Gadelica* is. In one word, [the only] objection to it is some would say you are not perhaps a classical scholar. Yet in giving a name to your collection you must not be *in any way* influenced by possibly silly sneers or afraid [of w]hat any one would say to get a catch at you. [M]en like Fionn [Henry Whyte (1852–1913), Easdale and Glasgow] or Neil Macleod [the Skye bard], good work as they may do, might think it ambitious. Prof. Mackinnon too, a naturally cautious man, might also say [you] chose a title from a language not very familiar to you. But you know enough Latin to see the meaning of these words . . . Your work is not meant for the uneducated or half-educated Highlanders and I would not be influenced by them but by the real merits of the case. I[t] would also baptize the work in the truth and also in a poetic light . . . You want a very comprehensive word indeed to include all the poems in your collection. Don't be blind to that. Many of them can't be rightly called Hymns, even in the large Greek sense . . .[27]

Nevertheless, Carmichael stuck to his guns, and 'Hymns and Incantations' appeared as the English subtitle in 1900. We may wonder, however, how Carmichael reacted to Henderson's fascinatingly candid comments about 'uneducated or half-educated Highlanders', and we may well ask who may have been the target of these comments. Here again we may be glimpsing one of the faultlines caused by differing views of 'education' after 1872, with distinctions being drawn between the 'old guard' of self-made 'Gaelic scholars', represented by Henry Whyte and Neil MacLeod (and even Professor MacKinnon?), and modern, 'state-of-the-art' scholars, who had been trained beyond Scotland, and were aspiring to greater things. There is more than a whiff of 'intellectual snobbery' in the attitude of Dr George Henderson, Ph.D. (Vienna), who was—perhaps!— aware that he was a degree above the rest of the pack.

Conclusion

When the first two volumes of *Carmina Gadelica* appeared in 1900, they represented a considerable achievement for Alexander Carmichael. They were, however, presented in a package very different from the rather unassuming initial outline suggested by the 1888 report of Carmichael's 'Uist old hymns'. The introduction to the first volume demonstrated that Carmichael had listened well to the views of Gaelic clergymen and scholars, and had absorbed their perspectives on what these hymns implied for the cultural qualities of the 'Celt'. 'Celtic Christianity' of a certain kind was indeed being manufactured and presented to the public, with the overall aim of liberating Highlanders from the stigma of incivility and barbarism attached to them by outsiders. As Henderson's damning but revealing comments about 'uneducated or half-educated Highlanders' indicate, the target readership for *Carmina Gadelica* lay beyond the Highlands.

The volumes were greatly pleasing to those who had helped Carmichael, and not least to George Henderson, who had contributed so much to the project. He must have known that he was, in part, polishing his own halo as adviser (at the very least) when he wrote glowingly to Carmichael in September 1900:

> The work will win itself friends, both by its contents and appearance. Your introductions are as good as anything in it and are very attractive and interesting both as to form and matter and I am happy you have got rid of diffuseness which I knew you were anxious to avoid . . . All Highlanders will be proud of your book and will look into it often and for many a long year . . . I hope Mackinnon will see you get your LL.D . . . [28]

Professor MacKinnon was evidently part of the overall plot. He appears to have done the needful. Carmichael did get his LL.D., and he climbed to subsequent fame as a result of his initial labours on 'Uist old hymns'. In the fulness of time, 'Uist old hymns', finessed to become the new, up-market and Latinate *Carmina Gadelica*, did 'win itself friends, both by its contents and appearance'. Transferred from the humble homes of crofters who lived perilously close to the edge of human existence, and relocated in libraries and ivory towers and even 'Middle England', it produced the building blocks of the contemporary, and supposedly 'indigenous', religious movement which we now call 'Celtic Christianity'.

A century after the published texts appeared, we are beginning to understand what went into the making of this foundational set of documents. To dismiss it as an outright fabrication is completely wrong, as *Carmina Gadelica* contains much genuine material, alongside some 'recomposed' versions, multi-layered specimens of contrived editing, and highly creative pieces by Carmichael himself, whose authorial powers were not insignificant, particularly when he was dealing with the sun, the moon and the stars; but, if we see it as an innocent, spontaneous, natural effusion of something beautifully and intrinsically 'Celtic', we merely delude ourselves in the other direction.

When it is set within the *Weltanschauung* of its own day, the making of the first two volumes of *Carmina Gadelica* appears to have been a consciously contrived 'project' with several agendas, some of which were contradictory and even disingenuous. It was creative and conservative, political and promotional, ecumenical and eccentric, and possibly even a little egocentric. Henderson's kindly—and well-founded—anticipation of Carmichael's forthcoming LL.D. reminds us that personal ambition was not, perhaps, wholly absent from this seemingly altruistic attempt to vindicate the 'uneducated and half-educated Highlanders', whom George Henderson (in a splendidly unguarded moment) evidently regarded as unworthy recipients of their own folklore.

The conclusion that the first two volumes of *Carmina Gadelica* were the culmination of a benign and well-intentioned scholarly conspiracy, involving numerous participants (most obviously Presbyterian clergymen), and aimed at vindicating the Gaels ('Hebridean Celts', no less) and their 'spirituality', as well as their 'education', in the eyes of outsiders, is borne out fully by the evidence presented in this paper. It might be said wryly in summary that, when making his way from his previous home in Scolpaig, North Uist, to his new abode in Royal Circus Gardens, Edinburgh, in 1882, Carmichael fell, not among the rude young men of Uist on this occasion, but among cultured scholars, who were only too willing to embroider (rather than steal!) his 'insular raiment', by means of grander, contemporary scholarly threads and artistic motifs. Carmichael was not, however, an entirely unwilling victim.

The desire to create, and to apply, an 'indigenous' form of spirituality continues today, for good reasons and bad. It is present most obviously in the brand of 'Celtic Christianity' currently being offered in comfortable paperbacks, whose contents have long been divorced from the plain, unadorned reality of their original Gaelic setting and the Celtic threads used in their subsequent embroidery. We—educated people of whom Dr George Henderson, Ph.D. (Vienna), would surely have approved, even if he did not approve of 'uneducated or half-educated Highlanders'—ignore the evidence of repackaging and reconstruction, and their consequences, at our considerable peril.

I am very grateful to Dr Domhnall Uilleam Stiùbhart for providing transcripts of relevant sections of John Francis Campbell's manuscripts in the National Library of Scotland, and also for identifying John Henry Dixon. I am no less indebted to Professor William Gillies, who read an earlier draft of this paper, and offered important insights into patterns of Celtic scholarship in the late nineteenth century. Professor Gillies also provided further information on Dixon. Mo thaing mhòr dhuibh le chèile.

---

[1] Ian Bradley, *The Celtic way* (London, 1993); Esther de Waal, *The Celtic vision: prayers and blessings from the Outer Hebrides* (London, 1988).

[2] Hamish Robertson, 'Studies in Carmichael's *Carmina Gadelica*', *Scottish Gaelic Studies*, xii(2) (1976), 220–65.

[3] D. Ellis Evans, 'The heroic age of Celtic philology', *Zeitschrift für Celtische Philologie*, 54 (2004), 1–30.

[4] Patrick Sims-Williams, 'The Visionary Celt: the construction of an ethnic preconception', *Cambridge Medieval Celtic Studies*, 11 (1986), 71–96.

[5] Report of lecture in Alexander Carmichael, 'Uist old hymns', *Transactions of the Gaelic Society of Glasgow*, i (1887–91), 34.

[6] Ibid., 44.

[7] Donald E. Meek, 'The Sublime Gael: the impact of Macpherson's *Ossian* on literary creativity and cultural perception in Gaelic Scotland', in Howard Gaskill (ed.), *The reception of Ossian in Europe* (London, 2004), 52–3, 64.

[8] AC, 'Uist old hymns', 44–5.

[9] William Grant, 'Alexander Cameron and Reliquiae Celticae,' in Michel Byrne, Thomas Owen Clancy, and Sheila Kidd (eds), *Litreachas & eachdraidh: Literature and history: papers from the Second Conference of Scottish Gaelic Studies, Glasgow 2002* (Glasgow, 2006), 203.

[10] Donald E. Meek, '"*Beachdan ùra à Inbhir Nis*/New opinions from Inverness": Alexander Macbain (1855–1907) and the foundation of Celtic Studies in Scotland', *Proceedings of the Society of Antiquaries of Scotland*, 131 (2001), 23–39.

[11] Lachlan MacKinnon (ed.), *Prose writings of Donald MacKinnon* (Edinburgh, Scottish Gaelic Texts Society, 1956), 264–70.

[12] AC, 'Uist old hymns', 46–7.

[13] Ibid. Note that William Jolly was the author of a booklet *The geology of Loch Maree and neighbourhood* (Edinburgh, 1886).

[14] Donald E. Meek, *The quest for Celtic Christianity* (Edinburgh, 2000), 61.

[15] *CG* i, xxix.

[16] Meek, *Quest for Celtic Christianity*, 45–53.

[17] *CG* i, xxix.

[18] John Francis Campbell (ed.), *Popular tales of the West Highlands* (1860–2: 4 vols, Paisley, 1890–3), iii, 119–26; iv, 209–26.

[19] NLS, Adv. MS 50.1.12 fo.333a.

[20] Ibid. fo.324.

[21] Ibid. fo.123.

[22] *CG* i, xxv–xxvi.

[23] *CG* i, xxxv.

[24] Kenneth MacLeod (ed. Thomas M. Murchison), *Sgrìobhaidhean Choinnich MhicLeòid: the Gaelic prose of Kenneth MacLeod* (Edinburgh, Scottish Gaelic Texts Society, 1988), 60.

[25] George Henderson (ed.), *Dàin Iain Ghobha: the poems of John Morison* (2 vols, Glasgow, 1893–6) ii, xxxix–xl.

[26] CW MS 527, not foliated.

[27] CW MS 528A, not foliated.

[28] Ibid.

6

Alexander Carmichael
and the Folklore of the MacMhuirich Poets

WILLIAM GILLIES

There are two main reasons why a paper on Carmichael and the poets is an appropriate ingredient to the proceedings of the present conference: first, because Carmichael was interested in the Clann Mhuirich bards, collected quite a lot of traditions about them, and moreover got most of his most important material in Uist; and second, because Carmichael's MacMhuirich material is reasonably self-contained and manages to capture, in miniature, all the main issues that scholars raise nowadays about his fieldwork and editorial methods. Clann Mhuirich provide, in short, an introduction to the man and his work, at a remove from the *orthachan* which have been at the centre of controversy.[1]

Why was Carmichael so interested in the MacMhuirich poets in the first place? Always allowing for the fact that he was interested in everything that the Gaels themselves were interested in, or which could illuminate their beliefs or way of life, two particular answers to the question suggest themselves. In the first place, the figure of the poet was a special one in Gaelic tradition, for reasons connected with his social standing and important functional role. There was a special curiosity about the slightly shadowy figures of the old professional poets, e.g. in connection with their powers to satirise people who displeased them, or the way in which their inordinate demands had to be satisfied by the chief on whose house they descended. They were part of what made Highland society distinctive. Traditional interest in the poets as a class is reflected in the number of stories and traditions, from all over the Highlands and Islands, about their doings, sayings and powers. They had long since become folkloric figures whose traditions contained their own range of recurrent themes and motifs, including a definite magical or supernatural dimension. As such, the poets could not fail to be of interest to Carmichael, whether as a collector of tales on behalf of Campbell of Islay, or as an investigator of unusual popular beliefs and traditions on his own account.

A second reason for Carmichael's interest in the poets, and especially in the earlier bardic poets, was their association with learning, literacy and manuscripts. As such, they could be seen as prime witnesses to the 'Golden Age' which, as Carmichael fervently believed, had existed before Clearances, Evangelicalism and Emigration destroyed the age-old continuum of traditional Gaelic society. In other words, the older poets could be seen as part of the economically simple, ecologically sound, spiritually harmonious world that gave rise to the *Carmina*. More specifically, they constituted a living rebuttal of the calumnies of pundits like Dr Samuel Johnson, and an antidote to the contempt felt by new-style *uachdarain* for Carmichael's 'beloved Highlanders'. The intellectual roots of this thinking, which surfaces most clearly in the 'Introduction' to the first volume of *Carmina Gadelica*, were tangled. They included, of course, Macpherson's Ossian; but also Dr Johnson's own picture of a patriarchal Highland society, which he went to seek, but did not find, in 1773. They included Rev. Donald MacNicol's rival version, contained in his *Remarks* on Johnson's onslaught on Macpherson. And they assuredly included Renan and Arnold on the Celt. In the same way that proverbs could be seen, not just as a window into the mind-set of the Gaels, but also as an indication that the Gaels possessed a mind-set worthy of the name, so the patronage, etiquette and cultivation of language and writing that was implicit in the practice of court poetry stood as a token of the civility of the Gaelic world.

It has to be admitted that poets and poetry in general do not figure largely in *CG*. That is partly because of the folkloric focus of the latter, which determines the content of the small number of references to poets in it. Alasdair Camshron (Bàrd Thùrnaig) is cited on account of the *ortha leigheis* ('curing charm') he knew and not because of any excellence in his poetry (*CG* iv, 302–3); and Iain Lom and Alasdair mac Mhaighstir Alasdair are quoted for their use of the phrase *Uidhist nan cràghiadh* 'Uist of the sheldrakes' (*CG* ii, 258) for ornithological rather than literary reasons. The Carmichael Watson Papers as a whole show many more references to poets and their works from different periods and different parts of the Highlands, including such 'big names' as Iain Lom, Mac Mhaighstir Alasdair, Rob Donn, Duncan Bàn and William Ross, together with many nineteenth-century bards, copious examples of *òrain luaidh*, and traditions of the *Cliar Sheanchain* and Aonghas nan Aoir.[2] But some of the material about the MacMhuirichs, exceptionally, found its way into *CG* (v, 305–19). Significantly, this material is placed next to a section containing poems and traditions relating to the drowning of Iain Garbh MacGilleChaluim of Raasay in 1671. That episode was notable for the widespread belief that the drowning was the result of witchcraft. And we shall see that such supernatural connotations were also present in the literature about Clann Mhuirich; for the archetypal Mac Mhuirich figure, sometimes simply called 'Mac Mhuirich (Mór)' by name, was often called on to engage with witches, or the devil, or an *uilebheist* ('monster') or *sìdhichean* ('fairies'). In his Editorial Note prefaced to *CG* iv James Carmichael Watson revealed the intended scope of the following volume: it was to contain 'a large body of prose and verse concerning fairies and other supernatural beings'.[3] That is a fair indication of the context in which Alexander Carmichael viewed the Clann Mhuirich material.

It may be useful at this point to step back and remind ourselves of some of the special attributes of poets and poetry in Gaelic tradition in general. The fundamental distinguishing feature of the poets is their special way with words. Not only do they have a fine turn of phrase, but they can 'cut a verse' extemporaneously when needed. This power can manifest itself competitively when two poets meet, but it is present in potential all the time, surfacing when circumstances challenge the poet to reveal himself, for example when the power of producing the right words is needed to respond to a personal or communal happening of significance. Sometimes the power shows itself at an early stage, when the precocious words of an infant or child indicate a poet in the making. Often one senses that the poet becomes somehow removed from the rest of us when composing poetry, whether he (or she) is in touch with something that we cannot be privy to, or is somehow 'possessed' by the spirit of poetry. Sometimes poetry is in the poets' genes, because we find that their people included similarly gifted people; and sometimes it lies dormant until brought into being by a life-altering event, such as illness or loss of sight or religious conversion or the death of dear ones. In traditional accounts of poets it is sometimes said that they owe their poetry to an encounter with otherworld beings, such as fairies or witches, who perhaps offer mind-transforming food or drink, or suggest a bargain in which something has to be pledged in return for the gift of poetry. (Similar stories are of course told about other types of artists, for instance pipers or story-tellers, with the same underlying premise that art is a magical or otherworldly gift.) Examples of poets possessing paranormal powers are also found: for example knowledge at a distance, or knowledge of things yet to happen. The cumulative effect of the many tales and anecdotes which assert these traits of the poets is to create and reinforce an image which emphasises how different they are from us 'ordinary mortals', and underlines their power to influence the course of nature by their gift of words. Because they can cause harm to those who displease them, they are potentially dangerous and we have to handle them carefully, even today.

The above characteristics are not meant to be exhaustive, but typical and indicative. They are freely associated with recent Gaelic bards, but in most ways they can also be shown, by unmistakably similar references in Early Gaelic literature, to have existed for centuries. Modern Irish folk tradition has many parallels. They may therefore be thought of as 'Gaelic' in the widest sense of the word. When one is dealing with the older, more learned sorts of Gaelic poet, the *filidhean* or *aos dàna*, one is more conscious of the arcane aspects of the poetic image—the 'mystery' or 'mystique' of their craft—and those aspects of their image which overlap with *fiosachd* 'foreknowledge, divination' or *buidseachd* 'witch-craft, wizard-craft'. I have suggested elsewhere that this magical or supernatural aura, as we find it in Gaelic popular tradition, reflects a self-protective patina deliberately cultivated by the freemasonry of the learned, professional poets.[4]

Armed with these general expectations we may now attempt to summarise the modern traditions about Clann Mhuirich which have appeared in print or been recorded on tape. It will be seen that they conform well to the expectations we have formed on general grounds, but with some interesting additions. I should add a warning at this point. This synopsis is based on a sample of what has been current in oral tradition about Clann Mhuirich since the mid-twentieth century. By then, interest in Gaelic folklore had been stimulated by a new generation of collectors like John Lorne Campbell, Margaret Fay Shaw, Calum I. Maclean and William Matheson. This in its turn had led to collections by 'insiders' like Domhnall Iain MacDhomhnaill (Domhnall Iain Dhonnchaidh) and Iain Mac a' Phì, and to systematic fieldwork by staff from the School of Scottish Studies. The involvement of the 'insiders', and the growing expertise of such fieldworkers as James Ross, Donald Archie MacDonald and John MacInnes in pinpointing the best informants and teasing out the 'best' and 'most important' information, give a timeless quality to the material captured in those pre-TV days. But it has two major shortcomings. First, it is at best a 'still', a snapshot of something that was intrinsically dynamic. And second, it is incomplete: the 'picture' we can assemble on the basis of what has been collected inevitably has pieces missing from it. Maybe a crucial informant was indisposed or absent when the School of Scottish Studies field-worker called, or was overlooked when the list of informants was being made up. For instance, Donald Alasdair Johnson, Àird Mhór, was completely overlooked until Angus John MacDonald knocked on his door in 1969. Neither the School's field-workers nor the local informants had thought of asking him for tales because he was outside the circle of people known locally as active tradition-bearers.[5] As a consequence of all this, my account may omit items or versions known to people today. My colleagues in the School of Scottish Studies and I would be the first to rejoice if such additional material were to come to light as a result of this volume.

In the research project which Barbara Hillers and I undertook in 1999–2000 we attempted to categorise the MacMhuirich material known to us from recorded, printed and MS sources. The main groupings turned out to be as follows:

1. Power over the Elements, represented by a widely known account usually entitled *Achain* (or *Achanaich* or *Athchuinge*) *Mhic Mhuirich Mhóir*, in which Mac Mhuirich is credited with the power to summon up a gale of wind.
2. Confrontation with other sources of supernatural power, in which Mac Mhuirich faces and outwits a Monster, or Witches, or the Fairies, or the Devil, or the King of the Cats.
3. Dealings in the human world, in which Mac Mhuirich sees through the deceit of a niggardly hostess, or outpoints another bard in verbal repartee, or sets up a clever way of ensuring that his guests do not lack food or drink; i.e. he displays superior discernment, mental agility and ingenuity.
4. *Seanchas* of Clann Mhuirich, in which we learn about the Red Book which was the key to the family fortunes, including how Mac Mhuirich learned to read it, and about its disappearance and possible location; also various items relating to the family, including the precocious verbal powers of individual family members, their tenure of land as Clanranald's poets and historians, and the location of their residence at Stadhlaigearraidh.

By comparison with material relating to other learned poetic families, the popular lore concerning the MacMhuirichs is copious. Nothing comparable survives in connection with the MacEwen poets of the Campbells, and only a little is preserved in relation to the Uí Mhuirgheasáin poets of the Macleans and MacLeods. This could be explained partly by reference to an earlier decline in the richness of Gaelic tradition in Argyll, and partly by the fact that the Clanranald chiefs continued to support a traditional Gaelic cultural ambience for longer than their counterparts in other parts of the Hebrides. Thinking of the Gaelic tradition as a whole, one could also suggest that the MacMhuirichs had come to be seen as the learned poetic family *par excellence*, in the same way that the Beaton physicians, the only other learned family with traditions as widespread as those of the MacMhuirichs, became the 'type' of the Gaelic medical family. Whereas stories about the majority of more recent poets, such as Iain Lom or Rob Donn, include some supernatural elements, they are on the whole more closely comparable to the stories about Mac Mhuirich having dealings in the human world. In other words, the more supernatural aspects of the MacMhuirich corpus and image are what is striking and distinctive for the image of the family.

The sources of our information about Clann ('ic) Mhuirich include some of the most revered informants of the twentieth century from the Hebrides as a whole: Nan Mackinnon from Vatersay, Ruairi MacPherson from Barra, Angus Mackinnon from Eigg, Donald Sinclair from Tiree, to name just a few. But when one looks more closely at the evidence, one finds that the densest concentration of information comes, not surprisingly, from South Uist and Benbecula. The further one goes beyond the 'homeland' of Clann Mhuirich, the more their lore is confined to the most famous stories (in particular the Raising of the Storm) and the most exceptionally learned informants. Conversely, the closer one comes to Stadhlaigearraidh, the more likely one is to find additional, less well attested stories and anecdotes and local legends. A similar point may be made at a more local level. Some of the most respected of Uist tradition-bearers are represented amongst those who have given MacMhuirich lore to the collectors: e.g. Angus MacLellan (Aonghas Beag), Donald John MacDonald (Domhnall Iain Dhonnchaidh), Mrs Mary Ann MacInnes and Michael Macintyre. But the most noticeable feature is the sheer density of informants, including people best known for songs or genealogy or place-names, who were able to give stories and *seanchas* about Clann Mhuirich. From my own enquiries, starting back in my student days, I can confirm this: there was a solid core of tradition about Clann Mhuirich, known at least in outline by just about everybody. I believe this is still the case amongst people of my own age or above, and comments at the Conference have borne this out. When one considers the depth of detailed knowledge now available about 'Who was Who' in Uist, and the exemplary detective work which Angus Macmillan and his colleagues in Taigh Eachdraidh Bheinn na Faoghla have done in regard to Carmichael's Benbecula informants, it becomes clear that we can greatly enhance our understanding of how our Gaelic tradition works by more minute research into specific areas of communal interest and pride like Clann Mhuirich.

We may now turn the clock back and look at what Alexander Carmichael found in the same locality a century earlier, and what he made of it in *CG*. In view of the questions that have been raised about his methods we shall exclude the published texts in the first instance and start with the texts recorded in CW, which show many signs of being authentic recordings, or nearly so. The first step will therefore be to ascertain how the items preserved in CW compare with twentieth-century oral tradition. Of the categories of Clann Mhuirich material outlined above, Carmichael's papers contain (1) two substantial tales telling of encounters with a supernatural creature termed *A' Bhéisd* or *A' Bhiast*, plus an additional version of the song sung by the Beast; (2) several other supernatural encounters (in brief or summary form); (3) stories about the origins of Clann Mhuirich; and (4) anecdotal and incidental information about the historical family as bards to Clanranald and Uist landholders.[6]

Carmichael's versions of the tale of Mac Mhuirich and the Beast are essentially the same as that summarised by Domhnall Iain MacDhomhnaill in his *Uibhist a Deas*.[7] They tell how Mac Mhuirich got power over the Beast by capturing her young, and forced her to perform magically aided tasks—for example, to build him a grand new byre and to build a causeway across Loch Langanais. Domhnall Iain's version is basically a report of a tale, but even so it contains some vivid language evoking the style of a fully formed tale. Carmichael has more of this, as in the following exchange between Mac Mhuirich and his wife, taken from 'Mac Mhuirich Mór' in CW MS 126(c):

> 'Gu de an creatair a ta agad an sin?' deir a bhean ris—boirionach mor mor briagha. 'An ta, tha creatair a fhuair mi fo sgath creaige a muigh anns a bheinn.' 'An ta, cuir a mach e, cuir a mach e, agus cuir a mach gu h-ealamh cuideachd e. Is e a chuireas a chrois ma do cheann agus an campar ma do chridhe.' 'Fagaidh mi mar seo fhein an trasd e, fiach ciamar a dh'eireas dhomh.' 'O,' ars a bhean, 'is beag 's fhios duit gu de thainig na bhuil, agus cuir uat e agus cuir uat gu brath cuideachd e.' Cha chuireadh ri a bheo no ri a mharbh easan uaithe an cuilein.

> *'What is that creature you have there?' said his wife to him—a great big handsome woman (she was). 'Well, a creature that I found sheltering under a rock out in the moor.' 'Well, put it out, put it out, and put it out quickly too. It will surely bring affliction on your head and vexation on your heart.' 'I'll leave it just as it is for now, to see how I get on.' 'Oh', said his wife, 'You little know what has come with it, so put it away from you, and put it away forever too.' Dead or alive, he would not get rid of the whelp.*

Note that the text of the tale is rough in many ways. (I have added some punctuation in the above passage, but the spellings are as in the MS.) Although one cannot absolutely exclude the possibility that the roughness is the result of artifice, I am strongly inclined to take these MS versions at their face value, as records of what Carmichael took down from his informants, with a small number of incidental and transparent 'notes to self', and no cosmetic or other editorial interference to speak of. The style of the *sgeulaiche* rings true in this excerpt.[8] And the same is true of the substance and purpose of the tale as a whole. It is convincing at three levels of explanation: (1) folkloristically, in that it fulfils the requirements for an international type of bargain tale, where a hero outwits a supernatural adversary; (2) aetiologically, in that it explains the origins of old ruins and an old causeway, part of the real landscape of Uist; and (3) 'mythologically', in that it contributes to a dossier of texts which perpetuate the image or 'legend' of Clann Mhuirich as something more than historical characters in Uist tradition.

Carmichael also took down an anecdote about Mac Mhuirich and Fairies; much more summary in its form, but with just a hint that it had once been a proper tale. I give it in full here from a loose leaf now tucked into CW MS 126(c), as a further illustration of the texture of the raw data.[9]

> Mac Mhuirich was losing his cattle le dosgaidh [call a chodach *added above line*] and what was left was only bodaich (fairy pha[n]toms of men app…). He ~~said~~ sat on a sithean thinking about his losses agus e n duil nach bitheadh ana toir air fhagail aig as an tsaoghail [am farrin air airinn air uachdar fuinn aige *added above line*] agus chual e gul agus caoidh san t-sithean fodha.
>
>   'Heist thus a lurain Huist a bhroin
>   'S d uair a shuitheachar clar fuinne
>   Mhic Mhuirich Mhoir
> Gheobh thus lan do leoir.'
> Thainig Mac Mhuirich dhachaidh a breineachadh air briathran a chual e. Chaidh e staigh dhan chitsin ge nach robh e a staigh riamh roimhe ann. Bha a bhean fhuine a toiseachadh ri fuinne. Thuiteadh cnap taois an drast agus cnap taois a rist uaipe agus cha leigheadh [*sc.* leigeadh] an naire leis an nighinn cromadh dan togail. Ach mu dheireadh thuit bredaig uaipe agus bha so mutha agus mor lethe chail agus chrom i ga togail–Bha slat do chaoil dubh an dorn Mhic Mhuirich agus thug e clibheag ~~san~~ an cul an duirn dha'n nighinn dhi. 'Fhad agus a sheasas tu an mo thaighs rid bheo mhaireann shaoghail na tog grcim a thuiteas bho'n chlar fhuinne Is ioma beul feumach tha a feitheamh air.' Cha ro la an deigh sin tuillidh nach robh Mac Mhuirich dol chon tullach nan sithean agus a dortadh a bhainne b fhearr mu mhullach an t-sithein dha na sithich. Cha do chaill Mac Mhuirich beothach le di no le dosgaidh riamh tuillidh.

The bilingual opening, the glosses and the false starts hardly appear contrived, and the simplest explanation is that the collector began by expecting to make a bare note of a snippet of lore, then found it expedient to slip into recording mode, and finally went over the beginning of the text adding in a couple of Gaelic phrases he recalled, having omitted them at the outset.[10] As for the story, it splices a commonplace item of fairy lore onto Clann Mhuirich. Its 'message' is that Mac Mhuirich was able to deal successfully with fairy depredations. The more fully recorded part contains snatches of a developed and effective oral narrative style.

We may turn now to the origin legends and *seanchas* about Clann Mhuirich. One of the most important texts, contained in CW MS 112 fos.86–9, is headed:

> Leabhar Dearg Chlann Mhuirich
> Seanachaidh Seonaid Nic Mhuirich
> Staoin~~braic~~ brig Uist D. aois 64
> Sgriobhta Faoilteach 24[mh] 1865

The text which immediately follows it in Carmichael's notebook (*Do'ull Gearr no Cearr*, contained on fos.89[v]–91[v]) carries the superscription *Bho an bhoiroinnach chiadna 24/2 1865* ('From the same woman . . .'); i.e. it was recorded on the same day as the preceding text. It concludes: *Chuala Seonaid Churri ('Seonaid Mhor') seo bho sheann duine, Do'null Currai Mac Mhuirich ann an Ormaclait'* ('Janet Currie ('Big Janet') heard this from an old man, Donald Currie

MacMhuirich in Ormacleit'). The degree of formality in the presentation of these texts, and the attention to sources, shows Carmichael took this material seriously. As for Janet Currie, not only was she of the family of the MacMhuirich bards, but her lore was explicitly associated with them. Hector Maclean, one of Campbell of Islay's collectors, who had visited Janet on 12 September 1860, wrote as follows in relation to her version of *Cànain nan Eun*:

> From Janet Currie Ston(e)y-Bridge, South Uist, who learnt it from her father about forty years ago. Her father died about 20 years ago and was past 85 years of age. He learnt it from Eachann Mac Mhurchaidh Mhic Alasdair D(h)omhnulla(i)ch, a maternal uncle of his who died before Quebec was taken by the English, which took place September 13th, 1759. This MacDonald learnt it in his youth from Niall Mac Lachuinn Mhic Dhomhnuill Mhic Mhic Mhuirich, and it came to him from Neil Currie the bard.[11]

Although this statement is not without its puzzles, the claim to authority is strong and plausible.

Leabhar Dearg Chlann Mhuirich ('The Red Book of the MacMhuirichs') tells how the original Muireach, the son of an Earl, was on the run after the death of his father and his father's people. Like Elijah in the desert, he was lying exhausted when he heard a voice which told him to uproot the clump of rushes on which his head was resting. On doing this he found the Book *cho glan agus cho tiorram agus ge do bhitheadh e ann an ciste* ('as clean and dry as though it had been in a chest'). He read the Book, *agus thainig a sin spiorad-[fh]iosaid (innsidh) thuige agus dh'innis an spiorad [fh]iosaid da cait an reachadh e* ('and then a spirit of discernment ([i.e.] telling) came to him, and the spirit of discernment told him where he should go').

> Thog a sin mac og an Iarla air agus cha d-rinn e stad no fois gus an d-rainig (tainig) e Uist-a-chinn-a-Tuath. Ghabh e tuinneachas an Uist-a-Tuath agus ann an am phos e agus b-e mhac Niall Mor Mac Mhuirich. Is e Muireach a b-ainm do mhac an Iarla. Is ann o'n fhear so thainig Clann Mhuirich agus sin mar a fhuaradh Leabhar Dearg Chlann Mhuirich.
>
> *Then the young son of the Earl set off, and he did not stop or rest until he reached (came to) North Uist. He settled in North Uist, and in time he married and his son was Niall Mór Mac Mhuirich. Muireach was the Earl's son's name. It was from this man that Clann Mhuirich are descended, and that is how the Red Book of Clann Mhuirich was found.*

At this point the story-teller interjected a short version of the story of Niall Mór's Three Wishes and the summoning up of the Storm, as found in more recent oral tradition. She then reverted to Muireach and the contents of the Red Book:

> Bha an leabhar ag innseadh mar a chruthaicheadh an saoghal agus na daoine bh'ann—bha fine agus slioc bha riamh ann o ghlun gu glun. Bha Muireach a falbh feadh Eirinn us Alba g-innseadh seanachais agus sloinneadh. Cha robh de[igh-]theach an Alba no'n Eirinn air nach robh cain bonna h-oc aig airson a bhi g-innseadh sloinntireac.
>
> *The Book told how the world was created, and the people who were in it–[every] tribe and race that ever existed, from generation to generation. Muireach travelled throughout Ireland and Scotland relating history and genealogy. There was not a noble house (?) in Scotland or Ireland from which he did not exact a payment of an eight-penny piece in return for reciting people's family trees.*

The narrative concludes with a note that at a subsequent time a stranger came and asked for a loan of the Red Book so that he could copy it. 'Mac Mhuirich gave the book to his kinsman, and nothing has been seen or heard of the Red Book from that time to this.' This episode has been taken as a folk memory of James 'Ossian' Macpherson's trip to the Highlands in 1760 in search of manuscripts containing ancient ballads which could count as the originals of the oral epics he claimed to have collected orally and translated. For present purposes, the point to note is that, although this is not stated explicitly, the implication is clearly that, just as the finding of the Book presaged the good fortune of the family, so its loss coincided with the end of their period of glory.

The second of Janet Currie's tales starts where the previous story left off, and explains how Muireach's son Niall Mór was living in North Uist but fell out with 'Lady MacDonald' and was expelled at her instance. He headed south to Mac Mhic Ailein, who welcomed him and gave him *còraichean* ('[written] rights, titles') but his son Domhnall lost these when his second wife burned them in order to prevent his first wife's children from inheriting his estate. Again, although this is not made perfectly clear in the narrative as we have it, the point of the episode is to assert that there was going to come a time when the lack of these *còraichean* would stand Clann Mhuirich in bad stead. Janet then went on to tell more about Domhnall himself, explaining how he had been sired by Niall Mór illegitimately during the course of his removal from North to South Uist. The outraged husband expelled his wife and her baby boy, who wandered until they met the legitimate daughter of Niall Mór, who recognised her sibling and brought the pair to her father. This enabled Niall Mór to make preparation, and effect a reconciliation between the woman and her husband. Finally, almost as afterthought, we are given some additional information regarding the outcome of Niall Mór's quarrel with MacDonald's lady:

> Mu'n d-fhag Niall Mor an Ceann a Tuath chaidh e stigh far an robh a ~~bhana~~ Bhan-mhorair agus shin e a lamh di agus thuirst—Slan leibh o na tha mi falbh cha'n eil toill agam a bhi'n droch run a dh'aon eir bith." Shin ise a lamh dha agus am priobaid cha ro falt eir a ceann no bian no inean eir a lamhan no eir a casan, nach d-fhag i agus dh-fhag Niall Mor a siod i na lo[bh]ran maol carrach rua.
>
> Chuir am Moraire a sin fios thun Mhic ic Ailein na geasan fo'n do chuir Niall Mor a bhaintighearna agus thug Mac ic Ailein eir dol eir ais agus a cruithioc fhein a thoirst thice. Chai Niall Mor ann eir ailios a Mhoraire—agus thug am Moraire dha or agus airgiod greidh agus tain gu leoir.

> *Before Niall Mór left North Uist he went in where Lady (MacDonald) was, and stretched out his hand to her and said, 'Farewell to you. Since I am departing I do not wish to be in a state of ill-will with anyone.' She stretched out her hand, and in a flash there was no hair on her head, and no skin or nails on her hands or her feet that did not leave her. And Niall Mór left her there, a bald, scurvy, ruddy leper. Lord (MacDonald) then informed Clanranald of the spells under which Niall Mór had put his lady, and Clanranald compelled him to go back and send her back her own form. Niall Mór went there at His Lordship's desire, and His Lordship gave him gold and silver, horses and cattle in plenty.*

The point of this closing section, though perhaps not of the tale as a whole, is clearly to emphasise the recurrent theme that it is dangerous to cross one's poet, and beneficial to be good to him. In folkloric terms it is a bit of a pastiche, but it has its part to play within the 'MacMhuirich Cycle' of tales.

If one takes the CW texts about Clann Mhuirich together, a similar point may be made. There are numerous folktale motifs around, but they tend to be of secondary importance, the credentials of the family being the fundamental preoccupation. I have argued in *Scottish Gaelic Studies* that we have here, in a slightly broken-down form, a group of family origin legends, of the sort we more frequently find underpinning an aristocratic dynasty, but in this case being applied to a poetic family. Such themes as the expulsion and wandering and the illegitimacy of dynastic originators are strongly reminiscent of the Heroic Biographical Pattern, as is the special gift of *fiosachd* and indeed the possession of the magically discovered Red Book. As to medium, we have glimpsed some of the stylistic traits of Gaelic oral story-telling, but in a less inflated and *bravura* style than the Gaelic heroic-romantic tales. In literary terms they may have stood somewhat as the Early Gaelic 'Cycles of Kings' did in relation to the Ulster Cycle of tales.[12]

An intriguing issue here, from the historical point of view, is the supposed North Uist phase of Clann Mhuirich, which is not paralleled in other sources for the family. In *Scottish Gaelic Studies* I took the line that one could explain it all away as literary *cum* genealogical fiction, and suggested that 'North Uist' might be no more than a cipher for 'pre-South Uist' in relation to the family's movements. I argued there that (1) this sort of dynastic origin legend needs a 'Wandering' phase before the founding hero finally arrives in the place his descendants will inhabit; and (2) there are suspiciously close parallels between the story of Niall Mór's rift with 'Lord MacDonald' (a problematic title in any case) and the rift between the family's eponymous ancestor, Muireadhach Ó Dálaigh, and Ó Domhnaill in Ireland. However, I had to admit that there could perfectly well be a grain of historical truth in the legend. For the period in question would have been the turbulent and sparsely documented sixteenth century; and if a MacMhuirich poet had briefly served with another branch of Clan Donald in those times, between leaving the service of the defunct Lordship of the Isles and taking up permanent residence with Mac 'ic Ailein, this episode might well not have a 'footprint' outside the memory of the family itself.[13] At the end of the day, it comes down to our estimate of the sources. If Carmichael went out of his way to consult the descendants of the MacMhuirich bardic family themselves, would the likes of Janet Currie have been so mischievously motivated, or could they have been so misinformed or mistaken, as to misrepresent the facts in this way? The difficulty is, of course, that the sort of families that had origin legends also had genealogies that were liable to pedigree making and faking of a more deliberate and sustained sort than is usual in oral-traditional family history.[14]

Turning now to the MacMhuirich material published in *CG*, we may begin our comparison between the manuscript and the published texts with the famous episode of Mac Mhuirich's Three Wishes and the Storm. In the CW story *Leabhar Dearg Chlann Mhuirich*, the story-teller's mention of Niall Mór, son of the eponymous Muireach, led her to interject an account of Niall, beginning *Be Niall Mor mac Mhuirich so aig an robh na tri iarrtais is an la fad a bheatha bho Dhia* ('It was this Niall MacMhuirich who had the three wishes per day all his life from God'). The passage describes briefly how Niall was moved to use his wishes, and is a summary of the tale found in *CG* and elsewhere. The suggestion that the wishes were God-given rather than 'druidical' is perhaps unusual. But this need not be a recent interpolation; it is reminiscent of the way the Early Gaelic saints cursed people with the preamble *Is cead liom más cead le Dia . . .* ('It's fine by me if it's fine by God . . .'). The style of the passage in CW is fairly bald and summary, though there are hints of a more polished sort of phrasing in the dialogue, and the wishes themselves are in verse. There are also some signs of disjointedness and other indications of field-work conditions, with the field-worker taking down a recitation and trying to cope with difficult words in the by-going. In all these respects the passage about Niall's Three Wishes is consistent with *Leabhar Dearg Chlann Mhuirich* as a whole. The concluding sentences show all these features.[15]

Thog iad a sin bho thir agus thainig stoirm agus doireann nan deigh an deigh dhaibh togail ri cua[n]. Thuirt a mhac a sin "Athair atharraichibh an soireas (soirbheas) mum bi sinn caillte." A bhalaich chan iarrainn-se an treas iarratas air mo Chruithear ga do bhitheadh-mid anns na liathagan. (Rud a bhitheas a cinntinn air ceann stamh)

Thainig a sin biorlainn (birlinn) nan sia rathach (ramhach) gu amar a Mhoile Tuath agus chaidh i na cliathan (na da-leth) ach leum na daoine aiste agus shabhaladh iad. Bha fios aig Niall Mor gun sabhailte iad Mar bitheadh dh-iarradh e an treas iarratas. B'iad an sgioba bha leis mac Mhuirich (a mhac fhein) Mac Mhairis Guinneach agus Loinneach Fionnla a ghille fhein. Cha'n abradh gach fear an sgioba ach taom a bhirlinn Fhionnlaidh Ach an la so chunnaig Niall Mor gun robh rud ri fhaotainn am Fionnladh agus thuirt e "Uam mac Mhuirich 's uam mac Mhairis uam na Guinnich s uam na Loinnich 's uam iad uil ach Fionnladh. (Sean-fhacall) (O nach fear sgiob thu taom an t-eathar)

I take the material in brackets at face value, as explanatory glosses and additions made by Carmichael at or near the time when he recorded this material from Janet Currie, on 24 January 1865.

When we turn to *CG* we find (v, 306–14), under the heading *Achain Mhic Mhuirich / MacVurich's Requests* two distinct tellings of the episode just reported from CW. What I will call Version A is at 306–9, and Version B is at 310–14. There are some clear verbal correspondences, though they also contain some divergences in detail, between CW, Version A and Version B, e.g.:

> Bha iad fichead la *ri port* ann an Cannaidh (CW)
> Bha e *ri post* [*with* '= port' *in footnote*] ann an Canaidh turas (Version A)
> . . . 'd é ach gun robh e *ri port* . . . (Version B)

Again, after Mac Mhuirich has summoned a breeze, his son says importunately that this is not enough:

> "*Is bog similidh d'iarratas* agus cathag oirnn" ars a mhac. (CW)
> '*Is bog similidh socharach a dh'iarr thu* a' ghaoth,' orsa fear dha na gillean. (Version A)
> Sin thubhairt an gille gun tonaisg: '*Is bog balbh t'iarratas*, athair' (Version B)

Both Version A and Version B show signs of the 'roughness' that we have seen in CW. Version A, for instance, has the footnote explaining that *post* is *port*, presumably indicating how Carmichael first heard the word and what he then realised it had to be. In both Version A and Version B the verse requesting a breeze has variants enclosed in square brackets in *CG*. Version A has:

> Soirbheas gun tiomadh gun abhsadh
>   [toirmeasg gun fhusadh]

Version B has:

> Gaoth gun fhusadh gun fhiar gun amhsadh
>   [fhùbhsadh; iorram, iorral, iorralt]

There is also a further version subjoined to Version A (*CG* v, 308) with the words *Dòigh eile air rainn mhic Mhuirich Mhóir* ('Another version of Mac Mhuirich Mór's verses'):[16]

> Soirbheas gun iomram gun abhsadh
> [chiorram]

We are not told whether these alternatives within each Version are variants reported by the informant to the field-worker, or variants known to the field-worker from elsewhere, or attempts by the field-worker to make sense of difficult words. But the impression that we are grappling with an old and difficult piece of text with traditionally known variants is unmistakable.

The same apparent roughness is evident also in the description of the storm-tossed boat's arrival in Uist in Version A, which has *An uair a rànaig iad Loch Einneort (Loch Sgiobort?)* . . . Why the doubt as to the place of landfall? The suggestion is that there were variant traditions. (Version B does not mention the place of landfall; CW, as we have seen, gave it as the Mol a Deas.) Again, in Version B the breeze is described as *ciùchar (ciabharan) beag bochd gaoith* (translated in *CG* as 'a low slow moan of wind'), where once again one gets an impression of alternative 'readings', and a suggestion that we are somehow near to the living moment of the recording of an old or difficult tale.

But can we draw the conclusions that are so clearly being suggested to us? The late Dr Alan Bruford published in *Scottish Gaelic Studies* some years ago a detailed analysis of the ways in which Carmichael re-wrote the version of *Eachdraidh Chlann Uisne* he had collected in Barra to create the text he published in *Deirdire*.[17] Bruford was able to do this because he had discovered an earlier transcription amongst the Carmichael Watson Papers. The categories of alteration in the case of the Deirdre story went well beyond editorial tidying up or scholarly rationalisation, though there were plenty of examples of these. Bruford demonstrated that, in effect, Carmichael had created a new literary tone, quite distinct from anything he could have recorded in Barra or anywhere else in the Gaelic world, and a whole new register of language to be its vehicle. We do not have such a clear-cut set of materials to work with, unless the 'originals' of Versions A and B should turn up in the Carmichael Watson Papers. On the other hand, I am in no doubt that some of the categories of alteration which Bruford diagnosed are present in *Achain Mhic Mhuirich*. A few examples should make this clear.

Note first some 'asides', in which the story-teller (as it were) interjects incidental comments to us, the audience:

> Thuig Mac Mhuirich gun robh am boireannach sgìth dheth fhéin agus dhe dhaoine—'s *a Mhoire's a Mhic, 's cinnteach gun robh an t-adhbhar aice!* (Version A)
> Thuig Mac Mhuirich gu robh am boireannach còir sgìth dhiubh—*agus m'anam fhéin, cha b'ioghnadh dhì!* (Version B)

Because the CW version is in such a summary form we need not be surprised that it contains neither the motivational explanation nor the exclamation. The former may or may not have been in the 'original', but the latter ('Mary Mother and Son, it is certain that she had (good) reason!' and 'Upon my soul, it was no wonder she (was)!') is almost certainly an editorial intrusion, designed to give a reader a sense of being near to the story-teller's performance of the tale. The same is true of the following:

> Thànaig a sin a' ghaoth, agus b'i sin a' ghaoth, agus dh'éirich a' mhuir, agus *a Mhoire, Màthair nan gràs, b'i sin a' mhuir ghrànda!* (Version A, not in Version B)

Exclamations like these do not occur in the MS versions in CW for the simple reason that there were more important, structurally essential things to write down.[18] There are also cases where the laconic narrative style of the CW *Leabhar Dearg Chlann Mhuirich* is replaced by a more modulated, literate tone. Where CW says that Mac Mhuirich was once at Canna, Version A adds *mar as minig a bha, a null agus a nall eadar Uibhist agus Mùideart* (translated 'as he often was when back and fore between Uist and Moidart'). In Version B this becomes even more a product of 'written' literature, despite the informal, conversational start to the sentence: *Turas bha sin bha Mac Mhuirich Mór a' tilleadh a dh'Uibhist o Mhùideart, o Chaisteal Tioram, rathad nach b'ainmig e a' siubhal . . .* (translated 'Once upon a time MacVurich Mór was returning to Uist from Moidart, from Castle Tirrim, a route he not infrequently travelled . . .'). Moreover, instead of being laid up at Canna, Version B has Mac Mhuirich *ri port rathad nan Garbhchrioch no rathad nan Eileana Caola—Canaidh Rum no Eige* (translated 'lying somewhere in the Rough Bounds or in the Small Isles—Canna, Rum or Eigg'). This is not oral story-telling but armchair travelogue with scholarly notes woven in for good measure.

In addition to this stylistic manipulation it is noteworthy that both Version A and B contain echoes of 'runs', i.e. formulaic passages of heightened description, for the setting off of the boat and the rigours of the storm. Version A has . . . *an t-eathar an dara turas a' froslaich nam faochaga dubh far feaman na tarraing ann an aigeal a' chuain, agus an turas eile shuas air farabharra nam beann* (translated 'the vessel at one time showering the black whelks from the draught seaweed at the bottom of the ocean, the next time up on the very tops of the mountainous seas'). And Version B has . . . *thog iad na siùil mhìne bhreaca bhaidealach ri barr nan crann fiùbhaidh fada fulannach* (translated '. . . they hoisted the smooth speckled towering sails to the tops of the tall enduring masts of wood'). These 'runs' and similar were a feature of the heroic-romantic tales, and were rightly seen by John Francis Campbell (1821–85) and his collectors as signs of antiquity and prestige. I do not think we should expect them to appear in tales of the present sort, and fear they may be interpolations by Carmichael, designed to give an inflated impression of the 'status' of the tale, but in reality a give-away that the editorial pen has been at work.

Equally worryingly, I have to report a similar unease in regard to some of the verse. In CW and in Version A (first alternative) the sequence of wishes is (1) wish for a breeze, (2) wish for a gale, and (3) refusal to wish for the gale to be stilled. By contrast, Version A (second alternative) inserts an additional wish between the breeze and the gale:

> 'Is lag leibideach a dh'iarr thu agus mi fhéin air an stiùir,' ars a mhac.
> 'Gaoth tuath co cruaidh ri slait
>   A' sineagaich ri bial a stuic   [ri bruaich
> Mar earba ruadh is i 'na h-airc
>   Teurnadh le ceann cam cruaidh cnuic.'

This is translated as:

> 'Weakly and contemptibly hast thou asked for it seeing I myself am at the helm,' said his son.
> 'A north wind hard as a rod
>   Bounding past her gunwale,
> Like a red roe in dire distress
>   Descending the hard rugged peak of a hill.'

I know that one can find in Gaelic poetry passages in which the boat races through the waves or the deer races down the glen with hounds in close attendance: poems like Murchadh

Mór mac 'ic Mhurchaidh's *An Làir Dhonn* and Domhnall mac Fhionnlaigh nan Dàn's *Òran na Comhachaig* come to mind. But this is not in the same league as those emorable passages in terms of poetic aptness. The idea of the wind (surely this should have been the wave?) 'bounding' is inappropriate to the 'wind like a rod', which is itself uneasy in Gaelic poetic terms; while the flight of the roe is equally unfortunate as an analogue to a biting wind, and quite unlike the sensually accurate imagery of traditional Gaelic verse. I am afraid this is a poetically inept fabrication. I have similar feelings about the corresponding passage in Version B, which retains the presumably original pattern of 'two wishes expended, one kept in reserve', but expands the son's comment into a verse:

> Sin thubhairt an gille gun tonaisg:
> 'Is bog balbh t'iarratas, athair,
>   Sinne 's an là d'ar tréigsinn,
> A' ghrian a' laighe air Heacala
>   'S gun trian dha'n astar 'nar déidh-ne.

Carmichael translated this as:

> Then the lad without sense said:
> 'Soft and dumb thine asking, father,
>   And the day fast forsaking us,
> The sun is setting upon Hekla
>   And not a third of the distance behind us.'

I take the superfluous incidental colouring of *gun tonaisg* as a warning sign that we are moving from oral tales to written literature. In the verse itself I am unconvinced by *balbh* 'dumb' as a descriptor of the 'request', and by the idea of 'the day forsaking us' ('fast' is not in the Gaelic). None of this is in CW, I need hardly add. It looks as though here too we may have evidence for Carmichael trying his hand as a versifier. To conclude, although we lack the means to make the direct comparisons that Bruford could make in the case of the Deirdre story, it can hardly be doubted that *Achain Mhic Mhuirich* as we have it in *CG* has been 'improved' by its editor. Reinforcement for this conclusion comes from *Mac Mhuirich Mór agus a' Bhéist*, to which we now turn.

Where the summary CW version of The Three Wishes corresponds to two (or two and a half) narratives in *CG*, the proportion is reversed for the story of Mac Mhuirich and the Beast: the CW MSS contain two separate accounts of this encounter, entitled respectively *Mac Mhuirich Mor* (hereafter *MM*) and *Mac Mhuirich agus A Bheisd* (hereafter *MB*), plus a separate and fuller version of *Port na Beisde* ('The Beast's Tune'). Moreover, the MS versions show signs of incoherence and syncopation of different narratives, while the printed tale has unity and coherence. Finally, it is to be noted that the latter concludes with the following editor's note (319): 'The above is a conflation of many MS. versions, some of them fragmentary.'

As its composite title hints, the printed text owes something to both *MM* and *MB*. Verbal correspondences with *MM* are the stronger at the beginning. In *CG* Mac Mhuirich finds a *creutair beag bìodach brònach* (*creatair beag biteach bronach MM*); having picked it up, *thug e dhachaigh leis isean na béist* (*thug e dhachaidh cuilein beag na biasta / beiste moire MM*); the Beast's repeated cry on completing the tasks set her by Mac Mhuirich was *A mach dhomh mo chuilein* (ditto *MM*). Again, Mac Mhuirich's request in *MM* for a causeway across the loch was for one *a bheir an nall an crodh*, which is embedded (though elaborated in a typical way) in the printed *a bheir a null agus a nall mo chuid chruidh agus chaorach*; and the three tasks in *CG* and in *MM* include bringing Mac Mhuirich's peats home. Similarly, at the conclusion of the tale, *CG* follows *MM* in having the Beast depart singing the song that is usually associated with the creature known as Colann gun Cheann, i.e. *Fada bhuam fhìn bonn Beinn Eadarra* or similar. In each of these instances the reading of *MB* is at a greater distance from *CG*.

But *MB* is also represented as the story proceeds. The Beast asks Mac Mhuirich to name his price for returning her whelp with the phrase *Cluinneam (do cheannach* or *do chùmhnant)*, which is found (though just once) as *Cluinim* (understand *do rogha iarrtais*) in *MB*. The whelp (*isean* or *cuilean*) is alternatively called *buiceallach*, *bucallach*, *buracallach* and *curralach* in *CG* (and *buaraclach* in a footnote in *CG*), corresponding to *guraclach*, *buraclach*, *buiriciollach* in *MB*. In *CG*, as the Beast built Mac Mhuirich's house, *cha robh ach an aon duan a' tighinn as a ceann*, and as she departed carrying her whelp *dh'fhalbh i leis an duan [seo] as a ceann*; in *MB* she departed with her whelp *agus an aon chullen binn briagh [seo] na beul*. The building song's concluding lines, *Sgrith sgrath sgolban etc.*, are taken from *MB* (though with embellishment: see below).

Conflation occurs too, as the composite title of the *CG* version indicates. A more substantial instance occurs in the Tasks: where in *MM* the Beast is asked to put a marvellous thatch on an existing byre, and in *MB* she is asked to build a new byre, in *CG* she is asked to build a new house with a marvellous thatch on it.

Did Carmichael have other MS sources in addition to *MM* and *MB*? Possibly the variety of terms used for the Beast's whelp indicates the presence of other versions. *CG*'s description of the colours in the wonderful roof, *air a thughadh le iteach ian agus gun an dà ite air an aon dath* (translated as 'thatched with birds' feathers, and no two feathers of the same hue'), makes sense of a passage which is garbled beyond sense in *MB* and does not appear in *MM*. This could imply the availability of another source. But some of the other elements in *CG* which are not in the MS texts are worrying. The poem that the Beast sings as she works begins as follows in *CG*:

> Clach air muin cloiche'
> Clach air muin a dhà;
> Càir mar sin na clacha
> 'S bidh am balla slàn.

This poem is clear and simple and reads like a children's poem. It is at odds, both metrically and in tone, with the obscure and garbled but pretty certainly authentic rhyme beginning *Sgrith sgrath sgolban / bior an tigh a' chealgair* in *MB*. In *CG* the intelligible part of *MB*'s rhyme is woven in at the end of the poem, replete with 'variants'. But the whole passage is unconvincing in my view; as is the following prose statement which occurs in *CG* alone: *Mar seo bha i a' seinn agus a' sireadh gon an robh crìoch air an taigh. Cha robh màthair eòin san ealtainn ghrinn ghuirm nach tànaig le ite gu cuideachadh tughadh an taighe leis an truas a bha aca ris a' bhéist*. This is translated as: 'Thus she sang and sought until the house was finished. There was not a brood-bird in the beautiful blue sky that did not come with a feather to help with the thatching of the house, out of compassion for the monster.' It is a pretty picture, but one would not expect this sort of sentimentality to be attributed to animals in traditional Gaelic oral narrative.

Once one admits the probability of tampering, other items begin to appear suspicious. In *CG* the hero has been out hunting and is carrying home a *làn-damh* (translated 'a royal stag') when he meets the Béisd, where *MM* describes him less grandiosely as looking for a way to get his cattle across the loch to pasture. *MB* has the Beast complete the roof *mun tainig lan a mheadhon oidhche*, but in *CG* she appears *mu mheadhon mharbh-thràth na h-oidhche*. In the same way 'morning' becomes *gairm-choileach* 'cock-crow' and *air a gualainn* ('on her shoulder') becomes *air fras-mhullach a guaillean* ('on the showery summit (?) of her shoulders'). Again, *CG* alone introduces a formulaic '*Och, och,' ors a' bhéist, 'ge cruaidh an ràdh is fearr a dhèanamh'* each time Mac Mhuirich imposes a task, which could be from another version of our tale, but could equally have been lifted from a different tale, or invented. And the same goes for interjections like *[T]hòisich i air a' chlachaireachd; agus a Mhoire, Mhoire,'s ann aice fhéin a bha an làmh ris!* (translated as '[She] began on the mason-work; and Mary, Mary! 'tis herself that had the hand for it!'), which may well have formed part of the narrative repertoire of some story-tellers and some sorts of tale, but hardly this tale. Parallels for all these sorts of addition and inflation are shown by Dr Bruford to be present in Carmichael's *Deirdire* when set beside the oral version of the same tale.

On the other hand, Carmichael also left out a lot of the material he had recorded in *MB* and *MM*, including whole episodes relating additional encounters with the Beast as a sea-monster, or with another sea-monster. In this case the desire for artistic unity may have led him to abandon material which probably represented the detritus of other Mac Mhuirich narratives that had become garbled and associated with these texts. At the same time, however, Carmichael also eliminated the well-motivated final Task contained in *MM*, perhaps because he had lost the thread when taking down the tale and could not recover it. (We can see what he should have recorded by consulting the independent version in Domhnall Iain MacDhomhnaill's *Uibhist a Deas*, 40.) Additionally, Carmichael sometimes eliminated the stylistically heightened language which was actually present in the original narrative, at the same time as adding his own brand of literariness to the tale. For instance, in *MB* Mac Mhuirich specifies the first Task as follows: *Thu dheanadh bathach naogh ceathail [= naoi ceangail] dhomh, gun mheang gun mhearachd gun mhur-bhith* ('You are to make a byre of nine couples for me without flaw, without mistake, without exception'). In the printed version Carmichael has *Thu thogail dhomh taigh tàmha agus naoi lànain 'na cheann*, translated as 'That thou build me a dwelling-house with nine couples in its roof', in which a nice example of the rhythm and rhetoric of traditional oral narrative is sacrificed, while at the same time Carmichael cannot resist putting in the more arcane word *lànain* to refer to the couplings (*ceangail*) in the frame of the building. Finally, an interesting insight is provided by the existence of a longer and more complete—or should we say padded-out?—version of the Beast's song in the manuscript notebook (CW MS 126(c)) which contains *MB* and *MM*. In this case the fuller version was not included in *CG*. Perhaps Carmichael had thought better of inserting a re-vamped version of the well-known words attributed to Colann gun Cheann.

To sum up, *Mac Mhuirich Mór agus a' Bhéist* shows Carmichael intervening in at least two sorts of way: editorially and creatively. The former is the easier to parallel and to understand, inasmuch as the two surviving specimens of the alleged 'many versions' of this story contained a jumble of additional material which—it might have seemed—cried out for editorial intervention. On the other hand, we may also see here examples of the more egregious traits identified by Dr Bruford: for instance, the replacement of commonplace with antique vocabulary, arguably to make the milieu more 'heroic' and 'aristocratic'; and the replacement of stylistic traits appropriate to this sort of oral folk narrative with styles appropriate to other genres (including the introduction of verse composed by the 'editor'). Bruford suggested that this activity could be explained in terms of a wish to sanitise and civilise his material according to a preconceived image of what would be acceptable to an external audience. The world described hence included elements of enhanced grandeur and dignity; but the mode of presentation also contained more 'hearth-side' features, designed to make his readership feel nearer to an idealised *seanchaidh* or *sgeulaiche*. The result was undoubtedly original in the creative sense. Occasionally one fancies one can detect the source of an image or phrase, and hence gain some idea of the way in which Carmichael's mind was working at a particular moment; and it would clearly be worth researching the relationship between his field-work copies and his printed texts wherever these can be identified. Although he destroyed many oral-traditional features of vocabulary, diction and narrative style which appear—apparently faithfully reproduced—in his MS versions, one can nevertheless detect a certain consistency, and indeed certain attractive features, in the styles he was evolving.

If the above sounds like a rather damning 'case for the prosecution', is there also a 'case for the defence'? I suppose one could argue in the first place that Carmichael, on reading over stories which he had taken down from dictation in long-hand, and punctuated by pauses and breaks and notes to self, might have felt that a combination of his own inadequacies as a transcriber, and the constraints imposed by the method of recording, had diminished the original stories, stifled the story-teller's art and threatened to perpetuate travesties of the tales as they had once been. It would be no more than they deserved (one might say) to present them as they might have been rendered in a performance by an expert tale-teller to a knowledgeable, appreciative audience.

In the second place, Carmichael might have thought, as some other scholars did, that the narratives he was collecting were already debased forms of literary artefacts that had once existed in a purer and more complete state; and this might have led him to gild the lily. If that was part of his motivation, he was one of a numerous company of gilders, including not just the creators of *Ossian* and *Seann Dàna*, but also such creative editors as John Mackenzie (1806–48) (*Sàr Obair*), Rev. Alexander Maclean Sinclair (1840–1923), Professor John Stuart Blackie (1809–95), Revs Angus (1860–1932) and Archibald (1855–1948) MacDonald, Rev. Kenneth MacLeod (1871–1955) and A. J. MacDonald (1900–75) (*Beyond the Farthest Hebrides*), to name but a few. The urge to gild the lily was connected in one way or another to the emergence of new, widely based, potentially unsympathetic audiences, though Bruford's canard of the 'inferiority complex of the urban Gael' is unduly narrow and limited. One can also argue that in Carmichael's day there was a special need for a 'dignified' and respectful view of the Gaels and their literature to be propounded as a corrective to a corrosive negative view which asserted itself in a number of contexts. Indeed, insofar as his choices were self-conscious, deliberate and systematic, one could argue that his position was not much different from that of a revisionist historian with a new thesis or agenda. A lot more research needs to be done on this whole area before final judgements are made.

On a different level of explanation, it would be interesting to explore the implications of an idea which has struck me on several occasions, namely the impact that Carmichael must have experienced on coming into contact with the riches of the Gaelic language and literary tradition in Uist, where the wealth and precision of register and dialect differentiation, the range of vocabulary and the 'purity' of idiom offered a heady mixture, and perhaps a vision of 'Gaelic as it was once in my own part', to visitors from the mainland such as John Francis Campbell. This experience could have led an enthusiast without scientific linguistic training, as Carmichael was, into hitting linguistic 'false notes', by missing register 'cues' and generally over-valuing 'rich and rare' by comparison with correct and accurate usage. This might explain some of the false notes we have detected when comparing the *CG* texts with those in CW.

The 'case for the defence' could also take into account the way the world had moved on between Carmichael's days collecting for John Francis Campbell in the early 1860s, and the 1890s. The status and image of Gaelic had changed, and artistic and intellectual expectations had grown apace by the *fin de siècle*. Celticising music and art movements took inspiration from the Celtic world eclectically and without feeling the need for authenticity on a more than intermittent basis. Literature could surely do the same. Indeed, as a minority began to say openly that Gaelic could have a future as well as a past, the question of new literary forms, in particular for the purposes of having a written literature, were beginning to be debated. Were Carmichael's editorial activities in principle less valid than Marjory Kennedy-Fraser's? Was the time not also ripe for experiments in writing?

The one insurmountable problem for the defender of Carmichael's methods lies, as it seems to me, in his apparent intent to convey the impression of scholarship. Just as James 'Ossian' Macpherson gave particular offence when he wrote learned notes showing parallels between conditions in ancient Scotland and Homeric Greece, when in fact the Gaelic 'parallels' had been shamelessly invented on the basis of Homer, so Carmichael's insertion of invented 'variants' into the traditional bit of the Beast's song in the *CG* version of *MB* strikes us as more heinous than his insertion of additional verses, composed by himself, into the same song. Given that Celtic scholarship had itself come of age between the 1860s and the 1890s, Carmichael's artifice appears as deliberate obfuscation, a step beyond the condonable. The publication of such books as *The Celtic Dragon Myth* (Edinburgh, 1911) by George Henderson (1866–1912) with illustrations by Rachel Grant Duff, showed that it was possible simultaneously to cater for a *celtisant* taste in illustrations and to observe rigorous standards of textual scholarship. Many of the Celtic scholars felt it necessary to be especially correct in their scholarship precisely because they feared being accused of inhaling too much 'Celtic mist'. It would therefore strain the powers of a 'defence counsel' to defend Carmichael's pseudo-variants successfully, though I suspect that they were actually intended to function visually or aesthetically rather than literally. We may remind ourselves, as a mitigating circumstance, that Carmichael was not in any way a trained scholar; but we must still admit that his judgement was grievously deficient if he thought that presenting the MacMhuirich texts in their *CG* form was a manifestation of scholarship.

To conclude this brief review, Carmichael gathered extremely valuable material about the Clann Mhuirich bardic family, both in the insights it gives us into the self-image of the family and in regard to the changes in texture and emphasis that have affected Gaelic traditions about the family over the century and a half since Janet Currie first told her tales to the early collectors. Some of this material is unique to the Carmichael Watson papers and, so far as I know, is no longer extant in oral tradition. In some ways the material which Carmichael did not choose to prepare for publication in *CG* is at least as interesting as what he did select. On the other hand, *CG* v was oriented towards the more overtly supernatural aspects of the poetic family, and in this light Carmichael's choices are understandable. The ways in which Carmichael subsequently interacted with the original Clann Mhuirich materials preserved in CW are revealing and thought-provoking. They show a spectrum of activity which supplements and complements what Alan Bruford found in his investigation of the background of *Deirdire*, and suggest that detailed textual research on texts like these this will be an important preliminary to serious scrutiny of the *Carmina* and the *orthachan*. Not the least important opportunity they offer is the facility to examine Carmichael's versificatory powers.

I wish to express my thanks to those who commented helpfully on the oral version of this paper, to Angus Macmillan for help with the North Uist MacMhuirichs, and to Donald Meek for reading and commenting on the written version. I am responsible for remaining imperfections.

---

[1] The Clann Mhuirich material was the subject of a research project undertaken by me in conjunction with my colleague Dr Barbara Hillers in 1999–2000. The findings were summarised in two unpublished research reports entitled respectively *Clann Mhuirich in oral tradition* (May 2000) and *Clann Mhuirich Legends in the Carmichael Watson Papers* (June 2000), and in two published papers: William Gillies, 'Alexander Carmichael and Clann Mhuirich', *Scottish Gaelic Studies*, xx (2000), 1–66; and Barbara Hillers, 'Poet or magician: Mac Mhuirich Mòr in oral tradition', in Joseph F. Nagy and Leslie Ellen Jones (eds), *Heroic poets and poetic heroes in Celtic tradition: A Festschrift for Patrick K. Ford* (Dublin, 2005), 141–57.

[2] The surviving papers of Alexander Carmichael form part of the Carmichael Watson Collection of papers lodged in Edinburgh University library after the deaths of Professor James Carmichael Watson in 1942 and William J. Watson in 1948. A provisional guide to their contents is contained in John Mackechnie, *Catalogue of Gaelic manuscripts in selected libraries in Great Britain and Ireland* (Boston, MA, 1973) i, 455–551; further information is recorded in Laura S. Sugg, 'Summary list of items 488 to 576 in the Carmichael Watson Collection', *Scottish Gaelic Studies*, xviii (1998), 131-65; and in Dr Anne Frater's handwritten annotations to Mackechnie's catalogue in Edinburgh University Library Special Collections. I am grateful to Dr Domhnall Uilleam Stiùbhart for supplying me with a working copy of his indexes to CW, which will in due course supersede Mackechnie's.

[3] *CG* iv, vi.

[4] See further Morton W. Bloomfield and Charles W. Dunn, *The role of the poet in early societies* (Woodbridge, 1989); Karen Ralls-MacLeod, *Music and the Celtic otherworld* (Edinburgh, 2000); Dáithí Ó hÓgáin, *An file* (Dublin, 1982), and 'The poet as hero', in idem, *The hero in Irish folk history* (Dublin, 1985), 216–56.

[5] See Donald A. MacDonald, 'Donald Alasdair Johnson', *Tocher*, 2 (1971), 36–7.

[6] See Gillies, 'Alexander Carmichael and Clann Mhuirich', 12–43, for translations of these texts.

[7] Domhnall Iain MacDhomhnaill, *Uibhist a Deas* (Stornoway, 1981), 39–40.

[8] It is true that triplication, as with *cuir a mach e* and *cuir uat e*, was listed by Dr Alan Bruford, in the article cited below, as one of the ways in which Carmichael elaborated the story of Deirdire in preparing it for publication. But Bruford's point was that this was a genuine feature overused or misused by Carmichael. The present examples could be (and I believe are) genuine manifestations of the device.

[9] For an English translation see Gillies, 'Alexander Carmichael and Clann Mhuirich', 25. Note that square brackets in quoted passages, unless otherwise stated, represent my editorial intrusions.

[10] The only possibly 'suspicious' note I can detect is the reference to Mac Mhuirich's never having been in the kitchen before, given the examples cited below of Carmichael's 'social cleansing' of Mac Mhuirich in the transition from CW to CG. But this 'hang-up' of Carmichael's may have predated the preparation of these MS materials for publication.

[11] Quoted from John G. Mackay, 'Cànain nan eun', *Scottish Gaelic Studies*, iii(2) (1931), 160–87 (180).

[12] Dr Domhnall Uilleam Stiùbhart's ongoing work on the Carmichael papers is throwing up additional valuable material, and this statement may need refinement when the full range of MacMhuirich material is identified and available.

[13] On the other hand, Angus Macmillan has reminded me of the late Dr Alasdair Maclean's suggestion ('Notes on South Uist families', *Transactions of the Gaelic Society of Inverness*, liii (1984), 491–518: 511), that the Uist MacPhersons may have belonged to the poetic family, and has drawn to my attention some distinctly early references to North Uist MacPhersons with South Uist connections.

[14] See, for example, 'The invention of tradition, Highland-style', in Alastair A. MacDonald, Michael Lynch and Ian B. Cowan (eds), *The Renaissance in Scotland* (Leiden, 1994), 144–56, in which I have shown some of the gambits and conventions used by the MacEwen poet-historians to the House of Argyll. It should be understood that in the meta-linguistic 'message' of a dynastic tale a statement that X, a founding father of a dynasty, left an illegitimate son in another place can be a way of asserting or validating a relationship between X's living descendants and real people in the other place. There is perhaps room for further research here.

[15] For an English translation see Gillies, 'Alexander Carmichael and Clann Mhuirich', 31.

[16] The translation given in *CG* (v, 309) is 'Variant versions of MacVurich Mór's verses'.

[17] Alan J. Bruford, '"Deirdire" and Alexander Carmichael's treatment of oral sources', *Scottish Gaelic Studies*, xix(1) (1983), 1–24. *Deirdire* first appeared in *Transactions of the Gaelic Society of Inverness*, xiii (1887), 241–57, and was published separately in 1905 with a reprint in 1914.

[18] The nearest example I can find in our texts is the interjection *boirionach mor mor briagha* 'a great big lovely woman', referring to Mac Mhuirich's wife, quoted above from the CW tale *Mac Mhuirich Mór*. This terse snapshot is much more like what one would expect in a genuine long-hand recording session. Yet the possibility remains that the texts I have discussed here are close to, but not identical to what Carmichael heard—that even here one may glimpse the blurring of the toles of collector and interpreter.

7

'Every Treasure You Chanced On':
Alexander Carmichael and Material Culture

HUGH CHEAPE

In *Dàin do Eimhir agus Dàin Eile*, brought to print in 1943 by his friend Douglas Young (1913–73), Sorley Maclean (1911–96) included his poem addressed to Alexander Carmichael, *Mhic Ghille Mhicheil*.[1] Though complex in its allusions and use of allegory, the simplicity of its 16-line appeal refocuses attention on the rich inheritance of Gaelic tradition, the seductiveness of this cultural inheritance and a prevailing sense of crisis:

> Mhic Ghille Mhicheil, 's tric mi smaointinn
> air gach faodail a fhuair thu:
> agus do shaoibhreas gach aon latha
> gun charachd gheur, gun bhruaillean . . .

Maclean later published his own translation of the poem although it has not attracted the same critical attention as his other work:

> Carmichael, I often think
> Of every treasure you chanced on,
> And of your wealth every day
> Without bitter wrestling and delirium . . .[2]

Sorley Maclean was familiar, probably intrigued as we are, with *Carmina Gadelica* and its wealth of material and inspiration. Significantly in this poem he invokes the *Ora nam Buadh* ('Invocation of the Graces') from the first volume of *Carmina* in which this dense and impressive charm is the third item.[3] It was attributed to Duncan MacLellan, Càrnan, South Uist, and further recorded as having been heard in the early-nineteenth century from Catherine Macaulay, a victim of the clearances on the east side of the island. The two volumes of *Carmina Gadelica* were published in a sumptuous format and style in 1900, with translations and annotations by Alexander Carmichael. These two volumes were reissued in 1928, the year before Sorley Maclean went to Edinburgh University. Volumes 3 and 4 were published in 1940–1, edited by James Carmichael Watson (1910–42), Alexander's grandson. Fascination with *Carmina* as a species of oral literature must have been current with their republication, and if the young professor's work was more than *pietas*, there was still an atmosphere of uncritical acceptance in academic circles in the 1930s.

Sorley Maclean's use of the key word *faodail* offers a prompt to take stock of the wider collecting interests of Alexander Carmichael. *Faodail* is 'treasure' in the sense of anything found, something chanced upon, arguably something with form and dimensionality, a term therefore happily reflecting the search and act of searching, what the eye alights on and what the acquisitive eye perceives then as treasure. With the standpoint of Carmichael studies being essentially within language and literature, little or no notice has been given to Alexander Carmichael's collecting activities in the round and in the sphere of material culture in which he engaged with a different circle of nineteenth-century scholars. A dichotomy emerges in our survey of Carmichael's work in this context, between, on the one hand, what were described as 'antiquities' and, on the other, what was recorded of the life and work of a perceived conservative and traditional society. The emphasis of this paper is on what Carmichael recorded and why, both in terms of language and of museum-type objects. Material culture, as is evident in Carmichael's own writings, supplies the background and the texture of life in all forms in the Hebrides in the nineteenth century and may (too often) be taken for granted while in fact no longer being appreciated or understood. It is something of an irony that the language of material culture, though self-evidently rich, was relatively undervalued by the recorders and early lexicographers, thus enhancing the importance of Carmichael's own word-lists and glossaries which offer remarkably detailed definitions and contextualisation. As he was to write in a letter of 1894 to Sheriff Æneas Mackay, for printing in the *Proceedings of the Society of Antiquaries of Scotland*:

> Gaelic is copious and descriptive in natural objects, and in the arts and sciences known to the old people.[4]

I

A life of collecting and serious research might have seemed Carmichael's birthright. His upbringing in Lismore, strategically located in Loch Linnhe and the Firth of Lorn and significantly bedded on Dalriadan limestone, gave him a rich inheritance in traditional and material culture. His parentage was clearly and strongly localised in Hugh Carmichael and Betty MacColl, both families obviously rooted in that district of Argyll. The Carmichaels belonged firmly to Lismore for generations and claimed descent from *an t-Easbaig Bàn*. Of more immediate significance was their role as historical landholders, according to Professor Donald MacKinnon (1839–1914), of the family of *Baran Taigh an Sgurrain*.[5] The Carmichaels are one of the older indigenous clans of the west coast although the English version of an older name had been adopted comparatively recently. They appear on record in Lismore in name-forms such as *Gille-colm Mac Gille-mhicheil* and *Kennethus Mac Gille-mhicheil*. Subsequently when the Stewarts came into Appin as feudal superiors, indigenous clans such as the Carmichaels gave them their allegiance in return for favour and protection. Such groups were referred to in the records as 'native men'.

The nineteenth century was a period of serious decline and emigration from the island of Lismore, and the mood of apparent demoralisation is symbolised by the departure of the pastoral staff of St Moluag, the sixth-century Irish cleric who founded a religious community there; this was the *Bachull Mór* which was handed to the Duke of Argyll in the late 1870s and kept in a private museum in Inveraray Castle.[6] The parish church of Lismore, dedicated to St Moluag, is what is left of the cathedral of the medieval diocese of Argyll and is, in spite of different stages of rescue and rebuilding, an important and impressive structure with early details still extant. The diocese was created about 1200 and Lismore was chosen as the bishop's seat. As in other instances in the ambit of the medieval church, there were hereditary

Fig. 1: Portrait in oils of Alexander Carmichael by the Edinburgh artist and designer, William Skeoch Cumming (1864-1929), later published in *Carmina Gadelica*.

custodians of the *Bachull* or staff, the Livingstones, and Alexander Carmichael recorded their traditional history in the *Celtic Review* in an essay which includes additional Lismore traditions.[7] The 'charter box' of the Barons of Bachuill, a small wooden box carved from the solid, was in Carmichael's possession and he deposited it in the National Museum of Antiquities of Scotland in 1870.[8] There are hints in *Carmina* of games known to Carmichael when a boy in Lismore; 'Kilmoluag' records a question and answer chant sung while a group swung one of their number by the head and heels and laid him successively in one or two symbolic spots. Carmichael's editorial comment is modest: 'The writer was an actor in this boyish drama, but what the drama represented he does not know.'[9]

Carmichael was an avid collector, probably curious and acquisitive since boyhood, and amassing a huge number of mainly small items, suggestive of portable *objets trouvés* or 'antiquities', noted while travelling the country and collected like words and phrases. On his death in 1912, a considerable personal collection was inherited by his family and this has survived. Its significance for us lies in the insights which it offers into Alexander Carmichael's longstanding collecting activities and a perception of the *faodail* that Sorley Maclean, who may well have been aware of these material collections, characterized thus in 1943. It comprised archaeological material, including an important bronze sword from South Uist, curiosities and exotic material, three wall-cases of remarkable plaid brooches and heart brooches, coins, a great many charms and amulets, for example a 'charm of deliverance' and 'stone rain charm from Creagorry, 1874', and many drift seeds so typical of the west side of the Long Island, obliquely and occasionally referred to in *Carmina*, jewellery and accessories such as needles and pins, and a collection of fabrics and textiles, mainly tartans collected in the islands in the late-nineteenth century.[10] Doubtless such fabrics appealed to contemporary interest and taste forming in the Arts and Crafts movement, but in assessing these fabrics, one may speculate that the same mind and attitude discovered and collected these fragments as collected fragmentary lore. The contemporary mind and eye perceived virtue in old portions of cloth, slightly tattered and torn, with their soft colours dyed, it was supposed, with locally sourced plant-dyes. The collection appears to have been offered for sale to the founders of the West Highland Museum in the 1920s, valued by the Glasgow collector Charles Whitelaw (1869–1939), to be held perhaps as a memorial to Alexander Carmichael and his work. No bargain was struck and James Carmichael Watson inherited the collection presumably following the death of his mother, Ella Watson, *née* Carmichael, in 1928. Following his own death in action in March 1942, the collection was deposited for safekeeping after re-valuation in Paisley Museum, possibly because of the preponderance of textiles in the collection and of the leading role of Paisley in Scottish textile history. Ownership of the collection then passed to another grandson of Alexander Carmichael, the late Michael Carmichael of Tigh-a-Bhet, Fort William, where the latter practised as a vet. He loaned the collection to the West Highland Museum and it passed by generous bequest into the museum collections in 1991.

II

The details of material culture were clearly a given for Alexander Carmichael but are carefully and consciously rehearsed by him where they explain, augment or interpret his case. This formed the backdrop and the concomitant of his work of recording the language and literature. His notebooks and fieldwork notes include a wealth of incidental detail on landforms, sites, buildings and objects and this feature still remains to be fully evaluated.[11] In the introductory essay in the first volume of *Carmina*, Carmichael makes clear the significance of material culture for his readers; he summarises Gaelic oral literature as widely diffused, greatly abundant and excellent in quality, and comparable to the classics of Greece and Rome, and concludes that the economic and social context particularly of crofting on the one hand and the céilidh house on the other contributed, perhaps uniquely, to this. He continues by describing from his own observation the 'institution' of the céilidh and its indigenous and characteristic background:

> In a crofting community the people work in unison in the field during the day, and discuss together in the house at night. This meeting is called 'ceilidh' … Let me briefly describe the 'ceilidh' as I have seen it. … The house of the 'story-teller' is already full, and it is difficult to get inside and away from the cold wind and the soft sleet without. But with that politeness native to the people, the stranger is pressed to come forward and occupy the seat vacated for him beside the houseman. The house is roomy and clean, if homely, with its bright peat fire in the middle of the floor. There are many present—men and women, boys and girls. All the women are seated, and most of the men. Girls are crouched between the knees of fathers or brothers or friends, while boys are perched wherever—boylike—they can climb. The houseman is twisting twigs of heather into ropes to hold down thatch, a neighbour crofter is twining quicken roots into cords to tie cows,

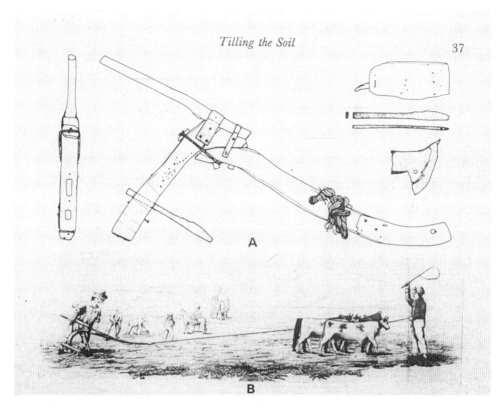

Fig. 2: Single-stilted plough or Crann-nan-gad collected by Alexander Carmichael and gifted to the 'Museum of Science and Art' (now the National Museums of Scotland).

Fig. 3: Stone vessel or 'font' from a probable former chapel site, Cladh Chrìosd, in Pabaigh, Barra Head, said to cure mental and physical illness, given by Alexander Carmichael to the National Museums.

> while another is plaiting bent grass into baskets to hold meal. … The housewife is spinning, a
> daughter is carding, another daughter is teasing … Neighbour wives and neighbour daughters are
> knitting, sewing or embroidering.[12]

Carmichael drew on earlier collecting work in the *Gàidhealtachd* in his emphasis on the céilidh house. He commented in the introductory essay in *Carmina* that he had 'the privilege of being acquainted with Iain F Campbell of Islay during a quarter of a century', in other words from the beginning of the latter's collecting activities in 1859–60 until his death in 1885.[13] The same inference of the importance of appreciating the social and economic context of storytelling is clear from the long introductory essay to *Popular Tales of the West Highlands Orally Collected*. John Francis Campbell of Islay (1821–85) was conscious of his socially exclusive birth and upbringing, and described in intriguing detail how he strove to be accepted by those whom he met on his collecting tours. Empathy with his informants was of the highest importance and also an understanding of their circumstances. Fluency in Gaelic was the principal means of gaining their confidence. Campbell of Islay prints in detail the descriptions of céilidh-houses in different localities as observed by himself and as given to him by his assistants, Hector Maclean (1818–93), Hector Urquhart and John Dewar (1812–72), and he notes the importance of appreciating material circumstances:

> In telling a story, narrative and dialogue are mixed; what the characters have told each other to
> do is repeated as narrative. The people in the story tell it to each other, and branch off into
> discussions about their horses and houses and crops, or anything that happens to turn up.[14]

Understanding and appreciation of context, of the material culture in oral narrative, is essential and of course is assumed by the narrator. The mind and eye read the story more readily, the message is the more potent, the irony more pointed, the metaphor more meaningful when the form and function of pot-hook, tether-pin, whey-stick and strike-a-light are known.

The material culture background looms larger in certain areas of *Carmina* where some understanding of the social and economic context is deemed essential for a proper appreciation of the oral material, for example where prayers or charms belong to particular phases of the seasonal round of work. *Laoidh an Triall*, the 'Hymn of the Procession', for example, was used for the day of moving stock from the townland to the shieling and Carmichael provides a useful account of this procedure. The procession is described in order of sheep, cattle, goats and horses, the last with creels slung across them for carrying the necessary gear for the weeks in the hill. The men carry tools and equipment for mending the shieling huts for the summer occupation and the women carry bedding, meal and dairy utensils. Women use a *crios-fèile*, a skirt-belt, to hold up their overskirts for ease of walking with loads on their backs through the heather of the hill. At the shielings, the huts are repaired, fires made and food prepared. The stock is counted in and the soumings set. This circumstantial detail is essential knowledge for understanding the process and for making sense of the lore which Carmichael prints.[15]

In this and other areas of *Carmina*, the material culture is the essential 'peg' on which the account seems to be hung. The author could be said to use an often florid prose, intended perhaps to elevate, even to glorify the mundane. Work and the daily round of course had its rich vein of poetry and music in work-songs or chorus-songs. The former wide usage of work-songs has tended to be elided to some extent by their categorisation as *òrain luaidh* or 'waulking songs', but it is important to note that they are well and properly integrated in *Carmina*. Alexander Carmichael includes a selection of work-songs, for example as used for working the quern or hand-mill. He described how he first saw the quern being used in October 1860 in Skye and in January 1865 in Barra, the first occasion to grind oats taken from the sheaf in the process of 'graddaning', and the second occasion to grind bere or barley in place of taking the grain to the mill.[16] The circumstances of each occasion are described in detail and evidently the more keenly observed since the use of the quern was almost certainly unfamiliar to him from Lismore. The process of *gradanadh* is carefully described and the use of the quern set on the floor on top of a sheepskin. In Barra, the quern was set on the floor on a cowhide and worked by two women sitting opposite each other, adopting a particular posture with the right leg stretched out and the left foot crooked in against the knee joint of the straight leg. Each held the *sgonnan* or handle to turn the quern and, as any would know who have turned a quern, the motion and pressure is eased as soon as the grain feeds between the quern-stones through the 'eye' of the upper stone—*sùil na bràthan*. The bere was held in what Carmichael has called a 'fan', that is a hallow circular sieve with cured sheepskin stretched taut over a wooden frame. The author adds some further historical detail about the destruction of querns on the orders of landlords in order to enforce compliance with and payment of mill dues, and fascinating ethnological detail about the discovery and re-use of stone mortars, which he calls *pollagan*, for grinding grain. This information bears the signs of community tradition and folk memory—on the destruction of querns for example—and the author's own extrapolation including perhaps 'invention' of the term for the stone mortar. Dwelly attributes this meaning to Carmichael while the older dictionaries make no mention of this specific meaning.[17]

George Henderson (1866–1912), close friend of Carmichael and later Lecturer in Celtic at Glasgow, saw *Carmina* in manuscript and urged the author against too much speculative etymologising. Another material culture detail may be cited that might prompt the same qualification: *iomairt* is given as the term defining a particular style of woven cloth but does not

Fig. 4: Stone font with elaborately carved outer faces, from the chapel site of St Maelrubha, Loch Aoineart, Skye, taken to South Uist and later gifted to the National Museums in 1870.

appear in the dictionaries in this sense except in Dwelly's where it is attributed to Alexander Carmichael.[18] This was cloth said to be with the colour set in the warp, the cloth thus being striped predominantly lengthwise. This has been a defining characteristic of the fine cloth of the woman's plaid or *earasaid*, a style of dress that was going out of fashion in the eighteenth century and finally disappeared with the advent of the Paisley Shawl in the nineteenth. The reference occurs in the section of *Carmina* devoted to 'Labour' and, naturally, material culture is strongly self-evident in this context of the oral lore. The processes of *calanas* or 'wool-working' are summarised by the author, sorting, washing and cleaning the wool, combing and carding, spinning the thread, dyeing the wool or the fibre, and the curious detail of setting up—*suidheachadh*—patterns for tartan on small pieces of wood. This may be a piece of creative thinking by the author. In this 'home industry', the people's experience, skill and intelligence were the requisite and the innate catalysts. His account is presented in general terms, some of which may be challenged, such as the division of labour, and does not bear the same signs of close or extended observation. Dyeing was said to be carried out with native plants and 'all Highland women are practical dyers, some more skilful than others'.[19] Carmichael, who had formed his own collection of tartan fabrics whilst in the islands, concluded that home-made tartans and other fabrics, made generations or, it could be said, sometimes centuries before, were very fine in texture and the colours remarkably bright and beautiful. The link back to homely and virtuous endeavour is implicit but dye analysis of these same objects in the National Museums in recent years has shown that the bright and colourfast tones were achieved with imported dyestuffs such as cochineal and that weavers in Benbecula obtained exotic dyestuffs through distant markets such as Inverness and Glasgow.[20]

In the second volume of *Carmina*, the 'Notes &c.' section of 152 pages includes definitions and citations, and many of the selected words and phrases are glossed with circumstantial detail and, for example, a wealth of ornithological information. This treatment reflects Carmichael's own interests and demonstrates his attention to material detail. Certain words are not previously noticed or similarly defined in the dictionaries, and this would require further refinement before conclusions are drawn. The following sampling from the section following its alphabetical order is noteworthy from the point of view of material culture and the contextualisation added by Carmichael: *ballan* is recorded for the first time in the sense of 'cupping' as a form of simple surgery used for rheumatism[21]; *calanas*, wool working; *ciosan*, basket; *crub*, a bed recess, 'not now seen except in the old dwelling-houses of St Kilda or in the shieling bothies of Lewis';[22] *fàileagan*, meadows, from *fàl*, turf or sod; *fitheach* includes Carmichael's own account of witnessing a 'raven dance'; *samh*, odour, augmented with *samh trom éisg*, 'that heavy odour from a great body of fish in the sea'; *sleabhag*, a small mattock 'used in digging up carrots and the roots of native plants used by the people in dyeing and tanning'; *smeòirn*, 'arrow-head, arrow-point, the destructive end of the arrow', and the comment that the dictionaries make 'smeòirn' 'the butt end'; *sola*, broken food or crushed shellfish used as bait, with the traditional circumstantial detail and comment that 'the Lady Amie, wife of John Lord of the Isles, sent men round the islands to make hollows in the rocks in which the people might break shellfish and prepare bait. Such pits are called 'toll solaidh', bait holes. These mortars resemble cup cuttings, for which antiquarians have mistaken them'; *streafon*, fringe, filament; *teiric,* herring hake, 'a triangular frame with spikes upon which herrings are hung up to dry in the smoke within or in the sun without.'

Fig. 5: Small sculpted cross-slab with an Old Norse inscription in runes on one face, seen by Alexander Carmichael at Kilbar in Barra, in 1865 and later sent to the National Museums.

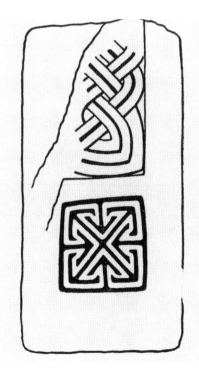

Fig. 6: Section of broken sculptured stone or cross shaft of gneiss from an early chapel site, Cill Aiseam, in Bearnaraigh, Harris, given by Alexander Carmichael to the National Museums.

III

Alexander Carmichael's collecting activities manifested themselves in Scottish museum collections from the 1860s. His contributions were symbolic of the contemporary museum movement. Profits generated by the Great Exhibition in 1851 led to the government-sponsored expansion of educational provision and the creation of public museums in the second half of the nineteenth century. The museum movement was a conspicuous element in education and in the provision for educational needs in a period of economic expansion. The Department of Science and Art was established as the agency of development, and the founding first of the South Kensington Museum (later renamed as the Victoria and Albert Museum) and then of the Royal Scottish Museum in 1854, as the 'Industrial Museum', followed. George Wilson (1818–59), Professor of Technology at the University of Edinburgh, was the first, though short-lived, Director (1855–9) of the Industrial Museum. The building of the cast-iron, stone and glass hall and pavilions in Chambers Street in Edinburgh in the 1860s, using some of the technology of the Crystal Palace, led to the expansion of displays and collecting activities and the significant renaming in 1864 of the new museum as the Museum of Science and Art. Material was drawn in for an 'Industrial Exhibition', filling the west pavilion and designed to demonstrate concepts and methods of progress in an era of rapid industrialisation. Deft (or crude) comparison offered evidence of progress and a number of Hebridean tools and implements were collected. Artefacts, as Wilson proposed, were 'the result of human industry.'[23]

Alexander Carmichael donated or 'deposited' in the Museum of Science and Art a *crann-nan-gad*, a 'ristle', and a *cas chrom*, each being regarded as archaic and unusual implements of cultivation. The *crann-nan-gad* was a single-stilted plough of light construction adapted for rocky and shallow soils (see Fig. 2). The 'ristle' was a horse-drawn implement used to prepare the ground for the plough or for the *cas chrom* which was a large heavy type of spade. Carmichael usefully glosses this in *Carmina*: 'The cas-chrom is well adapted for ground of tough surface, but not for ground already broken in and pulverised.' Each of these items given by Alexander Carmichael has survived, registered in 1879, transferred to the National Museum of Antiquities of Scotland in 1966 and now displayed in the Scottish Agricultural Museum at Wester Kittochside, East Kilbride.[24] At the same time they offered exemplars of 'Celtic' agriculture for the extraordinary *Book of the Club of True Highlanders*, and these very items were drawn by its London architect-author, C. N. McIntyre North, who acknowledged Carmichael's help in all things pertaining to the purposes of the Society, *Comunn nam Fior Gael*. The preface to the generous folio volumes published in 1881 explained that 'the record is of a modest Society which has indirectly exercised a great deal of influence on the Scotch residents in London by carefully fostering that enthusiastic love of country for which Highlander and Lowlander are celebrated, and by advocating the preservation (as precious relics) of all customs, manners and records that could in any way remind them of the Land of the Mountain and the Flood.' Two examples of the *cas chrom* are shown in the volume, one belonging to Carmichael and the other to John Francis Campbell of Islay, giving rise to the ingenuous comment in the text by the author reflecting typically the polymathic Islay: 'An implement similar to the cas chrom (we are informed by Campbell of Islay) is used in Japan in much the same manner as it is used in the Highlands.' These particular items and many others drawn by McIntyre North for the *Book of the Club of True Highlanders* were used by Edward Dwelly for illustrations for the *Gaelic-English Dictionary*.[25]

Carmichael's interests and collecting activities extended beyond human history and included natural history specimens which he also supplied to public museums; he gave a specimen from Taynuilt of the water shrew—*Crossopus fodiens*—to the zoological collections of the Royal Scottish Museum in 1900, although it is perhaps surprising to note that the Gaelic name was not recorded in the Museum's documentation. Natural history was one of the subjects of an extensive correspondence with the Rev. Alexander Stewart (1829–1901), minister of Onich, who contributed a column to the *Inverness Courier* under the name 'Nether Lochaber'. He introduced items of both science and folklore sent to him by Alexander Carmichael whom he variously described as his 'Uist Correspondent' or his 'Long Island Correspondent'. In May 1875, for example, writing in modest tones from Creag Goraidh, he sent the minister the skeleton of a species of dolphin, the detailed description and identification of which then filled a column of the newspaper. The letter hints at Carmichael's collecting methods:

> … The skeleton was found at Airdmore, Barra, about three weeks ago. Those who discovered it incidentally mentioned it to me, and I at once sent a man to secure it; and I have now much pleasure in sending it to you for examination. When discovered, the skeleton lay a few feet beyond the tide-mark (*Os cionn tùir an làin*) and was as cleanly dissected then as you now see it.[26]

IV

Alexander Carmichael's evident familiarity with many of the circumstances and details of everyday life and farming in the islands made him a ready candidate, as a literate Gael and a civil servant, to write about it for a general readership. In concluding his magisterial *Celtic Scotland: A History of Ancient Alban* in 1880, William Forbes Skene (1809–92) wrote: 'The author has to record his thanks to his friend Mr Alexander Carmichael for the instructive account of three of the Long Island townships embodied in the last chapter …' Skene's purpose was the scholarly one of providing a thoroughly researched account of early Scottish history and the historiographical one of correcting misapprehensions about so-called 'Dark Age' Scotland, together with his fundamental creed that the Pict was Gaelic, not Gothic. The final of his three volumes was titled 'Land and People', dealing with social conditions and organisation and as Skene suggests 'the real history of a country'. The last chapter, on 'Land tenure in the Highlands and Islands subsequent to the sixteenth century', is a careful history drawing probably on the foundations of Highland record scholarship laid by Donald Gregory (1803–36) and brought up to the nineteenth century, but the tone and style changes dramatically in the final section contributed by Carmichael. Strictly speaking his account of landholding, cultivation and animal husbandry appears on the whole anachronistic and sentimental, the tone set by the opening words: 'Old systems are tenacious. They linger long among a rural people, and in remote places. Of these is the land system of runrig …' Though runrig appears to have survived the sweeping changes of 'agricultural improvement' in some places, the author's focus on North Uist and Lewis fails to distinguish that runrig was abolished more or less wholesale in these localities in the course of the first half of the nineteenth century and survived in relict form only. There is a wealth of detail and terminology in his account, particularly looking at land division and allocation, animal husbandry and souming, but it lacks the qualification of distinctions between different localities and differentiation which would enrich it for modern scholarship. It is evident in his correspondence with Skene that Carmichael laboured long and hard on his text and re-wrote it and revised it several times in order to achieve a respectable standard. His message and purpose are clear, here as elsewhere, that is to represent the people of the islands in the best possible light for a contemporary Victorian readership.[27]

Justification did not have to be sought or offered since Carmichael's account was read by Lord Napier and Ettrick (1819–98), chair of the Royal Commission on the Highlands and Islands, that small committee charged in 1883 with the task of conducting the first official enquiry into crofting conditions. Lord Napier was known to have said that Carmichael's essay had enlisted his sympathy on behalf of the crofters. Napier himself requested that Alexander Carmichael write an account of crofting for the Royal Commission and a longer essay, 'Grazing and agrestic customs of the Outer Hebrides', was printed as a 31-page appendix to the *Report* of the Crofting Commission in 1884. Some offprints were printed by Neill and Company of Edinburgh and Carmichael distributed these. He included, in a Note prefacing the account, a patronisingly brief and anodyne testimonial from a 'Nobleman in London to Lord Napier': 'The account of the old customs is the most interesting thing in your Report; the old hymns are charming.' This essay is full of terminology and detail, for example a table of soums or *suimeachadh*, and distinctions are more carefully drawn between the different localities than in the earlier version so that for example, he makes clear that in areas such as Barra the arable had all been divided into crofts. The account is less vitiated by the tone of the earlier account in Skene's *Celtic Scotland* and includes several blunt references to clearances in Uist and Barra, and a plea to reverse permanently the status quo 'impoverishing the many to enrich the few'. By contrast, perhaps startlingly in this document where the author unequivocally blames his class, he singles out the North Uist factor for extraordinary praise: ' … a man endowed with more excellency of head and heart, without faults, than ordinarily falls to the lot of man, a man possessing the implicit confidence of proprietors and tenants alike, who daily injures himself to benefit them.' Carmichael concluded his Report with a representative selection of the oral lore which he had been collecting, the hymns, prayers and blessings which then appeared in later publications and in *Carmina*, and must have been the first extended pieces of authentic Scottish Gaelic in a British government publication.[28]

For his account of the three island townships, Carmichael later described how he had visited Lewis again to research his subject for Skene, but had found it difficult to gain his information. This he ascribed to a new distaste for talking about the past and about secular matters, including apparently material culture, and he drew an unhappy and sectarian division between the Protestant parishes to the north and the Roman Catholic parishes to the south:

> When I asked about old customs and old modes of working, I was answered, 'Good man, old things are passed away, all things are become new'; for the people of Lewis, like the people of the Highlands and Islands generally, carry the Scriptures in their minds and apply them in their speech as no other people do. It is extremely disconcerting to be met in this manner on a mission so desirable.[29]

V

Following the early death of his father, a boyhood ambition to join the army was supplanted by the expediency of a Civil Service career. He entered the Inland Revenue after schooling in Greenock and Edinburgh, and took up a position with the Customs and Excise in Skye where he was in communication with Campbell of Islay and Hector Maclean. This was followed by a posting to Cornwall between 1862 and 1864, then a return to Scotland and the posting to the Hebrides. Clearly this was most congenial to him, and his antiquarian and folklore interests brought him into contact with others working in this field at the time. Prominent among these was Captain Frederick W. L. Thomas who was responsible for the Admiralty Survey of the coasts of Orkney, Shetland and the Hebrides; he had been elected a Corresponding Member of the Society of Antiquaries of Scotland in 1850 and on his death in 1885 left a valuable collection of field notes and sketches to the Society. His survey vessel, HMS *Woodlark*, took him to many places rarely visited but with much to examine. Symptomatic of the time was his gift to the National Museum of Antiquities in 1861 of a stone incised with a cross from a ruined chapel on Taransay, the stone having been used in house-building close to the chapel site. The legitimacy of its removal is not discussed.[30] Researchers such as Thomas needed contacts such as Carmichael who, as a civil servant and a Gaelic-speaker, was qualified and 'respectable'. This accounts also for his involvement with the Ordnance Survey, introducing surveyors to local informants and commenting on and possibly 'correcting' the rendering of place-names in areas such as South Uist. This informal role is noted in the Ordnance Survey Name Books. Considerable correspondence between the two has survived and Carmichael also fulsomely acknowledged the friendship of Captain Thomas in his contributions to the *Proceedings of the Society of Antiquaries of Scotland*.

According to Alexander Carmichael's own comments, one of the strongest influences on his antiquarian and scholarly career was the Edinburgh lawyer and historian, William Forbes Skene. By inference, this influence steered Carmichael into more ambitious fields of study and collecting where we may see him perhaps even being exploited by the antiquarians. Alternatively, the attention given to Carmichael by men such as Thomas and Skene was flattering, as the tone he adopts in his letters to the two clearly demonstrates. Skene belonged to an Aberdeenshire family, the Skenes of Rubislaw, and was the son of James Skene of Rubislaw, advocate, antiquarian and close friend of Scott, and Curator of the Society of Antiquaries' Museum between 1819 and 1836.[31] William learnt Gaelic after staying, on the recommendation of Walter Scott, with the scholarly minister of Laggan, Rev. Dr Mackintosh Mackay (1793–1873), editor of the Highland Society *Dictionary* of 1828. Skene himself played a prominent role in the Society of Antiquaries having become a Fellow in 1833, and he formed an important friendship with the Society's Secretary, Donald Gregory, the author of the ground-breaking *History of the Western Highlands and Isles of Scotland* published in 1836. They formed the Iona Club and he edited, together with Donald Gregory, the Club's volume published in 1847 as *Collectanea de Rebus Albanicis*. Carmichael's own (signed) copy of *Collectanea* subsequently belonged to the late I. F. Grant. Skene's considerable scholarship and command of an extensive range of sources from Irish Annals to Norse Sagas is demonstrated by the *Collectanea*. He was also responsible for the collection of Gaelic manuscripts, having bought the so-called 'Black Book of Clanranald' on a Dublin bookstall and been given the Fernaig Manuscript by the executors of Dr Mackintosh Mackay. His contribution alone to the second volume of *Reliquiae Celticae* is therefore enormously significant. Skene published his *Highlanders of Scotland* in 1837 with its stated intention of reversing the 'general neglect of Highland history' and 'that extraordinary prejudice against the Celtic race'. His thesis that the Picts were Gaels opposed John Pinkerton's then fashionable theory that the Picts, as the founding nation of Scotland, were 'gothic' or Germanic.

An area of antiquarian endeavour which engaged Alexander Carmichael was the 'discovery' of early Christian monuments and stone sculpture such as were being located by Captain Thomas. This sphere of activity was particularly noted by Professor Donald

MacKinnon and, at this point, in a curiously detached style in his obituary essay: 'In the antiquities of the Outer Isles, Mr Carmichael took a great interest, and discovered several objects, the existence of which had been previously unknown, such as the runic cross from St Barr's in Barra, now in the Antiquarian Museum, Edinburgh.' While acknowledging Carmichael's success in this sphere, the author seems to convey a sense that this was not the world of the Gael. The Society of Antiquaries of Scotland had recognised the importance and quality of the early medieval sculpture of the West Highlands and Islands and was working on its recording and publication through the *Proceedings*. Knowledge of early stone sculpture and inscriptions had begun with Iona and gradually spread out from there to include most of the western seaboard. Notably drawings were published by men such as T. S. Muir, John Stuart, James Drummond, and Captain T. P. White, and the record began to be filled out in papers by Captain Thomas and communications from Alexander Carmichael, particularly relating to their discoveries in the Outer Isles. The first publication of a symbol stone from western Scotland, located at Hàcleit, Benbecula, was the work of Alexander Carmichael himself, having sent a tracing of its carved decoration 'upon cotton cloth' to Edinburgh. He described how 'the first time I saw it the slab formed the roof of a piggery' and the stone subsequently entered the collections of the National Museum of Antiquities.[32] Father Allan McDonald (1859–1905) was another valued source of information for the Society, for example reporting on the symbol stone on Pabbay, to the south of Barra. Much of this research was drawn together by the Society from 1881 in their sponsorship of Romilly Allen's and Joseph Anderson's *Early Christian Monuments of Scotland* published in 1903. This massive work had been devised as a study of Pictish monuments into which the early medieval West Coast sculpture did not ideally fit.[33]

The 'runic cross from St Barr's' was perhaps Alexander Carmichael's most significant discovery and legacy to the National Museums (see Fig. 5). He saw the Kilbar stone in 1865 in the former burial-ground of the medieval parish church of Cille Bharra, as mentioned by Professor Donald MacKinnon. This was a cross-slab, 1.36 m in height, with a cross and interlace flanked by scrolls and key pattern in low relief on the one face, and an inscription in Old Norse runes on the other. The runes are damaged and any reading still has to be speculative, although they include the names Thorgerth and Steinar and a commemorative formula, and these and the stylistic detailing suggest a late-tenth century date. Alexander Carmichael's wife Mary (whom he had married in 1868) drew the stone in 1875 and subsequently made tracings of the surfaces which were sent to W. F. Skene, who sent them to Captain Thomas who, in turn, sent them to Joseph Anderson, Keeper of the National Museum of Antiquities. Information and drawings were sent for interpretation and translation to Professor George Stephens (1813–95) in Copenhagen but the difficulty of deciphering the inscription led to the suggestion that a photograph of the stone could be sent to Professor Stephens. 'It seemed that the simplest and most satisfactory plan was to remove the stone to Edinburgh for this purpose, and after considerable delay (owing to the death of the proprietor of the island, Mr John Gordon of Cluny) the requisite authority was obtained through the good offices of Mr Alexander Ross, architect, Inverness, FSA Scot, who also kindly caused the packing and transport of the stone to be carefully superintended by his clerk of works. ... In August 1880 this costly block happily reached the Edinburgh Museum ...' The gift of the Kilbar stone to the National Museum of Antiquities was credited to Mrs Gordon (the then proprietor of the South Uist estates which included Barra) in 1880.[34]

The extent and significance of Alexander Carmichael's donations of 1870 have never attracted comment although undoubtedly they established Carmichael's reputation (or at least his usefulness) with the Society of Antiquaries. The contact from Carmichael in the Islands was usually made through W. F. Skene in Edinburgh who reported the finds to the Society. The font from Loch Aoineart in Skye for example was carefully described to a meeting of the Society by Skene himself, the details including the unfortunate information that the columnar pedestal had been left in the ruined St Maelrubha's chapel.[35] Skene then read a brief but entertaining paper from Carmichael describing how the font had come into his possession by gift of the incumbent of Ardkenneth in South Uist. According to Carmichael's information, the font had been removed by a crew of South Uist fishermen as 'too sacred to be left with the heretic Protestants of Skye.' (see Fig. 4) A further extraordinary donation was the upper section of a former cross slab with sculpture in relief from the island of Berneray, associated with a possible chapel site called *Cill Aiseam* (see Fig. 6). He recounted how this was part of a standing monument which had been broken about fifty years before: 'The old people of Berneray have told me that within their memory the base of the obelisk was surrounded with a heap of small, beautifully white and variegated pebbles, old coins, bone pins, and bronze needles, the offering of pilgrims at the shrine of St Asaph.'[36] The two sections had been used as building material and Carmichael traced one piece to the kitchen window lintel of the house of a Mr MacKillop:

> MacKillop was very reluctant to allow the slab to be removed for examination, although I twice offered to replace it at my own expense. Ultimately, however, he consented. But before removing it, I thought proper to inform the proprietor, the Earl of Dunmore, of its existence, and to ask his sanction to its removal from the island. His Lordship immediately wrote his factor to secure the slab and bring it to Rodail. Upon his Lordship's arrival in Harris he wrote me, expressing his interest in the stone, and giving his permission to make what use of it I pleased. I got the slab removed from Rodail to Lochmaddy, where it now lies.

A sense of serendipity emerges from the chronicle of Alexander Carmichael's collecting; we sense the frisson of the search consummated by the 'crack' of traditional information from local folks of advanced age: 'I got a minute description of this interesting work of antiquity from an old man who saw it in his boyhood' would be a typical tag put on his account. Carmichael's intense enthusiasm for these antiquities where he finds them may be effectively distracted in the end product, both published and unpublished, in loosely associated historical narrative in which distinctions between information derived from local informants or from book learning may be blurred. His account of St Michael's Chapel in Grimsay, North Uist, for example, is swamped by an elaborate account of its traditional builder, Amy MacRuari, the estranged wife of John, Lord of the Isles, and then of warring descendants in North Uist. His coloured sketch map of the site, sent to the Society of Antiquaries, was laid aside by them and filed in their manuscripts rather than being reproduced in the *Proceedings*. Of a comparatively different order though is his account of quernstones in the same essay. Carmichael, having sent the upper and lower stones of a quern from Dùn Gainmhich, Benbecula, to the National Museum, supplies his observations on the making of querns in Lochaber and Heisgeir and traditions regarding the term *Abrach*. He mentions that there is a cross carved on the upper stone and that there is a *beirt* (?) in the eye of the quern which, significantly, had been recently placed in position. These details satisfy the need for an accurate record of provenance for the quern but lack the name of the family who gave it to Carmichael and to whom he refers. The reader today of the nineteenth-century record realises that social attitudes and standards might have dispensed with such modest detail, or that we are glimpsing areas of complexity in

Carmichael's own make-up.[37] Another important item from the 1870 donation was the mortar-like stone vessel localised to 'Cladh Chrìosd, Harris', but with no further details in the Museum's records (see Fig. 3). It is by no means clear where this possible ecclesiastical site was or to whom this object belonged although it is described as 'formerly believed to be capable of effecting miraculous cures'. Whereas the lack of provenance in the printed record is frustrating, Alexander Carmichael's own manuscript notes give a very clear account of this item and it is a matter of conjecture why or how this information was 'lost'. In an extended and detailed essay, 'Contributions sent to the Museum not previously described', Carmichael writes over 800 words on the Font from Cladh Chrìosd, Island of Pabaigh, Barra:

> … This Font was for centuries an object of credulous belief to the inhabitants of Pabbay and the other southern isles of Barra. These simple people implicitly believed that the touch of this font like that of another stone in S. Mary's burying ground (*Cladh Naomh Moire*) in the neighbouring Island of Bearnaray (Barra-Head) was efficacious in preventing and removing many mental and physical disorders incident to themselves and their flocks. The lixivium found in the font was considered doubly consecrated, firstly through contact with the already consecrated Font, and secondly through the friendly agency of some invisible and mysterious power that presided over the scene. The virtues of this salinated water were deemed secondary only to those of the water consecrated by the priest.[38]

VI

From 1882 Alexander Carmichael and his family were permanently resident in Edinburgh and his collecting of Hebridean antiquities effectively stopped. He was able to participate more fully in Edinburgh social and scholarly occasions, and so, for example, he attended the meetings of the Society of Antiquaries. As a Corresponding Member of the Society, he enjoyed the same privileges of an Ordinary Fellow but was not liable for any fees of admission or annual contributions. A meeting of the Society on 12 February 1894 heard a paper by Sheriff Æneas Mackay on 'Pampooties or shoes of raw hide from Aran More, Galway Bay', and the printed version in Volume 28 of the *Proceedings* included a set of notes sent in a letter by Carmichael on words for shoe, different types of shoe and a wealth of circumstantial detail, folklore and song lyrics. He gives an account of words such as *bachaill, bròg, caiseart, cuaran, logais, mogais* and *slaopag*, the last defined as 'an old shapeless shoe' and a word unknown to the dictionaries picked up in a song from Bonawe.[39]

These were the years of what has been described as the 'Celtic Revival' or 'Celtic Renaissance', an aesthetic reaction to the industrialised society of the late nineteenth century. Similar influence can be seen in a variety of areas such as national romantic movements in the confused cultures of nascent industrial states elsewhere in Europe. Influence has more frequently been discussed in terms of the spiritual and the transcendental but material culture provided inspiration and access to a Celtic past to a degree not sufficiently appreciated. Art supplied the most familiar arena but attention focussed on material culture, on 'Celtic antiquities' in the collections amassed in the Royal Irish Academy and in the work of Sir George Petrie (1790–1866), in the contemporary publication of the Book of Kells, in the Rhind Lectures in Archaeology by Dr Joseph Anderson, and in the opening of the new National Museum of Antiquities in Queen Street, Edinburgh, in 1891. Scholars supplied authenticity and authority and fed an enthusiasm for 'Celtic art', both graphically and metaphorically. A spiritual and moral power seemed to be perceived in the arts and crafts of the Gael, and designers and decorative artists adorned their 'Fingals' and 'Ossians' with the recent finds of archaeology and the archaeological discoveries of the eighteenth and nineteenth centuries now available for viewing in the new public museums. The material culture of the prehistory of Scotland, identified as 'Celtic', for example in the lectures and publications of the Keeper of the National Museum, Dr Joseph Anderson, inspired the imagination of an urban generation and created a public and a market receptive to the studied finesse of *Carmina Gadelica* when it first appeared in 1900.[40]

Alexander Carmichael's enthusiasm for Ossian had been made public in the long letter to Campbell of Islay in 1861 and he continued to glorify this inheritance on behalf of Gaelic culture.[41] His most significant contribution in this context was the oral version of the tale of 'Deirdire', taken down in Barra in March 1867 from the telling of John MacNeil of Buaile nam Bodach, and published first in Gaelic then in English in the *Transactions of the Gaelic Society of Inverness*, xiii (1886–7), having been read at a meeting of the society. 'Deirdire' was very thoroughly rewritten by Carmichael before being published in Edinburgh in book form with Gaelic and English in 1905. Research has now shown how highly contrived this text is, and symbolic perhaps of this contemporary handiwork is the handsome engraved frontispiece by the Edinburgh artist, John Duncan (1866–1945).[42] This shared in the contemporary viewpoint and aesthetic articulated and inspired particularly in the Edinburgh circle of Patrick Geddes (1854–1932), biologist, town-planner, and visionary, and his group including William Sharp (1855–1905) (with his *nom de plume* of 'Fiona MacLeod'), Pittendrigh MacGillivray (1856–1938), Noël Paton (1821–1901) and John Duncan. He was also strongly influenced by the contemporary Irish authors Standish O'Grady (1846–1928), Lady Augusta Gregory (1852–1932), Douglas Hyde (1860–1949) and W. B. Yeats (1865–1939). Geddes published a review journal, *The Evergreen*, which appeared in four numbers only in 1895–7. This recalled Allan Ramsay and his patriotic espousal of a native poetic tradition. It also, in contemporary vein, gave form to new editions of *Ossian* in 1896 and offered new energy to the world to which the Ossianic balladry belonged. Alexander Carmichael appears to have had a new audience when he contributed an essay on 'The Land of Lorne and the satirists of Taynuilt' to the 'Spring' number of *The Evergreen*. His material was elaborately dressed but of much greater authenticity than most Celtic Renaissance prose and verse:

> The Land of Lorne is the cradle of Christianity in Scotland, of monarchy in Scotland, and so, in a way, of that merged monarchy on which the sun never sets. It was the home of Naoise and Darthula, of Ardan and Aille, of Fingal and Ossian, a home of epic poetry and song, of art and music . . .[43]

VII

Alexander Carmichael's account of material culture, both in 'antiquities' and in his fieldwork collecting, is important and valuable for the historical record. In fact his coverage of archaeology, social and economic history, language, and literature, and the contemporary community is unusual, if not unique, in the scholarly circles of his day. His award of the Honorary Degree of LL.D. by Edinburgh University, following the publication of *Carmina*, was an acceptable recognition of his longstanding efforts on behalf of Gaelic. He was a close observer of form and detail, of features and posture, of circumstances, a copious taker of notes, a keen collector and a champion of Gaelic and Gaels. The material culture was equally absorbed and transmitted by Carmichael as part of the whole picture which would serve to challenge and counter the disdain of late-nineteenth century society. He knew the value of *faodail* as his writings and collecting activities amply demonstrate but his own enthusiasm and writing style ultimately cloud the record and leave issues of material culture unresolved. There is a hint that the fellowship of Society and Museum did not take to his writings for their discursiveness, lack of control and eliding of detail. It may be surprising for posterity and in the light of Professor Donald MacKinnon's judgement on Carmichael's antiquarian career that there is only a single paper of Alexander Carmichael's exclusive authorship in the late-nineteenth century *Proceedings*. There is a tension detectable in his dealings with the Society of Antiquaries of Scotland, on the one hand, in a sometimes deferential, if occasionally obsequious tone rooted in an apparent sense of intellectual inferiority, possibly the burden of the Gael in the capital, or not being admitted or seeking admission to full fellowship of the Society, and on the other, his regarding the Society and National Museum as not fully appreciating the significance of the material that he laid before them. They appear to hold Carmichael slightly at arm's length, using him as a convenient agent in the Islands but limiting his contribution to the *Proceedings* to notes taken from letters to Captain Thomas and W. F. Skene. Added to this is the matter of the loss of vital detail with reference to his donations. A sense of disappointment or frustration suffuses areas of his work and from time to time is given voice. In a letter to his friend Captain Thomas, dated Lochmaddy, 28 March 1867, he writes in such terms; though doubtless not then specifically against the Society, his words serve to typify a lifelong embattled mood:

> I will be delighted if anything I can send will be of service to you. I trust I need hardly assure you of this. I am deeply interested in everything which concerns the Highlands and Islands and he who honestly endeavours to throw light upon the ancient habits and customs of these can at all times command my willing services to the extent of my humble abilities. I am so much in the habit of being discouraged in prosecuting my antiquarian predilections that your kind words of encouragement are to me what the shower is to the parched plant of summer. Those old people with the marvellous memories are the only parties from whom I have been in the habit of receiving any sympathy or co-operation. And this sympathy is perhaps all the more genuine because we are both proscribed—they openly and I silently.[44]

I am most grateful to Dr Domhnall Uilleam Stiùbhart for drawing my attention to relevant documents and passages in the Carmichael Watson Papers in Edinburgh University Library Special Collections and for providing me with copies of documents. I am also grateful to the Library for allowing me to quote from them. I would like to acknowledge the inspiration deriving from the lectures of my fellow speakers and from the company and learning of those sharing in the Conference at Sgoil Lionacleit in Benbecula, 22–25 July 2006.

---

[1] Somhairle MacGhill Eathain, *Dàin do Eimhir agus dàin eile* (Glasgow, 1943), 49.

[2] See Ronald Black (ed.), *An tuil* (Edinburgh, 1999), 303–5.

[3] *CG* i, 6–11.

[4] Æ.J.G. Mackay and AC, 'Notes on a pair of pampooties, or shoes of raw hide, from Aran More, Galway Bay, by Æ.J.G. Mackay, LL.D., F.S.A. Scot., Sheriff of Fife and Kinross. And on cuaran and other varieties of shoes used in the Highlands and Islands of Scotland, by Alexander Carmichael, Corr. Mem. S.A. Scot.', *PSAS*, 28 (1893–4), 143.

[5] Donald MacKinnon, 'Alexander Carmichael LL.D', *Celtic Review*, viii (1913), 112–15; Ian Carmichael, *Lismore in Alba*, (Perth, [1948]), 96–8; Derick S. Thomson, 'Alexander Carmichael', *Oxford Dictionary of National Biography*

10, (Oxford, 2004), 167–8.

[6] Carmichael, *Lismore in Alba*, 171–81. The Bachall of St Moluag was returned to Lismore in 1990.

[7] AC, 'The Barons of Bachuil', *Celtic Review*, v (1908–9), 356–375.

[8] *Catalogue of the National Museum of Antiquities of Scotland*, (Edinburgh, 1892), 300; National Museums of Scotland [NMS] H.KL 73; see also National Archives of Scotland, Skene Papers, GD 126/8/131 for a reference to the 'charter box' in a letter to William Forbes Skene.

[9] *CG* ii, 210–11.

[10] 'The Carmichael Collection' (typescript), West Highland Museum, Fort William. I am most grateful to Fiona Marwick of the West Highland Museum for bringing this to my attention. See also Trevor Cowie, 'Lost and found: a Late Bronze Age sword hoard from South Uist re-united', *Hebridean Naturalist*, 12 (1994), 9–18; drift seeds are considered in *CG* ii, 225.

[11] For example, see CW MS 116 fo. 4, noting details and names of parts of horizontal mills; see also Hugh Cheape, 'Horizontal grain mills in Lewis', in [Scottish Vernacular Buildings Working Group], *Highland Vernacular Building* (Edinburgh, 1989), 71–89.

[12] *CG* i, xxii–xxiii.

[13] *CG* i, xxxiv; John Francis Campbell, *Popular tales of the West Highlands* (second ed., Paisley, 1893) iv, 209–26 (for AC's letter of 28 November 1861 to John Francis Campbell regarding the strength of Ossianic tradition).

[14] Ibid. i, xlix; see also xix: 'Even the houses and the old agricultural implements, where they are still used, are peculiar.'

[15] *CG* i, 190.

[16] Ibid., 252–3; see also Alexander Fenton, 'Net-drying, pot-drying and graddaning: small-scale grain drying and processing techniques', *Saga och Sed* (Kungl. Gustav Adolfs Akademiens Årsbok: Yearbook of the Royal Gustav Adolf's Academy) (Uppsala, 1982), 85–106; Hugh Cheape, 'The graddan mill of John Grant', *Review of Scottish Culture*, 16 (2003–4), 158–61.

[17] Edward Dwelly, *The illustrated Gaelic-English dictionary*, (1911: Glasgow, 1967), 731.

[18] *CG* i, 302; iii, 352–3; John Lorne Campbell, '*Carmina Gadelica*: George Henderson's corrections and suggestions', *Scottish Gaelic Studies*, xiii (1981), 183–218.

[19] *CG* i, 294–5.

[20] Hugh Cheape and Anita Quye, 'Historical and analytical research of dyes in early Scottish tartans', in Rob Janaway and Paul Wyeth (eds), *Scientific analysis of ancient and historic textiles: informing preservation, display and interpretation*, AHRC Research Centre for Textile Conservation and Textile Studies 2004 (London, 2005), 202–7.

[21] See Hugh Cheape, 'Cupping', *Review of Scottish Culture*, 10 (1996–7), 135–9.

[22] See idem, 'The hearth and social focus in the Hebridean house', in Marion Wood (ed.), *The hearth in Scotland*, Scottish Vernacular Buildings Working Group Regional and Thematic Studies, 7 (2001), 25–49.

[23] Robert G.W. Anderson, 'Museums in the making: the origins and development of the national collections', in Jenni Calder (ed.), *The wealth of a nation* (Edinburgh, 1989), 1–17.

[24] Alexander Fenton, 'Early and traditional cultivating implements in Scotland', *PSAS*, 96 (1962–3), 264–317; idem, 'A plough type from the Outer Isles', *Tools and Tillage*, i(2) (1960), 117–28; idem, 'The cas-chrom: a review of the Scottish evidence, *Tools and Tillage*, ii(3) (1974), 131–48; see also CW MS 512, in which, *inter alia*, Carmichael describes buying a 'Crom-nan-Gad' from Norman Graham in Back, Lewis, for 5/-.

[25] Charles N. McIntyre North, *Leabhar Comunn nam Fior Ghàel. The Book of the Club of True Highlanders* (London, 1881), i, plate 27: 'Agricultural Implements'.

[26] Rev. Alexander Stewart, *'Twixt Ben Nevis and Glencoe* (Edinburgh, 1885), 68–73; see also idem, *Nether Lochaber* (Edinburgh, 1883), 201–3, 219–24.

[27] William Forbes Skene, *Celtic Scotland: a history of ancient Alba* (Edinburgh, 3 vols, 1876–80), iii, 378–93; see also Donald Gregory, *The history of the Western Highlands and Isles of Scotland* (1836: second ed., London 1881); National Archives of Scotland, Skene Papers, GD126/8/9.

[28] AC, 'Grazing and agrestic customs of the Outer Hebrides' in the *Report of the Commissioners of Inquiry into the Condition of the Crofters and Cottars in the Highlands and Islands of Scotland* (Parliamentary Papers 1884, xxxiii–xxxvi), 451–82; idem, 'Uist old hymns', *Transactions of the Gaelic Society of Glasgow*, i (1887–91), 34–47; see also Donald E. Meek, *The Quest for Celtic Christianity* (Edinburgh, 2000), for a discussion of the wide-ranging influence of Carmichael's collection of hymns and prayers.

[29] *CG* i, xxvii.

[30] *Catalogue of the National Museum of Antiquities of Scotland*, 300 (NMS X.IB 49); F. W. L. Thomas, 'Observations respecting articles collected in the Outer Hebrides, and now presented to the Museum', *PSAS*, 4 (1860–2), 115–17; [obituary notice] 'Capt. F.W.L. Thomas, R.N.', ibid., 20 (1885–6), 6–7.

[31] W.D.H. Sellar, 'William Forbes Skene (1809–92): historian of Celtic Scotland', *PSAS*, 131 (2001), 3–21.

[32] NMS X.IB 37; AC, 'Notice of Teampull Michael', *PSAS*, 8 (1868–70), 285–6; see also CW MSS 457: 'Contributions sent to the Museum not previously described'; and 362: 'Promiscuous Antiquities in the Long Island'.

[33] J. Romilly Allen and Joseph Anderson, *The early Christian monuments of Scotland: a classified, illustrated, descriptive list of the monuments with an analysis of their symbolism and ornamentation* (Edinburgh 1903), 110–11, 113.

[34] NMS X.IB 102; Professor George Stephens, 'Notice of a Sculptured Stone etc.', *PSAS*, 15 (1880–1), 33–6; Allen and Anderson, *Early Christian monuments*, 114–15.

[35] NMS H.KG 1; '[Donations to the Museum] By Alexander A. Carmichael Esq., Lochmaddy, through W. F. Skene Esq, F.S.A. Scot.', *PSAS*, 8 (1868–70), 237–9.

[36] AC, 'Notices of Teampull Micheal', ibid., 280–2; Ian Fisher, *Early medieval sculpture in the West Highlands and Islands*, (Edinburgh, Royal Commission on the Ancient and Historical Monuments of Scotland and Society of Antiquaries of Scotland, 2001), 112–13; CW MS 457 fo.7: 'Contributions sent to the Museum not previously described' and 'Sculptured Stones S. Asaph (*Cilleaiseam*), Island of Bearnaray in the Sound of Harris'.

[37] NMS X.BB 24-5; AC, 'Notices of Teampull Micheal', 282–3; see also Society of Antiquaries Manuscripts, National Museums of Scotland MS 522.

[38] NMS X.BA 25; *Catalogue of the National Museum of Antiquities of Scotland*, 74; CW MS 457 fos.1–6: 'Contributions sent to the Museum not previously described'.

[39] Mackay and Carmichael, 'Notes on a pair of pampooties', 136–50; see 143–9 for AC's contribution.

[40] Joseph Anderson, *Scotland in early Christian times: the Rhind Lectures in Archaeology, 1879* (Edinburgh, 1881): the title page figures an engraving of NMS X.KG 1, the font from Loch Aoineart in Skye credited to Carmichael; idem, *Scotland in pagan times, the Iron Age: the Rhind Lectures in Archaeology, 1880* (Edinburgh, 1883).

[41] John Lorne Campbell, 'Notes on Hamish Robertson's "Studies in Carmichael's *Carmina Gadelica*"', *Scottish Gaelic Studies*, xiii (1978), 8–9.

[42] AC, *Deirdire and the Lay of the Children of Uisne* (Edinburgh, 1905); Alan Bruford, '"Deirdire" and Alexander Carmichael's treatment of oral sources', *Scottish Gaelic Studies*, xiv (1983), 1–24.

[43] AC, 'The Land of Lorne and the satirists of Taynuilt', in *Evergreen*, i (Spring, 1895), 110.

[44] CW MS 472, fos.1–2.

8

The Visual Dimension of *Carmina Gadelica*

MURDO MACDONALD

My aim here is to draw attention to the first edition of *Carmina Gadelica* as the work of art that it is. In doing so I will consider both the visual sources for the initials and decorations, and also consider the tradition of Celtic-revival book design in Scotland of which *Carmina Gadelica* is the high point. *Carmina Gadelica* is one of the finest examples of book design and production published anywhere in the world in the years around 1900. To understand how this came about we need to consider a number of figures acknowledged by Alexander Carmichael in his introduction to the work. The first of these figures is Walter Blaikie (1847–1928) of the Edinburgh printing firm of T. & A. Constable.

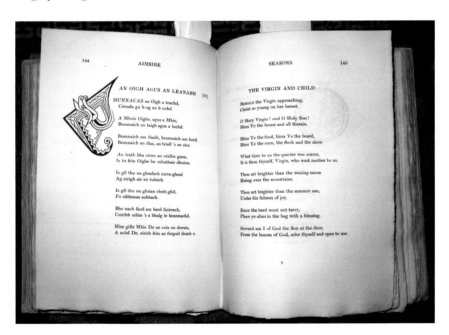

Fig. 1: *Carmina Gadelica* i, 144–5. The initial is derived from the Book of Deer (see Fig. 2)

A great book needs great production, and the firm of T. & A. Constable, under the stewardship of Walter Blaikie, was capable of precisely that. Blaikie is a fascinating character in his own right who deserves more research. He was an engineer by professional background, and came to publishing by accident in 1878. As director of T. & A. Constable, the impact he

Fig. 2: Detail of fo.85 of the Book of Deer, from John Stuart
(ed.), *The Book of Deer* (Edinburgh: Spalding Club, 1869)

made on the intellectual culture of Scotland was considerable. He numbered among his friends
both scientists such as D'Arcy Thompson (1860–1948) and Patrick Geddes (1854–1932), and
scholars of Gaelic language and culture such as Ella Carmichael (1871–1928) and Father Allan
McDonald (1859–1905). Indeed, it is to Walter Blaikie that we owe many of our photographs
of Father Allan. In his introduction to the 1983 reprint of volume one of *Carmina Gadelica*,
John Lorne Campbell discusses the initial difficulties of publishing the book, which were
resolved when 'Finally Fr. Allan McDonald's friend Walter Blaikie intervened and secured the
publication of the book by his firm T. & A. Constable in Edinburgh.'[1] Thus *Carmina Gadelica*
was secured by a man who had a real interest in the Gàidhealtachd for a firm which had some
of the highest design and production values in the world at the time. This was the time of the
high point of development of the Arts and Crafts movement, and Scotland was at the heart
of that movement.[2]

From the visual point of view the other key figure mentioned by Carmichael in that
introduction is his wife Mary (1841–1928). Her role in the eventual appearance of *Carmina
Gadelica* is crucial for, as Alexander notes, 'The Celtic letters in the work have been copied by
my wife from Celtic manuscripts, chiefly in the Advocates Library.' He continues: 'This has
been a task of extreme difficulty, needing great skill and patient care owing to the defaced
condition of the originals.' It is to these letters and their sources that I now turn, because they
are the defining visual feature of *Carmina Gadelica*. I would, however, reiterate the point that
these initials require good typographical design and good production to do them justice. Walter
Blaikie was fundamental here, but we should not forget another figure acknowledged by
Carmichael when he notes that: 'The letters have been prepared for the engraver with feeling
and insight by Mr. John Athel Lovegrove of H. M. Ordnance Survey.'[3] Although little is known
about Lovegrove, he was clearly a talented draughtsman.

So my first effort here is to identify the 'defaced' originals that Mary Carmichael copied and to address the issue of how much she copied directly and how much she modified. In his seminal article, 'The Gaelic manuscripts of Scotland', published in 1989, Ronald Black identified one of the manuscripts from the Advocates Library from which Mary Carmichael worked. This is a collection of several manuscripts of materia medica, written on vellum, and

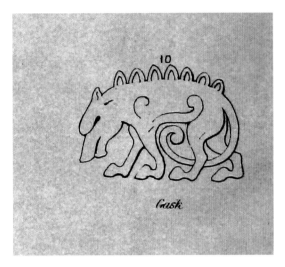

Fig. 3: The Pictish animal which Mary Carmichael used to conclude the
main text of *Carmina Gadelica* is closely based on this image from
Plate 23 of John Stuart, *Sculptured Stones of Scotland* ii
(Edinburgh: Spalding Club, 1867).

the particular initials that inspired Mary Carmichael probably date from the fifteenth century.[4] At present I am only aware of two examples and these occur near the beginning of the manuscript, at the beginning of page one and page two. The page one initial, the condition of which amply justifies Alexander's description 'defaced', is transformed with skill and sensitivity into the initial that occurs first on *CG* i, 72. Similarly, the page two initial from this manuscript is transformed by Mary into the initial which has its first occurrence on *CG* i, 26.

As Alexander Carmichael notes, the copying would indeed have been difficult due to the condition of the originals; it is also clear from her adaptation of these initials, however, that Mary Carmichael was no mere copyist. What she seems to have been doing was taking these designs, understanding their principles of construction, and making alterations to suit the purposes of her husband's book. That is to say, creating an exact copy was not her primary concern.

But there are several sources for the initial letters over and above the Advocates Library manuscript. What I want to do here is give an account of what I have come up with so far. One of the characteristics of the initials in *Carmina Gadelica*—when considered as a set—is their stylistic variety, and this is further extended when one notes the debt to Pictish art of many of the decorative features. Such visual diversity may be though of as an appropriate response to the variety of the verbal material, but it also implies a larger set of sources than Carmichael's comment that the letters in the work had been copied from 'manuscripts, chiefly in the Advocates' Library' might lead one to expect. Thus awareness of manuscripts with defaced initials in the Advocates Library collection was an important starting point for me, but it soon

Fig. 4: An initial from *Carmina Gadelica* which is either based on
an initial from fo.179ʳ of the Book of Kells, or on an
intermediate source.

became clear that this was not the whole picture with respect to Mary Carmichael's visual
sources. This is consistent with the fact that Alexander uses the word 'chiefly' when speaking
of Mary's sources, thus implying that some of the visual sources were not in fact from
manuscripts in the Advocates Library. One has to remember, also, that Alexander's comment
is made as an acknowledgement in an introduction, not as a description of specific sources.

So it is clear that Mary Carmichael was using a considerable variety of sources. In addition,
on a purely visual level I thought I recognised some of the initials. Celtic manuscripts are not
my everyday area of research, so I knew that if I did indeed recognise material, the likelihood
was that it was firmly in the public domain. This intuition bore fruit when I turned to the Book
of Deer, which would have been available to Mary Carmichael via the facsimile published by
the Spalding Club in 1869. Incidentally, since the current open shelf copy of this facsimile in
the National Library of Scotland bears the Advocates Library stamp, it seems reasonable to
suppose that this very facsimile would have been available to Mary in the Advocates Library.
There is an added interest here for Mary spent much of her childhood at Old Deer, so it is likely
that she had a personal interest in the history of this document. Two *Carmina Gadelica* initials
are near direct copies of letters from the Book of Deer. The first appears on *CG* i, 88, and is
clearly based on the initial from fo.2 of the Book of Deer. The second initial deriving from the
Book of Deer is to be found on *CG* i, 144. It derives, equally clearly from the initial on fo.85.

Also relevant to the wider decoration of *Carmina Gadelica* is another Spalding Club
publication from the 1860s, namely volume two of *Sculptured Stones of Scotland* by John Stuart
(1813–77), a book including several pages of Pictish symbols. A number of these provide
direct models for the decorations which divide sections in *Carmina Gadelica*, for example the
wolf-like creature which concludes the body of the main text, prior to the notes. This is directly
based on a Pictish image on a stone at Gask which appears on plate 23 of Stuart's volume two.
The same page of Stuart shows a salmon from Dunrobin which becomes, in the hands of
Mary Carmichael, the tailpiece for section two of *Carmina Gadelica* ('Seasons'). Similarly, an
eagle which appears in Stuart on plate 24, is the model for the tailpiece for
section four ('Incantations') of *Carmina Gadelica*. The Pictish crescent which appears on the

Fig. 5: An initial probably derived from an illustration in Owen Jones, *Grammar of Ornament* (London, 1856). The original is from the eleventh-century Psalter of Ricemarcus. Mary Carmichael inverts and reverses it.

Gaelic title page of both volumes of *Carmina Gadelica* is an inverted copy of an image on a stone at Rosemarkie, which appears in Stuart volume two on plate 21. Similarly the Pictish snake and Z-rod design which concludes both volumes is a direct copy of a design from Ballutheron which appears on plate 25 of Stuart.

In passing I want to note another set of possible sources, namely the lithographed copies of Irish manuscripts in the original Mackinnon Collection of the Department of Celtic and Scottish Studies at the University of Edinburgh. I have not had time to study these in detail, but at the very least there are some good analogies for letters in *Carmina Gadelica*. But the influence, if any, of that source requires more research to identify. A number of other letters in *Carmina Gadelica* have a loose relationship with the Book of Kells. Again I have not had time to study these links in detail, and there may well be some intermediary source here. There are, nevertheless interesting links for example initials in both works show a horizontal fish biting a vertical strut. Again initials in both works show a snake curved into the form of a figure of eight.

The variety of sources I have considered so far is considerable. We have manuscript art produced by Gaelic speakers dating from the early ninth century to the fifteenth century. We have Pictish rock engravings dating from the eighth century. And we find Mary Carmichael, like any good designer, using both originals and reproductions for her inspiration. Of particular interest, not least because it relates to an early definition of Celtic art, is an almost direct copy from a manuscript dating from the end of the eleventh century. This is the Psalter of Ricemarcus which is held at Trinity College Dublin. But the likely actual source of this initial for Mary Carmichael was nearer to hand, for this particular letter is reproduced in *The Grammar of Ornament* by Owen Jones (1809–74), published in 1856. In *Carmina Gadelica* the letter is inverted and reversed, but is otherwise a close copy.

The Grammar of Ornament has a wider relevance here for it was a comprehensive visual source book that helped to define ornamental style for the Victorian age. Jones attempted to gather examples from all cultures and all periods and to categorise them in an accessible way. One of Jones' categories was 'Celtic Ornament', explored in three pages of illustrations which contain images ranging from details of the Book of Kells to the Pictish cross slab at Aberlemno. Also of importance is the accompanying essay by the notable scholar John Obadiah Westwood (1805–93). It is quite possible that Westwood's earlier works are also sources for Mary Carmichael, but I have not yet researched this point. It is all the more likely that Mary Carmichael's source for this letter was Owen Jones, because Westwood's essay is drawn upon by her husband's older colleague John Francis Campbell of Islay (1821–85) to legitimise his use of the phrase "Celtic art" in volume four of his *Popular Tales of the West Highlands*, published in 1862. As Campbell says: 'It may be new to many to hear of 'Celtic art', but nevertheless it is classed [as such] in the Grammar of Ornament by Owen Jones, who is an acknowledged authority on such matters.'[5] So there is no doubt that Jones' work was part of the apparatus of the scholar as well as the designer. This point about scholarly interaction in this visual context can be underlined by noting that Westwood's essay includes in its bibliography volume one of Stuart's *Sculptured Stones of Scotland*, even though that book was only published in the same year as *The Grammar of Ornament*.

Thanks to *The Grammar of Ornament*, 1856 can be regarded as the date that Celtic art was recognised as a distinct style in an international context. I want to turn now to the use of that style, primarily in book design, in order to give context to the first edition of *Carmina Gadelica* as part of the material culture of Scotland. It will be clear by now that *Carmina Gadelica* is a high point not only of book design in general but of Celtic revival book design in particular. But it is worth pausing to consider this term 'Celtic revival' and what we might mean by it. In order for something to be revived, something of the original has to be engaged with in a systematic manner. This is exactly what we see happening in the decoration of *Carmina Gadelica* but, in order for that to happen a culture of serious visual analysis of Celtic art is a prerequisite. In short, you can't revive something unless you have a detailed engagement with what is being revived. If you don't have that detailed engagement you don't have a revival, you have a reference or an influence. Thus Celtic revival art depends on an appreciation of Celtic art, and an appreciation of Celtic art depends on careful drawing and measurement of that art. So the question is, when does the Celtic art of Scotland become adequately measured, drawn, printed, and of course published?

As good a date as any to begin such consideration is 1848 with the publication under the auspices of the Bannatyne Club of *The Ancient Sculptured Monuments of the County of Angus* by Patrick Chalmers (1802–54). This was, incidentally, another of the sources quoted by Westwood in his essay in *The Grammar of Ornament*. Chalmers makes his intention clear by noting the inadequacy of earlier representations of these primarily Pictish stones, and this book is a major advance on anything previously available. But even here the art is adequate rather than good, and the artist employed by Chalmers, P. A. Jastrzębski (misspelt in the volume as Jastrzcbski), was soon to be criticised for inaccuracy. For example on the eastern face of the Glamis stone it is hard to tell whether the animals are engraved or carved in relief.[6] So despite the fact that these images are a definite advance on what was available at the time, they lack involvement with the structure of the art depicted, and as such only partially achieve Chalmers' aim of moving on from the erroneous images of the past. This point can be clarified by noting that when some of them were reused in 1856 for the first volume of Stuart's *Sculptured Stones of Scotland*, the Aberdeen artist and lithographer Andrew Gibb made corrections.

In due course Gibb, who later became a Fellow of the Society of Antiquaries of Scotland, took over the illustrative project. In contrast to Jastrzębski he was consistently accurate and sympathetic to his subject matter. For example, his images of the Kildalton Cross, as well as being fine works of lithographic art, are immediate and reliable visual sources for the scholar. It is because of the shift from Jastrzębski to Gibb that Stuart's second volume, published in 1867 attains its extraordinary value as a visual source, not least for Mary Carmichael.

One has to distinguish here between the analysis of Celtic art which makes Celtic revival work possible and works of Celtic revival art and design in their own right. A key work from 1851 has both these characteristics. This is *The Archaeology and Prehistoric Annals of Scotland* by Daniel Wilson (1816–92)—the first use in English, incidentally, of the term 'prehistoric'— which has not only a very early Celtic revival cover, but includes within it detailed visual analysis of Celtic art: for example the frontispiece is an accurate engraving of the Hunterston Brooch. The original drawing here is by Wilson himself, an artist of considerable ability. As an academic work, his book is thus an example of the analysis required for Celtic revival art and design to come into being; as an object of material culture, by virtue of its cover, it is itself an early example of that Celtic revival art and design.

Visual analysis of Celtic art continued with, as I have noted, both Owen Jones' work and that of John Stuart. But another remarkable Celtic revival book cover from this period is the covers of John Francis Campbell's *Popular Tales of the West Highlands*, published in 1860 and 1862. This cover is an innovative adaptation of pre-Reformation West Highland School work, all the more appropriate when one recalls that, as I have noted, Campbell helped to establish the very notion of Celtic art as an academic category. This double process of analysis and revival continued in the early 1880s with the publication of classics of analysis such as the series of Rhind Lectures by Joseph Anderson (1832–1916), a series complemented by Celtic revival covers for other works. For example in 1885 one finds a Celtic border made into a decorative feature on the second edition of the intriguing *Loch Etive and the Sons of Uisneach* by R. Angus Smith (1817–84).[7] In 1889 a Celtic design is considered appropriate to represent the entirety of Scottish art, as the cover of Robert Brydall's *History of Art in Scotland*. Three years later, in 1892, the new illustrated catalogue of the Museum of Antiquities makes a nod to Celtic

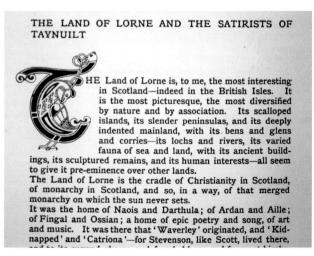

Fig. 6: The initial letter, by Helen Hay, of Alexander Carmichael's 'The land of Lorne and the satirists of Taynuilt', which appeared in Patrick Geddes' *Evergreen* in 1895. A precursor of Mary Carmichael's work for *Carmina Gadelica*.

interlace in its cover design and this ushers in the high decade of Celtic revival book design, which I date from 1895 to 1905. That decade has the publication of *Carmina Gadelica* at its heart.

Walter Blaikie has a significant role here for the publication which initiates this period in 1895 is Patrick Geddes' *Evergreen*, printed—like *Carmina Gadelica*—by Blaikie's firm of T. & A. Constable. The first issue of *The Evergreen* contains both Celtic revival design and illustration, and also, of particular interest for us here, a paper by Alexander Carmichael, 'The Land of Lorne and the satirists of Taynuilt', in which he speculates about the Gaelic background of Robert Burns' ancestors. This has an initial letter based on Celtic art. It is the work of Helen Hay (*fl.*1895–1940), one of a group of artists working with Geddes. With its links to both Carmichael as author and Blaikie as printer, it is possible that this single initial inspired the design of *Carmina Gadelica*. It is interesting to note also that it is used many years later, without acknowledgment, to introduce an obituary of James Carmichael Watson (1910–42) which was published in *CG* v in 1954. However by that time the grasp of who had done what for *Carmina Gadelica* was slack. The same volume makes the erroneous statement in the information on its back cover that 'the many ornamental initial letters, headpieces and tailpieces are the beautiful work and generous gift of Mr Robert Burns.' This statement is also made on the cover of *CG* iv, published in 1941, and it is telling that no one picked up on its inaccuracy before the issue of volume five. Some of the new designs for initials may well be by that artist, but most of the initials are repeats of Mary Carmichael's designs. The mention of Burns (1869–1941) is, however, interesting from a wider perspective because he was another of the artists who made a major contribution to Geddes' *Evergreen* in 1895 and this suggests enduring links between the circles of Geddes and Carmichael. Burns contributed one of the key Japanese influenced images to *The Evergreen*. Entitled *Natura Naturans* this work reminds one (if reminder were needed) that any consideration of the visual aspect of the Celtic revival must be seen in an international context.

The leading artist of the Celtic Revival was John Duncan (1866–1945) and one of Duncan's contributions to this first issue of *The Evergreen* has a high degree of interest, both with respect to the Celtic revival in general and with respect to the Carmichael family. This is his image *Anima Celtica*, which is an almost heraldic synthesis of Celtic and related symbolism: standing stones, the blind Ossian accompanied by Malvina, Fingal with the new-born Ossian, the awakening of Cuchullin, an ancient bronze sword of Celtic pattern, all centred on a Celtic muse. A further aspect is jacobite symbolism, which can be seen in the foreground, and takes the form of an eighteenth century dirk and a bonnet with a white cockade. The message is thus that the Celtic revival of the 1890s is part of a continuous Highland tradition, which leads back, via James Macpherson, via the jacobites, to the time of the Fenians and before. A few years ago I hazarded a guess that the central figure might be intended to represent Bride, a goddess and saint in whom John Duncan showed considerable interest. That may or may not be correct, but when I showed this image at a seminar of the Fine Art department at the University of Edinburgh, in April 2006, one of the audience, Abigail Burnyeat of the Department of Celtic and Scottish Studies, noted the similarly of the features of this central figure with none other Alexander Carmichael's daughter and amanuensis, Ella. There were definite links between John Duncan and Ella Carmichael a decade later, but considering Alexander's contribution to the *Evergreen*, it makes complete sense that Ella was part of the *Evergreen* circle in 1895.

When one compares *Anima Celtica* with Ella's portrait in the Celtic department of Edinburgh University, the visual evidence is convincing. What is more is that this portrait is signed

'Mackie', and I presume this to be Charles Mackie (1862–1920), another key member of the *Evergreen* group, indeed the designer of the covers among much else.

This identification leads one firmly into the cultural politics of the Celtic revival. Or to put it another way, it brings us to consider the contrast between Alexander Carmichael and William Sharp (1855–1905), also known as Fiona Macleod. The identification of Ella as the model for *Anima Celtica* bears on this because it sheds light on a well-known but rather strange letter written by William Sharp to Patrick Geddes. Sharp was closely involved in *The Evergreen*, so all other things being equal, one would expect him to be supportive of it, however he singles out John Duncan's *Anima Celtica* for particular attack, while at the same time complimenting other images by Duncan.[8] He does this under the guise of art criticism, which, as a friend of the likes of Rossetti, he was in a position to do, but I have always sensed a hidden agenda here. I had previously assumed that he saw John Duncan as a threat to his own aspirations—in the person of Fiona Macleod—as leader of the Celtic revival. But if the figure of *Anima Celtica* is indeed based on Ella Carmichael, then perhaps Sharp's hidden agenda is in fact directed against Ella. This is consistent with the fact is that Sharp preferred his cultures to be dead or dying. The idea of having to deal with real live Gaels—particularly young ones—was, I suspect, anathema to him. Furthermore the idea that the imaginary Fiona Macleod might have flesh and blood competition in the form of Ella Carmichael, was I suspect too much for him to absorb. He wanted Celtic culture in exactly the same condition as his other beloved culture, that of ancient Greece: namely dead but inspiring.

This cultural necrophilia comes out very clearly in his writings, but before I refer to these I want to consider the books published by Patrick Geddes and Colleagues with Sharp as advisor, because these have an important visual dimension. Just a year after the first volume of *The Evergreen*, Sharp was involved with a series called *The Celtic Library* for which Helen Hay designed covers, end-papers and the title-page decoration. A key work here was *The Centenary Ossian*, published in 1896. *The Celtic Library* became the point of origin for most of Sharp's Fiona Macleod works including *The Sin-eater* and *The Washer of the Ford*. Along with these were *The Fiddler of Carne* by Sharp's friend the Welsh writer Ernest Rhys (1859–1946), and *The Shadow of Arvor*, a book of Breton legends done into English by another friend, Edith Wingate Rinder (d.1952).[9]

The most intriguing of all the *Celtic Library* works was *Lyra Celtica*, 'an anthology of representative Celtic poetry' edited by Sharp's wife, Elizabeth (1856–1932). It contains almost two hundred individual works, followed by forty or so pages of notes. Contributions include ancient and modern work by poets from Scotland, Ireland, Brittany, Cornwall, Wales, and the Isle of Man. *Lyra Celtica* was emphatically pan-Celtic in its inspiration, ranging from Macpherson's *Ossian* to Yeats's *The Lake Isle of Innisfree*[10] via Duncan Bàn MacIntyre, Douglas Hyde, Sir Samuel Ferguson, Kuno Meyer, John Stuart Blackie, Hall Caine, T. W. Rolleston and Fiona Macleod. It was, however, a determinedly English-language presentation of the Celt: that was the key to Sharp's agenda for he wanted to claim the future of Celtic culture for English speakers like himself. In contrast to Sharp, Carmichael was, of course, a native Gaelic speaker, an attribute that Sharp was only able to claim for Fiona Macleod because she did not exist. In his introduction to *Lyra Celtica* Sharp quotes himself through the words of Fiona Macleod: 'The Celt falls, but his spirit rises in the heart and the brain of the Anglo-Celtic peoples, with whom are the destinies of the generations to come.'[11] Thus Gaelic for Sharp was something to be subjugated by English rather than a language to be presented in its own right.

Carmina Gadelica was published in 1900, four years after *Lyra Celtica* and Sharp, in the person of Fiona Macleod, reviewed it the same year in *The Nineteenth Century*. It is fascinating to see how he insists in this review that Carmichael's work is a wonderful elegy for a more or less dead culture, rather than an indication of any potential regeneration.[12] For Sharp, Carmichael can do no more than 'preserve awhile' a 'sunset beauty'. Having said that, he does not entirely misrepresent Carmichael here, for Carmichael himself saw his work as very much a reflection of an already passed age, in his own words 'a stone upon the cairn of those who composed and those who transmitted the work'.[13] But the difference lies in Sharp's emphasis time and again of a single outcome, that is to say the death of the culture that is held by Sharp to be inevitable. We must therefore distinguish Sharp's fantasy yearning for the death of the Gael from Carmichael's matter of fact recognition of loss.

In view of Sharp's advocacy of English as the language of the Celt, it is ironic to note that Alexander Carmichael's English text has an importance in its own right, indeed Carmichael can be considered the first of the great twentieth-century translators. His achievement in English should, I think, be seen alongside Rabindranath Tagore's translations of his own Bengali and Arthur Waley's translations of Chinese poetry. Perhaps this could be explored as part of *Carmina Gadelica*'s importance as a modernist project, to use Domhnall Uilleam Stiùbhart's description.

Whatever the complexities that William Sharp and his *alter ego* bring to the situation, one can underline the constructive links between the circles of Carmichael and Geddes by pointing out that when Carmichael published his dual language text of versions of the Deirdre[14] legend in 1905, the frontispiece was not only by John Duncan, it was the gift of the artist.[15] Duncan gives another indication of his closeness to the Carmichael family in a letter to Geddes, written some years later. He notes that the original of his drawing *St Columba on the Hill of Angels*, is in the possession of Ella Carmichael, who was by then wife of the Professor of Celtic at Edinburgh, William J. Watson (1865–1948).[16] This drawing was used by Geddes in 1912 as the frontispiece for *St Columba: A Study of Social Inheritance and Spiritual Development* by Victor Branford (1892–1941), but it was first reproduced in 1904 in *The St Columba Scrip*, a book issued to support the building fund of the Church of Saint Columba at Blackhall, Edinburgh. Duncan dedicates his image 'To my Celtic Muse in homage' and it seems likely that these words are addressed to Ella Carmichael.

So that is the wider context of *Carmina Gadelica* in terms of Celtic revival book design and illustration. It brings me almost to my conclusion, but there is one more Celtic revival artist I must mention. This is Archibald Knox (1864–1933), probably the greatest of all designers associated with Liberty's of London, not least for his Cymric metal work designs. Knox was born in the Isle of Man but his Scottish connections, and indeed his Highland connections, are strong. His father came from the Knox weaving dynasty of Kilbirnie in Ayrshire and his mother was a Carmichael from Lismore. When I became aware of this, thanks to my wife Lorna exploring the topic with Donald Black in Lismore in 2005, I began to wonder if Alexander Carmichael's fine gravestone in Lismore might be to the design of Archibald Knox. Again thanks to information from Donald Black, it seems that it is in fact to the design of Eoghan, one of Carmichael's sons. But the possibility of a link to Knox is worth exploring further not least because, as Ian Fisher pointed out to me, some of the decoration of *Carmina Gadelica* (including both spine and title page elements) is derived from Norse work found in the Isle of Man.

I would like to conclude by stating the obvious, namely that the high visual standard of the first edition of *Carmina Gadelica* is no accident, for it is abundantly clear that artists and designers were part of the Carmichael family milieu. In any consideration of the visual dimension of *Carmina Gadelica* we must give attention not only to the outstanding contribution of Mary Carmichael and to the backing of one of the most talented men in the book trade, Walter Blaikie. We must also take into account the circle of Patrick Geddes, which includes the Celtic revival designer Helen Hay. Ella Carmichael's links with that circle, in particular with the painters John Duncan and Charles Mackie, must also be given due weight. We should also consider the possibility of links with Archibald Knox. Whatever further study may reveal, research into this aspect of *Carmina Gadelica* enables one to appreciate much more deeply the interconnections between the oral, literary and visual culture in the time of Alexander Carmichael.

---

[1] John Lorne Campbell, 'Introduction to the 1983 Reprint', *CG* i (Edinburgh and London, 1983), xix.

[2] This is reflected by Walter Crane's endorsement of T. & A. Constable in his classic account *Of the decorative illustration of books old and new* (London, 1896).

[3] *CG* i, xxxi–xxxii.

[4] NLS Adv. MS 72.1.3: no.3 in Ronald I.M. Black, 'The Gaelic manuscripts of Scotland' in William Gillies (ed.), *Gaelic in Scotland: Alba agus a' Ghàidhlig* (Edinburgh, 1989), 154.

[5] John Francis Campbell (ed.), *Popular tales of the West Highlands* (4 vols, Edinburgh, 1860–2) iv, 382.

[6] Although Jastrzębski is a somewhat obscure character, it is to be presumed he was a European artist, making his living in various different countries—indeed he left Scotland for Australia in the 1850s.

[7] With notable lithographed illustrations by his niece Miss J. Knox Smith.

[8] NLS MS 10563 fos.13–14, published in Nicola Gordon Bowe and Elizabeth Cumming, *The Arts and Crafts movements in Dublin and Edinburgh* (Dublin, 1998), 43–4.

[9] For Wingate's role as the inspiration of 'Fiona Macleod', see Flavia Alaya, *William Sharp—'Fiona Macleod'* (Cambridge, MA, 1970).

[10] Given as *The Lake of Innisfree*.

[11] As a successful English-language writer, this demise of the Celt to be reborn as an English-speaker was very much in Sharp's interest and he notes W.B. Yeats as the leading poet of this new wave of English-language Celticism. Yeats nearly became an author in the *Celtic Library* (and, indeed, in *The Evergreen*) but, presumably due to the number of books being produced in 1896 and the concomitant financial pressures, Geddes had turned down a book proposal from the Irish poet. In a letter to Sharp of 30 June 1896, Geddes wrote: 'I have written to Mr Yeats to tell him that while we are in complete sympathy with him in his project, we cannot take up his book.' This letter is in the National Library of Scotland and is quoted in an informative footnote: John Kelly (ed.), *The collected letters of W. B. Yeats* ii (Oxford, 1997), 56n.

[12] Sharp writes of 'the bitter solace of absorption in the language, the written thought, the active, omnipresent, and variegated energy of the dominant race' and sees nothing but an ever more insistent silence for the Gael. Reprinted as 'The Gael and his heritage' in Fiona Macleod, *The winged destiny: studies in the spiritual history of the Gael* (London, 1904).

[13] *CG* i, xxxii.

[14] Carmichael uses the spelling 'Deirdire'.

[15] *Deirdire and the Lay of the Children of Uisne orally collected in the Island of Barra, and literally translated by Alexander Carmichael* (Edinburgh, 1905). The narrative was collected in March 1867, and first published in book form in 1905; the acknowledgment of Duncan's gift does not appear until the second, 1914, edition.

[16] Strathclyde University Archive, T-GED12/3/31, John Duncan to Patrick Geddes, 29 St Bernard's Crescent, Edinburgh, n.d. ? probably spring 1912.

9

Neil MacEachen, Marshal MacDonald, the Uists, and Alexander Carmichael

JEAN-DIDIER HACHE

The primary purpose of this paper is to tell a good story: that of Neil MacEachen (1719–88) of Tobha Beag/Howbeg, and of his son Marshal MacDonald (1765–1840). It is undoubtedly a long story—120 years long!—so, given the limited space available, I can only give a glimpse of it.

To begin with, without being disrespectful to the Outer Hebrides, it may be pointed out that by European standards, by British standards, and even by Scottish standards, these islands are perceived as remote. Nevertheless, within the Outer Hebrides themselves there are some areas which are considered even more so. Such is the case of Gleann Choradail, on the eastern coast of South Uist.

Gleann Choradail has no road access. It is surrounded by a chain of high hills— Beinn Mhór, Thacla, Beinn Choradail—which makes travel on foot a hard task. It has no proper anchorage, and any rough weather in the Minch makes the mooring in Bàgh Choradail very insecure. There are a few houses there, but no major population settlement. Therefore one would expect Gleann Choradail to be the kind of place where very little has ever happened.

Nevertheless, on the 1 July 1825 a ship dropped anchor in the bay, and a rowing boat brought a passenger ashore. He was no less than Étienne Jacques Joseph Alexandre MacDonald, Marshal of France, Duke of Tarentum, Arch Chancellor of the Order of the Légion d'Honneur, Chevalier Commandeur du Saint Esprit, Grand Croix de Saint Louis, French Minister of State, Member of the Privy Council of the King of France, Second Major General of the King's Bodyguards, and so forth—and, incidentally, Deputy Grand Master of the Freemasons in France.

The purpose of his presence was, firstly, to make a tour of the British Isles; secondly, to visit Scotland, since he was of Scottish origin; thirdly, and most importantly, to discover the land of his ancestors, since his father, Neil MacEachen of Tobha Beag, was a native of South Uist.

It is noteworthy that when he travelled to Uist, and the west coast of Scotland, Marshal MacDonald did so aboard a British Navy ship, the revenue cutter HMS *Swift*. He had been given the use of this ship on the direct orders of Robert Saunders Dundas, second Viscount Melville (1771–1851), First Lord of the Admiralty, and so during his visit he was a guest of the British Navy, with all the customary honours and salutes.

Had the same British Navy got hold of his father, some 80 years before, in the same area of Gleann Choradail, the treatment would have been somewhat different. Indeed, they may well have hanged him from the highest mast after forcibly extracting information on the whereabouts of Prince Charles Edward Stuart, since it was Neil MacEachen who was the very person in charge of arranging the Prince's escape in these islands, following the rout at Culloden. But thus are the changing fortunes of history.

*   *   *   *   *

The Marshal's visit to Scotland was well reported at the time. There were numerous articles in the London and Edinburgh press (for instance, in the *Caledonian Mercury*), as well as in the Highland newspapers (especially the *Inverness Courier*). A medal was even struck, and a pamphlet published recalling the details of the event.

It is not surprising therefore, that, some sixty years later, the attention of Alexander Carmichael was drawn to the story. Having had requests from various quarters, he dutifully collected memories of that visit, as well as correspondence relating to the Marshal's family connections in Uist. These may be consulted in the Carmichael Watson Papers in Edinburgh University Library, and I am indebted to Domhnall Uilleam Stiùbhart for kindly sending me transcriptions. I will mention some of these in due course. It must be said, however, that Carmichael only scratched the surface of these events. My main purpose is thus not so much to dwell on Carmichael's somewhat limited work on the subject, but rather to highlight 'what he did not say'.

In order to do so, I shall firstly consider who Neil MacEachen was—as far as we know— before going on to highlight some of the main features of his son's brilliant career in France. I shall then recount some details of the Marshal's tour of these islands in 1825, then conclude by drawing attention to some myths concerning him in general circulation.

I: Neil Étienne MacEachen (MacDonald) of Tobha Beag, South Uist (1719–88)

The life of Neil MacEachen has been recounted in Dr Alasdair Maclean's well known book *A MacDonald for the Prince*.[1] I shall briefly consider it here.

Neil was born in Tobha Beag, South Uist, in 1719. The MacEachens of Tobha Beag appear to have originated in Glenuig before the family settled in the Uists. They have been described by some as a sept of Clan Ranald, while others consider that they had MacLean origins. However, there is no doubt but that they had strong connections with Clan Donald, which is probably why Neil did not hesitate to change his name from MacEachen to MacDonald when he lived in France. It should be noted, of course, that MacDonald is considerably easier to pronounce and to spell in French than MacEachen!.

Neil has sometimes been described as 'a poor gentleman', but a glance at the ruins of the family's house in Tobha Beag indicates that the MacEachens were of some financial substance, at least by local standards. Seemingly they possessed lands not only in the fertile surrounding area, but also on the east side of South Uist, beyond the hills, where Neil was to hide later with the Prince.

How Neil was selected to be sent away for his education, and who exactly sponsored his studies—apparently for the priesthood—we do not know for sure. What we can ascertain is that in 1735, at the age of sixteen, Neil MacEachen left the islands in order to take up residence in the rather dramatically different surroundings of Paris, there to be educated at the Scots College.

The Scots College in Paris was not only a Catholic educational establishment, but also a hive of jacobite activity. Indeed, the list of its alumni at the time matches closely that of Prince

Charles Edward's army staff during the 1745. This alone may account for much of Neil's later involvement with the jacobite cause.

From the rather scant accounts we have touching upon Neil's stay at the Scots College in Paris—not, as is sometimes averred, at the college in Douai—the picture emerges of a pupil who is certainly intelligent; is sometimes absent on mysterious errands; and is not above playing a trick or two in order to get hold of some money.[2]

When he left the College after a two-year sojourn, Neil MacEachen was a man who could speak not only Gaelic and English, but French and Latin as well; he also had a good knowledge of Greek. On his return to Scotland, however, he did not become a priest as may have originally been intended. As evidence collected by Carmichael rather colourfully puts it: 'Neill came home without going under the hands of a bishop at all. Some of the vows of the priesthood were too hard for him to take and he came home without taking them at all…'[3]

What MacEachen did between 1737, when he left Paris, and 1746, is something of a mystery. Tradition has it that he set up some kind of private school in the Uists, and that he was the tutor to the children of his chief Ranald MacDonald (1692–1766), captain of Clan Ranald; it has certainly been said that he was tutor and guardian to his chief's son, Ranald the Younger (*c*.1722–76), while both young men were being educated in France.[4] What he did during the initial stages of the Forty-Five is also obscure. His son Marshal MacDonald was always convinced that Neil accompanied the Prince everywhere, indeed that he was present at Culloden; but there appear to be no historical sources extant which might confirm his assertion. What we know for certain is that when, in April 1746, the news reached Clanranald's house in Baile nan Cailleach/Nunton that the Prince, on the run since the defeat of Culloden, had just landed in the Roisnis peninsula in Benbecula, Neil was there, sitting at the table for dinner. The rest of the story is the stuff of legend. For the next two months, Neil took direct responsibility for the Prince's safety, guiding him through the remotest parts of the Uists, and eventually sailing with him 'over the sea to Skye'.

I do not intend to dwell on such an eventful and well-known episode, seeing that it has been described in detail in so many publications already—suffice to say that the most noteworthy, albeit regrettably incomplete, account of the affair is to be found in a manuscript probably composed by none other than Neil MacEachen himself, and discovered by a Scottish antiquarian in Paris in the mid-nineteenth century.[5]

There are stories galore of the Prince's hiding places in the Highlands—where almost every rabbit warren is supposed to have sheltered the distinguished visitor at one time or another— but the Uists can pride themselves on a number of clearly identified *bona fide* hideouts. The main ones were the cave at Gleann Choradail, and a hut in the Roisinis peninsula whose remains can still be seen.

Neil rejoined the Prince at Loch nan Uamh in September 1746, when two French ships, the *Prince de Conti* and *L'Heureux* managed to carry him back to France with a number of his followers, Neil MacEachen among them. Neil's involvement with jacobitism certainly did not end there, and there is strong evidence suggesting that he was back in Scotland again in 1747, engaged on a secret mission. However, France's involvement with the jacobite cause came to a (provisional) halt in 1748 when the Treaty of Aix-la-Chapelle was signed with Britain. A clause in the document stipulated that France put a stop to all further assistance to the jacobites, and expel the Young Pretender from its territory. Prince Charles refusing to comply, Louis XV of France was compelled to order his arrest, a decree entailing a massive police operation for fear of public riots in Paris. After a few days incarceration in the state fortress of Vincennes, Charles Edward Stuart eventually relented and left the country.

Legend has it that only one man, 'faithful Neil MacEachen', was allowed to keep the Prince company in jail, his other followers being imprisoned in the Bastille. There is no evidence whatsoever that such was the case, the more so given that Neil's presence in Vincennes does not appear to be mentioned at all in extant archives in France. Until more conclusive proof has been found, it is safer to suspect that the tale of Neil's incarceration with the Prince was simply part of a jacobite propaganda ploy requiring a 'witness' to testify to his royal master's fortitude during these difficult times.

What we know for sure is that, as did many jacobite exiles, Neil—now officially 'Neil Étienne MacDonald'—joined the French army's Scottish Regiments, becoming a lieutenant first in the Albany Regiment, and then in Ogilvy's Regiment. He pursued his career in the French army until 1763, when France disbanded this unit following the Treaty of Paris.

Having married a French wife, Alexandrine Gonant, by whom he had two surviving children—a boy, the future Marshal, and a girl, Eulalie Sophie—Neil retired on a meagre pension, first to Sedan in the Ardennes, and then to Sancerre in the centre of France. Living amongst a small Scottish jacobite community which had settled there with John Nairne, the jacobite second Earl of Nairne (1690/1–1770), it was there that Neil MacEachen ended his life in 1788, 'leaving to his son as estate only his name, and the example of his virtues'.

Neil MacEachen's life story is extraordinary enough as it stands, but it raises many questions. Was he a mere school teacher who was in the right place at the right time, who simply did his duty to the jacobite cause? Or was he, as Alasdair Maclean suggested in his book, a sophisticated jacobite agent—or perhaps even a French agent? My personal views on these matters are somewhat more circumspect than Dr Maclean's, but I agree that there is strong 'circumstantial evidence' that there was much more to Neil than met the eye. Indeed, other documents which I have unearthed in France also suggest that his family life was to say the least far from exemplary. But given that these assertions may have far-reaching consequences, further research is needed either to substantiate or to disprove them.

II: Étienne Jacques Joseph Alexandre MacDonald (1765–1840), Marshal of France, Duke of Tarentum

Neil MacEachen-MacDonald's son, Étienne Jacques Joseph Alexandre, was born in 1765 in Sedan, in the north-east of France. The life of the father is well worth a book; that of the son could fill a whole library shelf. The reader will forgive me if—once again—I cut corners and go straight to the essentials.

Alexandre spent most of his youth in Sancerre, where his family lived in a small house with apparently very scant resources. Nevertheless, the support of the more affluent members of Sancerre's community of exiled Scots, such as the Macnabs, enabled him to receive a proper education, and he was eventually sent to Paris for military tuition. The jacobite network was clearly of some use since, after a brief spell in Holland, Alexandre began his soldiering career in earnest in the French army serving in Dillon's Regiment, composed of Irish jacobites. Incidentally, it was this very regiment which played a decisive role in the Battle of Fontenoy, on 11 May 1745, when the French forces under Marshal Maurice de Saxe routed the British army led by William Augustus, Duke of Cumberland.

While Alexandre was keen on a military career, there is little doubt that his prospects at the time could not extend to ascending higher than junior officer rank. Under the French monarchy, the officer corps in the army, and especially its higher echelons, tended to be the sole preserve of the aristocracy: the more titled and fortunate, the better the prospects.

Alexandre was certainly not titled, and one may doubt that he would have been promoted much beyond the rank of captain were it not for the dramatic turn of events following the French Revolution of 1789, and the advent of the French Republic.

One of the consequences of the Revolution was that all privileges linked to title and rank were abolished overnight. Another was that the vast majority of the officer corps, composed as they were of aristocrats, fled into exile or lost their heads during the troubles. At the same time, France became embroiled in a long succession of wars, not only along its borders or in neighbouring countries, but also internally, with a bitter civil war convulsing those regions of the country where a majority opposed the Republic. The French army found itself desperately short of officers, but desperately needed them: for those who were competent and bold enough—given that the price of failure could mean the guillotine—the career prospects were boundless.

This is exactly what happened to Alexandre MacDonald who, having elected to remain in the army of the Republic, rose within two years from the rank of lieutenant to that of general, with an entire division under his command. Alexandre himself was astounded by the speed of his successive promotions, and even tried to object that he had never been properly trained for such high positions of command. In those days, however, one did not reject a promotion, for fear of being suspected of treason. Alexandre managed to develop his skills as a commanding officer during a succession of campaigns which took him to Holland, to Italy—where he was Governor of Rome—and to Switzerland, where he led his army in winter over the six thousand feet high Splügen Pass in the Alps. He also managed to develop his political survival skills, narrowly escaping the political purges during the Terror.

In 1797, with the Revolutionary years drawing to an end, France was governed by a corrupt and ineffectual regime. A political coup d'état was in the offing, but it needed a 'sword' to back it up. General Barthélemy Joubert (1769–99) was due to provide it, but he was killed in Italy. General Victor Moreau (1763–1813), hero of the Rhine, was then approached, but turned down the offer. General Alexandre MacDonald, was then asked—but also refused. Then General Napoleon Bonaparte, freshly landed from Egypt, was asked, and eagerly grasped the opportunity.

Thus came the coup d'état of November 1797, which saw the rise of Napoleon Bonaparte to power, with all its ensuing consequences. MacDonald, whilst refusing to lead the coup, nevertheless gave it his full backing, as did most of the army, and took an active part it. One may pause and wonder what would the history of France, Europe, and the Franco-British relationship have been, if the coup which ended the Revolution had been led by a General MacDonald instead of a General Bonaparte!

MacDonald's support for Bonaparte did not immediately further his career. The new leader was in fact quite anxious to sideline all those in the army who had the potential to oppose him politically, and so MacDonald was sent to Denmark on a diplomatic mission until 1803. He fell further from grace sometime later because of his relationship with General Moreau, who was himself suspected of being part of a plot to topple Bonaparte. As a consequence MacDonald was not given any command for a period of five years. During this time he lived under the watchful eyes of Napoleon's police in his country estate of Courcelles-le-Roy in the centre of France, where he acquired a keen interest in farming.

In 1809, however, with the French army experiencing difficulties, General MacDonald was recalled for active service in Italy. He immediately redressed the situation, then led his army towards Austria in order to rendezvous with the Emperor's forces at Wagram on the outskirts of Vienna.

The Battle which then took place in Wagram on 5–6 July 1809 has been described as the largest to have taken place in Europe, if not in the world, to that date. Some 360,000 soldiers from both camps fought for two days; at the end of the battle, casualties amounted to some 60,000. MacDonald's rôle in the French victory was decisive: he broke the enemy centre with a wedge of eight thousand troops and a hundred guns. In a what was a ferocious action, he led the action personally, his troops experiencing such devastating casualties that only 1,500 of them remained standing when victory was finally achieved. Acknowledging his bravery and decisiveness, Napoleon made MacDonald a Marshal of France on the battlefield itself—apparently the only known case of this kind—and awarded him the title of Duke of Tarentum.

It would take much too long to describe all the military campaigns in which MacDonald took part over the following years. Let us say simply that he fought all over Europe, from Catalonia to Russia, winning some battles, losing others, and narrowly escaping with his life on some occasions. But at last the pressure of fighting against all Europe proved too much for Napoleon, and the French army had to fight a defensive campaign on its own soil, ending with the seizure of Paris by the allied forces. Was Napoleon going to fight a last battle to regain his capital, and thus risk its ruin? Exhausted, the French army knew it could not do so, and MacDonald along with two other colleagues, was sent to the Emperor to entreat him to cease hostilities.

Marshal MacDonald then played a decisive rôle in negotiating Napoleon's abdication to the Allies, especially with the Czar of Russia. He did so with total loyalty—when many others were changing sides or signing individual truces—and ensured that Napoleon obtained the best possible terms according to circumstances. The Emperor handed his abdication formally to MacDonald at Fontainebleau in 1814, acknowledging that he had treated him unfairly in the past, and headed for his first exile in the small island kingdom of Elba in the Mediterranean.

Freed from his obligations, MacDonald then transferred his loyalty to Louis XVIII; he was as faithful to the new régime as he had been to the previous one. When Napoleon returned from Elba, MacDonald was sent by the king to oppose his advance on Paris, but did not succeed in doing so, his troops having rallied to the Emperor. He steadfastly refused Napoleon's offer to join him, and so did not take any part in the campaign which led to the latter's decisive defeat at Waterloo.

Upon the king's return and Napoleon's final exile to Saint Helena, MacDonald was rewarded for his loyalty. Considered a safe pair of hands, he was given the delicate task of disbanding the remains of the Imperial army, a task he accomplished with the best of diplomacy. Numerous honours came his way. He was nominated Minister of State, but refused the Ministry for War, in order to accept the position of Arch-Chancellor of the Order of the Légion d'Honneur. He was made a member of the King's Privy Council, a Peer of the Realm, and a second-in-command of the King's Bodyguards.

A political as well as a physical survivor, Marshal MacDonald died peacefully at his estate of Courcelles-le-Roy in 1840. Visitors to Paris will find memorials to him in various parts of the capital: his name written under the Arc de Triomphe, as well as given to an avenue, and his statue stands with those of other great men of France on the Louvre Museum façade on the Rue de Rivoli.

III: Marshal MacDonald's visit to the Uists, 1825

To put Marshal MacDonald's visit to the Uists in the summer of 1825 into perspective, it is necessary to emphasize the Marshal's continuing interest in Scotland in general, and in his MacDonald ancestry in particular.

This ongoing interest is perhaps nowhere more apparent than on his own coat of arms as Duke of Tarentum, which, with a lion rampant, a hand grasping a cross, and a galley with a salmon, as well as the motto 'My hope is constant in thee', were heavily inspired by those of Clan Donald. His determination to keep the Scottish dimension alive in his family can also be appreciated from a portrait of his young son commissioned from Horace Vernet, in which the four-year old French boy is seen clad in tartan, holding 'a Scottish sword of the MacDonald Clan'.

While the Marshal was born and bred in France, and undoubtedly a Frenchman, we have seen how the early years of the life were influenced by his Scottish and jacobite roots. These links seem to have been maintained till 1798, when the French Revolution and the ensuing Napoleonic wars interrupted exchanges with Britain more or less continuously until 1814.

After Napoleon's downfall, the Marshal's interest was rekindled, and he endeavoured to renew old contacts with Scotland and discover more about his family relations. Amongst his privileged contacts were the advocates Reginald Macdonald of Staffa (1778–1838) and Hector MacDonald-Buchanan (d.1835), two half-brothers, grandsons of Alexander MacDonald of Boisdale (1698–1768) who had been out with his own father Neil MacEachen in the cave of Gleann Choradail. They provided him with information regarding his ancestry, and with hospitality; indeed, Staffa acted as his guide during his trip to Scotland.

The choice of the year 1825 for the Marshal's visit corresponds to a watershed in his life: the untimely death of his third and last wife Thérèse Gasparine Bourgoing on 13 April of that year, leaving him with a baby son (MacDonald's first two wives, Marie-Constance Soral de Monloisir and Félicité (Françoise) de Montholon, had also died early, leaving him with three daughters). Greatly affected by his loss, the Marshal decided to overcome his sorrows by visiting the land of his ancestors, and so he undertook a two-month journey of the British Isles. Last but not least, he endeavoured to compose his 'Recollections', initially dedicated to his young son, which were published by his family only at the end of the century.[6]

Interestingly, the Marshal undertook this journey in the company of a member of the other branch of the MacEachen family, the Comte of Couëssin. The count was not only the Marshal's attending officer, but also the husband of one of his nieces.

The trip, which lasted two whole months, began on the 1 June and finished by the end of July. After a visit to London, the travellers followed the east coast route to Edinburgh; then north to Inverness, down the Caledonian Canal, and west to Arisaig. There the revenue cutter HMS *Swift* took the visitors to the Uists, Skye, down the west coast of Scotland, and on to Glasgow after a brief spell in Antrim. The journey continued southward by the western route, including a detour to Dublin. It is revealing that, of these two months in the British Isles, half of the Marshal's time was spent in Scotland; and much of that in the Highlands and the Hebrides.

The Marshal's trip cannot be recounted here in detail; indeed, it deserves a separate article. Let it simply be said that throughout, a strong emphasis was put on Scottish history in general, and that of Clan Donald in particular. While not an official visit, it was in many ways as close as could be to the real thing, and the Marshal met numerous personalities, including Sir Walter Scott.

Always curious about events relating to the 1745 Rebellion, the Marshal was nevertheless by no means starry-eyed, and made his views quite clear. On the Culloden battlefield, reported the *Inverness Courier* on the 29th of June 1825:

> …he expressed his surprise at the imbecility which dictated the choice of that spot for the position of the Pretender's army. No spot could be worse chosen for the position of an irregular body of men acting on the defensive against regular troops; and the wonder was increased, the General observed, when the neighbouring high grounds behind the water of Nairn afforded as fine a position as could be wished to obtain the objects and suit the circumstances of the Jacobite forces.

The Uist part of the journey lasted two days, from 29 June until 1 July. HMS *Swift* anchored in Loch Sgiopoirt, and an open boat took the Marshal to the North Ford. From thence, he went by cart to Tobha Beag, where he met a crowd of a few hundred MacDonalds gathered for the occasion, amongst whom were a number of direct relations.

According to evidence gathered by Carmichael, probably from Donald Macintyre, 'Domhnall mac Néill', aged 84, Tobha Beag, on 6 April 1877, when the Marshal came in sight of 'Faoghail Hough' he exclaimed, 'Ah! This is the river my fath[er] told me he used to be a breacach [trout, or salmon, fishing]!' 'There was a crowd & he went up & kiss[ed] an old man & said O seo m'athair—Al[e]x[ander] Maceachain & Neill d[itt]o sons of the two brothers— Raol was Alex[ander's] son.' There he visited the ruins of his father's house, apparently taking 'fill of a stocking of earth from "Tota na Bracha" which he brought back to France in order to be put in his grave. He also handed substantial sums of money to some of his relatives, and—according to what Carmichael recorded—devised a scheme to assist those who might be interested in following him to France to begin a career. 'Duke sharp', Carmichael notes, 'knew his relatives by sight.'[7]

The Marshal subsequently returned to the North Ford and crossed over to Benbecula, where he spent the night at the factor's house at Baile nan Cailleach. The next day he regained the ship and travelled to Gleann Choradail, where he met the local community and visited a cave used by his father and the Prince as a hideout in 1746. After this short stay, the Marshal sailed to Armadale Castle in Skye and to Castle Tioram in Moidart—where he was each time greeted by substantial crowds—then he continued southwards.

IV: THE MYTHS

The figure of Marshal MacDonald has given rise to a number of myths in Scotland. This is unsurprising, for he was a rather extraordinary blend: the scion of a jacobite family, but a general of the French Revolution; a Frenchman who had been one of the top officers of Britain's long standing arch-foe, Napoleon, but also a man who was, in his heart, strongly attached to Scotland and his Scottish origins.

Such myths existed well before his visit; five years before, during the 'Radical Rising' of 1820 in the Scottish Lowlands, rumours spread by the government *agent provocateur* John King suggested that five thousand expatriate Scots had landed under the command of Marshal MacDonald, a French general and the son of a jacobite exile. Having mustered at Campsie, the army would subsequently march to join up with others insurrectionists at Cathkin Braes, thence to spread revolution throughout the country—a most unlikely prospect, given that MacDonald was at the time a high-ranking dignitary in the restored French monarchy![8] Ironically, the official who presided over the brutal execution of two of the leaders of the Rising, the radical martyrs John Baird (1788–1820) and Andrew Hardie (1792–1820), was none other than the future escort of Marshal MacDonald, Reginald MacDonald of Staffa, Sheriff of Stirlingshire.

Another myth, which arose well after his death, was that the Marshal had left a substantial fortune to his Hebridean relatives. The story appears to have surfaced in the 1890s when the Marshal's direct descendants had his 'Recollections' published, first in French, and then in English. The book attracted some attention in the Highlands, and letters appeared in the local press. This gave rise to the notion that large sums of money were awaiting those who could claim some MacEachen descent—a forlorn hope, seeing that the Marshal, deceased over 65 years beforehand, had direct descendants in France. Nevertheless, poor Alexander Carmichael—who, having contributed a brief footnote to the *Recollections*, was now rumoured to be 'in the know'—was swamped by numerous letters from interested people, some of whom had only very tenuous connections with the Marshal.

Carmichael did his best to oblige by looking into the matter further. Indeed, judging by his archive, it appears that things went as far as the Foreign Office and the British Embassy in Paris. Of course, it was all in vain.

I shall not disclose the correspondents' names, as some of the petitioners may well have living descendants or relatives, but simply quote this extract from a series of letters sent to Carmichael by his contact, Alexander MacDonald, who was himself seeking more information concerning the Marshal's family. In a letter from Govan, dated 3 August 1892, he comments tersely:

> Only a congeries of old letters breathing nothing but a sordid craving for filthy lucre! Well well! I think I see you in your literary den at Raeburn Place smiling sardonically at my disappointment! … You can tell the parties who are bothering you about the Marshal's money or that of the late Duke that as they both left families no other parties can claim anything. If any special legacies had been made to anybody they would no doubt have been paid.[9]

The last myth, and my personal favourite, appears in a note in Carmichael's papers. It is attributed to the shipowner and folklorist Capt. Alexander Matheson (*c.*1833–97), Dornie, Kintail, compiler of the Dornie Manuscripts:

> I used to hear both on the Mainland and in Uist that the Duke of Tirentim after parting with Napoleon Bonaparte when he was made a state prisoner in the Elbe after the loss of his troops in Russia that he had never seen the Empourer afterwards and that he had taken the oath of allegenc to Lou[i]s Phillipic that he kept aloof from joining the Emperor on his return to France after his escape from his confinement in the Elbe.
> That he afterwards came into the confidence of the British Government privately, and that he had been in the millitary tent of the Duke of Wellington during the whole action of the British forces in Brussels in 1815 and knowing all the manuveries of the French army that he put up the Duke of Wellington to all the tactics of the French Army and that he had as much to do with the Battle of Waterloo to magnify the laurels of the Great Duke of Wellington as he had himself. This I use to heare from tratition but I cannot vouch for the correctness of the statement.[10]

The mind boggles at this picture of Marshal MacDonald, hidden in Wellington's tent, whispering advice to the latter on the best way to win the day at Waterloo!

In conclusion, I would like to draw your attention to the fact that I have had the privilege of rediscovering in the French archives the travel diary of Marshal MacDonald's 1825 visit to

Britain, Scotland, and the Uists. It has recently been translated and published by the Islands Book Trust under the title *The French MacDonald*.[11] I hope that it might be found a worthwhile read.

---

[1] Alasdair Maclean, *A MacDonald for the Prince: the story of Neil MacEachen* (Stornoway, 1982); also Alasdair Maclean and John S. Gibson, *Summer hunting a Prince: the escape of Charles Edward Stuart* (Stornoway, 1992).

[2] See, for example, Brian Halloran, 'Neil MacEachen at the Scots College in Paris', *Innes Review*, xliii (1992), 176–81.

[3] CW MS 363 fo.20: 'Thill Niall dachaidh gun dol fo lamhan easpaig idir. Bha cuid do bhoidean na sagartachd ro chruaidh leis ri ghabhail agus thill e dachaidh gun an gabhail idir.'

[4] Angus MacDonald and Archibald MacDonald, *The Clan Donald* (3 vols, Edinburgh, 1896–1904) iii, 235.

[5] 'The wanderings of Prince Charles in the Hebrides' in Walter Biggar Blaikie (ed.), *Origins of the Forty-Five and other papers related to that Rising* (1916: Edinburgh, 1975), 227–66.

[6] Camille Rousset (ed.), *Souvenirs du Maréchal Macdonald, Duc de Tarente* (Paris, 1892); translated as *Recollections of Marshal Macdonald, Duke of Tarentum* (London, 1892). The 1893 edition includes an extended footnote concerning the Marshal's visit to Uist by Alexander Carmichael: 'Note by Mr. Alexander Carmichael, of Edinburgh' in Camille Rousset (ed.), *Recollections of Marshal Macdonald, Duke of Tarentum* (London, 1893), 5–6.

[7] CW MS 108 fos.13^v–14, 14^v; see also *CG* ii, 325–6.

[8] Peter Berresford Ellis and Seumas Mac a' Ghobhainn, *The Scottish Insurrection of 1820* (1970: London, 1989), 29, 54, 149, 285.

[9] CW MS 527, not foliated.

[10] CW MS 363 fo.28.

[11] Jacques Ètienne Joseph Alexandre MacDonald, *The French MacDonald: Journey of a Marshal of Napoleon in the Highlands and Islands of Scotland* (Ness, Isle of Lewis, 2007).

10

Uist in the School of Scottish Studies Archives

CATHLIN MACAULAY

The School of Scottish Studies was set up in 1951 to collect, archive, research and publish material relating to the oral tradition and cultural life of Scotland: the people, their day-to-day lives and ways of being as expressed through song, music, poetry, beliefs, customs, narratives and tales. The establishment of the School at this time was no accident but could be seen as the culmination of a long history of collecting in Scotland.

By the eighteenth century collecting had become something of a vogue. At this time the mainland provided the principal source for Gaelic material, and one of the earliest collections of songs and ballads was made by the Rev. James McLagan (1728–1805) who was based in Perthshire. Many of his texts were published in *Sean Dàin agus Òrain Ghàidhealach* (1786), usually called the Gillies Collection. The infamous 'Ossian' published in the 1760s by James Macpherson (1736–96) is based on fragments of tales and verse which he first collected through the oral tradition in his native Badenoch, then further afield. This text was a seminal influence on the German Romantic movement and the interest in antiquarianism which followed. With the encroachment of English on the mainland Gaelic-speaking communities the locus of collecting shifted to the islands of the west and during the nineteenth and twentieth centuries the Uists, rich in Gaelic tradition, proved a fruitful source. Collectors who worked there include John Francis Campbell of Islay (1821–85), Frances Tolmie (1840–1926), Marjory Kennedy-Fraser (1857–1930), Father Allan McDonald (1859–1905), Amy Murray (1865–1947), and of course Alexander Carmichael himself. In the 1930s and 40s Margaret Fay Shaw (1903–2004) and John Lorne Campbell of Canna (1906–1996) collected and published many Gaelic songs and tales. They had established links with other Gaelic speaking areas in Ireland and Canada and helped found the Folklore Institute of Scotland in 1947. A year later the Linguistic Survey of Scotland was set up in the University of Edinburgh, its aim to record and study Scots and Gaelic speech.

Post-war, there was a great interest in issues of national and cultural identity symbolised in 1950 with the liberation of the Stone of Destiny from Westminster Abbey back to Scotland, an event which inspired much verse and song in both Gaelic and Scots. The time was right for the creation of a national institution which would collect and preserve Scotland's oral heritage, rather than leaving this task to the instigation of private individuals. Within the University of Edinburgh support for such an institution was led by Angus McIntosh (1914–2005) who had been appointed in 1948 as Forbes Professor of English Language and General Linguistics. He had a great interest in dialect. Working during the war on code-breaking activities in Bletchley Park, he was knowledgeable about new technology, the open reel recorder, soon to take over from wire and wax cylinders and disc recordings. There was strong impetus too from overseas.

Fig. 1: Calum Maclean and Angus MacMillan, Benbecula 1940s. *Courtesy of the UCD Delargy Centre for Irish Folklore and the National Folklore Collection*

Members of both the Irish Folklore Commission/Coimisiún Béaloideasa Éireann, which had been established by the Irish government in 1935, and the Institute for Dialect and Folklore Research/Landsmåls- och Folkminnesarkivet in Uppsala, founded in 1914, and funded through the Swedish Parliament, were keen to encourage a Scottish institute. Straddling the Norse and Gaelic worlds, it would complete a cultural triangle so placing the oral tradition, the folk life and folklore of Scotland, in a European context.

Funded by the Carnegie Trust for the Universities of Scotland and Edinburgh University, the School of Scottish Studies shared accommodation with the Linguistic Survey, for which Fred Macaulay (1925–2003) and Derick Thomson had already collected material in the Hebrides, and later the *Scottish National Dictionary* and the *Dictionary of the Older Scottish Tongue*. As a research archive the School employed a number of fellows each with a specific area of interest—Gaelic song, Scots song, music, oral narrative, place-names, customs, material culture. The first research fellow, Calum Maclean (1915–60), served his apprenticeship with the Irish Folklore Commission. In the late 1940s he had been sent to the Uists where he met Angus MacMillan (1874–1954) of Griminis, Benbecula, a retired crofter who could neither read nor write and had no English but who had 'a' Chrìosdachd de sgeulachdan', the whole Christendom of stories.

Here he describes this relationship to Alan Lomax, an American ethnomusicologist:

> Old Angus MacMillan was a storyteller with whom I worked in Uist for three years. I thought I would kill him before I'd finish with him, but he went much nearer to killing me before he finished with me. I sometimes recorded stories from him: I'd start at four in the afternoon: by

midnight *I'd* be exhausted but Angus MacMillan would show no signs of exhaustion. The longest story he ever told took nine hours to record. We started on Monday night and did two hours. We had to break off that night. We continued the story on Tuesday night and did two further hours. On Wednesday night we did another two hours and on Thursday we did another two hours again and we finished the story on Friday night. It took us an hour to finish the story. It took me fifteen days to write that story: it was the longest story I have ever written and I think it was really the longest story that has ever been recorded in the history of folklore recording. If I had had sufficient stamina Angus MacMillan would have continued the story uninterrupted for nine hours. I remember someone telling me that an old woman disappeared one night to the well to get a pail of water. It was seven o'clock on a winter's evening. By midnight she hadn't reappeared so a search party was sent out. They finally discovered her in a house where Angus MacMillan was telling a story.[1]

Once the stories were transcribed, it was the practice of the Irish Folklore Commission to scrape and reuse the wax cylinders. On starting work with the School of Scottish Studies in January 1951, Calum Maclean recorded more from Angus MacMillan, this time on open reel, and these stories remain in the sound archive. That summer Calum accompanied Alan Lomax, who had been financed by Columbia Records to create a library of world folk music, on his trip to the Hebrides. These recordings contain a wealth of songs and tales from South Uist and Benbecula and were among the first tapes to be deposited in the School. Lomax was inspired by his trip and described Gaelic culture as 'the finest flower in western Europe'.[2]

A decision was made early on by the School to archive the tapes themselves rather than to rely on transcription as was often the case among American archives and the early collections of the Irish Folklore Commission. Developments in technology during the 1950s meant that recordings were easier to make and to store. Open reel recorders could be cumbersome though and fieldwork trips involved various hazards, as Donald Archie MacDonald (1929–99) recollected:

In 1962 Iain Crawford and I made expeditions in the dark out to the house of Peter MacCormick and his wife who was a marvellous singer; he was a great storyteller. And I was very concerned with making good field recordings and instead of taking one of the smaller battery portables… we took out the full-sized Vortexion which… weighed almost as much as a sack of coal and was, I suppose, two and a half feet by two. Iain Crawford and I carried them in sacks on our back over to Hacklet [Benbecula] over the moorland in the dark using torches…

There's also … that remarkable man Peter Morrison at Sandbank in Grimsay. Well, Sandbank at that stage became an island at high tide. There was a road into it and you took the car out across the sands and stayed at the house until the tide went down again if it came up while you were recording.[3]

Over the years the portability of tape recorders has improved. Open reels were used until the 1990s when digital technology in the form of DAT and pocket-sized minidisc recorders arrived. Nowadays we have moved on to solid state recorders.

The School's policy of holding the source material in audio format, unedited and unembellished, protects the integrity and authenticity of the contributors' words. Dialects are maintained as are the nuances of the original story and the complexity of music or songs. The words of the fieldworker too, as intermediary, are transparent. Transcription always involves interpretation by the transcriber. The change in medium from oral to written takes away from us the subtleties of the original or even, unwittingly, changes it. How do you accurately reflect ornamentation in Gaelic song, for example, or an ironic comment?

The purposeful re-shaping of primary material is not unknown to some collectors, as with Carmichael, leading to controversy and debate as to what was actually said in the original version. This may well be kindly meant, an attempt to provide easy reading as in creating sense out of the material or making a composite from a number of variants. Publication of such material can, however, obscure the original sources, unless these too are given. The work of Marjory Kennedy-Fraser is, perhaps, a case in point. As is well known, Marjory Kennedy-Fraser visited the Hebrides to collect songs, then reorganised the tunes according to a western idiom, and the lyrics according to a rather loose, Celtic twilight translation supplied by the Rev. Kenneth MacLeod (1871–1955) who, incidentally had also worked with Carmichael. These were published as the collection *Songs of the Hebrides* (3 vols, 1909–21) and performed on the stages of the world's music halls. The songs were perceived by many as a direct translation of original Gaelic material and Kennedy-Fraser lauded for rescuing these remnants of a bygone age from oblivion.

Returning to original sound recordings of the songs enables us to trace her improvements'. Edinburgh University Library holds the original cylinders recorded by Marjory Kennedy-Fraser in the early years of the twentieth century. They were copied on to tape through the School of Scottish Studies in the 1960s and you can just hear the fragments of the original song underneath the steam-train chug of the recording machine. We also hold various versions of the songs recorded in the same areas, sometimes by the same singers. Whilst these recordings were made around 40 years after her cylinders, there is no evidence to suggest that these versions differed much from those given by her original contributors.

This brings us to the issue of the collectors as 'insiders' or 'outsiders'. The main collectors from the School in the Uists, Donald Archie MacDonald, Angus John MacDonald, John MacInnes and Ian Paterson in Berneray were all, as it were, natives and Calum Maclean became one by adoption. Knowledge of the community gave access to individuals, initiated greater trust and a sense of what was available. And of course speaking the language— Gaelic—was invaluable. The main disadvantage as far as I can see is that the common day-to-day aspects such as a curious anthropologist might have asked relating to domestic tasks such as what time people got up, who set the fire, and other such questions, were not sought. And scarcity of this domestic detail is, I think, particularly apparent in relation to women's lives.

Over the years since its foundation, the remit of the School has changed considerably. By the late 1960s it had become part of the Faculty of Arts in the University. For over twenty years there has been a full Honours degree in Scottish Ethnology and a graduate studies programme. Commitment to teaching meant that collecting, indexing, and research by fieldworkers were much reduced. However, the archives remain central to the degree programmes and coursework with students adding to the collections through their own fieldwork. Recent projects include oral transmission in North Uist, Hogmanay customs, second sight, tales and repertoires of North Uist story tellers. A study of piping in South Uist by Josh Dickson has recently been published by Birlinn.[4] In 2001 the School of Scottish Studies was amalgamated with Celtic to become Celtic and Scottish Studies, though the original nomenclature still applies to the archives. These are housed in the department where sound recordings and photographic material are kept in controlled environmental conditions to enable their preservation.

That is a somewhat potted account of the School's history. Before looking in more detail at the sound archive holdings I should like to turn briefly to material in other formats.

Manuscript Archive

There is a small manuscript archive concerned mainly with Gaelic and Scots song, tales, customs, and instrumental music, especially piping. Of particular interest are the Donald MacDonald of Eriskay manuscripts, donated by the Irish Folklore Commission, which contain material collected in the 1930s in Eriskay. Over 6,500 pages of South Uist tales, songs and traditions were collected during the 1950s by the renowned South Uist bard, Donald John MacDonald (Dòmhnall Iain Dhonnchaidh) (1919–86), son of Duncan MacDonald (Donnchadh Clachair) (1882–1954), himself a storyteller who was recorded for the archive.

Photographic Archive

The photographic archive holds over 20,000 images, mainly black and white photographs, but also including glass plates, lantern slides and colour slides and prints. Over 5,000 photographs were donated by Werner Kissling (1895–1988) who documented life in the Hebrides from the 1930s to the 1950s. He also directed the film *Eriskay: A Poem of Remote Lives* during the summer of 1934. In addition to Kissling's photographs, mainly portraying Eriskay, South Uist, and Benbecula, we have a number from North Uist taken in the 1960s by Iain Crawford who was examining the history of settlements, and some from the collection of Robert Atkinson, author of *Island Going,* who travelled round the Hebrides in the 1930s and 40s.

There is a wide range of pictures relating to crofting life in the Uists. Housing and buildings of various kinds and their interiors have been of perennial interest including the old houses with their turf or thatched roofs (Fig.2). There are many pictures of people working. Rope was a very important commodity in crofting communities. Horsehair, heather, straw and bent-grass were used, and the different kinds of rope served different purposes from horse bridles to tying down the roof. Rope-making occupied any spare moment (Fig.3).

Working the land and various aspects of cultivation also appear, from planting to harvest. With so many changes to the way of life, particularly after the war, many of these tasks have passed out of use, such as grinding corn with a quern stone (Fig.4).

Images of implements and techniques used for catching fish are also plentiful in the archive from examples of boats, lines, nets and creels to spearing flatfish (Fig.5).

Textile work was a mainstay too of the community, providing clothing, and there are various pictures of work with sheep, gathering crotal and other materials for dyeing as well as of spinning, weaving, and waulking the cloth. The small film (later video) project set up in the 1970s demonstrates a waulking in South Uist as well as various crafts and footage of singers Penny Morrison and Hugh Matheson, and storytellers Donald Alasdair Johnson, Donald John Stewart and Donald Allan MacQueen.

Material from the Photographic archive and from some videos, relating particularly to customs, is available on the SCRAN website (www.scran.ac.uk).

Sound Archive

The sound archive now contains over 20,000 items, around half of which were collected as part of the School's work. The Gaelic and Scots Linguistic surveys, and the Scottish Place-name Survey (with 37 tapes from this area, mainly North Uist) are also held along with many donated collections of music and oral history. The main concern of the early collectors was to undertake a cultural 'rescue' mission, to collect material from rural communities, in the language and dialect of the place, before the customs, practices, tales, songs and music died out completely. Recordings were undertaken in situ: in people's houses, in the field (literally), at céilidhs, at work, on boats. Tapes were used to their full capacity. While some contain material from only one individual, others captured the voices of a series of contributors or a group discussion, song, or musical performance.

Over 1600 tapes contain material from the Uists. Included in this count are the islands from Berneray to Eriskay as the landmass is now connected. There are a total of 656 fieldwork tapes containing contributors from North Uist, 642 from South Uist, 111 from Benbecula, 221 from Berneray and 25 from Eriskay (it should be noted that some tapes contained contributions from more than one island). The bulk of the material was collected during the 1950s, 60s and 70s and recorded in the islands themselves. At this time there was a studio available in the School and many of the 117 tapes by the Rev. William Matheson (1910–95), originally from North Uist, were recorded there. Songs feature on 57% of the tapes and 50% contain tales. One third have information on day-to-day life—crofting, fishing, work etc. Other material includes customs, beliefs, music, particularly piping, games, rhymes, riddles, charms, incantations, proverbs, sayings and prayers. Many of the contributors had more than one talent—they were singers, composers, storytellers, pipers and, perhaps, even dancers as well.

Many of the songs in the archive have a long history and appear in early 'national' manuscripts and printed collections. For example *'S daor a cheannaich mi an t-iasgach*, of which there is a version by Kate MacCormick of Benbecula and *'S fhad tha mi 'm ònaran* recorded by Ewen MacDonald from North Uist appear in the McLagan Manuscripts, the latter also in the Gillies collection. There are many versions of songs which feature in the more localised collections *Folksongs and Folklore from South Uist* and *Hebridean Folksongs*.[5] It is difficult to create a typology of Gaelic songs. They were sung in many different contexts. Theme (e.g. nature, homeland, love, elegy), function (waulking, milking) or structure (puirt à beul, pibroch) may prove the foremost feature, though there is much overlap.

The theme of love is central to Gaelic song and there are 400 tapes from the Uists containing love songs, many of which were composed locally, a tradition that continues to the present day. Songs by local bards were made for all occasions—elegies for friends, humorous local incidents such as a cow eating the washing, a midge attack, events like the local cattle market, the building of the rocket range. Some, of course, have become popular far beyond the islands, one example being the beautiful love poem *An Eala Bhàn* ('The Fair Swan'), composed from the trenches in World War One by Dòmhnall Ruadh Chorùna (Donald MacDonald (1887–1967)) from North Uist.[6]

The Fenian ballads, transmitted since medieval times, are renowned for their strong and colourful narratives. There are many manuscript versions but those in the archive, mainly from South Uist, are among the only extant oral versions. There are several examples of *Duan na Ceàrdaich*, the lay of the Smithy. Another interesting ballad is *Duan na Muilgheartaich*. John MacInnes describes the one-eyed hag who comes across the sea to fight the Féinn as 'a horrible apparition: bald, red, thick-maned; her forehead is dark-grey, charcoal coloured, her teeth red and slanting; she is one-eyed and the darting glance of her eye is keener than a winter star. The great bristles of her head are like withered brushwood covered with hoarfrost.'[7] She carries a rusty sword which she uses to swipe down the warriors. She is associated with the king of Lochlann, may be the foster mother of his son and has, according to the descriptive imagery of the verse, been seen as a personification of the sea, John Gregorson Campbell (1836–91) indeed called her 'the ocean itself in the flesh'[8].

The Arthurian ballad, *Am Bròn Binn*, the Sweet Sorrow, has been of great interest to collectors and scholars.[9] Variants exist in the McLagan Mss, the Dewar Mss and Carmichael himself collected several versions at least six from the Uists of which two texts are contained in *Carmina Gadelica*. It has been recorded by John Lorne Campbell and the School of Scottish Studies and reworked by Marjory Kennedy-Fraser as *The Sea Quest*, or *The Harp-Sorrow: Am Bròn Binn*. The version given below, comparable to Carmichael's version B[10] was recorded by Kate MacCormick from Benbecula by Calum Maclean in 1953. She in turn has passed it on to renowned singer, Catriona Garbutt.

Am Bròn Binn	*The Sweet Sorrow*
Chunnaic Rìgh Alba na shuain	*The king of Scotland saw in a dream*
An aona-bhean bu ghile snuadh fo'n ghréin,	*The woman with the fairest face under the sun*
'S gun b'fheàrr leis tuiteam dha cion	*And he preferred to succumb to love of her*
Na comhradh fir mar bha e'fhéin.	*Than to converse with his fellow man.*
Labhair Fionn Falaich ri Fian	*Fionn Falaich said to Fian*
'Théid mise ga h-ìarraidh dhut,	*'I will go and seek her for you.*
Mi fhìn 's mo ghille 's mo chù,	*I and my servant and my dog,*
'Nar triùir, a dh'iarraidh na mnà'.	*The three of us, will search for the woman'.*
Seachd seachdainean is trì mìos	*Seven weeks and three months*
A thug sinn ri siubhal cuain	*We spent travelling the ocean*
Ma facas fearann na fonn	*Before land or shore was sighted*
Aig an dèanadh a' long tàmh.	*Where the ship could berth.*
Steach gu iomall a' chuain ghairbh	*In by the edge of the rough ocean*
Chunnacas caisteal mìn-gheal gorm.	*A smooth-white blue castle appeared,*
Bu lìonar uinneag is stuadh;	*Numerous were its windows and gables;*
Bu lìonar air cuach is còrn.	*Numerous were its cups and drinking horns.*
'N am dhomh bhith teàrnadh ri bhun	*As I was going up to its base*
Thànaig slabhraidh dhubh a nuas;	*A black chain came down;*
Cha d'ghabh mi eagal na fiamh,	*I did not take fright or fear,*
Ghabh mi oirre 'nam ruith suas.	*I climbed up it at a run.*
Chunnacas a' bhean bhréid-gheal òg	*I saw the white-coiffed young woman*
Ann an cathair òir astaigh,	*On a seat of gold within,*
Stròl dh'an t-sìoda fo dà bhonn.	*Her feet resting on fine cloth of silk.*
Bheannaich mise dha gnùis ghil.	*I asked a blessing on her bright face.*
'A fhleasgaich a thànaig o'n chuan	*'Young man who came from the ocean*
'S fuar do bheannachadh oirnn!	*Cold is your greeting to us,*
Teann nall do cheann air mo ghlùin,	*Come and place your head on my knee*
Seinnidh mi dhut cruit is ceòl'.	*And I will play you music on the harp'.*
Cruit air uchd an aon-ghil ùir	*A harp on the lap of the fair bright one*
Is guirme sùil 's as gile deud—	*Of bluest eyes and whitest teeth—*
Thuit esan na shiorram suaint	*He fell into a deep sleep*
An déis bhith cuartachadh cuain ghairbh	*After sailing on the rough ocean.*
Ghoid i 'n claidheamh geur bho crios,	*She stole the sharp sword from her belt,*
Thilg i dheth gun fhiosd an ceann—	*She stealthily struck off his head—*
Siod agaibh deireadh gach sgeòil	*There you have the end of every tale,*
'S mar a sheinneadh am Bròn Binn	*And how 'The Sweet Sorrow' was sung.*[11]

Songs were often functional and accompanied work of all kinds, inside and out. The Uists are famed for waulking songs, *òrain luaidh*, and these are featured on 300 tapes, the majority recorded in South Uist and Benbecula.

Once taken off the loom the cloth was dipped in stale urine or liquid of a comparable chemical nature and pulled back and forth across a board to shrink it. The rhythm of the song created by pulling and kneading the cloth helped maintain the waulking which took around three hours. The songs were usually composed by women though often they remain anonymous. The subject matter includes love, tragedy, battles, humorous events, elegies. While the verse is usually sung solo, everyone joins in the chorus of meaningless but repeating vocables. Few of the songs are older than the mid sixteenth century apart from ballads, such as *Am Bròn Binn,* which have been adapted to this genre.[12] The last waulking in Uist took place at Loch Càrnan in 1955. However, in 1970 a reconstruction was filmed by the School of Scottish Studies by groups in Tobha Beag and an t-Ìochdar with well-known singers Kate Nicolson, Penny Morrison, Kate MacMillan, Penny MacLellan, Kate MacDonald and Isabel MacLellan.

Milking and butter churning songs were very common and cows were reputed to have their favourites. The rhythm of the milking songs is completely different to that of the *òrain luaidh* and in some recordings you can hear the milk going into the pail. Cradle and dandling songs too had their own rhythm.

There is a very close relationship between songs and music in these islands. The Uists are renowned for piping and pipe tunes often have songs attached to them as in the Lament of Glencoe and *Pìobaireachd Dhòmhnaill Duibh*, The Pibroch of Black Donald, a commemoration of the Battle of Inverlochy, 1431, of which there is a beautifully sung version by Alasdair Boyd of South Uist. *Puirt à beul* are reckoned to have developed when the pipes were supposedly proscribed after the jacobite risings as a means of memorising tunes used for dancing—strathspeys, reels and jigs. Normally the songs are short, fast and have fairly pithy, sometimes nonsensical lyrics. There are over 200 tapes containing *puirt* and renowned exponents include John Maclean, Ewen MacDonald, Roderick MacDonald, John MacInnes, John MacLeod, Alasdair Boyd and Kate MacDonald. There are also some examples of *canntaireachd*, vocables for teaching *ceòl mór* or *pìobaireachd*, using vowels and consonants to represent the notes and their ornamentation.

As well as songs such as the Fenian ballads which are, in effect, tales, there are songs which have congruent tales. For example, the song *Òran na Ròin* whose location is reputed to be Heisgeir sits alongside *Bean MhicCodrum*, The Seal Wife, of which there is a version recounted by Donald MacDougal from North Uist. Fairy songs are often associated with stories, *'S olc an obair* and *Uamh an Òir* being two examples.[13]

There is a large variety of tales in the archive. Overall, about half are supernatural involving fairies, witches, ghosts, mermaids, water horses, sea cattle or seal people. South Uist is a particularly prolific source of fairy stories some of which also feature in *Carmina Gadelica*. There are many hero and Fenian tales, and historical tales which are local to the area—for example stories of Clanranald, the elopement of Jessie of Balranald, the Battle of Carinish, clan battles, cattle raiding, Clearances, Vikings, strongmen and *Gille Pàdara Dubh*, a parallel to the tale of William Tell. Around a third of the tapes contain tales which may be categorised according to the Aarne-Thomson classification system denoting plots and archetypes which appear internationally, an example being the Cinderella story.

There are also tales about people, including a few about Carmichael. Here is one, 'Alasdair Bàn agus an Géidseir' ('Alasdair Bàn and the Gauger'), recounting how Carmichael was run out of the Uists. It was recorded from Andrew Nicolson of Griomasaigh in 1968 by Angus John MacDonald:

Alasdair Bàn agus an Geidseir
Sin, ma tha, 's bu mhath leam stòiridh innse dhuibh air fear ris an canadh iad Alasdair Bàn an eilean Ghriomasaigh a' Chinn a Tuath. Tha e coltach gu robh e math air deanamh uisge-beatha aig an àm. Tha cuimhn' 'am m'athair a bhith 'bruidhinn air an duine. Bha m'athair ma h-ochd bliadhna dh'aois nuair a thachair a' stòiridh a tha mi 'dol a dh'innse dhuibh. Rugadh m'athair ann an 1860.

A' latha bha seo bha Maighstir *Carmichael* air tighinn dhan dùthaich dhan a' *Chustoms and Excise* agus bha e air deanamh a mach gum beireadh e air Alasdair Bàn. 'S ghabh e droch shìde airson sin a dheanamh—thàinig e nuas air Fadhail Chàirinis air iom' bàthadh, agus nochd e 'n taigh Alasdair Bhàin gun for aca gu robh a leithid a dhuine 'dol a thighinn idir. Ach bha Alasdair Bàn a siod fhathast, agus thuirt e ri *Carmichael* gu robh e toilicht' fhaicinn aig a dhachaidh bochd, agus gu robh e duilich cho fliuch 's cho fuar 's a bha e.

'Agus, a dhuine chòir,' ars' esan, 'man téid sibh a lùib an taighe a rannsachadh bu toigh leam dram de dh'uisge-beatha math a thoirt dhuibh a bhlàthaicheadh sibh agus a chuireadh caran toileachas a's an inntinn agaibh.'

Agus rinn e sin. Thug e glainne dha, agus man do thàrr i bhith sìos dhùin na sùilean aig *Carmichael* agus dh'iarr e àit' a's a sìneadh e e fhéin. Agus fhuair e sin air a'bheingidh ann an taigh Alasdair Bhàin agus cuibhrige briagha Gàidhealach a shnìomh iad fhéin, 's a chàrd iad agus a dh'fhigh iad cuideachd, a chàradh air. Agus chaidil e airson ceithir uairean an uaireadair.

'Nuair a dhùisg e bha na bha 's an taigh air a chuir an dara taobh far nach fhaiceadh esan na duin' eil' e. Agus bha cuideachd a' phoit-dhubh, mar a chanadh iad, a bha pìos an tao' muigh dhen taigh aig Abhainn an t-Searraich, bha i air pìosan a dheanamh dhith aig a' bhodach, Alasdair Bàn Dòmhnallach, agus air a caitheamh dh'a' loch air beulaibh an doruis. Agus bha h-uile sìon dhe sin seachad nuair a dhùisg *Carmichael*, agus dh'iarr Alasdair Bàn air an taigh a rannsachadh 's rinn e sin. Chaidh e fo na leapannan fhéin, ma dheireadh, air a ghlùinean ach chan fhac' e sìon a sin. Cha robh dad ann—dh'fhalbh a h-uile sìon. Agus thuirt e gu robh e duilich gun do chuir e dragh air . . .

'Ach air an ath turus,' ars' esan, 'glacaidh mi sibh.'

'O,' ars Alasdair Bàn, 'cha bhi 'n ath turus ann, a charaide. An ath turus 's ann dhan ùir a bhios sinn a' dol, agus 's cinnteach gur e mis' théid an toiseach ann—tha mi sean có-dhiùbh.'

Ach beagan as a dheidh sin bha *Carmichael* air an fhadhail a' dol a null a Bheinn-a-Bhadhla. Agus bha taigh ann an Gramasdal an uair sen, taigh-òsda ris an canadh iad Taigh Ghramasdal—tha 'n tobht' aige fhathast ri faicinn—agus . . . Bha e'dol air adhart a null chon an taighe agus e air faighinn a mach gu robh deoch a' dol dhan taigh sin a feadhainn dhen fheadhainn a bha 'deanamh an uisge-bheatha ann a'falach aig na dachaidhean. Agus gun do thachair bràthair ris . . . an duine bha e 'rannsachadh an taigh aige beagan lathaichean roimhe sin—seann duine gasda aig an àm, Gilleasbuig mac Lachlainn Dòmhnallach, bràthair Alasdair Bhàin.

Thug e 'm pige far a mhuin agus bha e 'dol g'a thoir leis go Càirinis, ach rug Gilleasbuig mac Lachlainn air a' sgòrnan air agus thug e ruith mhath air agus chuir e 'na chadal e. 'S thug e air a mhuin e do dh'Eilean na Mnà Mairbhe, dhan Chaiginn, agus chaidil e ann a shin gu robh 'n ath tràigh ann, agus dh'fhalbh e air a shocair dh'a chois go Loch-na-Madadh. 'S ghabh e 'phacaid a' làr-namhàireach, 's chan fhacas tuilleadh an Uibhist *Carmichael*.

Sin sibh, ma tha.

Alasdair Bàn and the Gauger
Now then, I would like to tell you a story about a man who was called Alasdair Bàn, in the island of Grimsay, North Uist. Apparently he was good at making whisky at that time. I remember my father speaking about the man. My father was about eight years old at the time of the story I'm going to tell you. My father was born in 1860.

This day Mr Carmichael had come to the district for the Customs and Excise, and he had decided to catch Alasdair Bàn. And he had picked a bad day for doing this—he came over Carinish ford, nearly getting drowned in the process, and arrived at Alasdair Bàn's house where they hadn't expected that sort of person to come. But Alasdair Bàn was still there, and he told Carmichael he was happy to welcome him to his humble home and he was sorry he [Carmichael] was so wet and cold.

'And good man,' he said, 'before you go to the trouble of searching the house, I would like to give you a dram of good whisky to warm you, and perhaps give you a little pleasure.'

And he did this. He gave him a glass, and before it had gone down Carmichael's eyes were closing and he asked for a place where he could lie down. And he got this on the bench in Alasdair Bàn's house with a lovely Highland bed cover they had spun themselves, and carded and woven too, put over him. And he slept for four hours.

When he woke up anything that was in the house had been out of the way where neither he nor anyone else would find it. And the black pot as they called it [the still], which was a bit away from the house at Abhainn an t-Searraich, had been taken apart by the old man, Alasdair Bàn MacDonald, and thrown in the loch in front of the door. And this had all been done by the time Carmichael woke up, and Alasdair Bàn asked him to search the house and he did that. He even went under the beds, in the end on his knees but he saw nothing there—there wasn't anything there, it was all away. And he said he was sorry he had troubled him …

'But next time,' he said, 'I'll catch you.'

'Oh,' said Alasdair Bàn, 'there won't be a next time, my friend. Next time it's to the grave we'll be going, and I'm sure I'll be first to go—I'm old anyway.'

But a short time after that Carmichael was crossing the ford to Benbecula. And there was a house in Gramsdale then, an inn called Gramsdale House—the walls are still to be seen—and … He was going toward the house and he had found out that drink was being supplied to the house by some of the people who were secretly making whisky at their homes. And he met a brother … of the man whose house he had searched some days before—a fine old man at that time, Archie son of Lachlan MacDonald, the brother of Alasdair Bàn.

He [Carmichael] took the jar off his [Archie's] back and he was going to take it to Carinish, but Archie, son of Lachlan caught him by the throat and gave him a good going over and knocked him unconscious. And he carried him on his back to Dead Woman's Island, to the Caigeann [half way across the North Ford], and he [Carmichael] lay there until the next tide went out, and then he went quietly on foot to Lochmaddy. And he took the packet boat [out] next day, and Carmichael was never seen in Uist again.

There you are then.[14]

As well as collecting, the fieldworkers indexed the material and placed it in context. Various aspects of the oral tradition have been studied—the craft of storytelling, the role and function of tales within the community, transmission, the relationship of orality and literacy, the repertoires of storytellers and singers. Comparative studies have been undertaken into the origin and migration of tales looking particularly at Ireland, Scandinavia and Cape Breton.

Donald Alasdair Johnson, Àird Mhór, proved a very rich source of knowledge, appearing on 100 recordings. As well as a storyteller he was a piper, melodeon player, singer and composer. He indicated that when he was young he could fix a story in his memory on hearing it once. The issue of memory and storytelling is a fascinating one. Donald Alasdair Johnson talks of seeing images on the wall as he is telling a story like a film passing in front of you. Alan Bruford suggests that in South Uist one of the common ways of learning stories was memorising the framework or plot of the tale and much of the dialogue and runs but improvising the narrative.[15] Another area of great interest is the source of tales—how they passed into the tradition whether through manuscript or orally. Tales were often passed down through families and were heard in the céilidh houses and elsewhere. Sometimes everything would stop as the storyteller began. Otherwise work would be done at the same time. Here Kate MacDonald describes her uncle, the renowned storyteller Angus MacLellan[16]:

Chanadh cuideigin facal 's chanadh e 'Direach mar a bha leithid seo a dh'fhear no leithid seo a thé a bh'ann a' sgeulachd.' Bha e tòiseachadh air innse sin, a' sgeulachd a bha sin, 's mhaireadh i dà uair an uaireadair no barrachd gu math a sin… Bha e 'toirt astaigh eallach fraoich am beul na

Fig. 2: Thatching, Ceann a Deas Loch Baghasdail, 1936. Photo by Werner Kissling. *School of Scottish Studies Archives*

Fig. 3: Duncan MacDonald making rope with bent-grass, Peighinn nan Aoireann, 1953. Photo by Werner Kissling. *School of Scottish Studies Archives*

Fig. 4: Quern, Peighinn nan Aoireann, 1953. Photo by Werner Kissling. *School of Scottish Studies Archives*

Fig. 5: Spearing fish at Fadhail a Deas, 1936. Photo by Werner Kissling. *School of Scottish Studies Archives*

Fig. 6: Waulking, an t-Ìochdar 1970. Photo by Ralph Morton. *School of Scottish Studies Archives*

h-oidhche 'nuair a laiste 'lampa 's bhiodh e ann a shin gu aon uair deug 's chan fhaiceadh tu mu dheireadh ann a sìoman fraoich e, 'dol man cuairt air—air a shuainteadh man t-seidhear... e 'g innse sgeulachd 's a' gabhail òran greis ann a shin.

Someone would say something and he would say 'Just like such and such a man or such and such a woman in a tale'. He would start to tell it, that particular story, and it would go on for two hours of the clock or maybe a good deal longer ... He would bring in a load of heather when it was getting dark and the lamp was lit and he'd be there till eleven o'clock and you couldn't see him at last for the heather rope all around him—coiled round his chair ... he was telling tales and singing songs all the time there.[17]

As well as songs and tales, accounts of traditional life feature largely in the recordings and we have information about work and home from the nineteenth century onwards. All aspects of crofting are covered—cultivation, tools, house construction, furnishings, lighting, food, recipes, weather lore, and the proverbs and sayings that are part of the rituals of sowing and harvesting. Cures for various ailments are also discussed. Examples given by Donald Alex MacEachen from Benbecula include the common one of a spider's web to stop bleeding, liquid from boiled limpets for earache, the skin of an eel for a sprained ankle—fat side in—and, rather more dramatically, gunpowder and candlewax to fill cavities causing toothache.[18]

Various rhymes and charms celebrate seasonal events. There are versions of Hogmanay rhymes from all over the Uists recited by the *Gillean Callainn* as they went from house to house. Spiritual charms also feature. The genealogy of St Brigid, *Sloinneadh Ban Naomh Brìghde,* is recited below by Donald Allan MacQueen, Ìochdar to Donald Archie MacDonald in 1965. The charm is similar to versions in *CG* i, 164, and iii, 156–9.

Brìghde ni'n Duaghal Duinn	*Brigid daughter of Duaghal Donn*
'Ic Aoidh 'ic Aidh Ó Thuinn	*Son of Aodh son of Adh Ó Thuinn*
'Ic Fhiachra 'ic Earbra Chais	*Son of Fiachra son of Cairbre Cas*
'Ic Dhiarmaid 'ic Airt 'ic Cuinn.	*Son of Diarmad son of Art son of Conn.*

Fig. 7: Donald Alasdair Johnson, 1973. Photo by Ralph Morton.
School of Scottish Studies Archives

Bhon latha shloinneas mise Brìghde	*From the day that I can recite Brigid's*
Cha mhurtar, cha mharbhar, cha chuibhrichear,	*genealogy*
Cha loisg teine, grian, ola,	*I shall not be murdered, be slain or be*
Cha bhàth muir uisge no sàile mi.	*fettered,*
Tha mo choimprig-s' air caomh Mhoire:	*Neither fire, sun, nor oil shall burn me,*
'Se mo chaomh mhuime Brìghde.	*Neither a wave of fresh water nor sea water*
	shall drown me.
	Gentle Mary is my sanctuary:
	Brigid is my foster-mother.[19]

As can be seen there are various versions of material similar to that collected by Carmichael and memories too are given of the collector. One of the main strengths of the archives, in fact, is that there are so many different versions of the same tale, song or tune. This enables present day singers, storytellers and musicians, many of whom no longer learn their material directly through the oral tradition, to find the distinctive styles of their own local areas. so helping to counteract the tendency to homogeneity sometimes evident in contemporary Gaelic song and musical repertoires, resulting perhaps from a proliferation of commercial recordings which tend to create a 'standard'. As well as performers, users of the archive include teachers, féis tutors, authors, research scholars, students, local history societies and those seeking recordings by relations. Enquiries are welcome. As staff are in short supply, it is necessary to make an appointment—by phone or email—prior to visiting.

While the School of Scottish Studies Archives still has links with the various communities from which material was collected, it is archived in Edinburgh well away from its source. As a rescue mission, the focus in the early days was on getting material into rather than out of the archive. However, publication was also a priority with the journal *Scottish Studies* inaugurated in

1957. A series of commercial discs was launched in 1960, the format changing over time to cassette and CD and Greentrax now publish the Scottish Tradition series. Material from the Uists appears on *Music from the Western Isles*, *Clò Dubh Clò Donn*, *Gaelic Bards and Minstrels* and there is a cassette and book, *Ugam agus Bhuam*, of Peter Morrison telling stories. Stories also appear in *Scottish Traditional Tales* (Polygon, 1994). Independent publications include the very fine animation *Pìobairean Bhornais* created by Catriona Black using a story by Donald John Stewart, and the BBC made 50 programmes—*Sruth an Eòlais*—to celebrate the fiftieth anniversary of the School, many of which featured individuals from these islands.

The archive journal *Tocher* was established in 1971 and contains transcriptions (with translation and music notation) of songs tales and tradition. It usually focuses on a particular topic, collector or contributor. There have been many items from the Uists over the years. On-line access to the holdings commenced on a small scale in the mid 1990s with the creation of a digital archive through the PEARL project (Providing Ethnological Archives for Research and Learning) in which written transcriptions from *Tocher* were linked to the original audio (www.pearl.arts.ed.ac.uk). The story *Brìde, Muime Mhic Dé*, recorded from Donald Macintyre of South Uist in 1959 by Calum Maclean, is similar to a tale appearing in *Carmina Gadelica*; there are also various songs from the Rev. William Matheson.

Also conceived in the 1990s, the project called in Gaelic *Tobar an Dualchais* (Well of Heritage), and in Scots *Kist o Riches*, is of much greater magnitude incorporating not only the School of Scottish Studies Archives, but also complementary material from BBC Craoladh nan Gàidheal's radio archive, and the National Trust for Scotland's Campbell of Canna Collection, which contains mainly wire recordings and wax cylinders of Gaelic songs and tales. Supported by the Heritage Lottery Fund and matching funders, the project aims to preserve and create access to the archive by digitising 12,000 hours of audio recordings, recataloguing the material and making it available online. Complementing this, the Calum Maclean Project (funded by the Arts and Humanities Research Council) aims to digitise and put online the 10,000 pages of transcription of Scottish material he generated for the Irish Folklore Commission along with thirty fieldwork notebooks recording his work with the School. Both of these projects, are, of course closely related to the Carmichael project. Similar material from different time periods will create an on-line resource of outstanding historical and cultural significance.

As the massive changes of the twentieth century have virtually wiped out the oral tradition so the technological developments of the twenty-first will once again allow us to hear our songs, stories and narratives in the languages and dialects of the places from which they came. Once again, the voices of the people, those with such prodigious memories who so generously shared their knowledge, will provide a doorway into our personal and national heritage.

---

[1] 'Calum Maclean on Aonghus Barrach', *Tocher*, 31 (1979), 64 (SA1951/3/B1).

[2] Material from this trip is contained on *The World Library of Folk and Primitive Music* (Rounder CD143, 1998) and *Gaelic Songs of Scotland: Women at Work in the Western Isles* (Rounder CD1161-1785-2, 2006).

[3] 'Donald Archie MacDonald', *Tocher*, 57 (2003), 7–8.

[4] Josh Dickson, *When piping was strong: tradition, change and the bagpipe in South Uist* (Edinburgh, 2005).

[5] Margaret Fay Shaw (ed.), *Folksongs and folklore from South Uist* (London, 1955); John Lorne Campbell and Francis Collinson (eds), *Hebridean folksongs* (3 vols, Oxford, 1969–81).

[6] The archive contains a lovely version of the song by Ellen Morrison, North Uist.

[7] John MacInnes, 'Twentieth century recordings of Scottish Gaelic Heroic Ballads' in idem (ed. Michael Newton),

Dùthchas nan Gàidheal: selected essays of John MacInnes (Edinburgh, 2006), 200.

[8] See John Gregorson Campbell (ed.), *Waifs and strays of Celtic tradition, Argyllshire Series, no. IV: The Fians* (London, 1891), 131.

[9] See, in particular, Linda Gowans, *Am Bròn Binn: An Arthurian ballad in Scottish Gaelic* (Eastbourne, 1992).

[10] *CG* v, 100–5

[11] Translation by Donald MacAulay.

[12] Campbell and Collinson (eds), *Hebridean folksongs* i, 22.

[13] A number of examples of fairy songs are recorded in *Tocher* and on the PEARL website www.pearl.arts.ed.ac.uk.

[14] Andrew Nicolson, Griomasaigh, 'Alasdair Bàn agus an Géidseir', *Tocher*, 48/9 (1995), 413–16 (SA1968/223/A9).

[15] Donald Archie MacDonald, 'A visual memory', *Scottish Studies*, 22 (1978), 1–26; Alan Bruford, 'Recitation or re-creation: examples from South Uist storytelling', ibid., 27–44.

[16] Some of Angus MacLellan's tales have been published in idem, *Stories from South Uist* (London, 1961); and his life story in *Saoghal an treobhaiche* (Inverness, 1972), translated as *The furrow behind me: the autobiography of a Hebridean crofter* (London, 1962). Both volumes were edited and translated by John Lorne Campbell.

[17] Kate MacDonald, South Uist, 'Aonghus Beag ag innse sgeulachd', *Tocher*, 31 (1979), 64–5 (SA1969/69/A3).

[18] See Donald Alex MacEachen, 'Leigheasan/Cures', *Tocher*, 57 (2003), 40–51 (SA1963/52/A6–B1).

[19] Donald Allan MacQueen, Baile Gharbhaith, 'Sloinneadh Ban Naomh Brighde', *Tocher*, 48/9 (1995), 429–30 (SA1965/83/A5).

11

Future Plans for the Carmichael Watson Collection

MEGHAN COTE

INTRODUCTION

The Carmichael Watson Collection is one of the treasures of Edinburgh University Library Special Collections. At its heart are the papers of Alexander Carmichael (1832–1912). This enigmatic and controversial figure left behind a wealth of original manuscript material which offers unique, first-hand insights into the traditions, beliefs, language, and culture of Scotland's Gaelic-speaking communities, as well as the man himself. Writing in the *West Highland Free Press*, Ronald Black has stated that he regards the Carmichael Watson Collection as 'one of the seven wonders of Scotland, a great national treasure'. It is indeed one of the foremost folklore collections in the world. For nearly fifty years this invaluable resource has been underexploited due to its sheer volume and complexity, and the limitations of existing finding aids.

The Carmichael Watson Project aims to make the collection as accessible as possible, and disseminate its riches not just to the academic community, but to the wider public. Launched in 2005, the project is presently in its second phase, supervised by two departments at the University of Edinburgh—the Library Special Collections, and Celtic and Scottish Studies— under the leadership of Donald Meek, John Scally, Director of University Collections, and Arnott Wilson, Special Collections Manager and University Archivist. The project is still very much a work in progress at the time of writing, and therefore this paper can only provide the briefest overview of what is hoped to achieve.

THE COLLECTION

The Carmichael Watson Collection arrived at Edinburgh University in 1948 as one part of the larger 'Carmichael Watson bequest' left by Professors William J. Watson (1865–1948) and James Carmichael Watson (1910–42). William Watson, Professor of Celtic between 1914 and 1938, was Alexander Carmichael's son-in-law, having married his daughter Ella (1870–1928). James Carmichael Watson, William and Ella's son, succeeded his father as Professor of Celtic in 1938 but was reported missing and presumed lost in the Mediterranean some four years later. In addition to the manuscript material, the bequest also includes around 1400 volumes of printed books relating to Celtic and Scottish studies.

Physically, the collection occupies nine linear metres of shelf space in the library strong room. This includes 149 volumes of various sizes, including notebooks, scrapbooks, ledgers, and a few printed books, as well as some sixty boxes filled to the brim with an astonishing variety of materials, generally bundles of paper of various ages and conditions in envelopes or tied with cord.

The collection is an absolute mine of information. Reams of manuscripts, only a very few of which have been published, reflect Carmichael's long and prolific career as a folklorist. They offer us crucial insights into the creation of *Carmina Gadelica*, and into Carmichael's controversial editing processes. The project has uncovered Carmichael's original field notes in the form of small 'scrap books' which he used while travelling around the Outer Hebrides. These remarkable gems, previously more or less overlooked by scholars and hidden within the tangled strands of the collection, are gradually being brought to light through the project.

There is an extraordinary variety of material in the collection, demonstrating that there is much more to Carmichael than *Carmina Gadelica* alone. Carmichael's contributions to the study of the Scottish Gàidhealtachd cover topics as diverse as history, geography, botany, archaeology, and etymology, as well as folklore. These are vividly represented in the collection. A sampling of material from the box numbered 352–62 reveals this astonishing diversity.

CW MS 359 is an envelope containing assorted notes about saints, mainly on St Brìghde, or Bridget, and St Columba, mostly in Gaelic. It includes a letter of 12 December 1888 in English from Hector Maclean, John Francis Campbell's erstwhile tutor and colleague, and a major scholar in his own right, regarding various customs and traditions concerning St Brìghde. CW MS 361, on the other hand, is an envelope containing a diverse assemblage of notes on Shelta words reflecting Carmichael's long-standing interest in travellers' cant, as well as an article from the *Journal of the Gypsy Lore Society*, January 1891, 'On the Origin and the Age of Shelta'.

CW MS 362, an exceptionally important class of material, includes a letter from Carmichael explaining how in the second half of the 1870s he collected and edited Uist and Barra place-names for the Ordnance Survey, and also 'Promiscuous Antiquities in the Long Island, anciently known as Innis Cat and now known as Innis Fada', dated 27 April 1872. This major manuscript provides a history and description of churches and duns on the island, such as St Columba's in Benbecula. Also forming part of CW MS 362 is a folder containing assorted archaeological sketches, notes, and fascinating items of correspondence regarding antiquarian and archaeological features of the Outer Hebrides. Among these is a sketch by Carmichael labelled 'the Ancient Dun at Bearnary [Bearnaraigh], Barra', which he measured on 12 August 1867. This may well be the day on which he first met his wife Mary Frances MacBean.

Finally, CW MS 352 provides a delightful glimpse into Carmichael's role within the community. It reads 'First Annual Soiree of the Ossianic Society of Benbecula—held in Mr Gordon's Schoolhouse on Friday evening, 3 May 1878—A[lexander] A[rchibald] Carmichael in the Chair, tea on the table at 7 pm precisely', followed by an schedule of the evening's events. Attached to the programme is the text of a Gaelic speech delivered by Carmichael on the night.

Of course, there is much more to the Carmichael Watson collection than Alexander Carmichael himself. It includes material by the hands of William J. Watson and James Carmichael Watson, as well as other leading folklorists of Carmichael's day: a large cache of material by the Rev. Alexander Cameron of Brodick (1827–88), and additional papers of Father Allan McDonald of Eriskay (1859–1905) and the Rev. Charles Robertson of Jura (1885–1927). There are also contributions by Prof. Donald MacKinnon (1839–1914) of Edinburgh, Alexander Macbain (1855–1907) of Inverness, as well as the literary and genealogical historians the Rev. Angus MacDonald (1860–1932) and the Rev. Archibald MacDonald (1855–1948), in addition to many others.

THE CHALLENGES

The Carmichael Watson Collection's enormous value to Gaelic scholarship is clear. However, it also presents significant challenges which limit its full accessibility and exploitation. The physical arrangement of the collection has been somewhat muddled over the years, with the work of numerous individuals often dispersed apparently at random across the collection. Given the collection's lack of an underlying structure, it is often difficult to determine the context and significance of an item. Indeed, one major challenge is to identify the different categories of material. As discussed previously, the collection includes original field notes by Alexander Carmichael, as well as neat transcriptions and 'worked-up' versions prepared for publication. The distinction, however, is not always evident without scrupulous inspection. In addition, the material itself can be very difficult to interpret. Carmichael's handwriting is often barely legible, he tends to employ idiosyncratic spellings and abbreviations, and he frequently switches between English and Gaelic, sometimes within the same sentence.

For a number of years, handlist H28, available for reference in the Special Collections Reading Room, has served as the primary guide to the collection. The handlist is based around the relevant section the Rev. John Mackechnie's somewhat idiosyncratic *Catalogue of Gaelic Manuscripts in Selected Libraries in Great Britain and Ireland* (2 vols, Boston, 1973), in which items numbered 1–487 are identified and enumerated. The handlist's copy of Mackechnie's work was helpfully annotated and expanded by Dr Anna Frater. In 1992 it was discovered that a further 122 items, many of them relating to *Carmina Gadelica*, had not been included in Mackechnie's list. Items 488–576 were then listed, summarised and published by Dr Laura Sugg in *Scottish Gaelic Studies,* xviii (1998), a copy of which is bound with the handlist.

While handlist H28 has certainly served as a valuable resource over time, it has its limitations. Above all, it is purely manual and lacks an adequate indexing system. The researcher is thus forced to trawl through over one hundred extraordinarily dense pages, one at a time, in an attempt to locate any relevant material. In addition, Mackechnie's descriptions often fail to represent the full depth and breadth of information embedded within the collection, sometimes leaving significant material overlooked and in some cases inaccurately described. For example, Mackechnie has identified CW MS 439 as an 'Account written by Alexander Carmichael of his visit to the Glasgow Exhibition, 1901', even though it clearly relates to a visit to London in 1864. Many of the item's creators are unidentified, and in some cases inaccurately identified. The first three items in the collection, notebooks of traditional tales probably compiled by John Ewen MacRury and the Rev. Kenneth MacLeod, have been incorrectly attributed to Carmichael. In addition, Mackechnie often excludes crucial information such as relevant dates, not to mention details concerning location and informant, all of which Carmichael, trained by John Francis Campbell, was usually careful to record.

THE PROJECT

Recognising these challenges and the critical need to unlock such a hugely significant resource, the Carmichael Watson Project is intended as a means to create a dynamic, comprehensive online resource to the collection. The project comes at an exciting time for Gaelic scholarship, when numerous other Gaelic resource enhancement projects are currently underway. We are currently liaising with the *Tobar an Dualchais* and Calum Maclean projects under the auspices of the School of Scottish Studies, with the expectation that this will facilitate integrated research and highlight the underlying connections between these outstanding collections.

From the outset of project planning, it was evident that the obstacles posed by the collection could only be surmounted by a carefully designed, phased approach. Phase One, a preliminary scoping study, was completed in 2005, assisted by seed corn funding from Bòrd na Gàidhlig. Undertaken by Dr Domhnall Uilleam Stiùbhart, this pilot phase allowed for a critical examination of the collection and its existing finding aids. An elementary guide to the papers of Alexander Carmichael was compiled, accompanied by a thematic index providing initial pathways into the collection. Phase One also revealed the requirements for developing the collection, thus enabling the methodology and project plan for Phase Two to be devised.

Phase Two of the project officially commenced in May 2006 with generous assistance from the Carnegie Trust for the Universities of Scotland. This intermediate stage is being used to test the methodological principles and professional practices involved in developing the collection, as well as exploring and stimulating its potential for collaborative research and inclusion in teaching. It is focused on developing and testing a set of online research resources and tools which will open up access to the collection. At the end of Phase Two a detailed project proposal will be submitted to a major funding council, and we hope that the resulting Phase Three will expand and enhance the range of resources tested throughout the previous phase.

The primary resource and the major output of Phase Two is a scalable, fully searchable online catalogue, which will serve as the principal gateway into the collection. The catalogue should conform to ISAD(G), the General International Standard for Archival Description, in accordance with Special Collections procedures for cataloguing archival material. Developed by the International Council on Archives (ICA), ISAD(G) is currently the foremost standard of archival description and is centred on the concept of multilevel, or hierarchical arrangement. The catalogue will be prepared for online delivery by use of Encoded Archival Description (EAD), which is compatible with ISAD(G). Developed by the Library of Congress and the Society of American Archivists, EAD is an XML compliant Document Type Definition (DTD) used by a growing number of archival repositories to facilitate inter-repository data exchange.

At the start of Phase Two, it was initially hoped that the collection could be rearranged into logical sets of sub-fonds and series in accordance with the hierarchical cataloguing structure prescribed by ISAD(G). Sub-fonds are subdivisions of a collection (or 'fonds') containing the related records of one creator, while series are groups of documents maintained as one unit because they result from the same activity, have the same form, or some other relationship. A re-arrangement and renumbering of the collection would then follow. However, after carefully evaluating the collection it was determined that such divisions do not clearly exist, and that to force them material into artificial groupings would be arbitrary and archivally unsound. The collection will instead retain its present arrangement and numbering system as recorded in Mackechnie's catalogue, and employed in Gaelic scholarship for some decades. This approach is clearly beneficial, avoiding the confusion and frustration likely to be caused by assigning new identifiers to items. Recognising that an 'item' as identified by Mackechnie can represent one single document or a box filled with bundles of papers, letters or notebooks, lower, more detailed levels of description will be added as necessary.

As Phase Two is an intermediate testing stage, only a selected proportion of the collection is being catalogued at this time. Most descriptions are likely to relate to Carmichael material, although attempts will be made to demonstrate the breadth of the collection. Catalogue entries will include links to related material within the collection where possible, thus enabling Carmichael's editing process to be examined in detail. For example, Carmichael's original field recording of 'Deirdire' in field notebook CW MS 114 will be linked to a transcription of it in the 1872 notebook CW MS 154; to notes he made on the piece at CW MS 434; and to the polished and to some extent recreated version of it transcribed onto paper sheets at CW MS 437. Descriptions will also include references to published material, such as the published version of 'Deirdire' in the *Transactions of the Gaelic Society of Inverness*, xiii (1886–7), and material in other archive collections. Phase Two also incorporates an experimental investigation of bilingual catalogue descriptions.

Comprehensive and consistent indexing of the catalogue will enable users quickly to locate relevant material, and also to link related items. The Carmichael Watson catalogue must be congruent with overall Special Collections procedures for cataloguing and indexing, and therefore will incorporate the National Council on Archives rules for the construction of personal and corporate names, and draw index terms from Library of Congress Subject Headings (LCSH). However, LCSH often lacks the scope to meet the unique requirements posed by a Gaelic folklore collection. We will also incorporate specialised indexing systems developed through the related School of Scottish of Studies projects. This collaboration will help ensure the viability of searching across the three resources simultaneously via a future federated search engine.

The project also includes a programme of digitisation, an approach increasingly used as a means to broaden access to archive collections. During Phase Two, 200 key items from the collection will be selected and digitised to international standards by the Library's own Digital Imaging Unit, with a further 300 images created by the digital scanning of pre-existing microfilms of material. These images will be made available through an online image gallery, and will also be linked to the corresponding item's catalogue entry. Transcriptions and translations of key material will also be provided where possible, to the great benefit of users.

Additional research aids designed to increase access to the collection will also be developed. During Phase Two an online guide to Carmichael's challenging handwriting will be compiled and launched, incorporating step-by-step tutorials to his letter forms and the common abbreviations he employed in his fieldwork. Other resources currently being explored include an index to the types of paper commonly found within the collection. An approach linking and analysing items written on the same type of paper could provide vital clues to Carmichael's working methods, for example suggesting when and where he collected material, and help pinpoint the various levels of editing which are demonstrated in the collection.

All the resources—the fully searchable catalogue, the digital images, transcriptions and translations, and the handwriting guide—will be available through the bilingual project website, found at www.carmichaelwatson.lib.ed.ac.uk, providing a comprehensive online gateway to the collection.

The project is designed to be holistic and provide an inclusive enhancement of the collection; therefore conservation needs will also be addressed. Phase Two includes an assessment of the collection's condition based on the method devised by the National Preservation Office, with a view to professional conservation of vulnerable material during Phase Three. Phase Two also includes unskilled conservation measures such as basic cleaning and rehousing of the collection in archive quality boxes and folders.

Alongside the resource development work is an active programme of dissemination, in order to illustrate the outputs and benefits of the project to the wider community. Project findings and progress are being distributed through a bimonthly, online newsletter, available to be accessed at the project website. Seminars demonstrating the rich potential of the collection will also be planned. As Phase Two is a testing stage, research outputs will be evaluated as they emerge throughout the project by the Project Support Group, an advisory committee comprised of Celtic scholars from leading institutions throughout Scotland. A formal evaluation will take place at the end of the project and an evaluation report will be produced, which will feed directly into the construction of Phase Three. This final stage will then fully develop the resources tested in Phase Two, and see the collection readily available for full exploitation.

CONCLUSION

The papers of Alexander Carmichael make up an incomparable archive, one of the great treasures of Edinburgh University Library. The collection allows us to trace the compilation and editing of one of most important but controversial books ever published in Scotland, *Carmina Gadelica*. It spans over fifty years of Carmichael's recording career, embracing not just the folklore and traditions, but also the archaeology and the natural history of the Scottish Highlands. Nevertheless, much of it remained unpublished and relatively inaccessible. It is hoped that the Carmichael Watson Project, using the latest means of archival resource enhancement through digital technology, will bring this valuable collection to the academic community, to the many communities where he collected his material, and to the wider world.

12

Memories of Families Who Gave Carmichael Material

Clann 'ic Ruairidh, Tòrlum, Beinn a' Bhadhla

CALUM LAING

The MacRury family of Tòrlum, Benbecula, gave much material to Alexander Carmichael when he was staying on the island, and they continued to do so after he and his own family moved to Edinburgh. Iain Eòghann, born 1853, was the major contributor, whom Carmichael describes in *CG* ii, 381 as 'A highly intelligent man, for whose knowledge of old lore I am greatly indebted in this work.' Although the index in *CG* vi has five items attributed to Iain Eòghann—*Tàladh* (*CG* ii, 194–200); *An Dealan-Dè* (*CG* iv, 4); *Frìth* (*CG* v, 294); *Duan Calaig* (*CG* v, 380); and *A' Gheàrr* (*CG* v, 394)—it is clear from the Carmichael Watson papers that between 1887 and 1895 he supplied Carmichael with a significant amount of material he himself had collected in Uist and Benbecula from the 1870s onwards, including almost an entire notebook of material. Not only that, but evidence in the manuscripts suggests that he had a hand in composing many of the entries making up the final part ('Notes etc.') of the second volume. He probably gave in at least some of this material in person, as we have evidence that Iain Eòghann was a frequent visitor to Edinburgh during the period. In the *Northern Chronicle,* 2 February 1888, there is the song he composed, *Òran an Taigh Mhòir*, recorded as by Mac Thormoid Oig from Duneideann—that is, Edinburgh. Tormod Òg was his father. We know that Iain Eòghann was in Edinburgh in 1895 from a letter sent to Carmichael, dated 7 March 1895, from his younger brother and my grandfather, Eòghann C. MacRury, enquiring about him as he knows he is a frequent visitor to Carmichael's house [CW MS 488A fos.1–2]. In the letter my grandfather gives Carmichael the tale of Mac Mhuirich's meeting with 'Isean na bèiste' and his three wishes to it.

Eòghann was born in 1859, so was fairly young when Carmichael was in Benbecula, but he had a great interest in local folklore and corresponded with Carmichael after the latter had moved to Edinburgh. Eòghann and his wife moved to Stadhlaigearraidh, South Uist, in 1890 in order to run the Post Office there. Stadhlaigearraidh was a place very rich in folklore, being the residence of the MacMhuirich bards. He remained there all his life, dying in 1924. In 1907, however, he went to visit his sister Ciorstaidh, who had emigrated to Saskatchewan, Canada, in 1884. He kept a daily diary from when he left Glasgow until he returned, demonstrating his desire to record things in writing. He also composed a Gaelic song when his son Norman went to Canada in 1911. His sister Ciorstaidh also wrote a Gaelic song on the Boer War which appeared in *Mac-Talla* in 1900.

The oldest of the brothers was Iain. Born at Tòrlum in 1843, he was to become one of the most prolific Gaelic writers of his generation. Iain MacRury had the good fortune to be educated before the Education Act of 1872, a measure which made no provision for Gaelic whatsoever. He was educated at a parish school in Dùn Sgealair, North Uist, which prepared pupils to enter University. When he was there I am not quite sure, as in the 1861 Census he is living at home in Tòrlum, and his occupation is given as merchant. He went to Glasgow University in 1867. Very interestingly, in the 1871 Census he is in Cradhlastadh, Ùig, in Lewis as a schoolmaster, and his brother Iain Eòghann is staying with him as a scholar aged 17. After this Iain went back to Glasgow University to read Divinity, and he became a minister of the Church of Scotland in Islay in 1877. From there he went to Tiree in 1879 and remained there until 1886, when he moved to Snitheasort, Isle of Skye. He was Church of Scotland minister there until his death in April 1907. He first started writing to John Murdoch's newspaper *The Highlander* in July, 1873, just after it had started. He always wrote in Gaelic and under the name Iain. His pieces included tales, as well as the songs of his uncle, Domhnall MacRuairidh, the Tòrlum bard, who lived on the same croft as his own family. He was often also complimenting *The Highlander* on how it was drawing attention to the poor lot of the crofter, and how they were oppressed by the estate and those in authority. Iain was also advocating the greater use of

Iain Eòghann MacRury
Portrait in possession of Calum Laing

Gaelic, which would make people prouder of it and also give them greater confidence. Writing in that paper at the same time from Benbecula was Alexander Carmichael. In *The Highlander* of 17 January 1874, we have one example of a *Duan Callainn* from Carmichael, writing from Benbecula, and another one from Iain, writing from the North of The Long Island—that is, Lewis. Although Iain was not living in Benbecula most of the time Carmichael was living there, it is safe to assume that they would have corresponded. *An Dealan-Dè* and *Duan Calaig* are recorded under the name Iain in *Carmina Gadelica*, so it may have been himself, and not his brother Iain Eòghann, who gave these items to Carmichael. We do know, however, that there was much cross-fertilisation between the two brothers, and in his writings he sometimes says that he got the tale he is relating from his brother Iain Eòghann.

Iain MacRuairidh himself was to become one of the most productive Gaelic writers of his generation. He composed thirteen Gaelic lectures for the Gaelic Society of Inverness, more than anyone else in the history of the Society. He wrote regularly in *Mac-Talla*, the Gaelic newspaper published in Cape Breton, Canada, from 1893 until it ceased publication in June, 1904, as well as for the *Northern Chronicle* from 1886 until shortly before his death in 1907. In these two newspapers he put his Gaelic translations of the *Arabian Nights*, a mammoth work which took nearly seven years, and his Gaelic translation of Defoe's *Robinson Crusoe*. From 1886 until his death he edited the Gaelic Supplement of the Church of Scotland magazine *Life and Work*. Iain also wrote two books: *Eachdraidh Beatha Chrìosd*, the four gospels combined to form a biography of Christ; and a Gaelic translation of William Mair's *History of The Church of Scotland*. He was also a composer of Gaelic songs and hymns.

On 3 May 1878 a cèilidh was held at Tòrlum Schoolhouse, chaired by Alexander Carmichael—indeed, it may well have been held in his honour. This occasion, whose running order is recorded in CW MS 352, was the first—and quite possibly the last—Annual Soirée of the Ossianic Society of Benbecula. Among those taking part were Domhnall the Bard, and Iain Eòghann, who sang three songs, one of them composed by his brother, Iain. One can safely assume that my eighteen-year-old grandfather and his sister, Ciorstaidh, would have been in the audience.

Margaret MacDonald (Mairead Aonghais Duinn) 1791–1874

ISA MACKILLOP AND NORMAN JOHNSON (NORTH UIST)

Margaret lived in Gearraidh Iain, Malacleit, North Uist. She was the eldest child of Angus and Marion MacDonald. The other members of the family were Effie, Alexander, Allan, Hugh, and Angus (our great-grandfather), also known as Aonghas Donn. Incidentally, we have been told that he was a fiddle and chanter player.

In 1870 Mairead gave Alexander Carmichael a version of the ballad *Am Bròn Binn* which was later published in William Mackenzie, 'Leaves from my Celtic portfolio, sixth series', *Transactions of the Gaelic Society of Inverness*, ix (1879–80), 71–4. We were told various facts about the family but, unfortunately, very little about Mairead. Our theory is that the influence of the church and the clergy was the reason why the family did not mention the contribution she made as a tradition bearer. At the recent conference, we were very pleased to learn from Domhnall Uilleam Stiùbhart that she contributed much more to Alexander Carmichael than appears in his *Carmina Gadelica*.

Her father Aonghas Donn (senior) operated a fulling mill in Gearraidh Iain, probably for the landlord. The ruins of this mill can still be seen in that area. This place would probably be a hive of activity where Mairead could have heard many songs and sgeulachdan. For many years she worked for the MacDonalds of Vallay whom she held in high regard.

We believe Aonghas Donn's forbears originally came from Skye (probably from the Kilmuir or Staffin areas), so we may find some Skye traditions in amongst her contributions. We look forward very much to studying the other contributions Mairead gave to Alexander Carmichael once these are published.

∗ ∗ ∗ ∗ ∗

The short time Alexander Carmichael spent living with his young family at Trumaisgearraidh Manse during 1870–1 allowed him to get to know better the people and traditions of the northern part of North Uist; hitherto his work had taken him mainly to the south and west of the island. One of his main informants in the area was Margaret MacDonald, Mairead Aonghais Duinn, Gearraidh Iain, Malacleit. It appears that Alexander Carmichael first recorded her, then aged 79, on 10 February 1870 [CW MS 150 fos.47ᵛ–51ᵛ]. He describes her as '[a] poor old woman in a hut who had been at service in Vallay for a long time & who is eloq[uen]t upon the old style of gentlemen.' On that occasion Carmichael wrote down two songs from her: *Mac Iain 'ic Sheumais* and *Am Bròn Binn*, a favourite of his, indeed the first item he ever recorded in the Uists, from John MacLeod of Ìochdar on 10 January 1865 [see also Linda Gowans, *Am Bròn Binn: an Arthurian Ballad in Scottish Gaelic* (Eastbourne, 1992), 10, 22–3]. The two clearly established a rapport with each other: six months later, on 4 August 1870, with Mairead now 'close up 80', Carmichael recorded her again [CW MS 116 fos.28ᵛ–32ᵛ]. This time he took down the following songs: *Tàladh Dhomhnaill Ghuirm*; *Ceud soraidh Mhaol-dòmhnaich*; and a song headed *Am beinn 's an coille 's aig a' bhaile/Mi fo chirb do bhreacan baile* ['She heard this 60 [years] ago']. After her songs, Mairead told of the awful punishments meted out to those caught 'faobh-bhleoghann': 'milking the cows at night aft[er] they had been milk[ed] before—stealing'. It is possible that she also told the stories which follow in Carmichael's notes, traditions concerning the Morair Bàn and Sìol Ghoraidh. Having recorded *Tàladh Dhomhnaill Ghuirm*, Carmichael writes: 'The old woman sang this song very well, considering her age. Also vowed from our previous meeting that she would give me all the old things she had.' Later on that same year, possibly on 6 October, Carmichael returned to Malacleit and recorded from Mairead a magnificent version of *Craobh nan Ubhal*—headed as *Craobh an Iubhair* [CW MS 116 fos.35–6]. He may have visited her on another occasion, although we have no record of it in the extant notebooks, for printed in *Carmina Gadelica* is her charm to heal a cow's udder, *Eolas At Cioch* [*CG* ii, 8–9]. Alexander Carmichael clearly had a great regard for the songs of Mairead Aonghais Duinn, transcribing most of them into other notebooks. He had her version of the *Bròn Binn* published with other variants in the *Highlander*—its text appeared on 18 March 1876. As we have seen, it was later published by William Mackenzie in the *Transactions of the Gaelic Society of Inverness*. Carmichael's move south in 1871 to Ìochdar, then to Creag Goraidh, coupled with the pressures of work, bringing up a young family, and supervising the renovation of his new home, meant that he was unable to continue intensively collecting lore in the Ceann a Tuath. For the rest of the decade he spent what time he could recording the traditions of Benbecula, South Uist, and Barra.

Domhnall Uilleam Stiùbhart

Alexander Carmichael and the Morrisons of Rucaidh

PETER MORRISON

In 1870–1 Alexander Carmichael lived with his young family in the old manse of Trumaisgearraidh, about half a mile from Rucaidh [Ruchdaidh, Ruchdi]. Rucaidh was the home of John Morrison (1802–86), crofter and stonemason, and his wife Ann Ross (1813–93), who came from Liubhras, Broadford in Skye. Their son John Morrison (*c.*1842–1909), after being a seaman, and then a diamond miner in South Africa, farmed at Torinturk near Oban. His son Donald John was my father.

There are three items in *Carmina Gadelica* which were provided by my great-grandmother, my great-grandfather and my grandfather, although there is nothing in Carmina Gadelica to suggest that these people were related. At *CG* i, 158–9 is *Beannachadh Bliadhna Uir*, a prayer to be repeated 'the first thing on the first day of the year.' Carmichael gives the reciter as Ann Morrison *née* Ross, from Skye, 'Mason's wife, Trumsgearry, North Uist'. Ever since I found this in *Carmina Gadelica* twenty or thirty years ago, I have repeated it at the stroke of midnight at each New Year.

At CG iv, 320–1 is *Mac Shiamain*, a poem about 'the good husbandman, diligent and God-fearing.' It is stated to be from Iain Mac Ghill-Mhoire/John Morrison, Rucaidh, Uibhist a Tuath. When my father was speaking Gaelic he gave his name as Moireasdan; I do not know whether his father and grandfather used MacGilleMhoire or whether this is Carmichael's antiquarianism.

The very last item in the very last volume of *Carmina Gadelica*, even after the indices, is a list of the names of my grandfather's cows, headed 'Seo ainmean a' chruidh aig Iain Mac Gille Mhoire, Torr an Tuirc, an Latharna'. When I told this at Lìonacleit someone—and I have been racking my brains to remember who—spoke up who had sent a copy of the list to a friend in New Zealand in response to a request for suitable names for a herd of Highland cattle. So the tradition continues on the other side of the world.

Marion Campbell, Mòr bean Nill (the sister of Angus Beag MacLellan whose autobiography John Lorne Campbell published as *Saoghal an Treobhaiche/The Furrow Behind Me*), worked on my grandfather's farm at Torinturk until 1893 and was really my father's nurse. I visited her in 1967 when she was 100. Although I had little Gaelic then and she had no English we managed a good conversation. I asked her for a lullaby and she sang a little of *Griogal Cridhe*. I taped it and a lady who had sung in opera in her youth asked, on hearing it, whether she had been a professional singer, so good was her control of her breath. I think the School of Scottish Studies has about a hundred tapes of Bean Nill's singing.

There was a tradition at Rucaidh that a tinker wife came when some of my Grandfather's sons were there and recited a long piece of old Gaelic which contained several words that even she did not understand. My uncle Sandy was the best Gaelic scholar among the boys and he wrote it down. It was shown to Carmichael on his next visit but he was not very interested, saying that it was a well-known piece of Ossian. This must have been after Carmichael had left Uist, for Sandy was born in 1886.

* * * * *

From CW MS 87 fos.22–3 we can see that on 14 September 1885 Alexander Carmichael recorded from 'Ann Morrison, nee 'Anna Ros', Rucaidh, Trumsgearridh N. Uist' the song *Mo ghaol, mo ghaol, mo ghaol fhéin thu*: 'Composed by his father's 'banachaig nan gobhar' to the heir or Rararseidh, who afterwards became his wife, and who made an excellent wife.' This was Janet MacLeod, Baintighearna Dhubh Osgaig, the second wife of Malcolm MacLeod of Raasay, whom Johnson and Boswell met when they visited the island in 1773.

Domhnall Uilleam Stiùbhart

13

Under the Mantle of Holy Bride

THE VERY REV. ANGUS JOHN, CANON MACQUEEN

Given at the ecumenical service in Griminish Church on Sunday, 23 July 2006

In my early twenties I came across *Carmina Gadelica* for the first time and before long it replaced the bible as my bedtime book. It brought to life for me in a special way the joyful message of the Old and New Testament.

In our village of eight thatched cottages nestling comfortably on the north-western corner of South Uist, the world had passed us by and I realised that we were still living in the world of Carmichael, moving gently to the rhythm of the passing seasons, conscious of the hand of God guiding our path, at a time where everyone was poor but never short of the necessities of life and everyone was content.

On the first of February, the feast of Bride, my father would gather the family round the kitchen table to recite the genealogy of Bride who would protect us for the year from the dangers of fire and water. Bride would remind the Lord that the earth had rested well through the winter and that it was time to breathe new life into the soil. My father would remind us all of the importance of being under the mantle of holy Bride for the months ahead when we would take turns in herding the cattle on the machair while experiencing the wealth of nature, tasting the nectar collected by the bees 'under the protection of Holy Mary and our gentle foster mother our beloved Bride'.

Our prayer life guided us as we moved the sheep to the moor at Beltane while the cows grazed daily on the machair in order to preserve the croft pasture for the long winter months. Butter and cheese were made and stored while the fruits of the sea like carrageen were preserved, and peat was brought home for the fire and every moment of life was punctuated by the old who had a prayer for all that happened.

Alexander Carmichael captured the passing moments of the day and as I turn the pages I realise how sensitive his approach to our prayer life was, as if he were eavesdropping on the private life of those old folk who included their God in every passing moment of the day.

Michaelmas brought the work on the land to a close, and his feast was the joy of the cottages of the village. Once again my father would gather the family together round the table. The Struan would be blessed and, after we were reminded of the fruits of the land, he would break the bread and together we would eat the cake. Father would have ground the first barley on the quern stone for the flour which was the centre section of the Struan.

Then came winter—the quiet time, the reward for the active seasons and the cosy time when the thatched cottages were unaware of the howling gales outside.

My most beautiful memory is of my mother after our night prayer, spreading the dying embers of the fire and laying a dampened peat across the top of the fire with the smooring prayer, making the last chore of the day a religious rite.

Index